Essays on
the Philosophy and Science
of René Descartes

Essays on the Philosophy and Science of René Descartes

Edited by
STEPHEN VOSS

New York Oxford
OXFORD UNIVERSITY PRESS
1993

Oxford University Press

Oxford New York Toronto
Delhi Bombay Calcutta Madras Karachi
Kuala Lumpur Singapore Hong Kong Tokyo
Nairobi Dar es Salaam Cape Town
Melbourne Auckland Madrid

and associated companies in
Berlin Ibadan

Published by Oxford University Press, Inc.
200 Madison Avenue, New York, New York 10016

Library of Congress Cataloging-in-Publication Data
Essays on the philosophy and science of René Descartes /
edited by Stephen Voss. p. cm.
In English, with some essays translated from French.
Includes index.
ISBN 0-19-507550-1; ISBN 0-19-507551-X (pbk.)
1. Descartes, Rene, 1596–1650. I. Voss, Stephen, 1940–
B1875.E87 1993 194—dc20 92-6596

2 4 6 8 10 9 7 5 3 1

Printed in the United States of America
on acid free paper

To

Karen, Amarantha, Serenity, Tamara, and Julie

Acknowledgments

I am grateful to many people for valuable assistance with this book. Michelle Beyssade, Alan Gabbey, Daniel Garber, Douglas Henslee, and Dalia Judovitz made up an invaluable advisory board. Earlier, in the days of the Sainte Claire, so did John Etchemendy, Peter Galison, and Mark Olson. Wonderful and varied contributions were made by Margaret Wilson, Karen Voss, Frederick Van De Pitte, Fred Sprat, Elizabeth Sonnier, LaVonne Simpson, Jean-Jacques Servain-Schreiber, Richard Schubert, Dennis Rohatyn, Vernon Read and the Collegium Musicum, Charles Paul, David MacNeil, Peter Koestenbaum, Richard Keady, Michael Katz, Barbara Jeskalian, Marilyn Holland, Thomas Hicks, Donna Gustafson, Kathy Eldred, Lucius Eastman, Rob Daigle, Ed Curley, Peter Collins, Vere Chappell, Cornelia Brenneis, Carolyn Black, and Roger Ariew. Thanks to Cynthia Read and Angela Blackburn for their editorial vision and labors. My especially enthusiastic gratitude to the authors whose work appears here.

Veyrins, France S.V.
May 1992

Contents

Abbreviations

Works frequently cited in text and in notes have been identified by the following abbreviations:

AT — Charles Adam and Paul Tannery, eds. *Oeuvres de Descartes.* 11 vols. Paris: new presentation: CNRS and Vrin, 1964–76 (referred to by volume, page, and, sometimes, line).

CSM — John Cottingham, Robert Stoothoff, and Dugald Murdoch, trans. *The Philosophical Writings of Descartes,* 2 vols. Cambridge: Cambridge University Press, 1985–86.

CSMK — Cottingham, Stoothoff, Murdoch, and Anthony Kenny, trans. *The Philosophical Writings of Descartes.* Vol. 3: The Correspondence. Cambridge: Cambridge University Press, 1991.

HR — Elizabeth Haldane and G. R. T. Ross, trans. *The Philosophical Works of Descartes.* 2 vols. Cambridge: Cambridge University Press, 1931.

Notes on Contributors

MICHELLE BEYSSADE, *Maître de Conférences* at Université de Paris I, is author of *Descartes* (1972); "La problématique du 'cercle' et la métaphysique du Discours de la Méthode," in H. Méchoulan, ed., *Problématique et réception du Discours de la méthode et des Essais* (1988); and "System and Training in Descartes' Meditations," *Review of the New School for Social Research* (1988). Her work on Hume includes an edition *L'Enquête sur l'entendement humain* (1983) and an essay "Hume et les miracles," *Revue de l'enseignement philosophique* (1987). She is translator of Descartes's *Méditations métaphysiques,* in an edition containing the Latin text and the original French translation (1990). With Jean-Marie Beyssade she is editor of Descartes's *Méditations métaphysiques, Objections et Réponses* (1979) and *Correspondance avec Elisabeth* (1989).

JEAN-MARIE BEYSSADE, Professor at Université de Paris IV, is author of *La Philosophie première de Descartes* (1979); "Création des vérités éternelles et doute métaphysique," *Studia Cartesiana* (1981); and many essays on Descartes, Spinoza, Rousseau, and other modern philosophers. He is translator of *L'entretien avec Burman* (1981).

EDWIN CURLEY, Professor of Philosophy at the University of Illinois, Chicago, is author of *Spinoza's Metaphysics* (1969); *Descartes Against the Skeptics* (1978); "Descartes on the Creation of the Eternal Truths," *Philosophical Review* (1984); and *Behind the Geometrical Method* (1988). He is editor and translator of *The Collected Works of Spinoza* (1985–   ).

WILLIS DONEY, Professor of Philosophy at Dartmouth College, has written "The Cartesian Circle," *Journal of the History of Ideas* (1955); and translated Malebranche's *Entretiens sur la métaphysique et sur la religion* into English (1980). He is editor of *Descartes: A Collection of Critical Essays* (1967), *The Philosophy of Descartes* (25 vols., 1987), *Eternal Truths and the Cartesian Circle* (1987), and *Berkeley on Abstraction and Abstract Ideas* (1989). With Vere Chappell he has compiled the bibliography *Twenty-Five Years of Descartes Scholarship, 1960–1984* (1987). He is presently writing a commentary on Descartes's Fifth Meditation.

ALAN GABBEY, formerly Reader in History and Philosophy of Science at Queen's University, Belfast, teaches philosophy at Barnard College, Columbia University. He is author of "Force and Inertia in the 17th Century: Descartes and Newton," in S. Gaukroger, ed., *Descartes: Philosophy, Physics, Mathematics* (1980); "Philosophiae Cartesiana Triumphata: Henry More 1646–1671" in T. Lennon et al., eds., *Problems of Cartesianism* (1982); and "The Mechanical Philosophy and its Problems" in J. Pitt., ed., *Change and Progress in Modern Science* (1984). He is currently preparing an edition of the More-Descartes correspondence and a study of the mechanical philosophy. Alan Gabbey is a *membre effectif* of the Académie Internationale d'Histoire des Sciences.

DANIEL GARBER, Professor of Philosophy at the University of Chicago, is author of *Descartes' Metaphysical Physics* (1992), cotranslator of *Leibniz: Philosophical Essays* (1989), and coeditor of the *Cambridge History of Seventeenth-Century Philosophy* (1993). He is also the author of numerous articles on seventeenth-century philosophy.

MARJORIE GRENE, Professor Emeritus at the University of California, Davis, and Adjunct Professor and Honorary Distinguished Professor at Virginia Polytechnic Institute and State University, is author of *A Portrait of Aristotle* (1963), *The Knower and the Known* (1966), *The Understanding of Nature* (1974), *Philosophy In and Out of Europe* (1976), *Sartre* (1983), *Descartes* (1985), and *Descartes among the Scholastics* (1991).

GARY HATFIELD, Professor of Philosophy at the University of Pennsylvania, is author of "Force (God) in Descartes's Physics," *Studies in History and Philosophy of Science* (1979); "The Senses and the Fleshless Eye: The Meditations as Cognitive Exercises," in A. Rorty, ed., *Essays on Descartes' Meditations* (1986); "Science, Certainty, and Descartes," in A. Fine and J. Leplin, eds., *PSA 1988* (1989); "Metaphysics and the New Science" in D. Lindberg and R. Westman, eds., *Reappraisals of the Scientific Revolution* (1990); and *The Natural and the Normative: Theories of Spatial Perception from Kant to Helmholtz* (1990).

MICHEL HENRY, Professor Emeritus at Université de Montpellier, is author of *Généalogie de la psychanalyse: le commencement perdu* (1985) (English translation, D. Brick, Stanford University Press, 1992), *Marx* (1976), *Philosophie et phénoménologie du corps* (2nd ed. 1987), *La barbarie* (1987), *Voir l'invisible: sur Kandinsky* (1988), *Phénoménologie matérielle* (1990), and *L'essence de la manifestation* (2nd ed. 1990). He has written three novels, one of which, *L'amour les yeux fermés* (1976), won the Prix Renaudot.

EVERT VAN LEEUWEN, who teaches philosophy and ethics in the Faculty of Medicine of the Free University of Amsterdam, is author of *Descartes' Regulae: De eenheid van heuristische wetenschap en zelfbewustzijn*

(1986). Recent articles in English include "Neurosemiotics—the Loss of Reference," in T. Sebeok, ed., *Approaches to Semiotics* (1991); "The Right to Genetic Information," *Journal of Medicine and Philosophy* (1992); and "A Case Study in Bioethics," in A. W. Musschenga et al., eds., *Morality, Worldview and Law* (1992). He is presently working on philosophical and ethical questions raised by neuroscience and genetics, and preparing work on Von Tschirnhaus and Malebranche from this perspective.

JEAN-LUC MARION, Professor at Université de Paris X, is coauthor of *Index des Regulae ad directionem Ingenii de René Descartes* (1976), translator from the Latin into Descartes's French of the *Règles utiles et claires pour la direction de l'esprit en la recherche de la vérité* (1977), and coeditor of *La passion de la raison* (1983) and *Le Discours et sa Méthode* (1987). He is author of *Sur l'ontologie grise de Descartes* (1975; 2nd ed. 1981), *Sur la théologie blanche de Descartes* (1981; 2nd ed. 1991), *Sur le prisme métaphysique de Descartes* (1986), *Réduction et donation* (1989), and *Questions cartésiennes* (1991). He has written several works in theology, including *L'idole et la distance* (1977; 3rd ed. 1991) and *Dieu sans l'être* (1982; 2nd ed. 1991), translated into English by T. Carlson as *God without Being* (1991). Articles in English include "The Essential Incoherence of Descartes' Definition of Divinity," in A. Rorty, ed., *Essays on Descartes' Meditations* (1986); "On Descartes' Metaphysics," *The Graduate Faculty of Philosophy Journal* (New York; 1986); "L'Interloqué," *Topoi* 7 (1988); "The Idea of God," in M. Ayers and D. Garber, eds., *The Cambridge History of Seventeenth-Century Philosophy* (1993); and "Descartes' Methodology and Metaphysics: Descartes' Theory of Ideas," in J. Cottingham, ed., *Cambridge Companion to Descartes* (1992). Jean-Luc Marion has received awards from the Académie des Sciences Morales et Politiques (1977) and the Académie Française (1982).

GENEVIEVE RODIS-LEWIS, Professeur Honoraire at Université de Paris IV, is editor of numerous works of Descartes, Leibniz, and Malebranche (in particular the two-volume Pléiade edition of the latter). She has contributed widely to collective works, ranging from entries in dictionaries and encyclopedias to articles in the *Grande Antologia filosofica* (1968) and the Pléiade (1973) and Ueberweg (1992) histories of philosophy. Professor Rodis-Lewis is author of dozens of articles on art and on the philosophy of antiquity and the past four centuries (over sixty on Descartes and Cartesianism), and has gathered some into the collections *Idées et vérités éternelles chez Descartes et ses successeurs* (1985), *L'anthropologie cartésienne* (1991), *Le développement de la pensée de Descartes* (1993), and *Ecrits sur l'art* (1993; with complete bibliography of her writings). She is author of the following books: *L'individualité selon Descartes* (1950), *Le problème de l'inconscient et le cartésianisme* (1950; 2nd ed. 1984; these two theses appearing under the name "Lewis"), *Nicolas Malebranche* (1963), *Descartes, Initiation à sa philosophie* (2nd ed. 1964), *La Morale de Descartes* (3rd ed. 1970), *La morale stoïcienne* (1970), the classic *L'Oeuvre de Descartes* (2 vols., 1971), *Platon et la "chasse de l'être"* (4th ed.

1972), *Epicure et son école* (1976), *Descartes: Textes et Débats* (1984), and *Descartes et le rationalisme* (6th ed. 1992).

In 1985 Geneviève Rodis-Lewis was awarded the Grand Prix de l'Académie Française for the totality of her work on Descartes. Her current project is a biography, *Descartes sur le chemin de la vérité.*

MARLEEN ROZEMOND, author of "Descartes' Conception of the Mind" (UCLA dissertation, 1989), teaches philosophy at Stanford University. Her research centers on Descartes's conception of the mind, with particular reference to Aristotelian scholasticism—for example, on the First Meditation, the arguments for dualism, and errors about the mental.

JOHN SCHUSTER, is Associate Professor (Reader) in the Department of Science and Technology Studies at the University of Wollongong, Australia, and Coordinator of the University's Research Program in Science and Technology Analysis. He is author of "Descartes and the Scientific Revolution—1618–34: An Interpretation" (2 vols., Princeton dissertation, 1977); "Descartes' *Mathesis Universalis,* 1619–28," in S. Gaukroger, ed., *Descartes: Philosophy, Physics, Mathematics* (1980); "Cartesian Method as Mythic Speech: A Diachronic and Structural Analysis," in Schuster and R. Yeo, eds., *The Politics and Rhetoric of Scientific Method* (1986); and "The Scientific Revolution," in R. Olby et al., eds., *The Companion to the History of Modern Science* (1990). He is coauthor of "The Feminine Method as Myth and Accounting Resource," *Social Studies of Science* (1989) and of "Natural Philosophy, Experiment and Discourse in the 18th Century: Beyond the Kuhn/Bachelard Problematic," in H. Legrand, ed., *Experimental Inquiries* (1990). He has served several terms as President of the Australasian Association for the History, Philosophy and Social Studies of Science.

DENNIS SEPPER teaches philosophy at the University of Dallas. He is author of *Goethe contra Newton* (1988); "Imagination, Phantasms, and the Making of Hobbesian and Cartesian Science," *The Monist* (1988); and "Descartes and the Eclipse of Imagination," *Journal of the History of Philosophy* (1989). He is finishing a guided study of Newton's optical writings, writing a book on the evolution of Descartes's conception of imagination, and fitfully developing a hermeneutic theory of science.

JEAN-PIERRE SERIS, Professor at Université de Paris I and Director of the Institut d'Histoire et de Philosophie des Sciences et des Techniques, is author of *Machine et communication* (1987), which analyzes the genesis of the science of machines between the baroque age of the "*Théâtres des Machines*" and the postrevolutionary institution of the teaching of industrial mechanics, and which won the 1990 Prix Jean Cavaillès. His essay in this volume gives a glimpse of developments in his most recent book *Machine et Langage aux XVIIe et XVIIIe siècles* (1993), which aims to understand and place within the structure of their historic problematic the projects of "*physique de la parole*" and "mécanique des signes" which accompanied the rise of a classical science of language and of languages, and to evaluate the possibility of applying to the knowledge of signs the methods that have been applied to gain knowledge of the natural world.

STEPHEN VOSS is coauthor of "The Structure of Type Theory," *Journal of Philosophy* (1980) and author of "Understanding Eternal Life," *Faith and Philosophy* (1992). He has produced English editions of Descartes's *The Passions of the Soul* (1989) and *The Leibniz-Arnauld Correspondence* (forthcoming). His current project is *Metaphysics, Morals, and Passion,* a book on developments in Descartes's thought after the *Meditations*.

STEPHEN I. WAGNER, who teaches philosophy at St. John's University, Minnesota, has presented work on Descartes at numerous conferences, seminars, and institutes on both sides of the Atlantic. He is author of "Descartes' Cogito: A Generative View," *History of Philosophy Quarterly* (1984) and is writing a book on Descartes's *Meditations*.

MARGARET WILSON, Professor of Philosophy at Princeton University, is author of *Descartes* (1978), as well as many articles on seventeenth and eighteenth century philosophy. Her recent interests include the relation between the history of philosophy and contemporary philosophy, and the intersection between metaphysics and theories about perception in early modern thought.

Essays on
the Philosophy and Science
of René Descartes

1
Introduction

In his philosophy and science, René Descartes was able to construct a world so capacious that anyone who studies his ideas well can live there—can acquire a unique understanding of our common world by examining it from his perspective. The community of scholars inhabiting the Cartesian world is now more than 350 years old. Each generation, in its distinctive way, discovers new resources in Descartes's world and makes its own contribution to our understanding of it. The present book is rich with such contributions, at once expressive of the present moment in scholarship and of the immutable natures specified by the Cartesian text.

This volume's publication helps celebrate the 350th anniversary of the second edition of the *Meditations*. It originated in my conviction that Americans ought to join in celebrating the 350th anniversary of the *Discourse on Method*. As Henri Gouhier observed in 1987 in opening a major conference in Paris, "three and a half centuries after the publication of the *Discourse* and the *Essays*, the land of Descartes is not simply the one we know today as France." In that spirit I arranged a similar conference in 1988 at the old Sainte Claire Hotel in San Jose, which created an opportunity to advance Descartes scholarship by bringing together an immensely diverse range of people linked by interest in Descartes's world. This book is inspired by that conference.

These essays move the cutting edge of work on Descartes. They provide new answers; sometimes they even ask new questions. In this Introduction I enumerate some of the new currents in Descartes scholarship—the new approaches to Descartes's world—which they exemplify.

Above all, this book conveys a sense of history that is new to Descartes studies. Decades ago Etienne Gilson, in *Études sur le rôle de la pensée médiévale dans la formation du système cartésien,* and then Ferdinand Alquié, in *La Découverte métaphysique de l'homme chez Descartes,* called attention to a decisive development in the philosopher's thought around 1629. Here their hypothesis is strikingly extended: a third of these essays—those by Dennis Sepper, Jean-Pierre Séris, John Schuster, Evert van Leeuwen, Geneviève Rodis-Lewis, Gary Hatfield, and Daniel Garber—independently document specific developments in his thought at that time.

Several authors shed light on Descartes by pointing to relations with his historical context. Marleen Rozemond, Stephen Voss, Alan Gabbey, and Marjorie Grene display for comparison the views of authors who worked with

Descartes's questions—predecessors, contemporaries, and successors. To take one example, Rozemond investigates the relation of Descartes's doctrine that the mind is incorporeal to the rest of his work, and employs above all the historical setting of his thought about mind in considering whether he aimed more at refuting attempts to explain mind mechanistically or at correcting scholastic defenses of immortality.

These essays reflect a steady growth in catholicity within Descartes scholarship during the past decade or two, as Anglo-American and continental scholars have sought to learn from one another. Thus, two of the most important recent interpretations are Jean-Luc Marion's *Sur la théologie blanche de Descartes* and Jean-Marie Beyssade's *La Première philosophie de Descartes.* Each investigates the consequences of a fundamental doctrine—respectively, the creation of the eternal truths and knowledge of God, and the continuity of time. These books are not written only for French scholars or read only by them. In the same way, in the decade since Edwin Curley's *Descartes Against the Skeptics* and Margaret Wilson's *Descartes* appeared, their results have been incorporated into continental scholarship. A glance at the notes in this volume will show the acceleration of that cross-fertilization. In particular, Stephen I. Wagner develops the French scholar Martial Gueroult's interpretation of the distinction between a substance's power and its modes in an entirely new direction, by demonstrating its capacity to dispel some of the air of mystery from the doctrine of mind–body interaction. Séris enters into dialogue with those Anglo-Americans who imagine Descartes to anticipate theories of the convergence of machine and language. Sepper incorporates continental studies to shed light on the conceptions of imagination in the early writings. Schuster does the same in arriving at an understanding of the early writings about method. Grene fruitfully extends Gilson's comparison between Descartes and Harvey on the heart and blood. These essays provide especially vivid models for dialogue between what used to be two largely distinct interpretive traditions.

This book significantly advances such dialogue. For it is still true that only a tiny proportion of the output of continental scholars is available in English. Even linguistic adepts find that work with foreign languages requires downshifting. So we are proud to be able to present six works originally written in French. Sometimes these articles stem from continental scholarly traditions; see the essays by Henry, Marion, and Rodis-Lewis. Sometimes they make use of traditions pioneered in the English-speaking world; see the essays by Jean-Marie Beyssade, Michelle Beyssade, Jean-Pierre Séris, and once again Rodis-Lewis. Thanks to their essays here, these six authors become more accessible to the English-speaking part of the land of which Henri Gouhier has spoken.

In particular, this book makes newly available in English a radical approach to Cartesian phenomenology. In a series of studies that includes the present essay, Michel Henry has asked whether Descartes's text supports a distinctive phenomenology that posits nonrepresentational conscious states prior to the *ekstasis* separating consciousness from its object. Jean-Luc Marion examines the application of this strategy to the passion of generosity portrayed in *The Passions of the Soul,* aiming to produce a broader understanding of Descartes's *cogito.*

The book represents growing catholicity in another way. Historians of philosophy on the one hand and historians and sociologists of science on the other speak and listen to one another here. It is increasingly clear that Descartes's philosophy cannot be understood apart from his aims and achievement in physics. He told Mersenne on 28 January 1641 that his metaphysics was meant to contain the foundations of a new physics, and destroy the foundations of the old. He wrote in the 1647 preface to the *Principles of Philosophy* that his philosophy was like a tree—its root was metaphysics, its trunk was physics, and all of the fruit of his philosophy grew on branches sprouting from that trunk. Voss argues that one of the metaphysical principles governing mind–body interaction has specific implications for physics as well. Daniel Garber investigates how Descartes can consistently make use of experience in science and as a rationalist require certainty of scientific belief. Rodis-Lewis and Gary Hatfield scrutinize the fundamental question of the theological validation of scientific knowledge.

We are now witnessing a burgeoning interest in Descartes's rhetoric. It arises in part from a new concern in general among philosophers, critics, social scientists, and historians with rhetorical aspects of texts; and in part from an older but persistent concern about Descartes's sincerity. Sincerity is, perhaps, some kind of relation between intention and text. But many kinds of intention are possible and Descartes writes many kinds of text, from dialogue to treatise to manual to mediation to letter to, most interesting of all, discourse. He clearly intends to teach a method for doing science, but in what manner and with what self-consciousness and sincerity does he mean to teach it? Is there a connection between the narrative style of the *Discourse* and the respective claims it makes for philosophy and science? What is it about his historical falsehoods concerning his career in science that makes them look true? What is it about his intentions that might make his falsehoods means to realizing them? It is such questions that Evert van Leeuwen and John Schuster raise in their studies of the central works in which Descartes advertises a scientific method.

To take the *Rules for the Direction of the Mind* as an accurate depiction of Descartes's scientific procedures may stand in the way of understanding them. To take the *Discourse* either as autobiography or as treatise on method in science may obscure the place it reserves for philosophy. Understanding the structure of the false historical claims that Descartes makes for his method may help us understand their rhetorical success. Understanding the genres he employs in recommending his method may help us understand his conception of the way in which philosophy provides the foundation for science.

We are beginning to gain a clearer view of the organic relation between Descartes's outlook and its intended human benefits. Three branches—mechanics, medicine, and morals—sprout from the trunk of physics, each yielding its own kind of fruit. Gabbey, Grene, and Marion examine topics within these respective branches, and each helps us see more clearly Descartes's way of approaching such practical topics. Gabbey considers how the author could have described mechanics both as part of the trunk and as a branch. By tackling this structural aspect of the tree, he brings unexpected clarity to the status that mechanics came to possess after the Middle Ages.

Descartes's aim to preserve human life is now acknowledged as a significant motive for his work. In Part VI of the *Discourse* he articulates a vision of a "practical philosophy" which might be used to "make ourselves, as it were, masters and possessors of nature"—a philosophy desirable "most importantly for the maintenance of health, which is undoubtedly the chief good and the foundation of all the other goods in this life" (AT VI, 62; CSM I, 142–143). The value of medicine rests directly on the applicability of physics to the human body. But Grene shows that we have as yet only an incomplete understanding of the approach to the body that generated Descartes's specific doctrine about the circulation of the blood, and his specific objections to that of Harvey.

In the end, as he wrote to Chanut on 15 June 1646, Descartes came to think that his thought was fruitful above all in morals: "What little knowledge of physics I have tried to acquire has been a great help to me in establishing sure foundations in morals. Indeed I have found it easier to reach satisfactory conclusions on this topic than on many others concerning medicine, on which I have spent much more time. So instead of finding ways to preserve life, I have found another, much easier and surer way, which is not to fear death." (AT IV, 441–442; CSMK, 289) If he writes his last major work, the *Passions,* "as a physicist" (AT XI, 326; CSM I, 327) he intends it to serve as a prolegomenon for morals. The passions are means for gaining what is of intrinsic value in human life—the determination to make good use of one's free will, a determination which is the prime prerequisite for the master passion of generosity. Marion tests Henry's distinctive interpretation of Cartesian phenomenology by applying it to generosity as well. If the Second Meditation presents the fact of appearance nonrepresentationally, might not the *Passions* present free will similarly? Might it then begin to approach the traditional philosophical ideal—apparently abandoned twelve years earlier in the *Discourse*—of a wisdom whose domain includes both fact and value?

Finally, the book represents a heightened courage to examine the text more carefully, to place more weight upon it, to submit to more exacting standards of interpretive validity. For example, Edwin Curley sheds new light, by a close examination of familiar passages, on the idea of metaphysical certainty and the idea of a valid ground for doubt. The doctrine that clear and distinct perception in the case of the *cogito* provides a criterion for truth in general has often disturbed readers, but Michelle Beyssade's exquisite care with the text reveals unsuspected subtlety and strength into Descartes's conception. Henry displays a sensitivity to the Second Meditation that is comparable to her sensitivity to the Third, in developing a distinctive account of the uniqueness of *cogito*-like situations. Willis Doney examines the Fifth Meditation's a priori argument for the existence of God, in the light of a dispute between Descartes and Caterus over its nature; and by adjudicating the dispute he reveals with greater clarity the outlines of the argument. And Jean-Marie Beyssade devotes characteristically sensitive scrutiny to Descartes's accounts of the ways in which it may, and may not, be possible to understand God's nature, and demonstrates that allegations of contradiction are premature.

According to a well-known passage in Part V of the *Discourse,* language is a sure sign of mind. But Séris extracts a distinctive doctrine about language from texts less thoroughly studied, and displays its role in Descartes's doctrine of the distinction between humans and machines. Margaret Wilson devotes typically careful study to passages concerning the perception of primary and secondary qualities, in search of Descartes's doctrine about what the senses and the intellect each contribute to knowledge. Rodis-Lewis, as is her style, uncovers meaning in phrases that the most scholarly are accustomed to ignoring.

All nineteen authors impose upon their work standards of fidelity to Descartes's text that are higher than those typical only a generation ago. Some devote such care to the text that they break new ground in the understanding of passages we thought we knew already. All in their own way constitute good reason to celebrate anew the world of René Descartes.

I

CARTESIAN PHILOSOPHY: ITS FOUNDATIONS IN THE *COGITO* AND THEOLOGY

2

Certainty: Psychological, Moral, and Metaphysical

Edwin Curley

My purpose in this paper is to comment critically on the program elaborated in Peter Markie's recent book, *Descartes's Gambit,*[1] and to respond to criticisms Markie there makes of my own book, *Descartes Against the Skeptics.*[2] My hope is that this exchange may actually shed some light on Descartes, but each reader must judge that for herself.

The "gambit" Markie refers to in his title is Descartes's attempt to deduce a metaphysical theory of the self from premises about his knowledge of himself. The epistemological premises are that I am certain that I think, that I am certain that I exist, and that I am uncertain that I have a body. The metaphysical theory of the self derived from these premises is, roughly, that I am a thinking, nonextended substance capable of existing apart from its body. Markie maintains that Descartes himself held that these metaphysical conclusions could be deduced from these epistemological premises without establishing God's existence and veracity, provided we are willing to settle for something less than absolute certainty about our conclusions.[3] The bulk of his book is an attempt to show how this might be done, drawing on various definitions, epistemic principles, and metaphysical assumptions,[4] but not drawing on any of the specific metaphysical assumptions about causality and perfection familiar to students of Descartes from the Third, Fourth, and Fifth Meditations.

I shall be concerned with this larger project only tangentially. Markie maintains that the key to Descartes's gambit is his position on the nature and content of certainty. This, he says,

> is the basis for his defense of his premises about self-knowledge. . . . It provides the principles that enable him to move from those premises to intermediate conclusions about the logical possibility of his existing in some ways and not others, from which he derives his theory of the self. (p. 30)

Most commentators on Descartes, he thinks, have overlooked the importance of his theory of certainty to his overall strategy, and those who have not overlooked its importance have still not given a proper account of Cartesian certainty (p. 30). Whether or not this is an accurate assessment of the current state of Cartesian scholarship, Markie clearly does give an account of Cartesian certainty more detailed than, and quite different from, any I am aware of in the literature. It raises some very interesting questions, which deserve to be discussed, even if, as I think, Markie's approach to these questions is thoroughly wrong-headed.

Three Species of Certainty

Markie distinguishes three species of certainty which Descartes recognizes—psychological, moral, and metaphysical—and offers the following definitions of these kinds of certainty:

> *p* is psychologically certain for *S* = df *S* believes *p* and *S* is unable to doubt or deny *p*. (p. 56)
>
> *p* is a moral certainty for *S* = df (1) believing *p* is more reasonable for *S* from the standard epistemic perspective than denying *p* or doubting *p*, and (2) believing some proposition *q* is more reasonable for *S* from the standard perspective than believing *p* only if *q* is a metaphysical certainty for *S*. (p. 37)
>
> *p* is a metaphysical certainty for *S* = df (1) believing *p* is more reasonable for *S* from the standard epistemic perspective than doubting or denying *p*, and (2) it could never be more reasonable for *S* to believe some proposition *q*, than it is at present for *S* to believe *p*. (p. 39)

To doubt *p*, here, is to neither believe it nor deny it. By the standard epistemic perspective Markie means the perspective of someone who accepts the imperative: believe all and only the truth with regard to the matter under investigation. According to Markie's Descartes, the standard epistemic imperative is the appropriate one to follow when we engage in practical affairs (p. 60). But when we engage in an inquiry into truth, we ought to adopt a further policy, combining the standard epistemic imperative with what Markie calls the Cartesian imperative: place under the special heading of "science" all and only what is metaphysically certain and true (p. 60). We still aim to believe all and only true propositions, but we classify our beliefs as scientific only if we think them also metaphysically certain.

Markie has arranged his definitions in such a way that metaphysical certainty entails moral certainty, but not conversely. All metaphysical certainties are moral certainties, but not all moral certainties are metaphysical certainties (p. 39). And there is, as he puts it, "a void between moral and metaphysical certainty," in the sense that no morally certain proposition is more reasonable than another unless it is also metaphysically certain.

There are no logical connections between psychological certainty, on the one hand, and moral and metaphysical certainty, on the other. The latter two concepts involve an evaluative element:

> To tell someone a proposition is a moral or metaphysical certainty for her is to tell her that, from the standard epistemic perspective, she *ought* to believe it . . . (p. 56),

even though a morally certain proposition (unlike a metaphysically certain proposition) might be false (p. 53). Psychological certainty, by contrast, is a purely factual concept, with no evaluative implications. So psychological certainty is neither a necessary nor a sufficient condition for either moral or metaphysical certainty, at least insofar as this is a matter of definition and logic (p. 56). It is, in fact, the case that all metaphysical certainties are psychological certainties, but this is not because of the nature of these concepts. It is because God has so arranged it (p. 57).

Psychological Certainty

Now, although Descartes does not have the label "psychological certainty," it's clear that he uses a concept like the one Markie defines, and that it is a very important concept in the *Meditations*. So, for example, Descartes writes in the Fifth Meditation,

> I am of such a nature that, so long as I perceive something very clearly and distinctly, I cannot but believe it to be true. . . . E.g., when I consider the nature of a triangle, it appears most evident to me, imbued as I am with the principles of Geometry, that its three angles are equal to two right angles, and I cannot but believe this to be true, so long as I attend to its demonstration.[5]

Although the example here is of a proposition which is perceived clearly and distinctly as a result of a demonstration, elsewhere Descartes gives examples of propositions which

> are so clear and at the same time so simple that we can never think of them without believing them to be true, e.g., that I, while I think, exist, that what is once done cannot be undone, and others concerning which it is manifest that we have this certainty.[6]

So some propositions are psychologically certain in their own right, without consideration of any other propositions. Others are psychologically certain because we are psychologically certain that they follow from psychologically certain propositions.

One thing particularly interesting here is the connection between clear and distinct perception and psychological certainty. Later in his book (pp. 187–190) Markie gives an account of clear and distinct perception in terms of psychological certainty, an account which has the consequence that all and only clear and distinct perceptions are psychologically certain.

I have no problem with Markie's definition of psychological certainty or with the connection he makes between it and clear and distinct perception. I defined essentially the same concept myself—though I spoke of descriptive indubitability or assent-compelling propositions (DATS, 94n, 119, etc.)—and

I made essentially the same connection Markie does between psychological certainty and clear and distinct perception (DATS, 119). My main criticism of Markie would be that the notion of psychological certainty enters into his account of Descartes's theory of certainty rather as an afterthought,[7] and that perhaps as a result, he does not give it enough of a role to play. I think it is much more closely connected with metaphysical certainty than he does. My grounds for holding that will appear as we proceed.

Markie on Moral and Metaphysical Certainty

Markie's main textual support for his definitions of moral and metaphysical certainty is a passage toward the end of Part IV of the *Discourse on Method:*

> Finally, if there are still people who are not sufficiently persuaded of the existence of God and of their soul by the reasons I have adduced, I want them to know that all the other things which they perhaps think they are more sure of, such as their having a body, or there being stars and an earth, and things of that kind, are less certain. For although one may have a moral assurance of these things, which is such that it seems that one cannot doubt them without being extravagant, nevertheless, when it is a question of metaphysical certainty, one also cannot deny, without being unreasonable, that there is sufficient reason for not being entirely sure of them, from having noticed that in sleep one can, in the same way, imagine that one has another body, and that one sees other stars, and another earth, without there being any of these things. (AT VI, 37–38)

This is, I think, an interesting passage, but it does not give us very much to go on. Descartes here deploys the distinction between moral and metaphysical certainty without really explaining it, as if it were a philosophical commonplace which stood in no need of explanation.

Still, it would seem we could say, on the basis of this passage, that if you have only moral certainty, then you have something less than complete or perfect certainty; there will be some reason for not being entirely confident of the proposition you are morally certain of, even if it may not be the sort of reason you would ordinarily pay much heed to, such as the possibility that you might be dreaming. Nevertheless, if you've got moral certainty about something, you're in a pretty good epistemic situation. It would be extravagant to deny the proposition you are morally certain of. It must be more than just more probable than not.

These considerations would seem to me to speak against arranging the definitions of moral and metaphysical certainty in such a way that metaphysical certainty implies moral certainty. That is a feature Markie seems to think an advantage of his account (p. 39). But when you have metaphysical certainty, you have no reason to doubt the proposition you are metaphysically certain of. When you have moral certainty, you do have some reason for doubt, or at least you can, in the sense that there is a reason someone could propose to you, even if you haven't thought of it yourself, and might even have been incapable of thinking of it yourself.

Markie fleshes out his account of moral certainty (p. 35) by appealing to a passage in the First Meditation in which Descartes says of the beliefs which have been challenged by the dream and deceiver arguments that they are

> indeed, in some measure doubtful . . . but nevertheless, very probable, and such as it would be much more consistent with reason to believe than to deny . . . (AT VII, 22)

and appealing to a passage early in the Sixth Meditation in which Descartes says (of the hypothesis that there is some body to which the mind is so joined that it can apply itself to examine it whenever it pleases)

> I easily understand, I say, that the imagination can be produced in that way, if the body indeed exists; and because no other equally appropriate way of explaining that presents itself, I conjecture from that with probability that [some? this?] body exists, but only with probability . . . (AT VII, 73).

Descartes does not in fact use the terms "moral certainty" or "metaphysical certainty" in either of these passages, but Markie comments that he "might have put his point differently," by saying that the beliefs in question were morally but not metaphysically certain.

I have some difficulty about Markie's construction of these passages. In the case of the First Meditation passage, at that point of the argument the beliefs in question have supposedly been rejected, in conformity with the methodological requirement that we should withhold our assent from any proposition we find some reason for doubting (AT VII, 18). Descartes acknowledges that it is in fact very difficult to comply consistently with this requirement, so strong is the force of habit and so strong is the evidence for the beliefs. But if we take him at his word, he does not at that stage believe that he has a body, that there is a sky, earth, and so on. If at that stage in his reflections he no longer believes these things, I would have thought it would follow that he is no longer morally certain of them, though he no doubt was morally certain of them initially. It seems to me just anomalous, as a piece of linguistic usage, to say "I am morally certain of that, but I don't believe it." The most we should say of the passage in the First Meditation, I think, is that Descartes's evidential situation is such that, if he did believe the propositions in question, he would be entitled to claim moral certainty about them.[8]

As regards the passage in the Sixth Meditation, it seems to me that, given his own definition of moral certainty, Markie should hesitate to cite that case as one where Descartes would claim moral certainty. Moral certainties are supposed to be *much* more reasonable to believe than to doubt or deny, so much so, according to Markie, that they fall just short of being metaphysical certainties. But all Descartes says in the passage in the Sixth Meditation is that at that stage of the argument his evidence for the existence of bodies makes it a probable conjecture that there are bodies. So in that case believing that there are bodies may not be much more reasonable than denying or doubting it.

The Background of the Cartesian Distinction

Earlier I observed that in the *Discourse* Descartes seems to deploy the distinction between moral and metaphysical certainty as if it were a commonplace, which stands in no need of explanation. And indeed, Descartes is using terms here which he might expect a philosophically sophisticated audience to be familiar with. As Gilson points out in his commentary on the *Discourse,* where the French has ". . . *une assurance morale* . . . ," the Latin has ". . . *certitudo, ut loquuntur Philosophi, moralis* . . . ," a certainty of the kind the philosophers call moral.[9] Neither in his commentary nor in his *Index Scholastico-Cartésien*[10] does Gilson cite any philosopher earlier than Descartes in whom the concept of moral certainty is found. But in the *Index* he does cite a passage from Chauvin's *Lexicon*[11] in which a threefold distinction is made:

> An act of the intellect is said to be morally certain when it assents to a truth which, although it can happen otherwise, is nevertheless so constant that doubt about it is contrary to good principles of action [*bonis moribus*] . . . , [I am said to be] physically certain when I assent to an object firmly, on account of an immutable principle in nature, or . . . to a truth which, although it is possible to think otherwise, is most constant, so long as the order of nature remains the same . . . and [I am said to be] metaphysically certain when I assent firmly to an object which is presented to me in such a way that it cannot be otherwise even by the absolute power of God, or when I assent to a truth which cannot even be thought otherwise. (*Index,* 334)

Though this *Lexicon* is post-Cartesian, it clearly records scholastic usage, since it conceives judgment as an act of the intellect rather than the will. One interesting question it raises is "why is it that what had been a threefold distinction in the scholastics becomes a twofold distinction in Descartes? That is, why does Descartes recognize a distinction between moral and metaphysical certainty, but not between these two kinds of certainty and the physical certainty which for the scholastics had been intermediate between them?"

Now I think we can see why this might have happened if we look at the scholastic manuals whose usage Chauvin's *Lexicon* records. Consider the following passage from Arriaga:

> Certainty is three-fold, moral, physical, and metaphysical. Moral certainty is what we have when our reasons are indeed fallible physically [i.e., scientifically], though infallible morally speaking, i.e., almost infallible, as, for example, the certainty I have about the existence of Naples, from what has been said by so many knowledgeable and honest men who assert it and make me certain that Naples exists, although, because it is not physically impossible that they should all lie, I am not physically certain of this existence. . . .

> Physical certainty is what rests on physical principles [*principiis physicis*] which cannot, in accordance with the nature of the thing [*res*], be otherwise, as, e.g., the certainty I have about Peter's running, which I see; for the thing [*res*] really can be otherwise, at least by [God's] absolute power, insofar as God can miraculously make it appear to me that Peter is running, even though he is not really running; and he can do the same in other matters; therefore, that certainty is not called metaphysical and supreme, but natural or physical. Finally, metaphysical certainty is that by which the object is presented in such a way that in relation to every power it cannot be otherwise, as the certainty I have about God's existence, or about such principles as *Each thing either is or is not,* or *Things which are the same as a third thing are the same as each other,* and the like, or about all the mysteries revealed by God, which cannot be false, even in relation to God's absolute power.[12]

I think we can see why a passage like this might have seemed problematic to the author of the First Meditation. It assumes that perception generates a belief which is highly reliable, that we are entitled to have a confidence in it just short of the confidence we have in the existence of God or the truths of logic. Presumably this is the case because perception operates according to natural laws (e.g., the laws of optics) which cannot be otherwise, and which naturally produce veridical perceptions. We can readily imagine Descartes objecting: first, there are perfectly natural processes (e.g., dreams)[13] which produce experiences intrinsically indistinguishable from the experiences of ordinary perception and which are nevertheless not veridical; second, if we allow the possibility that God could have supernaturally produced deceptive experiences intrinsically indistinguishable from veridical ones, then it does seem that we need some ground for supposing he has not done this before we assign our experiences a particularly high level of credibility; and finally (to focus only on the issue of physical certainty), if our confidence in the operation of the physical laws involved in the production of these experiences rests on the assumption that they cannot be otherwise, we need some explanation of how this can be so, compatibly with God's omnipotence. Descartes, of course, thinks *he* has an explanation, viz. that the laws of nature are necessary truths because they are an expression of the will of an omnipotent God whose will is immutable. But he does not think his scholastic opponents have any good explanation of this.[14]

By focusing in this way on Arriaga, I do not intend to suggest that *he in particular* influenced Descartes or that he was *the* or even *a* source of the hypothesis of a deceiving creator. Though his *Cursus philosophicus* antedates the *Discourse* and the *Meditations* by several years, there's reason to believe that Descartes had not paid much attention to scholastic philosophy in the twenty-year period between 1620 and 1640.[15] His casual use of the concept of moral certainty in 1637 reflects a reading he had engaged in long ago. I do assume that what we find in Arriaga could be found in other scholastic textbooks, among them those Descartes read at La Flèche. But I do not at present have the time to verify that conjecture.

Descartes on Moral and Metaphysical Certainty

What is most surprising about Markie's account of the concepts of moral and metaphysical certainty is his total neglect of Descartes's most explicit discussion of the distinction, the passage at the end of the *Principles of Philosophy* (IV, aa. 205–206), in which Descartes claims that his physics should seem morally certain even to those who do not accept his metaphysics. I'm going to quote from the French version of this passage here. There are interesting differences between the Latin and French versions, so much so that I find it hardly credible that the translator would have taken such liberties on his own authority. I'll follow Adam and Tannery in italicizing those parts of the passage where the French and Latin differ.

Descartes has just finished saying that at the very least his explanations of the phenomena show how things could have happened, and that even Aristotle did not profess to do more than that:

> Nevertheless, in order not to do wrong to the truth, *by supposing it to be less certain than it is, I shall distinguish here two kinds of certainty.* The first is called moral, i.e., sufficient *to guide our practices [moeurs] or as great as that of things we are not accustomed to doubt* regarding the conduct of life, although *we know that it could happen, absolutely speaking that they are false.*[16]

At this point Descartes gives two examples of moral certainty. People who have never been to Rome do not doubt that it is a city in Italy, even though they know this only by hearsay, and the people who have told them this may have deceived them. And a person who finds a key to a cryptogram which makes it convey a meaningful message will not doubt that he has found the true meaning of the cryptogram, even though it could be that the author of the cryptogram may have intended a different meaning. This would be so unlikely that it is not morally credible, particularly if the message is a long one.

Only the second of these examples is given in the original Latin version. The addition of the example of the knowledge that Rome is a city in Italy—as possessed by those who have never been there—should by now remind us of Arriaga (whom Descartes may, in fact, have read in his research for the *Principles*). But what is particularly interesting is the assimilation of the two examples. Descartes will go on to claim that his explanations of the phenomena are so comprehensive that they are comparable to the decoding of a *very* long cryptogram,[17] so long that it is not credible that we should be mistaken. And yet, good as Cartesian science is, it is merely in a class with good hearsay, in the absence of the divine guarantee. Only when we have that guarantee, do we have metaphysical certainty:

> *The other kind of certainty is when we think that it is not at all possible that the thing should be other than we judge it.* And it is founded on a *very sure* principle of Metaphysics, *which is* that God being supremely good and the source of all truth, *since it is he who has created us,* it is certain that the *power or* faculty he has given us to distinguish the true from the false is not

> deceived at all when we use it well and it shows us *evidently that* a thing *is true*. (IV, a. 206: AT IX–2, 324; cf. AT VIII–1, 328)

Descartes goes on to contend that someone who accepts his metaphysical foundation will have this kind of certainty about mathematical demonstrations, the existence of the material world, and about demonstrations regarding the physical world which are equivalent in their evidence to those of mathematics, a category which he takes to include at least the principal and most general propositions he has argued for in the *Principles*.

Curley on Moral and Metaphysical Certainty

What conclusions can we draw from this passage? I think it's clear that a person who has moral certainty believes the proposition he is said to be certain of, and that though his evidence is not sufficient to compel belief (since there are grounds available which would lead him to doubt the proposition), it is quite strong.[18] How strong? This is a question Markie had asked in connection with the passage he relied on from the First Meditation: how *much* more reasonable must belief be than nonbelief? His answer (not really supported by any textual argument) was that it must be so reasonable that the only thing more reasonable to believe (if anything was) would be a metaphysical certainty. But the example of the person who believes that Rome is a city in Italy on the basis of hearsay suggests that it need not be that strong. And the reference to its being sufficiently strong to guide our conduct (common to both the Latin and the French versions) also suggests a lower standard. I would propose the following definition of moral certainty:

> I am morally certain that *p* = df I believe *p* and my evidence for *p* makes it sufficiently more probable than *not-p* that it would be extravagant (at least foolish and perhaps insane) for me not to act on my belief that *p* if I were in a situation in which I had to act either on the belief that *p* or on the belief that *not-p*, although I have, or could have, some valid reason for doubting *p*.

This picks up the idea (particularly strong in the French version of the *Principles*) that I would violate ordinary standards of prudence if I did not act on my belief that *p* in a situation where *p* was relevant to some choice I had to make, and the idea (common to both the Latin and the French versions) that, although I believe *p*, I am not absolutely certain of it.

I take it to be an implication of this definition that we cannot say in general what level of probability a belief must have in order to be morally certain, and in particular that we cannot say that it must fall just short of absolute certainty. Whether or not it will be extravagant not to act on a perceptual belief will depend in part on the content of the belief and what is at stake if it is true. If my senses incline me to believe that there is a precipice before me, I would be foolish not to act on that belief, even though I may have good grounds for doubting the evidence of the senses in general, and even if special features of the particular perceptual situation seem to supply additional grounds for doubt. (It may be dark and foggy, but by God that certainly looks like a precipice in front of me.)[19]

> I am metaphysically certain that *p* = df I am psychologically certain that *p,* and I have no valid reason for doubting *p.*

This is essentially the way I defined metaphysical certainty in *Descartes Against the Skeptics,* though in some passages there I spoke of it under the heading of "normative indubitability" (cf. DATS, 111–112, 118–123). Both of these definitions make use of the notion of a valid ground of doubt, a notion which will have to be clarified presently.

Markie on the Role of Moral Certainty in Descartes's Argument

However we may define the notion of moral certainty, Markie's account of Descartes's argument surely gives it a crucial role in the structure of the *Meditations;* that is one of the defects of his account. In addition to the definition of metaphysical certainty cited earlier, Markie also provides us with a criterion of metaphysical certainty:

> *p* is a metaphysical certainty for *S* if and only if *p* is a moral certainty for *S* and *S* has no reason to doubt *p.* (p. 42)

In the subsequent argument of *Descartes's Gambit* it is this criterion, rather than his definition, which does the work. So, for example, in introducing his solution to the *cogito* puzzle, he writes,

> I argue . . . that Descartes' claim . . . to be metaphysically certain that he thinks has two parts: he is morally certain that he thinks, and he has no reason to doubt that he thinks. His claim . . . to be metaphysically certain that he exists is similarly complex: he is morally certain that he exists, and he has no reason to doubt his morally certain belief that he exists. Since Descartes' claims are complex, his defense of them must be so, too. He must explain what makes him morally certain he thinks and exists, and why no hypothesis casts doubt on those morally certain beliefs. (p. 165)

So he constructs arguments which he ascribes to Descartes, arguments which yield the conclusion that Descartes is morally certain of his existence and his thought. These arguments rely on the principle that all our clear and distinct perceptions are morally certain, a principle which Markie admits Descartes never states explicitly, but which he thinks we must attribute to him to understand the relation between Descartes's clear and distinct perception that he thinks and exists and his moral certainty regarding those facts.

I see no reason to suppose that it is an important part of Descartes's argument in the *Meditations* to show that he is morally certain that he thinks and exists, or even that he makes any attempt to do so. Forget about the fact that he never explicitly states the principle on which the argument is supposed to rest, the principle that all our clear and distinct ideas are morally certain. Where does he ever state the conclusion of the argument Markie attributes to him? For that matter, where in the *Meditations* does Descartes ever make any explicit use of the concept of moral certainty?

Metaphysical Certainty and Psychological Certainty

If the definition of metaphysical certainty which I have offered is correct, however, it would be a part of Descartes's argument in the *Meditations* to show that he is psychologically certain of his existence. That would be an important first step in establishing the metaphysical certainty of his existence. I suggest that this is the way we should understand what is happening in the first three paragraphs of the Second Meditation. Descartes does not begin by establishing that it is (much) more probable than not that he exists. Rather, he discovers that he *cannot* believe in his nonexistence by examining a series of grounds of doubt which have in the First Meditation proven effective in enabling him to suspend judgment about his other beliefs, such as the beliefs in the existence of the external world and the truths of mathematics. So when he writes that

> it must be maintained that this proposition, *I am, I exist,* is necessarily true, as often as I express it, or conceive it in my mind (AT VII, 25),

the "must" here expresses a psychological certainty, engendered by the failed attempt to find grounds for doubting my existence, and reaffirmed in the fourth paragraph of the Third Meditation:

> As often as I turn my attention to these things which I think I perceive very clearly, I am so completely persuaded by them that I spontaneously break out in these words: let whoever can deceive me, he will still never bring it about that I am nothing, so long as I think that I am something. . . . (AT VII, 36)

As I argued in *Descartes Against the Skeptics* (93–95, 123–124), I do not think Descartes claims metaphysical certainty, even of his own existence, at this point in the argument of the *Meditations*. Unlike many interpreters of Descartes, I take quite seriously the conclusion of this paragraph, where Descartes writes that so long as he does not know whether God exists and can be a deceiver, he does not seem able ever to be completely certain of any other thing (*non videor de ulla alia plane certus esse unquam posse*).

So I take psychological certainty to be a necessary, but not sufficient, condition for metaphysical certainty. Markie almost agrees. He grants that in fact, according to Descartes, all our metaphysical certainties are psychological certainties, but holds that this is a contingent fact stemming from the way we have been created by God, not a necessary truth which the definitions of the various kinds of certainty ought to reflect (pp. 56–57). Nevertheless, I think that for Descartes the connection between metaphysical and psychological certainty was so close that it was definitional. Markie writes that Descartes "tends to conflate metaphysical and psychological certainty," and as evidence of that fact cites a passage from the Second Replies which has often been stressed by Frankfurt:

> As soon as we think we have perceived something correctly, we spontaneously persuade ourselves that this is true. But if this persuasion is so firm that we can have no reason for doubt regarding what we thus persuade ourselves of, there is nothing further to be sought. We have everything we could reasonably desire. (AT VII, 144–145)

Markie comments that

> Descartes' talk of persuasion suggests a concern with psychological certainty; his talk of reasons for doubt and all the certainty that can reasonably be desired makes it clear that he is also concerned with metaphysical certainty. (p. 56)

But it seems reasonable to talk of conflation here only if you assume that Descartes wants to make a sharper separation between these concepts than it seems to me that he does. As the passage continues, Descartes deliberately identifies metaphysical certainty, what he calls here "the most perfect certainty," with "a firm and immutable conviction":

> For we are supposing a persuasion so firm that it cannot be removed in any way, which persuasion therefore is absolutely the same as the most perfect certainty. But it can be doubted whether there is any such certainty, *or* [*sive*] firm and immutable conviction. . . . (AT VII, 145)

Now I don't suppose that a firm and immutable conviction is the same thing as psychological certainty. I might believe *p* now and be unable now not to believe *p,* and yet my conviction that *p* might not be immutable. Further reflection or new evidence might lead me to doubt *p*. So psychological certainty does not entail metaphysical certainty. But surely metaphysical certainty entails psychological certainty. If my conviction that *p* truly is firm and immutable, then I cannot but believe *p,* not only now but forever more. So psychological certainty ought to be an element in the definition of metaphysical certainty, and it is a defect in Markie's account of metaphysical certainty that it is not.

Reasons for Doubt

Markie's criterion for metaphysical certainty differs obviously from my definition of that concept in substituting moral certainty for psychological certainty in the first branch of the definition, and seems to agree with my definition in accepting the idea of an absence of valid grounds for doubt in the second branch. I say "seems to agree" because Markie gives quite a different explanation of what a (valid) reason for doubt consists in than I had and he is sharply critical of my explanation. In *Descartes Against the Skeptics* I had offered the following analysis of this concept:

> Someone has a valid ground for doubting a proposition, *p,* if and only if he can think of some other proposition, *q,* such that
> (i) *q* is incompatible with *p* or with some principle, *r,* which provides the basis for his assent to *p;* and
> (ii) (a) if either *p* or *r* is not assent-compelling, then he can think of no assent-compelling proposition incompatible with *q,* and
> (b) if both *p* and *r* are assent-compelling, then so is *q;* and
> (iii) *q* explains how he might have erroneously thought *p.* (DATS, 122)

Markie characterizes this as a "purely psychological account" and that seems appropriate, since its central concept, that of an assent-compelling proposition, is a psychological concept. It was just my way of getting at the notion of what we have been calling here psychological certainty. Markie writes that my

> interpretation has two problems common to all purely psychological accounts of how reasons for doubt are ruled out. It has no textual support—Curley provides none, and I do not know of any—and it chains Descartes to an incorrect position. It is silly to think that by merely changing our psychological state we can change our epistemic position and so rule out a reason for doubt and make a mere moral certainty into a metaphysical one. Suppose you have a reason to doubt a morally certain, non-assent-compelling belief, and you want to make your belief into a metaphysical certainty. Curley's Descartes says: Just think of an assent-compelling proposition incompatible with your reason for doubt. . . . Surely more is required. You must increase your belief's reasonableness if you want to make it a metaphysical certainty, and that entails finding evidence against your reasons for doubt. Curley's Descartes might say that the assent-compelling propositions he has in mind will contain such evidence, but even if that is so, it is the evidence's status *as evidence,* not its assent-compelling nature, that causes your epistemic state to change. (p. 44)

So Markie proposes an alternative, epistemic account of what a (valid) reason for doubt consists in:

> *q* gives *S* a reason to doubt *S*'s morally certain belief *p* if and only if (1) *q* is a metaphysical possibility for *S,* and (2) either *q* indicates to *S* how *p* might be false despite *S*'s evidence for *p,* or *q* indicates to *S* how an essential part of *S*'s evidence for *p* might be false despite *S*'s evidence for that essential part. (p. 49)

Roughly speaking, this account differs from mine in that it drops the first condition in my account, offers a version of the third condition which is more complicated but essentially the same in spirit, and uses, in the second condition, the notion of metaphysical possibility rather than that of an assent-compelling proposition. It's this last difference which seems to me most important.

Up to a point I have some sympathy with Markie's proposal. The fundamental question, as it seemed to me when I wrote *Descartes Against the Skeptics,* and as it still seems to me, is "what are the requirements for something's being a reasonable or valid ground of doubt?" That's the natural question to ask for someone who was as much influenced as I was by the work of Gewirth and Frankfurt on the circle. So in *Descartes Against the Skeptics* I wrote:

> The first thing to notice is that it is not necessary that a proposition which is offered as a reason for doubting be itself very probable or even supported by a substantial body of evidence. It is sufficient that there not be any intellectually compelling evidence against it. (p. 85)

In support of this I strongly emphasized a passage from the Seventh Replies:

> For those reasons are valid enough to force us to doubt which are themselves doubtful and therefore not to be retained. . . . They are indeed valid so long as we have no others which induce certainty by removing doubt. (AT VII, 473–474, cited on pp. 85, 106–107 and 116)

And though I didn't cite it in the context of my defense of my analysis of the notion of a valid ground of doubt, I did expect that careful readers would recollect my discussion of the dream argument, in which I argued that

> the premises of the skeptical arguments of the First Meditation need not be ones Descartes knows to be true, or is certain of, or even believes without question . . . (p. 50),

pointing out that the hypothesis of an omnipotent God is introduced simply as "a certain old opinion implanted in my mind" (AT VII, 21) and later characterized as a "preconceived opinion" (AT VII, 36).[20]

I argued that it was because Descartes had set the evidential requirements for a valid ground of doubt so low that he was prepared to characterize the reasons he offers for doubting as very slight and metaphysical (AT VII, 36) and to admit that the beliefs they cast doubt on are nonetheless very probable (AT VII, 22). The point of setting the evidential requirements so low, I said, was "a strategic one. The weaker the criteria for a valid ground of doubt the more dramatic and persuasive it is if a valid ground of doubt cannot be found" (116). Descartes's dialectical situation vis-à-vis the skeptic requires him to make it very easy for the skeptic (or the skeptic in himself) to come up with a valid ground of doubt.[21]

Now insofar as Markie too adopts a very weak evidential requirement, I think he shows a correct appreciation of the Cartesian strategy. If the only evidential requirement a reason for doubt has to satisfy is that it be a metaphysical possibility for the inquirer, that is equivalent to saying that it must not be metaphysically certain for him that the proposition offered as a reason for doubt is false (DG, 44). So Descartes would be saying that no matter how improbable a reason for doubt is, it will count as a valid reason for doubt so long as it is not known with absolute certainty to be false. And that seems to me to be in the right spirit.[22]

Nevertheless, even though Markie's requirement seems initially to be along the right lines, I think it is a mistake to define the evidential requirement for valid grounds of doubt in terms of metaphysical possibility. That notion is in turn defined in terms of metaphysical certainty. I want to use the notion of a valid ground of doubt to define the notion of metaphysical certainty. After all, that seems to me to be what Descartes himself does in the Second Replies (AT VII, 144–145). If we turn around and define the notion of a valid ground of doubt in terms of metaphysical certainty, we generate an infinite regress. To exclude a proposed ground of doubt as invalid because of its failure to satisfy the evidential requirement we'll have to be able to say that it's metaphysically certain that it is false. And to establish the metaphysical certainty of that falsity, we will need to inquire into the metaphysical possibility of propositions which might be proposed as grounds for doubting it, and so on.[23]

Markie says I provide no textual support for my interpretations and that I chain Descartes to an incorrect position. Indeed, he says, it is "silly" to think that merely by changing our psychological state we can change our epistemic position and so rule out a reason for doubt and make a mere moral certainty into a metaphysical one.

Now I thought I had supported my interpretation textually by citing that passage from the Seventh Replies which runs

> For those reasons are valid enough to force us to doubt which are themselves doubtful and therefore not to be retained. . . . They are indeed valid so long as we have no others which induce certainty by removing doubt. (AT VII, 473–474)

I see now that this passage is not sufficient to establish everything I wanted it to prove. It *is* sufficient, I think, to rule out any understanding of the notion of a valid ground of doubt which would require that valid grounds of doubt satisfy some strong epistemic requirement, such as being known to be true, or even being more probable than not. So it's a good text if our only purpose is to show that Descartes has been relevantly misunderstood by such philosophers as Moore and Prichard and Austin and Walsh, philosophers who have urged against Descartes what I call "the Procedural Objection" (DATS, 48–49). But it is not sufficient to rule out an understanding of the notion of a valid ground of doubt which requires only that a valid ground of doubt satisfy a weak epistemic requirement, such as being a metaphysical possibility.[24] For someone like Markie might say that when Descartes talks about inducing certainty by removing doubt, he means that we induce metaphysical certainty by becoming metaphysically certain that our former reasons for doubt were false. How, he might ask, could anything less than metaphysical certainty that those grounds of doubt are false yield metaphysical certainty about the proposition they were introduced to cast doubt on?

It's tempting to answer this question with another question: If we have to have metaphysical certainty that our grounds for doubting a proposition are false before we can be metaphysically certain of the proposition they cast doubt on, how can we ever be metaphysically certain of anything? Markie's way of thinking seems to lead inevitably either to the circle or to an infinite regress. But I take it that Markie would not think this an objection to his interpretation, since his view seems to be that Descartes is stuck with the problem of the circle as soon as he tries to go beyond metaphysical certainty regarding his thought and his existence (p. 162, n. 12).

Nevertheless, I persist in thinking that we have, in principle, a way out of the circle if we allow that we can exclude reasons for doubting by becoming psychologically certain that proposed reasons for doubting are false. And I do think this was Descartes's way out. In *Descartes Against the Skeptics* (121–122) I tried to support this textually by appealing to that passage in the Second Replies in which Descartes grants that an atheist might perceive clearly and distinctly that the three angles of a triangle are equal to two right angles, but contends that, so long as he remains an atheist, he cannot have true *scientia* of this proposition (AT VII, 141), "since no knowledge which can be rendered doubtful seems rightly to be called *scientia.*" I take it to be agreed between Markie and myself that, in lacking *scientia,* the atheist lacks metaphysical certainty of what he clearly and distinctly perceives (cf. DG, 159–160). And the question is: what would the atheist have to acquire in order to turn his clear and distinction perception into metaphysical certainty?

In *Descartes Against the Skeptics* I took it for granted that, according to Descartes, it would be sufficient for him to be metaphysically certain of this clearly and distinctly perceived mathematical proposition if he came to perceive clearly and distinctly that God exists, that God is not a deceiver, that God would be a deceiver if he permitted his creatures to be mistaken about things which they could not help but believe, and hence, that all his creatures' clear and distinct perceptions are true. Descartes certainly does not say all that in the passage in question. All he says is that the atheist will never be safe from doubt concerning the things which seem most evident to him until he first recognizes God. But what I took for granted still seems to me a reasonable gloss on what he says, so I'm going to continue to take it for granted.

The question I then raise is: What does this clear and distinct perception consist in? Markie explains it in terms of psychological certainty (DG, 186–192), and that seems to me to be the right way to proceed. I have argued elsewhere that it is characteristic of the analytic method of the *Meditations* that important concepts are introduced not by means of formal definitions, but by means of examples.[25] The concepts of clarity and distinctness are introduced in the *Meditations* in connection with the example of the piece of wax, which we originally grasp in a way which is imperfect and confused and then, after a thought-experiment, in a way which is clear and distinct (AT VII, 31). My idea of the wax becomes clear when I realize that there are certain things I am compelled to ascribe to the wax (that it is something extended, flexible, changeable). It becomes distinct when I realize that the other things I might initially have been inclined to ascribe to the wax—that whiteness, that fragrance, that shape, and so on—are things I am not compelled to ascribe to it.[26] I make my idea of body distinct by eliminating from it whatever is not clear, just as in the *Principles* (I, 45) I make my idea of pain distinct by eliminating from it the unclear thought that there is something in my body like the sensation of pain in my mind.

So if I perceive clearly and distinctly that God exists, is not a deceiver, etc., then I am compelled to assent to those propositions, and recognize that I am not compelled to assent to other, related propositions (such as the proposition that it would be incompatible with God's goodness for me to be deceived about things I do not perceive clearly and distinctly). And if that is all clear and distinct perception consists in, then my becoming psychologically certain that God exists, is not a deceiver, etc., will be sufficient to remove the doubt based on the possibility of deception by an omnipotent being. What the atheist needs, to turn his psychological certainty about the mathematical proposition into a metaphysical certainty, is the psychological certainty that an omnipotent being is not deceiving him.

Perhaps the most explicit recognition of this comes in that passage cited earlier from the Second Replies in which Descartes identifies the most perfect certainty with a "persuasion so firm that we can never have any reason for doubting what we are so persuaded of" (AT VII, 144). Descartes asks rhetorically,

> What is it to us if perhaps someone feigns that that very thing of whose truth we are so firmly persuaded appears false to God or to an angel, and therefore, absolutely speaking, is false? What do we care about that absolute falsity, since we don't believe in it in any way, or even suspect it? (AT VII, 145)

Harry Frankfurt used to take this passage to indicate that Descartes was forswearing any interest in the concept of absolute truth, that is, in truth understood as correspondence with reality.[27] But it seems to me rather that he is forswearing any interest in proposed grounds of doubt which he cannot in any way, even to the slightest extent, believe in.

Is it "silly to think that by merely changing our psychological state we can change our epistemic position and so rule out a reason for doubt and make a mere moral certainty into a metaphysical one"? I don't see why (though I would prefer it if the question were framed in terms of turning a psychological certainty into a metaphysical one). I take it that the First Meditation illustrates how changes in our psychological state entail changes in our epistemic position. I start out thinking that my senses only deceive me concerning small or distant objects, and that I cannot doubt sense-based beliefs concerning things that are neither small nor distant. Then I recall that I have often had experiences while asleep which were as deceptive as those of madmen. My first reaction to this is to say that experiences as distinct as I am now having would not happen to someone who was asleep. But then I remember how distinct some of my dreams have been. My psychological state is constantly changing, and as it changes, my epistemic position changes with it. What it is reasonable for me to believe at each stage of this reflective process is at least partly a function of the beliefs I consciously hold at that stage of the process.

I say "partly" because I don't think Descartes holds it to be necessary that a valid ground of doubt should be something the enquirer believes. He treats the hypothesis of the evil demon as a valid ground of doubt, even though he does not believe in the demon. But he does think that facts about what we do and can believe have epistemological significance. Once I reach the point where I cannot believe in the demon, I have exorcised that ground of doubt. But that is not an easy thing to do. Markie writes as if it were: "Just think of an assent-compelling proposition incompatible with your reason for doubt." Unfortunately it's not that easy for us to change our psychological state, or for someone else with finite powers—an author, say—to change it for us. Descartes spent at least two meditations trying to work out an argument which would leave us unable to give credence to the possibility of the demon. He did not succeed. But a proper understanding of the criteria for a valid ground of doubt should help us to see that this was, at least, not a project which was doomed from the start because of problems about circularity.

It may, of course, be in trouble for other reasons. If my reading of Descartes is correct, there is a kind of naturalistic fallacy at work in his theory of certainty, as my use of the labels "descriptive" and "normative indubitability" was meant to suggest. Descartes does not simply equate psychological certainty with metaphysical certainty, but he does think that if we're psychologically certain of something, and psychologically certain of the falsity of any ground we can think of for doubting that proposition, and if we've conducted a sufficiently rigorous search for grounds of doubt, and adopted a sufficiently liberal criterion for a valid ground of doubt, we're entitled to say that we're absolutely certain. It may be that the project of testing our beliefs by seeking grounds for doubting them is not one which we can ever pronounce to be finished. The subsequent history of science, which has involved rejection by the scientific community even of some mathematical propositions Descartes took to be metaphysically certain, would seem to suggest that psychological certainty is too weak a reed to support the enterprise, no matter how much it may be supplemented by methods of doubt. But if the project does fail for that reason, it seems to me a more interesting kind of failure, a more honorable failure, than that which we attribute to him by committing him to the circularity Markie's interpretation involves.

Notes

1. Ithaca: Cornell University Press, 1986 (henceforth abbreviated DG). Page references not otherwise identified will be to this work.

2. Cambridge: Harvard University Press, 1978; (henceforth abbreviated DATS).

3. Cf. DG, 29–30, citing AT VII, 226.

4. The definitions and epistemic principles are conveniently listed in an appendix at the end of the book (pp. 271–274). The metaphysical assumptions are not given equal prominence, but are there nonetheless. So, for example, Markie's "gambit defense" of the claim that "I am essentially thinking" assumes that thought is a nonrelational property and that some property is essential to me (p. 235). His defense of the claim that "I am not extended" assumes that if I am extended, I am necessarily extended (p. 249). And so on.

5. Cited by Markie, 55. I follow the Latin text (AT VII, 69–70). The French (AT IX–1, 55) is slightly different.

6. Cited by Markie, 187. Cf. AT VII, 145.

7. This seems quite literally to be true. Not only does Markie offer his account of psychological certainty quite late in his chapter on certainty, but also, in two earlier articles which anticipated most of what he has to say about moral and metaphysical certainty, there is no mention of psychological certainty. Cf. "Dreams and Deceivers in Meditation One," *Philosophical Review* 90 (1981): 185–209, and "The *Cogito* Puzzle," *Philosophy and Phenomenological Research* 43 (1982): 59–81.

8. It is not an inadvertent feature of Markie's definition of moral certainty that it permits moral certainties not to be believed at the very time when they are moral certainties. Cf. DG, 58. In comments on an earlier draft of this paper, read at a conference in Cincinnati in the fall of 1987, Markie replied that he did not see anything strange about saying that someone is morally certain of something he does not believe. "It seems to me that we can and do sometimes fail to believe what we have good reason to believe." But that's not the point. The question is whether we should say of such a person that he is morally certain of the thing he does not believe, just because he has good reason to believe it. To me that seems a perverse use of the term "certain."

9. René Descartes, *Discours de la méthode, texte et commentaire,* ed. Etienne Gilson (Paris: Vrin, 1976), 358.

10. 2d ed. (Paris: Vrin, 1979).

11. *Lexicon rationale sive Thesaurus philosophicus* (Rotterdam, 1692).

12. Roderigo de Arriaga, *Cursus philsophicus* (Antwerp, 1632), 226, col. 1. I owe this very interesting reference to Peter Dear.

13. Dreams, however, are not the only example, only the most familiar example. Cf. AT I, 21: "There is a part of mathematics which I call the science of miracles because it teaches us how to use the air and light in such a way as to provide the same illusions which they say magicians produce with the aid of demons." Cf. AT VI, 343–344.

14. I have discussed this issue in "Descartes on the Creation of the Eternal Truths," *Philosophical Review* 93 (1984): 569–597, reprinted in *Eternal Truths and the Cartesian Circle,* ed. Willis Doney (New York: Garland, 1987).

15. This is the conclusion Roger Ariew reaches in "Descartes and Scholasticism," in the *Cambridge Companion to Descartes,* ed. J. Cottingham (Cambridge University Press, 1992). A key bit of evidence is Descartes's letter to Mersenne of 30 September 1640 (see esp. AT III, 185).

16. IV, a. 205: AT IX–2, 323. Cf. AT VIII–1, 327–328, well-translated in CSM. Note that our word "moral" and the French word "*moeurs*" both derive from the Latin "*mos, moris,*" meaning practice, custom, habit, etc. So a connection with action is implied in the label.

17. We must, I think, interpret Descartes as referring to types of phenomena, and not to individual phenomea, when he claims comprehensiveness for his explanations. So his science is supposed to be complete in that it explains how magnets work in general, not each particular instance of magnetism at work (of which there might be infinitely many).

18. One interesting variation between the French and the Latin, omitted by my abridgment of the text, is this: in the Latin it is said that the person who decodes the message may "know this only by conjecture"; this gets eliminated in the French, which recognizes that his initial decision to try a certain key was a conjecture, but that after he has found that key to yield a sensible message, he has something more than a mere conjecture. Cf. AT VIII–1, 352 (of the re-edition).

19. The example is suggested by the Fifth Replies (AT VII, 350–351), and dis-

cussed (unsatisfactorily, it seems to me) by Markie (DG, 40). The whole topic needs further exploration. Among the passages which need to be taken into account are the reply to Hyperaspistes (AT III, 422–423), the *Passions of the Soul* II, 146, and the letter to Elisabeth of 6 October 1645.

20. In the same vein I might have cited another passage in the Seventh Replies in which Descartes writes that when the context is a theoretical one rather than a practical one "whatever can produce even the slightest suspicion must be taken to be a sufficiently valid reason [for doubt]" (AT VII, 460), or that passage in the Second Meditation in which Descartes writes that he will once again attempt the same path he had entered on the day before "by removing whatever admits of even the slightest doubt, no less readily than if I had found it to be completely false" (AT VII, 24).

21. I am pleased to find an appreciation of this point, arrived at independently, in James van Cleve's "Foundationalism, Epistemic Principles and the Cartesian Circle," *Philosophical Review* 88 (1979): 62.

22. I don't think Markie keeps consistently to that point of view. Later on, for example, when he comes to discuss Moore's objection to the dream argument (DG, 129–132), he rightly rejects Moore's contention that Descartes's use of the premises of that argument implies knowledge that those premises are true, a knowledge he cannot have if the conclusion of the argument is correct. But then, from my point of view, Markie spoils this reply by saying that "the Dream Argument needs only reasonable premises to accomplish its purpose" (132). He doesn't define "reasonable," but if we assume that a reasonable premise must at least be more probable than not, I think this is too strong a requirement. Markie's earlier discussion of the dream argument suggests that by "reasonable" in this context he means "morally certain." See p. 110, n. 5, and p. 111.

23. Markie acknowledges this as a prima facie difficulty in p. 51, n. 11. He evidently thinks that his ch. 5 deals with the difficulty, but I don't see that it does. Markie says there are some propositions which resist all reasons for doubt right from the start. I suppose he means that in the case of some propositions (e.g., "I think" or "I exist") all proposed grounds of doubt can be excluded as invalid not for failure to satisfy the evidential requirement but for failure to satisfy the explanatory requirement, so that we don't need to face the question whether they satisfy the evidential requirement. But though this might work for propositions like "I think" and "I exist," it won't work in general. I.e., it won't work for most of the propositions Descartes claims to be metaphysically certain. And if what I have argued in DATS (pp. 93–95) is correct—that even the existence of the self is not metaphysically certain until after the arguments of the Third and Fourth Meditations validate the inferential principles used to derive his thought and his existence from skeptical hypotheses—then it won't work even for "I think" and "I exist."

24. The same might be said of the other passages I cited earlier (AT VII, 21, 24, 36, and 460).

25. Originally I argued this in "Spinoza as an Expositor of Descartes," in *Speculum Spinozanum,* ed. S. Hessing (Routledge and Kegan Paul, 1977), 133–142, but I have developed it more fully in "Analysis in the *Meditations,*" in *Essays on Descartes' "Meditations,"* ed. A. Rorty, (University of California Press, 1986), 153–176.

26. Cf. DATS, 197, 212–215.

27. *Demons, Dreamers and Madmen* (Indianapolis: Bobbs-Merrill, 1970), 179–180.

3

The *Cogito:* Privileged Truth or Exemplary Truth?

Michelle Beyssade

TRANSLATED BY STEPHEN VOSS

Et comme elle a l'éclat du verre,
Elle en a la fragilité.

Antoine Godeau, *Ode à Louis XIII*

It may be surprising to see how Descartes, in the *Discours de la Méthode* and the *Meditationes,* after having gained the certainty of his existence as a thinking thing, derives from this first knowledge the general rule that allows him to become certain of any thing, that is to say, to recognize truth, the rule which is often called the criterion of truth (a phrase which Descartes himself does not use).

There is no doubt that this first knowledge is incontestably a truth: it resists doubt and presents itself as indubitable. But it appears as a truth which is privileged and, properly speaking, exceptional: it is an exception to doubt because the recognition of one's existence is the condition of this doubt. If it eludes doubt, this is because it always follows from the doubt, which, in the very exercise, affirms it.

But if it is exceptional, can it serve as an example? Can one extract from it the general criterion of truth? Can the exception provide the rule? How is it that this privileged truth can also be exemplary?

Truths and the Criterion of Truth

First we must observe that the criterion derived from the new truth is not a new criterion.

Part II of the *Discours de la Méthode* formulates four precepts, which issue from reflection on logic and certain branches of mathematics; and the first of them, which explicates the notion of evidence in terms of those of clarity and distinctness, already proclaims the criterion of truth.[1] The *Regulae ad directionem ingenii,* taking arithmetic and geometry as its model, attributes the same characteristics to the *intuitus mentis,* that fundamental act of the understanding by which we gain true knowledge. We observe that in this work the pair "clear and distinct" is not yet the frozen, canonical expression which it is to become from the *Discours* on for Descartes and still more for his translators. But if it does not appear in Rule III, which associates "easy" with "distinct," it is certainly present in the focal passage in Rule XI.[2]

The demands of metaphysics place in question, or rather in suspense, the certainty of the method. The universal metaphysical doubt in Part IV of the *Discours* and in Meditation I suspects all of our thoughts of falsity, and makes no exception of those evident truths whose clarity and distinctness provided the criterion of truth in Part II of the *Discours* and in the *Rules.*[3] This very criterion loses its significance: within the throes of metaphysical doubt, clarity and distinctness are no longer the sign of truth.

But it is precisely at this point, within the very heart of the trial by doubt, after the affirmation of a truth, that of my existence as thinking thing, that Descartes recognizes anew, on reflection, clarity and distinctness as the criterion of truth.[4] A new truth allows the recovery of the old criterion, which until then has been held in suspension by doubt. What could be more satisfying? We may inquire about the exact meaning of the *quaedam* which, in the Latin text of the *Meditationes,* accompanies the word *clara* (*clara quaedam et distincta perceptio*). Does it express some hesitation in the choice of the term to be associated with *distincta,* or does Descartes wish to emphasize that this first knowledge is an example of clear and distinct perception? In any event, in both texts—the Third Meditation and Part IV of the *Discours*—the movement is the same: a newly won truth is the stimulus for the release of the criterion of truth which the demands of metaphysics had briefly detained. Cartesian reflection has altered its model; but the criterion is not altered, and it seems even to be confirmed.

But in what sense confirmed?

Doubt and the Criterion of Truth

This new explication of the criterion does not for all that reestablish the truth of mathematics, or more generally our confidence in the validity of the criterion.

The *Discours de la Méthode*

If this is not immediately apparent in the *Discours de la Méthode,* it is made manifest a little later, when, after having demonstrated the existence of God, Descartes adds, "what I have just now taken as a rule, namely, that the things we conceive very clearly and very distinctly are all true, is secure only because God is, or exists."[5] The general rule was not secure so long as the existence of

God was not established. Descartes had only made use of it, "*taken it as* a rule [*prendre pour règle*]." At the moment when he enunciated the rule, he was not sure of its validity, although he did not mention the fact and may not even have been aware of it. It is the knowledge of God which "renders us certain"[6] of this rule. Since the *Discours* does not formulate the hypothesis of a deceiving God, Descartes has not previously been warned of this lapse of certainty.

The meaning of this belated doubt is explained in the *Meditationes*. But the text of the *Discours* invites a rigorous vocabulary, especially if we use other terms than those Descartes uses. *Je pense, donc je suis* is not the criterion of truth, but an example of truth which is taken as a *model*. In this sense it may be called exemplary. As such it supplies the *criterion* of truth, but not the *guarantee* of truth—the assurance that the criterion is a good one.

The *Meditationes*

In the *Meditationes,* the persistence of the universal doubt, with the exception of the *cogito,*[7] and the continued doubtfulness of mathematical truths, in spite of their clarity and distinctness, are completely manifest.

The Statement of the Rule (Paragraph 2)

At the moment when he derives the general rule from his first knowledge, and even before he enunciates it, Descartes expresses what certainly appears to be a restriction, or at least a fear: "which truly," he says, speaking of clear and distinct perception, "would not be enough to assure me that it is true, if a thing I conceive clearly and distinctly in this way could ever turn out to be false." Even though it is expressed in the contrary-to-fact present tense, as the Latin text shows (*non sufficeret . . . si posset*),[8] this hypothesis of the falsity of what is clear and distinct limits in advance the assurance which the rule might have been able to provide.

The Application of the Rule (Paragraph 4)

The development that follows, introduced by "Yet I previously accepted" (AT IX, 27, l. 33; CSM II, 24), moderates still further our hopes for the growth of knowledge. It is here that Meditation III goes beyond the *Discours*. No doubt we may take it that the third paragraph[9] (AT IX, 27, l. 33–28, l. 11) explains the remark which follows the *Discours*'s statement of the rule: "But there remains some difficulty in ascertaining which ones we conceive distinctly." For Descartes in fact observes here that the bits of knowledge too quickly accepted at first as certain are complex wholes, often grasped confusedly, within which doubtful affirmations on the one hand must be distinguished from indubitable elements on the other. But the next paragraph (AT IX, 28, ll. 12–34; CSM II, 25, through "a manifest contradiction") focuses on simple and easy things, of which mathematics provides examples—objects of the *Regulae*'s *intuitis mentis,* to remind us that there has been reason to doubt them, namely, the hypothesis of the deceiving God, and reason even now to exercise doubt about that which definitely seems to be evident, simple and easy, clear and distinct.

> Every time this previously conceived opinion of the supreme power of a God is presented to my mind, I am constrained to confess that it will be easy for him if he wishes to do things in such a way that I am mistaken even in the things I think I know [*mentis oculis . . . intueri*] with a very great degree of evidence.

The criterion of truth just now extracted is useless. My clear and distinct conceptions risk being deceptive. If the *cogito* is certain, and has been posited as certain in spite of the doubt stemming from the hypothesis of the deceiving God, it might now seem that it is not its clarity and distinctness which makes it certain. Its certainty must derive from something that other clear and distinct conceptions lack, from some privilege, and in any case not solely from its clarity and its distinctness. Its certainty must accrue to it by virtue of its entirely exceptional resistance when threatened by the deceiving God. If we take up the formula and the terms of the *Discours, je pense, donc je suis,* we should then have to say that it is not only on account of the clarity and the distinctness of the relation between the *je pense* and the *je suis* that this truth cannot be threatened by the most extravagant suppositions of the skeptics.[10] And yet Descartes says the opposite: "And having observed that there is *nothing at all* in *je pense, donc je suis* which assures me that what I say is true *except* that I see very clearly that in order to think it is necessary to be. . . ." He says the same thing in Meditation III before formulating the rule in the second paragraph: "In this first knowledge *nothing* is to be found but a clear and distinct perception of that which I know."

How can all of this be made consistent? How can we unite the exceptional character and the exemplary character of the *cogito?* We may hope that Meditation III, whose fourth paragraph, as we have just seen, raises this problem more explicitly, also contains, if not its solution, at least the principle of a solution or the elements for a solution.

The Privilege of the *Cogito*

The Privilege Forgotten?

Curiously, no privilege seems to be granted to the *cogito* in the fourth paragraph of Meditation III, where in the sentence that follows the one we have just cited the *cogito* appears on the same plane as a mathematical truth:

> And on the other hand every time I turn to the things I think I conceive very clearly I am so convinced by them that I find myself spontaneously breaking out in these words: Let him who can deceive me, he can never bring it about that I am nothing while I think I am something . . . ; or that two and three added together make more or less than five. . . .

In the presence of clear and distinct conceptions I am persuaded by their evidentness, and affirm them. The *cogito* is not presented here as an exception; two other truths are joined with it, as two examples among others ("or similar things"). It has at most the privilege of coming first.

It may even be asked whether these three examples may not stand in the same relation to the two sentences "And whenever my preconceived belief . . . a manifest contradiction" (AT IX, 28, ll. 21–34; CSM II, 25) and whether they cannot be transported into the previous sentence to be considered retrospectively as examples of the evident things cast into doubt when the hypothesis of a deceiving God fills my thought. In this case the *cogito* would no longer enjoy any privilege: like mathematical truths, it would fall under the blow of doubt. The difficulty then simply increases. We cannot see why Descartes substituted it for mathematical truths as a model of all truth. It is treated like them—affirmed in present evidentness, wavering in the presence of the hypothesis of the deceiving God. Have we gained nothing in the Second Meditation? Is what happened there only illusion?

The Privilege Recovered

The privilege of the *cogito* is recovered, and the difficulty raised is dissipated, if we re-read this passage, taking it as a time of experience and not of demonstration, or, if you wish, as a moment of "exercise" and not a moment of "system."[11] From the point of view of system, isolated from the movement which provides it, the last proposition cannot be justified: it is false that "let him who can deceive me" two and three make five. But Descartes here is not recalling what he has gained in the previous meditations, and is no longer attempting to make progress in the construction of the system. The first two sentences of the paragraph (mistranslated in CSM II, 25 as three) have been recollections: the recollection of the certainty spontaneously accorded to clear and distinct conceptions, objects of intuition; and the recollection of the doubt which next (*postea*) assaulted these evident things when I formed the hypothesis of the deceiving God. But these two sentences, whose verbs are in the past tense ("I considered," "I did not conceive them," "I judged," "it occurred to me")[12] are followed by two sentences whose verbs are in the present tense ("comes to mind," "I cannot but admit," "I turn," "I am convinced")[13] and which express the present effect on the meditating subject of the previous meditations. After the time of doubt and the time for acquisition of a certainty, the subject experiences alternatively doubt and certainty, and sometimes certainty in the very exercise of doubt. But what certainty? It is here that we must follow attentively the experience or the exercise of the subject. Descartes recovers, with its exceptional form and its exceptional force, the certainty of his existence. And it is here that this certainty entails other ones, in the same movement: the affirmation of the omnitemporality of truth, an example of mathematical truth—all this is affirmed in spite of the hypothesis of the deceiving God, which is somehow staved off without being forgotten. Grammatically, "that two and three added together make more or less than five" is a subordinate clause, which depends on the main clause "he can never bring it about";[14] this means that philosophically speaking mathematical certainty here limits the power of the deceiver. Mathematical truths are raised here to the level of the *cogito,* and their truth is affirmed with equal force. This extension of certainty, which is incomprehensible from the point of view of system, may be comprehended easily from the point of view of exercise. Every success tends to extend itself; exceptions rarely remain exceptions, but possess an expansive force. Far from being forgotten, the exceptional certainty of the *cogito* manifests its force by communicating it to clear and distinct conceptions in the presence of which I never in reality have any doubt. This is not a matter of demonstration. It is a matter of the effect of previous experiences and meditation on the meditating subject who has seized hope again, and in whom clear and distinct conceptions recur with greater force.

But not with the greatest force: a certain difference is maintained between the *cogito* and mathematical truths. In fact the original Latin text introduces truths like "two and three make five" with the phrase *vel forte etiam,*[15] which may be translated as "or perhaps even," which indicates the difficulty they have in pulling themselves up to the level of the *cogito.* The French version, with its simple *ou bien,* which omits the *forte* and the *etiam,* neglects this difference in level, which leaves mathematical truths in retreat, and lower in rank. This negligence in the translation confirms the ascetic character of the text: the translation is a re-reading, distant from lived experience, which allows this nuance to escape, a nuance insignificant or troublesome for the system, but essential and clarificatory within experience.

It must therefore be recognized that the *cogito*'s privilege is not denied. Instead of saying that the *cogito* is lowered to the rank of mathematical truths, we must say that mathematical truths tend to become elevated to the rank of the *cogito,* while not yet reaching that rank and causing the *cogito* to lose its privileged position. This position is that of having the power to reactualize itself while being threatened by the deceiving God, a power of which mathematical truths are in themselves incapable, even if the *cogito* here lends them force in manifesting its own. We cannot say that Descartes is neglecting the specificity of the *cogito* here.[16] What we need to see is that its privilege tends to become foundational.

Have we discovered the unity of its privileged character and its exemplary character? We understand at least their association with one another. Retrospectively, after this moment of exercise, we understand better what the explanation of the general rule signifies within the system. No matter how exceptional the situation in which the truth of the *cogito* arises, and even if it is true that this first truth can arise only in this exceptional situation, it is just its clarity and its distinctness that enables me to recognize it as such. In reality there can be nothing but this—clarity and distinctness—whereby I recognize truth. We understand that a truth gained back in an exceptional manner within the process of doubt—but with a clarity and a distinctness comparable to that of the manifest (*perspicuae*) truths of mathematics, which are suspected of falsity only if I suppose a deceiving God—constitutes an example allowing us to explicate clarity and distinctness as signs of truth, and to confirm their validity.

But the confirmation is not total. The situation remains unstable. Deception is always possible. We have not found the perfect foundation or guarantee. It is necessary to ask whether the privilege of the *cogito,* which we see has not been denied, is such that it resists doubt absolutely, or if there is not a certain fragility within the *cogito* itself. Paradoxically, it is perhaps in grasping its fragility that we shall see how the exceptional and the exemplary are joined within it.

An Exemplary Fragility

The privileged status of the *cogito* must not cause us to miss its fragility. Even if we renounce the thought that it too is suspected of falsity "whenever this opinion, just conceived, of the supreme power of a God is present to my thought," the rest of the text of the Third Meditation will remind us that something is lacking. "Without the knowledge of these two truths," writes Descartes, "I cannot see that I can ever be certain of anything." Is the *cogito* therefore not certain? To be sure, the Latin text is different: *Hac . . . re ignorata, non videor de ulla alia plane certus esse unquam posse.*[17] If some differences do not seem to us of much consequence (*hac re* becoming *ces deux vérités; ulla alia* translated by *aucune* and not by *aucune autre*),[18] the presence of *plane,* omitted in the French, demands our attention. This adverb, modifying *certus,* in effect explains that it is absolute certainty that is denied to the *cogito,* as it is to all other knowledge. It suffices nonetheless to underscore its fragility. But why is it not completely (*plane*) certain? It is true that, by contrast with mathematical truths, it resists doubt, over which it always emerges victorious; but this victory is never won. It is true that its certainty *can* always be reactualized through doubt; but this *must* always be done. It is always subject to this necessity, to this condition. It resists the hypothesis of the deceiving God, but this hypothesis, and the threat it carries, remain. It does not dissipate them. The deceiving God always causes it to tremble. It always resists the attack, but does not destroy the adversary. It is always at war—victorious, but at war. It is too much to say that it is shaky,[19] but it is unstable. It is not *plana,* equal and full.

We see that the *cogito* is also fragile. It too must certify its certainty in that of the existence of a nondeceiving God; it too requires the divine guarantee. From this point of view it is one truth among others. Its lack of certainty becomes apparent by comparison with the certainty of the existence of a nondeceiving God which would itself destroy the hypothesis of a deceiving God and be affirmed in a stable manner as true science and not simple persuasion,[20] no longer knowing either threat or fear. The *cogito* is most definitely more certain than the mathematical truths which cannot stand against the hypothesis of a deceiving God, but it also possesses a certain fragility. It is definitely an example of truth, manifesting both the weakness and the strength of that which is evident.

It suffers its fragility still more than any other evident truth. It suffers it, in fact, at the same time as its privileged character, and in as vivid a manner; it suffers its fragility in its status as exception, which must manifest itself as such when it arises from the very exercise of doubt, as the very condition of that doubt.

It is thus that it recovers a privileged character, because it is, if not the most fragile of evident truths, at least the most manifestly and consciously fragile; and because (more profoundly and positively) in calling for superior assurance, it finds that assurance. Like all other evident truths, it needs that assurance, but it differs from them because it seeks it and finds it, and it finds it within its own depths. In fact, it is in becoming better known and more familiar to itself[21] that the thinking thing or the mind discovers within itself the idea of God, and thereby acquires the certainty of the existence of a God whose perfection rules out deception. The *cogito* leads to God. Its unstable certainty leads, in a continuous and uninterrupted act of thought, to the stable certainty which is the foundation of all certainty. Born from doubt, in an experience of imperfection and finitude, it plumbs its own depths to find within itself the idea of the perfect and the infinite, for which it cannot account otherwise than by positing the existence of the infinite and perfect being. If it is not in itself what provides the foundation, it leads to that foundation, something no other evident truth can do. That is its privilege—a privilege linked to that of its exceptional manner of arising from within doubt; it is the extension of that first privilege. Because the extension feels fragile, it seeks assurance; and it finds it.

In the same way, at the same time, we recognize in the *cogito* something of the exemplary: no longer simply in the fact that it manifests the characteristics of truth, but also in the fact that it leads to that which assures and founds truth, raising truth to what it necessarily must be, and showing it the way to its own fulfillment and plenitude (*plane certa*). The *cogito* is exemplary in that it *provides the example,* and not only in that it is itself an example. The exemplary, here, falls within the exceptional. It is not that the exception gives the rule; it is rather that the exception founds the rule.

The privilege of the *cogito* is that it is born directly from metaphysical doubt; to that extent it is not exemplary, but exceptional. If it can be called exemplary beyond this point, it is so in this sense: its clarity and distinctness confirm a criterion which is always felt if not explicitly recognized: it gives *an* example, not *the* example. Its clarity and distinctness have nothing exceptional about them. And its evidentness reveals itself as fragile and unstable, menaced by the ever-present possibility of deception. But just because this fragility and instability are more manifest in and for it than for all other evident truths, and because the doubt which gives birth to it also carries it to God, the *cogito,* as exceptional, *gives the example* of truth which gains its assurance by seeking and finding its foundation: the ground of the truth of the clear and distinct, its guarantee within the recognition of the divine veracity. It is thus exemplary in that it truly gives the example of what truth is, that is, of what it necessarily must be. Its privileged or exceptional character and this exemplary character are closely linked here. It is not a truth among others, but it shows the way to truth.[22]

Notes

1. *Discourse on Method* II: AT VI, 18; HR I, 92.

2. Rule III: AT X, 368, ll. 15–17; HR I, 7. Rule XI: AT X, 407, l. 16; HR I, 33.

3. *Discourse* IV: AT VI, 32; HR I, 101. First Meditation: AT VII, 21; AT IX, 16–17; HR I, 147–148; CSM II, 14–15.

4. *Discourse* IV: AT VI, 33; HR I, 102. Third Meditation: AT VII, 35, ll. 7–15; AT IX, 27; HR I, 158; CSM II, 24.

5. *Discourse* IV: AT VI, 38; HR I, 105.

6. *Discourse* IV: AT VI, 39; HR I, 105.

7. Following tradition, by *cogito* I understand the certainty of my existence as a thinking thing.

8. Third Meditation: AT VII, 35, ll. 10–13; AT IX, 27; HR I, 158; CSM II, 24.

9. We have in mind the paragraphs of the French text of 1647. (The Latin text of 1641 and 1642 does not break the first three Meditations into paragraphs.)

10. Cf. AT VI, 32, ll. 20–21; HR I, 101.

11. I borrow from Michel Foucault the pair of terms *système* and *exercise*. Cf. *Histoire de la folie à l'age classique* (NRF, 1972), 2, pp. 593–594.

12. In Latin, *considerabam, intuebar, judicavi, veniebat.*

13. In Latin, *occurrit, non possum, me converto, persuadeor.*

14. The French version faithfully follows the construction of the Latin sentence: *ut duo et tria simul juncta plura vel pauciora sint quam quinque* (AT VII, 36, ll. 19–20) is dependent on *nunquam tamen efficiet* (l. 16).

15. Ibid., ll. 18–19.

16. F. Alquié says this in a note to his edition of the *Meditations* in *Descartes, oeuvres philosophiques* (Paris: Garnier, 1967), II, 432–433.

17. Third Meditation: AT VII, 36, ll. 28–29; AT IX, 29.

18. Since *Hac re* designates the thing that is God, in his existence *and* in his veracity, it may be translated by *ces deux vérités*. The omission of *alia* (*de ulla alia*) in the translation (*d'aucune chose*) does not seem to us to falsify Descartes's thought. *De ulla alia* means nothing other than God, and not, as H. Gouhier says in *La pensée métaphysique de Descartes* (Paris: Vrin, 1978), 315, "d'aucune chose autre que le *cogito,* c'est-à-dire l'*ego* comme *res cogitans.*" The same formula is found at the end of the Fifth Meditation (AT VII, 71, ll. 5–6) and in the French translation of the *Principles of Philosophy* I, 13 (title of article).

19. So says Martial Gueroult, *Descartes selon l'ordre des raisons* (Paris: Aubier, 1953), I, 155.

20. Cf. Descartes to Regius, 24 May 1640: "Quae duo ita distinguo, ut persuasio sit, cum superest aliqua ratio quae nos possit ad dubitandum impellere; scientia vero sit persuasio a ratione tam forti, ut nulla unquam fortiore concuti possit; qualem nullam habent qui Deum ignorant" (AT III, 65, ll. 3–8). The CSMK translation: "I distinguish the two as follows: there is conviction [*persuasio*] when there remains some reason which might lead us to doubt, but knowledge [*scientia*] is conviction based on a reason so strong that it can never be shaken by any stronger reason. Nobody can have the latter unless he also has knowledge of God" (p. 147).

21. Third Meditation: AT VII, 34, ll. 17–18; AT IX, 27; HR I, 157; CSM II, 24.

22. I am very grateful to Stephen Voss for his translation of the original French text of this essay.

4
The Soul According to Descartes

Michel Henry

TRANSLATED BY STEPHEN VOSS

We wish to attempt a phenomenological elucidation of what Descartes understands by the soul. We shall not apply the presuppositions of classical phenomenology, either Husserlian or post-Husserlian, to his thought. Instead, quite to the contrary, we shall appropriate the Cartesian concept of the soul and thereby give the idea of phenomenology a radical meaning still unnoticed today.

What makes the character of the *cogito* fascinating even today is that it is the search for the Beginning in a radical sense. What is it that begins in a radical sense, if not being? Being, without which nothing would be unless it had previously unfolded its proper essence so as to gather into it all that is. In a more precise way what does the standing-at-the-beginning (*l'initialité*) of this radical beginning consist in? What is already there before the appearance of every other thing, but appearing (*l'apparaître*) itself as such? Appearing alone constitutes the standing-at-the-beginning of the Beginning, not insofar as it fashions the appearing of what appears, but only insofar as it appears first of all itself, in itself. It is only to this extent that appearing is identical to being—insofar as it catches fire and illuminates itself, insofar as this luminous trail of light, as the illumination of itself and of nothing else and as the appearing of appearing, expels nothingness and takes its place. It is the phenomenological efficacy of pure appearing in its capacity to constitute an appearance by itself and in itself, it is the field traced out and circumscribed by the auto-appearing (*auto-apparaître*) of appearing, it is the appearance of this pure field that is being. This is the beginning—not the first day, but that which is first of all.

In his own language Descartes calls appearance as such "thought" (*pensée*). And just because the initial unfolding of appearance in its own auto-appearance—thought—is identically the unfolding of being, Descartes thought he could find the radical beginning he was seeking: *je pense, je suis.*

So let us quash a number of misunderstandings at the start. First, the critique Heidegger leveled at the *cogito* in his *Sein und Zeit* period, namely, that the Cartesian beginning is not a radical one because it presupposes something—a prior, at least implicit, ontological understanding; for if I did not know confusedly what being is, how could I ever say "I am"? But Descartes does not say "I am"; he says "therefore I am." Far from arising without presupposition, his affirmation results from the systematic elaboration of the indispensable prerequisite from which alone the proposition of being is possible. This prerequisite is nothing other than the appearance which Descartes calls "thought." The determination of this prerequisite is the content of the *cogito*. "We are *only by virtue of the fact that* we think [*Nous sommes par cela seul que nous pensions*]."[1]

That the affirmation of being in Descartes arises only from the projection of the appearing in appearing, and thus from its immersion in itself, is attested to by one of Descartes's cutting replies to Gassendi:

> It is also surprising that you maintain that the idea of a thing cannot be in the mind unless the ideas of an animal, a plant, a stone, and all the universals are there. This is like saying that if I am to recognize myself to be a thinking thing, I must also recognize animals and plants, since I must recognize a thing or the nature of a thing.[2]

Descartes knows what a thing in general is insofar as he knows what a thinking thing is, that is, a thing whose entire essence is to think, that is, whose substantiality and materiality are the substantiality and materiality of pure phenomenality as such.

The idea of phenomenology at work in this Cartesianism of the beginning—and by this we do not mean that of the *Rules for the Direction of the Mind* but this unique and fantastic moment in Western philosophy when thought holds the Beginning in its view and tries to become its equal—the idea of phenomenology at work here therefore provides us three of its components, the first two being (1) phenomenological reduction as reduction to pure appearance, achieved (2) by putting being (*l'étant*) to one side. This division between appearing and being is the Cartesian differentiation between soul and body. The soul finds its essence in appearing and properly speaking designates it, whereas the body is, in principle, properly devoid of the power of manifestation. This is why all corporeal determinations, for example the eyes, are blind. What we call Cartesian mechanism signifies primitively nothing but this radical heterogeneity of being in relation to manifestation. Because the soul signifies original appearing, the thought whereby Descartes constitutes the essence of the soul has nothing to do with what we call "thought" today—thinking that, considering that, together with something as a *meinen*. Doubt is a thought in this sense—a considering that things are doubtful; so is certainty—a considering that things are certain. The *cogito* has nothing to do with doubt or certainty or the exchange of one for the other, as Descartes shows in the Replies to the Seventh Objections when he criticizes Bourdin for having substituted for the essential difference between things that think and things that do not the inessential difference between those that "think that they think" and those that "do not think that they do."[3] Let it be said in passing that most of the critiques of the *cogito* repeat Bourdin's confusion, for example, the confusion of the

Lacanian who takes himself to refute Descartes's "I think, I am" by affirming "I am not that which I think, I am that which I do not think."

But now a third component of the idea of phenomenology has already arisen before us, even if we failed to notice it. It alone matters to us, and we must turn our attention in its direction. (3) The *cogito* finds its ultimate formulation in the proposition "*videre videor*"—it seems to me that I see. Let us recall the context where this decisive assertion appears. Descartes has practiced a radical *epochē* from the world and from himself as a man, from his body, from his eyes. But then what does "see" mean for a being who has no eyes? *At certe videre videor, audire, calescere*—Yet I certainly seem to see, to hear, and to be warmed.[4] Isn't what remains at the end of the *epochē* that pure vision, reduced to itself, in abstraction from any relation to presumed eyes, an alleged body, a supposed world? But if pure vision exists as such as "phenomenon," doesn't what is seen in it also exist as such, as "simple phenomenon"—these sensible appearances just as they appear, grasped precisely in that way? To this question, heavy with consequences, the Cartesianism of the beginning responded in the negative. These appearances are not as I believe I see them, for I believe I see real forms even though they perhaps belong to the universe of dreams, where nothing is real. But a vision that is not of the eyes sees something entirely different than such appearances: it sees that two plus three make five, that in a triangle, etc.—and all of this also falls within the provisions of the reduction. But if such clearly perceived contents are nevertheless false, this can only be because the vision is itself fallacious, because the seeing is not a seeing.

The well-known path of Cartesian *epochē* gives way beneath our feet. What it accomplished by the rejection of everything that appears was, we thought, the liberation of appearing as such as the ultimate foundation. But it is this foundation that is unsteady now—appearing itself, insofar as this appearing is a seeing. Seeing is challenged because what is seen is not as we see it. What is it to see? To see is to hurl oneself outside oneself into a horizon of light which is this very exteriority; it is to ek-sist in the ecstatic Dimension of ek-sistence which Descartes calls the natural light and which according to Rule I's famous declaration illuminates each thing without being exhausted or modified by it. And now this very light becomes clouded. For doubt can accomplish the subversion of essences, for example, only if it implicates something else beforehand—the region of visibility in which they bathe. It is therefore the condition of the possibility of all seeing; we can say that it is *ek-stasis* which the reduction brusquely abandons. But what remains then; what can the reduction claim to have left standing?

At certe videre videor—yet I certainly seem to see. Descartes holds that this vision, however fallacious it may be, at the very least exists. But what is it to exist? To exist, according to the presupposition of the Cartesianism of the beginning, means to appear. "*Videor*" designates nothing else; "*videor*" designates the primitive semblance in which vision originally manifests itself and gives itself to us, whatever credibility or veracity it may properly be accorded as vision. Consequently, there arises before us the crucial question that lies at the very heart of Cartesianism and perhaps all true philosophy: is the semblance that prevails in the *videor* and renders it possible as the original appearing and as the appearing to itself by virtue of which the *videre* first appears to itself and gives itself to us—by virtue of which it seems to me that I see—is this primary semblance identical to the one in which seeing unfolds its essence and constitutes itself properly as a seeing? Is the original essence of revelation reducible to ek-stasis?

A formulation that is equivalent to "*videre videor*" in the Cartesianism of the beginning is "*sentimus nos videre*"[5]—"we are aware that we see"—an assertion all the more interesting because Descartes makes it in the course of opposing the vision of animals, who properly speaking see nothing at all, to "human" vision, that is, to actual vision, which thus does not consist only in *videre* but counts as such only if *sentimus nos videre*.

What is it to be aware (*sentir*)? For, after all, seeing is a mode of awareness, on a par with hearing and touching, and falls under it. But awareness is not simply homogeneous with seeing: it leads us back to it, if it is true that visual awareness, experiential awareness in general, rests on a transcendental seeing. Therefore, we mean to say not only that the perception of men passing in the street with their hats on presupposes a vision of the idea of thinking substance, but also that this vision itself becomes possible only in ek-stasis.

Three Cartesian theses concerning the beginning render impossible any reduction to the *videre* of ek-stasis of the awareness or feeling that is immanent in thought and constitutes its original semblance. The first, which we have set forth at length, is that seeing is deceptive. The second is that the soul cannot be felt. What this thesis excludes is in no way the empirical nature of feeling, a nature somehow barred by the reduction, but rather "the mere thought of seeing and of touching"; it is the pure structure of this thought, its ecstatic structure, that is placed out of bounds.

The third thesis, which is irrefutable, was formulated as luck would have it when Descartes was directly confronted with the precise question that we are raising; this occurred when Gassendi, rising for once above his coarse sensualism, or, what came to the same thing, thinking it as it truly was, enunciated in his own language the ek-static structure, as he saw it, of all possible awareness. This extraordinary text declares that the tip of the finger cannot touch itself, that the eye cannot see itself, that the understanding cannot conceive itself. The structural ontological condition insisted on by Gassendi, under which the fingertip, the eye, the understanding, the mind may enter into experience and be something rather than nothing, the structural condition for appearing as such, is the oppositional structure of ek-stasis: it is the coming outside the self wherein the eye can be before itself and thus itself see itself. To the question "Why and how is it that the eye cannot itself see itself, or that the understanding cannot conceive itself . . . ?" Gassendi answers, "since this faculty is not outside itself, it . . . cannot produce any notion of itself." Moreover, "Why do you think that the eye can see itself in a mirror although it cannot see itself in itself? It is because there is a space between the eye and the mirror. . . ." And the same is true for the mind: "Therefore give me a mirror . . . [and] you will then be able to see yourself and know yourself."[6]

Descartes's radical rejection of these presuppositions of Western philosophy, that is, of ecstatic phenomenality at least in its claim to be originary, finds its positive expression in all of the technical definitions of thought and idea which the philosopher tirelessly and vainly proposes. All of these definitions carry out the theme of immediation, that is, appearing's original appearing to itself in such a way that, by excluding the mediation of ek-stasis, it consists in thought's primitive awareness as the awareness of self in which thought experiences itself as it is. "By the term 'thought' I understand everything that is within us in such a way that we immediately perceive it," ". . . everything that is in us in such a way that we perceive it [*l'apercevons*] immediately by ourselves."[7] Insofar as thought in its immediate awareness of itself excludes the exteriorization of exteriority, it manifests its essence as a radical interiority. The Cartesian definitions of thought are indicators of this interiority consubstantial with its essence and identical to its power—". . . everything that is within us in such a way . . ."—and lead us to "the kind of internal knowledge that precedes acquired knowledge," a proposition cited so often that perhaps the time has come to try to understand it.

Internal knowledge is "knowledge of the soul"; acquired knowledge is "knowledge of the body." But in knowledge of the soul and knowledge of the body what is in question is neither the soul nor the body, and still less knowledge that concerns soul and body in turn. Moreover, as far as the latter—that is, the being—is concerned, it falls under the provisions of the reduction. The expressions "knowledge of the soul" and "knowledge of the body" must each be put in quotation marks, for they each designate two pure modes of appearing and its fulfillment. Knowledge of the body is ek-stasis, which also falls under the provisions of the reduction; knowledge of the soul is "that kind of internal knowledge," "immediate" knowledge, which our question now concerns.

Among the insubstantial objections addressed to Descartes by his illustrious contemporaries there is a philosophical question. It is from Hobbes, and it is worth quoting:

> It is quite certain that the knowledge of the proposition "I exist" depends on the proposition "I am thinking," as the author himself has explained to us. But how do we know the proposition "I am thinking"?[8]

The reply to this crucial question—it is the question of the *cogito*—is in fact the technical definition of "idea": "*Idea.* I understand this term to mean the form of any given thought, immediate perception of which makes me aware of the thought."[9] Thoughts belong to appearing; they are its crystallizations; it is here that they differ fundamentally from bodies, that is, from being. But appearing appears only insofar as it appears to itself. Each thought is thus a thought only insofar as by revealing itself to itself, it arrives within itself and rejoins its proper being. "Thought" for Descartes, therefore, does not only mean what it means for us, thought in a kind of external sense, but that by which thought originally arrives within itself and is then found as such to be thought. Now how does thought arrive within itself? For the second time the technical definition of "idea" gives us the answer: it is not by an ek-stasis. On the contrary, the original arrival which traverses all thought and constitutes its essence is not an arrival outside itself, in exteriority, but an arrival of each thought within itself, which returns it upon itself, delivers it to itself, gives it to itself—thus being its auto-revelation, the revelation of thought itself and not of anything else, any alterity, any objectivity whatever. The idea, understood in this absolutely original sense, enables us to understand what its formal reality is: not the simple form of a content situated outside itself, but in the absence of all exteriority its unity with this radically immanent content which the idea is itself insofar as it is identical to it, to thought. The reason this is so is that the idea in itself reveals nothing other than thought; the examples used by Descartes to circumscribe the idea as original essence of thought are limited to immanent modalities of thought: "I am taking the word 'idea' to refer to whatever is immediately conceived by the mind. For example, when I want something, or am afraid of something, . . . I count volition and fear among my ideas."[10] All the immanent modalities of thought—sensations, feelings—must be considered "as ideas which are only in our soul." The proposition "I think" seems too simple to articulate this auto-reference of appearance and this immersion of it into itself, this immanence and this return of thought upon itself. For an adequate formulation of the *cogito* it is necessary to wait a long time, to wait for Nietzsche, who will say, not "I am," but in a more rigorous and fundamental way "I am who I am,"[11] thereby laying the foundation for all the great analyses of Nietzsche's thought during the last period.

Descartes affirms of knowledge of the soul not only its irreducibility to knowledge of the body but also its primacy over the latter—a primacy so essential that the Second Meditation is dedicated to establishing it. What we are therefore given to understand is that "knowledge of the body," that is, seeing in itself and as such—whether it be the seeing of the eyes or what remains of it after reduction, a touching, an imagination, or an inspection of the mind—in any case presupposes, as the vision of what it sees, as the projecting of what is found to be projected into its presence, the appearing to itself of this very vision, the auto-revelation of its ek-stasis, although as distinct from it and as its prerequisite. It is only in this way that "the knowledge that we have of our thought precedes the knowledge that we have of the body,"[12] for if it were identical to it as knowledge, that is, in the essence of its appearing, how could it be its presupposition?

It is here that the third component of the idea of phenomenology challenges us. We have already alluded to it in the course of showing, in connection with the thinking thing, how the substantiality and materiality of this "thing" are the substantiality and the materiality of pure phenomenality as such. I call "material phenomenology" a phenomenology that takes into account the phenomenological materiality of pure phenomenality, that is, pure phenomenality in its efficacy. Such a phenomenology does not have to do with "phenomena," that is, with the contents of consciousness, inquiring in particular which of them are susceptible of being posited, in virtue of the mode wherein they are given to us, with a given degree of determinate validity. Its unique concern is this mode of being given, and ultimately the pure phenomenality in which it consists: its task is to take account of this latter, and to relate it to appearance. But in truth pure phenomenality as such already relates itself to appearance in virtue of its own power. Material phenomenology has no other purpose than to read in this completed phenomenality the structure of its mode of completion—that is, its phenomenological materiality.

The structural opposition between the *videor* and the *videre,* in which the Cartesianism of the beginning is exhausted, is philosophically grounded only if the opposition of the two primitive modes in which phenomenality is realized signifies that what differs in the two cases is the appearing, in the materiality of its appearing. Moreover, if the Cartesian project aims at establishing not only a radical dissociation between these two modes of phenomenality, but also a hierarchy between them such that only one escapes reduction, then what must be shown is how in fact in such a primitive upheaval of phenomenality everything that becomes a phenomenon in it and belongs to it shows itself as it is, in its reality. For only if we recognize in the mode of its effective presentation and in the pure phenomenological materiality of this presentation something like an omni-exhibition of itself can we maintain that such a manifestation of it absolutely and indubitably is one. Did Descartes ever, even once, designate the phenomenological substance of appearance as auto-attesting to itself, as auto-presenting itself in itself and as it is, as the foundation and the essence of all absolute truth?

Article 26 of the *Passions of the Soul* answers this last question. Developing a prescientific problematic in conformity with the general thesis of the treatise, namely, the action of the body on the soul by the mediation of nerves and animal spirits, and thus hewing to the antithesis of reduction, he abruptly returns to it. Once again the state of sleep is evoked, but also that of wakefulness, the one not being distinguishable from the other. What the sleeping or waking person thinks he sees or feels, for example in his body, is rejected; the claim of seeing and feeling to attain the truth is again challenged and thrown out. By contrast, one's awareness of oneself, or rather its pure phenomenological materiality and substantiality, that is, the affectivity of this original auto-affection, both this affectivity in general and all of its modalities, suddenly turn out to be marked with the seal of the absolute. The passions reveal themselves in the substantiality of their proper phenomenality, in their affectivity and by it, as they are in themselves, and no illusion has any power against them.

> Thus often when we sleep, and sometimes even when we are awake, we imagine certain things so vividly that we think we see them before us, or feel them in our body, although they are not there at all. But even if we are asleep and dreaming, we cannot feel sad, or moved by any other passion, unless the soul truly has this passion within it.[13]

Thus the crucial opposition within the Cartesianism of the beginning between the *videor* and the *videre* is repeated, in a material phenomenology, determined or rather grounded by the phenomenological substantiality of the fundamental modes of appearing. Now it takes the form of the opposition between passion and perception:

> We may be deceived concerning perceptions that have reference to objects outside of us, or those that have reference to parts of our body, but . . . we cannot be deceived in the same way concerning the passions, inasmuch as they are so near and so internal to our soul that it is impossible that it should feel them without their being truly such as it feels them.[14]

As the ultimate possibility of thought, that is, of appearing, affectivity reigns over all of its modes and secretly determines all of them. Do we not see the reign of passion curiously extended for Descartes himself? Not only the passions *stricto sensu* which "have reference to the soul," but also those which have reference to external objects and to our body are circumscribed by Descartes, not only, it is true, in virtue of their intrinsic affectivity, but also as we know by the transcendent construction of the *permixtio*.[15] But the body falls under the provisions of the reduction. Or should we say that it does so only provisionally? Far from it: as eidetic variation, the doubt liberates what is left. As far as the relation of affectivity to the body in the sense that Descartes has in mind is concerned, reduction signifies this: the "body" is not and never will be comprehended in the phenomenological materiality of the pure phenomenality of the original appearing, insofar as this materiality is affectivity, and within the phenomenological dimension constituted by it. Moreover, in general all the attempts to explain affectivity are ludicrous, insofar as they inevitably presuppose the very thing they claim to explain. Whatever the case may be for the dogmatic content of Cartesianism and its theories, do we not see passion extended far beyond the domain assigned to it, to the point, for example, where it includes the infinite will, insofar as it is considered in its innermost possibility, that is, precisely in its possible inherence in thought? "And although with respect to our soul it is an action to will something, it may also be said that it is a passion in it to perceive that it wills."[16]

Now when confronted by this blinding intuition of affectivity as constituting the first approach of appearing to itself—the original auto-affection in which it appears to itself and emerges into the appearance of its proper phenomenality—the Cartesian gaze turns away: affectivity is not the essence of thought, or its substance—viz. the phenomenological substantiality of pure phenomenality. Affectivity befalls thought not in virtue of what it is and as identical to the power that produces it, but as an accident constraining it from without, as a disorder of it, in such a way that the principle of reduction is again mocked.

Cartesianism then falls prey to an inexorable dialectic, which also possesses an absolutely general significance going far beyond it. If it is no longer affectivity that constructs appearing from the inside and renders it in its first semblance possible, granting it the efficacy of its phenomenological material, then where is the power to be found by which phenomenality comes about; what is the phenomenological substance of this first occurrence? It is ek-stasis; it is the light of exteriority which pro-poses itself as the unique reference of the concept of phenomenality and consequently of phenomenology itself. The immanence prescribed by all the Cartesian definitions of "thought" and "idea" is nothing but a simple prescription, and it becomes fragile as soon as its phenomenological foundation gives way. It is light, rather, the light of ek-stasis and of all that it grounds, the light of representability and of ratio, which must supply this foundation and, substituting itself for the immediation of appearing, take its place—a place which appearing always leaves vacant in its invisible retreat from the world. Thus the forgetfulness of the beginning and its loss take place. The *cogito* is dismembered; the first semblance of the *videor* is suppressed in favor of the semblance of the *videre*. Cartesian "thought" is no longer the soul and no longer life, but its opposite: it becomes the thought of the moderns, knowledge.

For Descartes how does the *videor* become obscured by the *videre* and progressively forgotten? The end of the Second Meditation, undermined by a profound contradiction, already shows how this comes about. On the one hand, the point there is to show that knowing the soul is easier than knowing the body and that all the powers used for knowing the body must first, within a more original semblance, be known in themselves. On the other hand, under the pretext of better grasping this knowledge of the soul, and precisely because it is immanent in the knowledge of the body, it is knowledge of the body which becomes the theme. The faculties of the soul become faculties of knowledge, and are evaluated as such.

The Third Meditation accentuates this slide. In the first place a decisive substitution is made, the substitution for the *cogito* itself of its relation to the *cogitatum*. It is this relation, or rather the *cogitatum* itself, that becomes the theme of the analysis. The issue is the increase of knowledge, and the first task is to ground it definitively—as though the *cogito* had not already done this. Once the *videor* is forgotten, as the immediation of the *videre* which had originally revealed it to itself as an irreducible and incontestable seeing, it can freely be replaced by an entirely different project, that of mediately legitimizing the *videre* by the divine veracity, which must be read into the idea of God as *cogitatum* and which thus leads to the inventory of *cogitata* and to the problem of their status. The *cogitatum* must avoid reduction by itself—which means that being thought or being represented or being seen is indubitable if we confine ourselves to it as thought or represented or seen. But being-seen as such, the fact of being seen considered as a phenomenological condition, in abstraction from that which is seen, is sight itself; it is seeing deployed in its luminous space. With the original semblance of its essential immediation unperceived within it, the *cogito* is nothing more than such a seeing, and its appearing is that of the *cogitatum*—the appearing in which the *cogitatum* exists *qua cogitatum*. The Heideggerian reading of the *cogito* in *Nietzsche* II, with its explicit and deliberate reduction of the "I think" to an "I represent to myself," is on this level. But we would never finish if we set out to cite all the interpretations that draw the phenomenality of the *cogito* back to the light of Rule I—for example, that of Gueroult, by the end of which the Cartesian *cogito* is already a Kantian, or even a Fichtean, *cogito*. Behind these mistakes stands an absolutely general presupposition: deprived of its dimension of radical interiority, reduced to a condition of objectivity and representation, or rather constituting this condition, the subjectivity of the subject is no longer anything but the objectivity of the object.

What the Third Meditation brings about is therefore something entirely different from the thematic displacement of the *cogito* by the *cogitatum;* it is the reduction of the former to being nothing but the condition of the latter. Such a reduction, in which the essence of life is lost, is not carried out surreptitiously; it is not somehow unknown to Descartes or his reader: it is asserted when the *cogito* becomes, as "clear and distinct perception" of what is known, the criterion of all possible truth, and when the *cogito* itself becomes the first of these truths, even if this be the opposite of what it is, namely, something evident.

But the immediation of appearing, because it is also the immediation of knowing, cannot be so easily forgotten, and Cartesianism in its most striking statements returns to it. There thus arises a unique situation on the plane of philosophically technical Cartesianism: all the key concepts of Cartesian phenomenality—thought, idea, apperception, perception, clarity, distinctness, confusion, obscurity—refer by turns to the two modes according to which phenomenality becomes a phenomenon, and to their specific materiality. From this constant amphiboly there results a text that is readable only within the frame of reference a material phenomenology provides. For it is not only the content of these concepts that constantly varies; the interplay among them also changes depending on the dimension of appearing whose laws they seek to fix. Thus to circumscribe the original phenomenality, which excludes ek-stasis, Descartes must use the language of ek-stasis and knowledge, subsuming two irreducible orders under a single unvaried terminology. As for the interplay among these amphibolous concepts, we limit ourselves here to the following facts:

(1) Clarity is identical to confusion and obscurity in the case in which it designates the immediation of appearing, that is, a single essence, clear insofar as it carries out the work of phenomenality, obscure insofar as the phenomenological material of this work is affectivity. So it is in *Principles* I, a. 46, where Descartes declares, "When someone feels an intense pain, the perception he has of this pain is very clear." This perception should not be confused with the false judgment which makes someone imagine that he feels the pain in the injured part of the body "even though he perceives nothing clearly but the feeling or the confused thought within him." It belongs to clarity and obscurity, as identical in the original essence of appearing, to be incapable of changing into one another, being always the Same—namely, that dimension in which phenomenality unfolds itself into the invisible in such a way that

nothing that grows within it ever goes outside it, just as nothing outside it ever makes its way inside, so that what is living lives forever.

(2) The clarity that is opposed to confusion and obscurity is that of ek-stasis, and it therefore marks a unique essence—clear insofar as it opens up the place where light is concentrated, but obscure insofar as this illuminated place is surrounded by shadow, namely by the nonthematizable horizon of every ecstatic ex-position. Being (*l'étant*) is clear or obscure depending on the condition of the object, so that being never possesses those characteristics itself, but only in its ex-position and through it. Clarity and confusion are here pure phenomenological determinations, consubstantial to the phenomenality of ek-stasis and prescribed by it. Together they construct the phenomenality of the world, whose essential finitude the Cartesian method movingly attempts to exorcise.

Therefore the *cogito* does not mean one thing but two, not merely different but heterogeneous—so much so that their co-appearance at the origin and their being-together in this co-originarity is without any doubt one of the major problems of philosophy. Is it not extraordinary that Malebranche, that most Cartesian of Cartesians, was led to say of the irreducible and incontestable phenomenon which the doctrine explicitly provided as point of departure and as sure support exactly the opposite of the formulation provided by its author, Descartes—namely, that the *cogito* is not evident or the clearest thing of all, but an abyss of obscurity; that it is not knowledge or the first of all things known, but that of which we have no solely conceivable knowledge; that the soul consequently is not easier to know than the body, but on the contrary unknowable, and furthermore that any knowledge that we are in a position to acquire on that subject can only be by analogy with knowledge of the body and on the basis of that knowledge; that finally the idea of the soul, rather than constituting the precondition and foundation of all knowledge can play no such role, ultimately for the reason that it does not exist, in any case not for us? But what is no doubt most surprising is that with such propositions and in spite of their word-for-word opposition to the cardinal theses of Cartesianism, Malebranche, far from avoiding those theses, proposes for the first time and perhaps the last a radical repetition of them which goes to the very beginning of the Beginning which Descartes had glimpsed, delivering it in an abrupt flash of metaphysical vision.

The Cartesian definition of man as soul, that is as pure phenomenality, poses many serious problems. Very broadly, the cultural world to which we belong takes its departure from these problems and from its inability to provide an adequate solution for them. Can it be an accident if today in almost all domains research defines itself by an implicit or explicit rejection of the *cogito,* but if those domains also share as common ground a total incomprehension of it? The problems posed by a phenomenological definition of man are no less serious, and often take on the look of insurmountable difficulties. Perhaps only a material phenomenology is in a position to confront them; perhaps only such a phenomenology possesses the means suited to such tasks.

Notes

Earlier versions of this essay were read at Yale University and Osaka University (Japan), and a version was published in French under the title "Le cogito et l'idée de la phénoménologie" in Osaka University's journal *Cartesiana,* 1989.

1. *Principles of Philosophy* I, a. 8 (French version): AT IX–2, 28; CSM I, 195. Emphasis added.
2. Replies to the Fifth Objections: AT VII, 362; CSM II, 250.
3. AT VII, 559; CSM II, 382.
4. Second Meditation: AT VII, 29; CSM II, 19.
5. To Plempius, 3 October 1637: AT I, 413; CSMK, 61–62.
6. Fifth Objections: AT VII, 292; CSM II, 203–204.
7. Replies to the Second Objections. Arguments proving the existence of God . . . : AT VII, 160; CSM II, 113. *Principles* I, 9 (French version): AT IX–2, 28; CSM I, 195.
8. Third Objections: AT VII, 173; CSM II, 122.
9. Replies to the Second Objections. Arguments proving the existence of God . . . : AT VII, 160; CSM II, 113.
10. Third Replies: AT VII, 181; CSM II, 127.
11. *Genealogy of Morals* III, §14.
12. *Principles* I, a. 11 (French version): AT IX–2, 29; CSM I, 196.
13. AT XI, 348–349; CSM I, 338.
14. AT XI, 348; CSM I, 338.
15. Sixth Meditation: "Nature also teaches me . . . that I am not merely present in my body as a sailor is present in a ship, but that I am very closely joined and, as it were, intermingled [*permixtio*] with it . . .": AT VII, 81; CSM II, 56.
16. *Passions of the Soul,* a. 19: AT XI, 343; CSM I, 335–336.

5

Generosity and Phenomenology: Remarks on Michel Henry's Interpretation of the Cartesian *Cogito*

Jean-Luc Marion

TRANSLATED BY STEPHEN VOSS

No doctrine recovered from the history of metaphysics could grasp us as an authentic thought, as opposed to a monument to a completed disaster, unless it intervened, always and without reservation, in the play of the thought being thought at present. Conversely, an older thought cannot gain such relevance unless the thought being thought today is carried out in essential dialogue with it. Such encounters do not always consecrate metaphysical doctrines; the richness and rigor of many of them possess no contemporary interest or significance—mortality must be acknowledged for thoughts as well as for people. Among those rare bodies of thought which are reborn from one century to the next, and never cease to call for exegesis because they first impose their own hermeneutic upon us, that of Descartes, powerful in its enigmatic simplicity, at once apparent and real, makes the most intimate contact with contemporary philosophy, which in turn mounts an attack upon its living works.

And so even today the interpretation of the *cogito, ergo sum* calls into play the most essential resources of phenomenology. This involves two dialogues. In the first, we may pose the question as follows: "What does *sum* mean; in particular, what does *esse, being,* contribute to the formula *cogito, ergo sum?*" Saying "being" is really not enough, if we wish to think what being gives to thought; hence the interrogation which Heidegger addresses to Descartes, in the form of a critique—that Descartes, at the very moment when he enunciated *cogito, ergo sum,* "left undetermined . . . the *meaning of the Being of the 'sum'*."[1] Since this first dialogue has been examined elsewhere, we need not resume the discussion of it here. In the second dialogue, we may pose the question as follows: "What does *cogito* mean; in particular, what does *cogitare, thinking,* contribute to the formula *cogito, ergo sum?*" Saying "thinking" is really not enough, if we wish to think what thinking might be. Thus

Michel Henry's interrogation, concerning the indeterminacy of *cogitare* in the Cartesian *cogito,* at least as the latter is usually interpreted. We shall resume this discussion here, for it matters as much to Cartesian studies as it does to the most determinate advances of contemporary phenomenology.

The *Ego Cogito, Ergo Sum* as the "Transcendental Spectator"

How can we think the *cogitare, thinking?* In all phenomenological rigor, this question is prior to the double interrogation concerning the link between the *cogitatio* and the *esse;* to be more precise, the link itself depends on the link between the *cogitatio* and, in general, everything it cogitates. In fact, as Husserl emphasizes, the *cogitatum* reveals itself from the start as already included in the *cogitatio;* deprived of the *cogitatum,* it would have neither meaning nor possibility of its own, having no object. Therefore,

> the expression *ego cogito* must be expanded [*erweitert*] by one term. Every *cogito* contains a meaning: its *cogitatum,* as that which it grasps [in intentionality] [*als Vermeintes*]. . . . *The fundamental property of modes of consciousness, in which I live as my own self, is what is known as intentionality.* Consciousness is always consciousness of something.

Again,

> The transcendental heading, *ego cogito,* must therefore be broadened [*erweitert*] by adding one new member. Each *cogito,* each conscious process, we may also say, "*means*" [*meint*] *something or other* and bears in itself, in this manner peculiar to the *meant* [by intention; *Gemeinten*], its particular *cogitatum.* Each does this, moreover, in its own fashion.[2]

I think always signifies that thought is ecstatic, standing out from the *I* by a displacement originating with it, in the direction of that which it posits as its object. It is only within this relation that intentionality makes possible representation. The *cogito,* intrinsically structured by intentionality, includes within itself its necessary other, the *cogitatum.* To be sure, there is a unity within the "dual expression *cogito—cogitatum* (*qua cogitatum*) . . . ,"[3] wherein the two elements become indissociable, precisely in virtue of intentionality; but these two terms define the primitive ecstasy of representation which makes possible objectivity. The displacement that intentionality opens up—the fact that I never think without an other in my thought, therefore an other from my thought, within the depths of thought—accrues to representation by running from the *cogitatum* to its *cogito;* taking what intentionality ecstatically makes of my thought, representation runs through the displacement, as though against the grain, from the object to the thought that objectifies it. I represent (*vorstellen*) the *cogitatum,* and therefore the intentional object; to be sure, I render it present to myself as given in flesh and blood (*leibhaftig*), but I do so in such a way that I represent it only by its ambassador, if not by proxy (*vertreten*). The represented—truly so called because with it there comes to me an other than me—remains decidedly other than the *I* which represents it.

But why should anyone be surprised at the intentional structure of the representative displacement? Is it not simply the condition of objectivity, as the theory of constitution will one day definitively certify it? No doubt this is the case, but something more has to be said: Husserl also imposes the intentional structure on a very specific case of thought—namely, thought thinking itself. Even if he recognizes that we have in this case a "paradoxical fundamental property," Husserl admits and even emphasizes that consciousness—which is already intentional, and already has its objects—apprehends its own self only by a *re*doubled intentionality, or if you will, an intentionality folded back on itself:

> The "object" of consciousness, the object as having identity "with itself" during the flowing subjective process, does not come into the process from outside; on the contrary, it is included as a sense in the subjective process itself—and thus as an "*intentional achievement*" [*intentionale Leistung*] *produced by* the synthesis of consciousness.

In fact,

> these modes of appearance of the internal consciousness of time are themselves *intentional components of conscious life* [*intentionale Erlebnisse*];

the consciousness of intentional lived experiences is therefore itself grasped intentionally—intentional self-consciousness as consciousness that is already intentional. Thus arises a redoubling of intentionality, at which Husserl, in spite of everything, marvels in the very act of naming it:

> . . . the ego's astonishing being-for-itself: here, in the first place, the being of its conscious life in the form of reflexive intentional relatedness to itself [*Auf-sich-selbst-intentional-zurück-bezogen-seins*].[4]

One cannot help asking here: Is consciousness related to itself by the *same* intentional relation that it bears to its other *cogitata?* Is intentionality capable of applying its ecstasy to thought itself, on the same grounds whereby it does so to every other object? Conversely, does consciousness bear no more intimate relationship with itself than intentional ecstasy according to the displacement of objectivity which representation traverses? Can the *ego* be defined only as the "impartial spectator of itself [*unbeteiligter Zuschauer*]"?

For his part, Husserl does not hesitate to justify this assumption, even at the cost of a stupifying schizophrenia within the *I:*

> Phenomenological reduction thus tends to split the I [*Ichspaltung*]. The transcendental spectator [*transzendentale Zuschauer*] . . . sees himself both in control and also as the previously world-immersed I.

In this schizophrenia, phenomenological intentionality ecstatically exiles the *ego* from itself—"the *ego* phenomenologically mediating as transcendental spectator over its own being, and its own life. . . ."[5] Husserl persisted in thinking the thought of the *cogito, ergo sum* on the model of intentionality, and therefore as a representation of the power of representation. He thus exposed himself to formidable aporias, both of temporal consciousness and of the transcendental reversal of phenomenology—no doubt in strict fidelity to the intentional interpretation of all thought in general, which was itself regarded as integral to phenomenology. Whatever the specifically Husserlian aporias induced by this radical *Ichspaltung,* it must be observed that this analysis would ascribe to Descartes primary responsibility for the redoubling of intentionality upon itself, and in this sense would render him, as having anticipated one of its most fragile paradoxes, the precursor of phenomenology.

It is this point that Heidegger contests. In fact, for *Sein und Zeit* intentionality remains from the very start a provisional moment in the return to the very things which lead back most radically from consciousness to *Dasein* and thereby to the *Seinsfrage.* So intentionality restrains phenomenology within metaphysics even more than it lets it take the initiative. Nevertheless, this fundamental dispute with Husserl does not keep Heidegger from agreeing with him on the only point that matters to us here: he consistently agrees to interpret Descartes's *cogito, ergo sum* in terms of intentionality, in terms of the displacement which its ecstasy brings about, in terms of the representation which runs through intentionality. Only one difference remains. At the point where Husserl acknowledged an anticipation of phenomenology, Heidegger denounces a form of metaphysics. But whether they approve or disapprove of intentionality, they give the *cogito, ergo sum* the same interpretation in terms of it. And therefore,

> the representing *I* [*vorstellende Ich*] is if anything more *essentially* and necessarily *co*-represented, in every "I represent," namely as something toward which, back to which, and *before* which every re-presented thing is placed.[6]

Thus Heidegger attributed to each Cartesian *cogitatio* the same ecstasy that Husserl attributes to it; thinking, *cogitare,* is equivalent—whether by an already phenomenological intentionality or by a decidedly metaphysical representation—to putting thought at a distance as an object. The fact of its being called up by and before the *ego* could impose no return on the *cogitatum,* no renewal or reduction, if no ecstatic displacement had already been opened; *re*-presenting presupposes that representing has taken place.

On this understanding how can Heidegger comprehend the *cogito, ergo sum?* Obviously, necessarily once again as a redoubling of representative ecstasy, centered on itself. Representing always implies representing *to oneself,* and therefore representing precisely myself *to myself,* as the condition of the possibility of every other representation. For what is represented itself, the representation of that which represents must precede the representation of that which is represented; what is represented thus discovers, in all rigor, within that which represents (namely, the *ego*), that which represents it—the "lieutenant" which represents it by first presenting itself. Consequently, it must be said that

> we encounter [*one* feature of the essence of *cogitatio*] when we consider that Descartes says that every *ego cogito* is a *cogito me cogitare;* every "I represent something" simultaneously represents a "myself," me, the one representing (for myself, in my representing).[7]

All the dignity of the Cartesian formula would thus derive from the fact that it deploys—under the guise of a reasoning that attempts to establish the existence of a particular being—the ultimate requirements for representation, for in running through intentional ecstasy (as Husserl had seen), it presupposes the priority of that which represents to that which is represented. But how can we ignore the fact that in reasoning in this way Heidegger repeats the *Ichspaltung* in which Husserl's interpretation was implicated? No doubt he conceals this aporia better than his master does: Heidegger has no need to recast the Cartesian *ego cogito, ergo sum,* since he undertakes only to "destroy" it on the basis of the analytic of the *Dasein;* he therefore no longer has any need to preserve its logical and ontic pretensions. But the fact remains that, given the presupposition that *cogitare* is equivalent to *vor-stellen,* the redoubling of the thought of the self into one ecstasy from another can lead only to the dissolution of the *cogito* (*me cogitare*), in an exodus from the self without end or assurance—at least of the ontic variety.

Even though they lead to precisely opposite conclusions, the interpretations of the *cogito, ergo sum* proposed by Husserl and Heidegger agree on one postulate: like all other *cogitationes,* the *cogitatio sui* submits to intentionality, to its ecstasy, and therefore to representation. In fact it doubtlessly submits to them with greater rigor than other *cogitationes* do, since it alone redoubles within itself what is represented on top of what represents, as it disengages what represents, which is presupposed elsewhere but always concealed. The *cogito, ergo sum* redoubles an ecstasy, whether that of intentionality or that of representation. In this perspective, even without taking into consideration the opposing judgments that Husserl and Heidegger contrive to make about it, we must immediately emphasize just which aporia it is that renders the *cogito, ergo sum* absolutely impracticable: intentional and representative ecstasy rends with an impassible caesura the transcendent from the immanent, and the represented from what represents; the being which carries out the *cogito* remains separated from the being which it knows as its *cogitatum,* whatever it may be. Therefore the *ego,* far from becoming reconciled to itself by reconciling itself to a certain existence—which Descartes certainly meant to establish—must admit that it gains thereby only an empirical existence, and not the pure *I,* which remains alienated by itself from itself. Transposed into Cartesian terms, the aporia of a *cogito, ergo sum* interpreted intentionally would be formulated as follows: if doubt disqualifies the relation between every idea (every representation) and its *ideatum* (what is represented), and if the existence of the *ego* or even its performance of thinking constitutes an *ideatum,* then how are we to certify that the representation of that *ideatum* and it alone constitutes an exception to the disqualification of even the most present of things that are evident? In short, if the *cogito, ergo sum* heightens representation, then it too, like all representations, must be vanquished by the blow of doubt. For why should it be certain that I think, that I am, if I also represent these things to myself?

Since the ecstasy which intentionality institutes is exercised henceforth between the *ego* and itself as its own *cogitatum,* it must be acknowledged that what the representing *ego* represents no longer coincides with this *ego,* since what we have here first is that which is represented: no *cogitatum,* not even that of the *ego,* may be identified with a *cogitans.* Kant saw this consequence and made it one of his themes, marking in advance the final contradiction in an interpretation of the *cogito, ergo sum* in terms of representation. The *I,* always comprised within the horizon of representation, must "accompany" every representation; but in order to remain itself, it must remove itself from that arena, and never be counted as an object:

> The *I think* must be *capable* of accompanying all my representations, for otherwise something would be represented within me which absolutely could not be thought, which amounts to saying that the representation would either be impossible or at least be nothing for me.

As "correlate of all our representations," the *I,* to be sure, "is capable of accompanying" all representations of objects. But in virtue of the very fact that it remains a simple traveling companion of objectivity, it can never itself claim to be an object.[8] As representation's traveling companion, the pure *I* makes representation possible, without for all that benefiting from it, or obtaining existence from it. If the appelation of representation may sometimes be conceded to the *I,* this is always subject to a restrictive condition:

> . . . the simple representation *I,* for itself empty of all content, which can never be said to be a concept, but only a pure consciousness which accompanies all concepts.[9]

Kant concludes by disjoining precisely what Descartes intended in all rigor to conjoin. On the one hand, the *ego cogito,* understood as the transcendental *I,* exercises to be sure a primitive unity; but as this spontaneity is not sensible, and as only sensible intuition is given, the primitive unity of the *I* can never be given to us in a representation; and therefore the transition from the *ego cogito* to an actual *sum* can never be legitimate: that which thinks can never be represented as existent.

On the other hand, what could be represented in the case of the *I* would have to be registered within sensible intuition, and therefore satisfy the conditions of objectivity within experience, in order to appear within it as phenomenon and as object. If the *I* is to think itself as existent, it must become other than itself—an objectivized *i;* if the *I* is to be (according to existence), it must be (in its essence) only an *i:*

> *I,* as intelligence and *thinking* subject, know myself as object *thought,* insofar as I am also given to myself in intuition—but only as I know other phenomena, that is, not as I am for the understanding, but as I appear to myself.[10]

And like other phenomena, the *i* reduced to objectivity must attain an existence that is conditioned, and therefore in Cartesian terms uncertain. The constraints of objectivity, which determine all of existence as empirically given, therefore constrain the *ego* either to objectify itself in order that it may exist, and thus to alienate itself from its primary status as origin, or not to exist according to objectivity in order that it may exercise its primary status as origin representing objectivity. This celebrated dilemma marks not so much an innovative thesis of Kant's as the inescapable aporia for every attempt to interpret the *cogito, ergo sum* on the model of representation. Representation, which by intentionality ecstatically separates what is thinking from what is thought, *noesis* from *noema,* can never conjoin them, even if it uses the same term in both cases to refer to them.

Cogito, from Intentionality to Auto-affection

The aporias of interpretations of the *cogito, ergo sum* in terms of intentionality and representation are now patent. They all lead to the same contradiction: what the *ego cogito* reaches by way of existent being immediately becomes other than that *ego,* since it amounts to the object represented by itself, but as objectivized by representation. This is therefore already no longer the *ego—cogito, ergo est* [*aliquod objectum* = *me*]. Moreover, the object that is in this way can be only conditionally, like every other object transcendent of the representing consciousness. It is not only that the *ego* never recognizes itself in what appears to it under its intentional gaze; what it does recognize it recognizes only hypothetically, not absolutely. All the critiques directed against the alleged "substantialism" of the *ego cogito,* from Kant to Husserl, may therefore be inverted: they prove only the fundamental impotence of the common (representative or intentional) interpretation when it comes to thinking and repeating the Cartesian foundation of the first principle. They are beyond all doubt far from invalidating it.

Furthermore, the very enterprise of interpreting the *cogito, ergo sum* in terms of representation and intentionality may be contested as mistaken in principle. It would seem incoherent on the one hand to admit (with Hegel, Husserl, and Heidegger) that all modern thought concerning subjectivity ultimately depends on the *ego cogito* which Descartes originated, and on the other hand to claim to interpret this very subjectivity with the aid of concepts which, far from being prior to it, ultimately derive from it—just such concepts as intentionality and representation.

If the *ego cogito* alone makes possible the depiction of representation, and thereby that of intentionality, we must then *exclude* in principle the idea that the model of representation or that of intentionality could suffice to make the *ego cogito* intelligible. If the *ego cogito* engenders intentionality, then intentionality can neither comprehend nor confirm it; above all, it cannot count against it.

A third reason above all enjoins us from maintaining the representative or intentional interpretation of the *cogito, ergo sum:* the fact that Descartes condemns it *expressis verbis.* If we retain Heidegger's formula—that *cogito* means *cogito me cogitare*(*rem*)—we observe that Descartes uses it to the letter at least once, but precisely to condemn it, leaving no opportunity for appeal.

> My critic says that to enable a substance to be superior to matter and wholly spiritual (and he insists on using the term 'mind' only in this restricted sense), it is not sufficient for it to think: it is further required that it should think that it is thinking, by means of a reflexive act, or that it should have awareness of its own thought. This is as deluded as our bricklayer's saying that a person who is skilled in architecture must employ a reflexive act to ponder on the fact that he has this skill before he can be an architect. [Item cum ait non sufficere quod substantia aliqua sit cogitans, ut sit posita supra materiam, et plane spiritualis, quam solam vult vocari mentem, sed insuper requiri ut actu reflexo cogitet se cogitare, sive habeat cogitationis suae conscientiam, aeque hallucinatur ac Caementarius, cum ait Architecturae peritum debere actu reflexo considerare se habere illam peritiam, priusquam esse possit Architectus.][11]

This statement is quite unambiguous: for thinking substance to be established as such—immaterial, spiritual, in short, irreducible to extension, to the sphere of the world—it need not redouble its *cogitatio* by a reflected, second-order *cogitatio,* as in a *cogito me cogitare,* any more than an architect must redouble his expertise by consciousness of it in order to build competently. Thought is prior to reflection on thought: ". . . that internal awareness which always precedes reflective knowledge . . . [*cognitone illa interna, quae reflexam semper antecedit*]" (AT VII, 422, ll. 13–14, CSM II, 285); therefore, the *cogito* in act is prior to the *cogito me cogitare.* Without lengthy explanation, but with the greatest clarity, Descartes leads the *cogito me cogitare* back to the simple *cogito,* rejecting in advance Heidegger's inverse procedure. In its essence, *cogitatio* excludes all reflection, for it is accomplished by and for the sake of immediacy (AT VII, 160, ll. 8 and 15; CSM II, 113). But this unambiguous statement of his position does not entirely settle the question, first of all because even if Descartes takes exception here to a reflexive interpretation, it remains no less true that the *cogito, ergo sum* may, and for many interpreters must, be understood (if only implicitly) in terms of the ecstasy of representation or of intentionality: once attention is drawn to the ambiguity, it persists all the more. Furthermore, we still need to see what other conceptual model could provide terms wherein the immediacy of *cogitatio* might be exhibited phenomenologically.

These motives converge in a single demand: if we are to think the *cogito, ergo sum* in such a way that it allows intentionality, we must deploy a more radical phenomenology than one that intentionality allows. We are indebted to the powerful thought of Michel Henry for the possibility of such a phenomenology, presented under the label "material phenomenology."[12] In this perspective, consciousness does not at first think of itself by representation, because in general it does not think by representation, intentionality, or ecstasy, but by receptivity, in absolute immanence; therefore, it thinks at first in immanence to itself. Consciousness thinks, and thinks of itself, fundamentally by auto-affection. Before any other operation consciousness experiences itself, with an absolute immediacy, without which it could never experience anything else. This auto-affecting of consciousness is therefore accomplished before any reflexivity of representation, precisely because it precedes even nonreflexive representation. With the aid of a dazzling analysis of an enigmatic Cartesian formula—"Yet I certainly *seem* to see, to hear, and to be warmed . . . [*At certe videre videor, audire, calescere*]" (AT VII, 29, ll. 14–15; CSM II, 19)—Michel Henry seeks to carry out a hermeneutic of Descartes's *cogito, ergo sum* that is nonreflexive because nonintentional, relying on the principle that "Cartesianism is a phenomenology . . . a material phenomenology."[13]

We cannot undertake here either to sketch an examination of "material phenomenology" or even to test its pertinence for the hermeneutic of Cartesian thought in general. We can, however, set for ourselves a limited objective: to determine whether it is possible to understand the *cogito, ergo sum* after the manner of Michel Henry, without having recourse to intentional ecstasy or incurring its aporias, taking as a clue the notion of the auto-affection of consciousness.

Within the Cartesian text, which conceptual arguments might authorize us to take *cogitatio* as auto-affection, and therefore as immediate sensing? First of all, the reasoning already cited from the Second Meditation: it is also the same "I" who has sensory perceptions (*Idem denique ego sum qui sentio* [AT VII, 29, l. 11; CSM II, 19]); I am now seeing light (*jam lucem video* [AT VII, 29, l. 13]); but this mediated perception (*tanquam per sensus* [AT VII, 29, l. 12]) may be exposed as false if I am sleeping. Nevertheless, Descartes adds immediately, even if I am sleeping, and this mediated (that is, intentional) representation is disqualified, ". . . *certe videre videor, audire, calescere*" (AT VII, 29, ll. 14–15)—it remains indubitably certain that it seems to me that I am seeing, hearing, and feeling heat; the immediacy of *videor,* "it seems to me," remains valid and incontestable, even when doubt disqualifies *videre* (and all other forms of representation). Even if no intentional object completes my intention, it remains no less true that I am immediately affected by the appearance of a representation, which may be void of anything represented. The *ego,* even when deceived, does not deceive *itself,* since it affects *itself* just in that immanent appearing—and then deception, the intentional's lack of intuitiveness, fails to occur. What precedes the disqualified representation, and resists it, is not a first representation, but an affection with no transcendent cause—the absolute immanence, therefore, of auto-affection. This redoubling of mediate perception by auto-affection may be expressed by the redundancy *videre videor* (as also at AT VII, 53, ll. 18–22; CSM II, 37) or more strongly by explicit reference to pure phenomenological sensation: ". . . *sentimus nos videre*. . . ." And Descartes clarifies: by contrast with animals who see like automata without actually thinking what they mechanically perceive, we, who are thinking *egos,* sense what we perceive; that is, we think only by sensing, since "to sense" means here to allow oneself to be immediately affected:

". . . to see as we do, i.e. sensing or thinking [*videre . . . ut nos, hoc est sentiendo sive cogitando*]."[14] So Descartes does not hesitate elsewhere to emphasize this equivalence: ". . . the mind, which alone has the sensation or thought that it is seeing or walking [*mentem, quae sola sentit sive cogitat se videre aut ambulare*]" (*Principia Philosophiae* I, a. 9); when it thinks what it sees, the *mens* does not represent it to itself, but senses it, that is, presents it immediately to itself—or, better, presents itself (offers itself, exposes itself) to what affects it, in conformity with its capacity for sensing. It cannot be emphasized too strongly that what is at issue here is not only the inclusion of sensation among the other modes of *cogitatio* on which the *Meditations* so often insists;[15] it is above all Descartes's radical interpretation of all *cogitatio,* as such, as ". . . the primitive sensing of thought."[16] It is only on the foundation of this immediacy to itself that *cogitatio* may, at the precise moment when in doubt it challenges reflection and its intentional objects, first assure itself with certainty of itself, and then experience that, as long as it *experiences itself* and hence auto-affects itself, it is, it exists (AT VII, 25, l. 12; 27, l. 9; CSM II, 17, 18).

This interpretation of the *cogito, ergo sum,* no doubt provocative if only because it is illuminating, arouses several further questions: (1) Is a nonintentional phenomenology even possible?; (2) the dispute among various types of phenomenology may, no doubt, be approached by reference to the interpretation of the Cartesian *cogitatio,* but that provides no positive indication that the auto-affecting of thought constitutes a properly and authentically Cartesian concern; and (3) finally, can an absolutely nonintentional *cogito, ergo sum* be identified in the Cartesian texts? Michel Henry seems to have doubts about the first of these; he sagaciously exhibits Descartes's own failure to understand his most profound discovery, favoring a notion of the primacy of representation to which he finally succumbed.[17] The first of these questions does not bear on our present purpose; the second, a question of right, presupposes the third, a question of fact. It is therefore fitting to inquire whether a nonecstatic, nonrepresentative, and nonintentional determination of *cogitatio* is to be found among Descartes's texts. This inquiry may be regarded both as homage, in the form of an examination of "material phenomenology," and as a contribution to the history of the *cogito, ergo sum* over the course of Descartes's thought.

Passion of Oneself

Among the functions of the soul Descartes distinguishes "two genera: the first, namely, are the actions of the soul; the others are its passions" (*Passions de l'Ame,* a. 17). How should these passions be characterized?

> All the sorts of cases of perception or knowledge to be found in us can generally be called its passions, because it is often not our soul that makes them such as they are, and because it always receives them from things that are represented by them. (ibid.)

According to this definition, the passions appear first of all to consist of "perceptions," "cases of knowledge," "representations"; they are imposed on the soul by "things" which act on it; it is consequently passive. Thus, the passions, far from constituting an exception to the general ecstatic displacement of representation, precisely repeat it.

Nevertheless, a more attentive reading of this definition discloses the indication of an exception within it: given that the passions are "generally" "perceptions," Descartes specifies that the soul "often" submits to them because of external things. Why does he add "often" here? The answer, of course, is that this is not *always* the case. Circumstances could be found in which cases of perception and knowledge are found "in us," and therefore received passively, but in which it is still the soul that makes them "such as they are." It is "often," not always, that the soul suffers passions that it does not cause. We must conclude that "sometimes" it causes passions (or representational perceptions) by itself, which it nevertheless suffers—in short, that "sometimes" the soul affects itself.

Is there textual confirmation for such a conclusion? Certainly. For, when he examines "what the first causes of the passions are" (a. 51), Descartes attempts to specify what it is that most closely determines

> the last and most proximate cause of the passions of the soul . . . the agitation with which the spirits move the little gland in the middle of the brain.

Among these "first causes" he distinguishes first "the temperament of the body alone" (with no external object) and, chiefly, those "external objects" themselves which are the most common and principal cause of the passions; but then he admits another cause, which is indeed exceptional but which is undeniable:

> though they [the passions] may sometimes be caused by the action of the soul. . . .

Sometimes the soul causes its own passions. That is why it was correct to say that it is only *often* and not *always* that the soul does not make them what they are.

Other texts confirm this rare but undeniable production by the soul of its own passions. Thus, while the soul's absolute power over its volitions may be opposed to the independence of the passions, which "depend absolutely on the actions [of objects] that produce them," an exception must be maintained: the soul suffers its passions "except when it is itself their cause" (a. 41). Hence the soul can indeed cause its own passions, in certain exceptional cases, without external objects. So, strictly speaking, it indeed affects itself, by itself; it suffers the passion of self. In short, it is auto-affected.

But since this possibility is only realized "sometimes" (a. 51), and as an exception, can it have any significant uses and examples? Descartes appears to have pointed out at least two. (1) The auto-affecting of the soul is undeniably confirmed in the case of volitions, since they can be called "excitations of the soul which have reference to it, but which are caused by it itself" (a. 29).

Nevertheless, when volitions are in question, as they are here, it is impossible for us to discern a paradigm of the passions as such, at least at the present stage of the analysis. We therefore pass on to the second example. (2) Parallel to the passions proper, "which always depend on some motion of the spirits" and hence on a cause external to the soul, Descartes admits, as "different" and yet "similar," "inner excitations, which are excited in the soul only by the soul itself" (a. 147). In this case the soul suffers only what it does to itself—in brief, it is auto-affected. The example par excellence of such an internal excitation is that of "intellectual joy" (a. 147)—"the purely intellectual joy which comes into the soul by the action of the soul alone, and which can be said to be a delightful excitation, excited in it by itself" (a. 91). What we have here is, with no ambiguity, a passion, which owes nothing to the will, but which owes nothing either to a (first) cause external to the soul, such as the "impressions of the brain [which] represent to it" some other good as its own. Thus the soul indeed causes on its own a passion within itself, an "excitation excited in it by itself" (a. 91).

We are therefore perfectly justified in speaking of an auto-affection of the soul, without ecstasy or displacement between cause and effect, represented and representing, intention and intuition. This is our first result: Descartes admits that there is "sometimes" an auto-affection of the *ego*. Two ambiguities remain. First, does auto-affection concern certain passions or volitions or both? Second, does not the auto-affecting which the soul accomplishes still remain within the horizon of representation, so that its ecstasy is simply transposed into the heart of the *ego* itself?

A Representation Without Something Represented

This last query is all the more significant because the definition of the passions with which we began specified without exception that "it [the soul] always receives them from things which are *represented* by them" (a. 17). In other words, no passions—not even the passions aroused by auto-affection—can occur without the representation of an object. The conclusion seems inevitable that even the soul's auto-affection in certain passions maintains an ecstasy (an intentionality, a representation), and is therefore vulnerable to the resulting aporias. Nevertheless, this conclusion would be a fragile one, for the very concept of "things . . . represented" remains to be determined and expressed precisely. In fact, will and perception (or passion) must each be divided in two.

(1) Volitions may have their terminus in the body, and will then be related to an object of representation; but they may also "have their terminus [*se terminer*] in the soul itself." In this case—for example in the volition to love God—thought is applied "to some object that is not material" (a. 18). Such a volition neither admits of nor requires any object external to the soul: love of God is neither another body nor the representation of an abstract concept, but a demeanor, a volition, a modality. It is more than a representable object; it is

an *objective* which the soul acknowledges for itself, within its very heart. Can we then still speak of ecstatic (or intentional) representation of another object? Does will, when its terminus lies inside the soul itself with a nonmaterial object, represent that object, whatever that object may be, according to the ecstatic definition of representation, that is to say as *res,* even the least of which is in reality foreign and objectifiable? Doubt on this score seems permissible—especially in the light of the second division.

(2) Perceptions can also be understood in two ways. Either they have bodies as cause, and then assume their ordinary status, or they have only "the soul as cause," and are immediately classed as pure "perceptions of our volitions" (a. 19), since in fact volitions are defined as being caused by the soul alone. The question, consequently, is modified, and becomes this: Can a perception of such-and-such a volition be assimilated to the ecstatic representation of an object? Here again doubt is permissible, for at least two reasons.

(a) Perception adds no object to a volition which might destroy that volition's immediacy to itself. On the contrary, "this perception and this volition are really only a single thing" (a. 19); again,

> we cannot will anything without knowing that we will it, nor could wc know this except by means of an idea; but I do not claim that this idea is different from the act itself [*nous ne saurions rien vouloir, sans savoir que nous le voulons, ni le savoir que par une idée; mais je ne mets point que cette idée soit differente de l'action même*]:

finally,

> because we cannot will anything without understanding what we will, and we scarcely ever understand something without at the same time willing something, we do not easily distinguish in this matter passivity from activity [*nihil unquam volumus, quin simul intelligamus et vix etiam quicquam intelligimus, quin simul aliquid velimus, ideo non facile in iis passionem ab actione distinguimus*].[18]

The distinction between a volition and the perception of that volition is not real (in the Kantian sense of the term); instead, it amounts only to a difference of modalities, not one of content, essence, or object. A volition, viewed in juxtaposition with the soul's perception of it, is bare. The convertibility between certain perceptions and certain volitions each having the soul as cause immediately rules out the possibility of opposing them on the schema of representational ecstasy, which would distinguish the object from the thought of that object.

(b) When bare will wills, does it always will an object? In one sense, it certainly always wills a quasi-object, which serves as its objective—"something which is solely intelligible." Now what specific example of this does Descartes give? "For example to attend to its own nature" (a. 20). The example is surprising, for we already know that when perception and volition are "really only a single thing" (a. 19), perception has "the soul as cause." Here will has its own nature—hence, itself again—as object, so that in the end what we have is a volition causing itself, willing itself—hence, as such, indiscernibly from a perception of the will's own circularity, which is to say the soul's.

In the closed circle of a thought perfectly perceiving and willing itself, where are we to introduce an object on the schema of the ecstatic displacement of representation? If we still wished to apply the concept of representation, we would at the very least have to amend it radically, the result being a representation without any object other than the objective of a volition caused by itself and made to will its own nature. But would not such a representation of a nonobject be equivalent to a nonrepresentation? It matters little where the negation crops up (as representation *without* object or as *non*representation), provided that it appear clearly that the perception of a volition focused on itself emphatically exceeds the exercising of ecstatic representation, and of intentional displacement. And so the second result is achieved: Descartes admits, in certain cases of volition, a perception without a real object other than the soul itself—a perception without ecstatic representation.

Generosity, the Last Formulation of the *Cogito, Ergo Sum?*

Can the two features that we have just isolated in certain passions—auto-affection and nonecstatic perception—be reunited in any single passion? And could we, in the case of this passion, sketch a formulation of the *cogito, ergo sum* without representational ecstasy, by auto-affection? We will attempt to furnish the elements of a positive answer by examining the particular passion of generosity. Let us recall that generosity depends on the passion of esteem, which is itself one of two "species of wonder" (aa. 150 and 54). Since wonder constitutes "the first of all the passions [*la première de toutes les passions*]" (a. 53), its primacy infects generosity, which issues directly from it.[19] Generosity, deriving from or rather deploying wonder as such, is the beneficiary of its primacy in the order of passions and therefore in morals. Is this ethical primacy related to the metaphysical primacy which the *Discours de la Méthode* recognized twenty years earlier in its *premier principe*—"*je pense, donc je suis*" (AT VI, 32, l. 19; CSM I, 127)? The internal coherence of Cartesian thought requires that a relation be acknowledged between these two primacies. But is it one of rivalry or rather of identification? We shall now try to show that the ethical primacy, far from being opposed to the metaphysical primacy, in fact repeats and so fulfills it.

But generosity also preserves, within its own definition, the global architecture of the *cogito, ergo sum,* wherein thought, in the very remarkable case in which it is a thought related to itself, becomes a principle, and hence an existence. Generosity is defined similarly, by a like reference of the self to itself: "it is our own merit that we esteem or scorn" (a. 151); "true generosity . . . makes a makes a man esteem himself as highly as he can legitimately esteem himself" (a. 153). Generosity therefore repeats the act of the *cogito,* but it does so by rescuing it from any risk of ecstatic or intentional interpretation, since it dispenses with any trace of representation, in virtue of four aspects of the concept.

It is therefore appropriate for us to examine these characteristics. (1) Generosity is marked first by a perfect auto-affection of the soul: "we can thus esteem or scorn our own selves" (a. 54); "one can esteem or scorn oneself" (a. 151). This is not a passion provoked by an external object, since it is born of self-satisfaction—in Descartes's words, a "*satisfaction de soi-même*" (aa. 63 and 190). If we still wish to speak of an effect, we shall have to specify that this is an effect on the soul of which the "cause depends only on ourselves" (a. 190), for this cause is "[nothing] other than the volition we feel within ourselves" (a. 158). And these "causes are . . . marvelous" (a. 160) indeed, since in this exceptional case they and that which suffers their effects form but a single thing. The circle of *cogitatio* of self by self is repeated and maintained, but now in the form of an affecting (an action or causation) of self by self. This, it must be admitted, might be described as auto-affecting.

(2) But would not generosity, if it remains a passion,[20] still need to be assigned an object—and a real one? In answering this question it will help to refer again to wonder, from which generosity issues. If wonder is born of "the first encounter with some object," it must be provoked more by the object's novelty and unexpectedness than by the object itself. In fact, "if the object presented has nothing in it that surprises us, we . . . regard it without passion" (a. 53): the object of wonder therefore is not the object *qua* real (and really given), but rather the (unreal) modality of its presence—"to be new, or very different from what we knew in the past or what we supposed it was going to be" (a. 53).

The object disappears behind the modality of its presence; in other words, the object of wonder is already no longer an object but a (necessarily unreal) modality of objectivity. The first passions derived from wonder, namely, esteem and scorn, again contribute to this distancing of the object: here too, what is in question is not the object, but "the greatness of an object or its smallness" (a. 54); greatness and smallness do not constitute objects, but only qualities of objects, and therefore the objectivity of the object tends to vanish. The tendency is accentuated when esteem is directed to "other objects which we regard as free causes, capable of doing good or evil" (a. 55), for such a capacity for choice constitutes, in itself, neither a being (*un étant*) nor an object—a fortiori "when we refer [esteem and scorn] to ourselves—that is, when it is our own merit that we esteem or scorn" (a. 151). In fact, if the object to which we direct our esteem coincides with our own merit, it is no longer distinguished in any way from that which the *ego* apprehends. Furthermore, this merit itself is constituted by "a single thing . . . , namely the use of our free will and the dominion we have over our volitions" (a. 152); hence, a man's understanding of his merit consists in "his understanding that there is nothing which truly belongs to him but this free control of his volitions, and no reason why he ought to be praised or blamed except that he uses it well or badly" (a. 153).

The object disappears behind a double unreality: first that of the estimation of the quality or modality of that object (more than of the object itself); and then that of a will (which is unobjectifiable by definition)—or rather of a use or a disposition (hence, a modality) of this will. Generosity has no other object in the soul except the soul itself, but the soul in turn understood as the pure use of a will. In the passion of generosity, what Descartes calls "good will [*bonne volonté*]"[21]—which might be defined as a volition to make good use of the will, in short a doubly unreal volition to will—is substituted for every real object. Thus auto-affection no longer confronts any impediment in the veil of an intermediate object. It is always the soul, alone and unique, which causes and suffers—and is assured of itself in experiencing itself under the mode of esteem.

I Esteem, Therefore I Am?

Two difficulties still remain which weigh upon the credibility of our hypothesis. One has to do with the exercise, or lack thereof, of *cogitatio* by the *ego* affected by generosity; the other has to do with the ontic relevance of generosity—whether it still allows the *ego* to say *sum*. These must be examined separately.

(3) The *cogito, ergo sum* is accomplished according to *cogitatio,* in all of its originality. But does generosity provide for the *ego* it affects a way in which it might itself be affected according to something which somehow or other arises from *cogitatio,* and which possesses as clearly as *cogitatio* does its nonreflexive, nonintentional character?

The following consideration suggests a positive answer. Generosity is understood in terms of wonder (as wonder referred to the self); but wonder in turn admits, as two sister variations, esteem and scorn (aa. 149–150), and esteem is defined as "an inclination the soul has to represent to itself the value of the thing esteemed" (a. 149).[22] *To esteem* is therefore equivalent, in a way still to be defined, with *to represent,* and hence with *cogitare.* But only in a certain way, for whereas I usually represent some thing (a being, a proposition, etc.), in esteem I represent "a thing's value" (a. 149) more often than a thing. Esteem still represents a thing, but precisely through the mode of its value, and hence it inevitably incorporates appreciation; this is what makes esteem a *cogitatio.* When one thinks the value of a thing and not that thing directly, one must think it by esteem (as one sometimes must navigate by estimation), and this entails a lack of precision and rigor, for "often this belief is only a very confused representation in [the soul]."[23] Moreover, esteem also allows that which positively surpasses comprehension to be represented: "The greatness of God . . . is something which we cannot grasp even though we know it. But the very fact that we judge it beyond our grasp makes us esteem it the more greatly."[24]

In fact, the modulation which esteem imposes on ordinary *cogitatio* is a double one: not only does esteem concern the "value" of a thing more than the thing itself, but it concerns not so much simple value as a thing's "true value [*juste valeur*]"[25]—a value of a value: "one esteems oneself only at one's true value" (a. 161). "True value" is distinguished from simple "value" by a clear and distinct criterion; true value relates a thing's value to the *ego* which is representing it:

> If it [the soul] knew distinctly their [things'] true value, its contentment would always be in proportion to the greatness of the good from which it proceeded. I observe also that the greatness of a good, in relation to us, should not be measured only by the value of the thing which constitutes it but principally also by the manner in which it is related to us.[26]

Thus, "to examine the true value of all the things that we can desire or fear" or "to examine the true value of all the goods whose acquisition seems to depend in some way on our conduct"[27] still remains a work of *cogitatio*—one, moreover, which is not a derived or secondary use, but a work of the "true office of reason."[28] Reason always officiates by the exercise of *cogitatio,* but *cogitatio* does not always represent objects objectified ecstatically, with intentionality; it can also take as quasi-objects "value," or better "true value," which is doubly unreal, and hence doubly immediate to the *ego.*

This is, in fact, why only such a nonecstatic representation can provide access to generosity, inasmuch as generosity is constituted by an esteem of self according to a representation of *res cogitans* as will by *cogitatio* as esteem. For only a *cogitatio* comprehending itself in the mode of auto-affection could attain the auto-affecting of the *res cogitans* esteeming itself. Only the presentation of *cogitatio* in esteem is suited to the auto-affecting of the will, which is immediate to self in the generosity in which a man feels "within himself a firm and constant resolution to use it [that will] well" (a. 153). Will knows and represents itself only as "the volition we feel within ourselves" (a. 158); hence it thinks itself only in the mode of esteem. When the "soul" knows itself as will, and auto-affects itself by its "good use," it thinks according to esteem, as an absolutely nonintentional modality of *cogitatio;* therefore, in esteeming *itself,* it thinks itself nonintentionally, it "feels" itself, in short it auto-affects itself. Thus esteem appears as the modality of *cogitatio* that is most expressly appropriated to generosity, understood as a primitive formulation of the *cogito.*

A final difficulty remains. (4) The *cogito* leads to a *sum,* sometimes redoubled by an *existo.* Can we find an equivalent ontic result in generosity—which seems strictly limited to the field of ethics?

In spite of appearances, generosity has direct implications in several respects for the ontic status of the *ego.* (a) First, like every other passion, generosity modifies the manner of being (*d'être*) of the being (*l'étant*) "man": it "even alters the countenance, the gestures, the walk, and in general all the actions of those who contrive a better or a worse opinion of themselves than the usual" (a. 151). The manner of being of the *ego,* at least insofar as incarnated, thus depends on its self-estimation, and hence on its auto-affection. It becomes in a way its own quasi-object: "according as it is the greatness of an object or its smallness we are wondering at. And we can thus esteem or scorn our own selves" (a. 54): the *ego* esteems itself as, so to speak, its own object.

(b) But the passions also concern the very fact of being (*l'être même*), *qua* pure actuality. For example, since unvirtuous humility consists "in believing we cannot *survive* by ourselves" (a. 159), and since generosity has precisely "opposite effects" (a. 158), we may infer that it allows us to survive by ourselves.[29] In fact, it assures the *ego*'s actuality by the power of the will "never to lack the volition to undertake and execute all . . . things" (a. 153); moreover, will redoubled by generosity assures an independence of actual being for the *ego,* due to its lofty mastery of itself.[30] The will indeed governs the *ego*'s survival and possible independence only insofar as that will *is,* as an essential characteristic of the *ego:* ". . . the good will . . . which they [men] suppose *to be*—or at least to be capable of *being*—in every other man" (a. 154). Hence, generosity also determines the (surviving) being of its subject—in short, its actuality.

(c) Finally, since it concerns "the greatest and most solid contentment in life," and the "means of making oneself happy,"[31] generosity determines the well being, and hence also the being, of the *ego,* as, indeed, all the other passions do as well. In bestowing on the *ego* "a species of joy . . . which is the sweetest of all [the passions]" (a. 190), "an inner satisfaction which is the sweetest of all the passions" (a. 63), generosity not only effects the happiness of the *ego,* it confers upon it the highest possible perfection of existence, that of depending only on itself; hence, it indeed effects its being, ontically, under the ethical modality of happiness. Therefore, generosity concerns the manner of the being, the survival of the being, and the perfection of the being of the *ego,* for which it thus explicitly sanctions the *sum.*

Thus interpreted, generosity might for the first time make it possible to overcome the separation, so often lamented, between the theoretical work and the *morale par provision* which in 1637 unbalanced the Cartesian enterprise. For, on our hypothesis, it would be the *cogito* itself, in its final formulation—at once the best concealed and the most radical—which would reunite with the ethical demand. The metaphysical *premier principe* would assure the final completion of morals. Existence immediately apparent to itself by thought (in auto-affection) would culminate in esteem of self, with *res cogitans* repeating and reaffirming itself through the modality of its will. In this way it would gain the existence of the *ego,* by carrying out auto-affection in the mode of a volition, that is, by carrying out a perfect auto-affecting of the soul taken in the mode of a volition esteeming itself; by consequently interpreting representation (of self) as an esteem (of self); and by undoing all objective mediation of any object whatever by the redoubled unreality of the will. The aporias of an ecstatic interpretation of the *ego cogito, ergo sum* deriving from representation and intentionality would thus be dissolved in the immediacy of the auto-affection accomplished by generosity.

No doubt "material phenomenology" should be examined further for its own sake, according to its own difficulties and requirements. No doubt the possibilities of Descartes's hermeneutic, interpreted according to the "material phenomenology" proposed by Michel Henry, can be developed and defended along other lines. Let it suffice, in this first attempt, to emphasize not only that this particular line gives access to an original and powerful understanding of the *cogito, ergo sum,* and not only that its phenomenological repetition pulls the Cartesian *ego* out of the aporias for which the greatest interpreters—Kant, Nietzsche, Husserl, Heidegger—had opposed it, but above all that this line opens absolutely new perspectives on the whole of Descartes's work. In particular, it would in this way seem possible to reestablish, in the "I think, therefore I am" which generosity finally effects, the unity long missing between the love of wisdom and the search for truth.[32]

Notes

An earlier version of this essay was published in French as "Générosité et phénoménologie," *Études philosophiques,* 1988. Another earlier version was presented in English under the present title at the 1988 San Jose conference.

1. Martin Heidegger, *Being and Time,* trans. John Macquarie and Edward Robinson (New York: Harper and Row, 1962), §6, p. 46. German text at *Sein und Zeit,* 24, ll. 22–24. See our study "L'*ego* et le *Dasein.* Heidegger et la 'destruction' de Descartes dans *Sein und Zeit,*" *Revue de Métaphysique et de Morale* 92, no. 1 (1987).

2. Respectively, Edmund Husserl, *The Paris Lectures,* trans. Peter Koestenbaum (The Hague: Nijhoff, 1964), 12–13; and *Cartesian Meditations,* trans. Dorion Cairns (The Hague: Nijhoff, 1960), §14, p. 33. German texts in *Husserliana: Edmund Husserl, Gesammelte Werke,* ed. S. Strasser (The Hague: Nijhoff, 1950), I, 13 and 71 (henceforth abbreviated *Hua*).

3. Husserl, *Cartesian Meditations,* §15, p. 36 (translation modified). *Hua* I, 74.

4. Ibid., §18, respectively, pp. 42 and 43 (translation of the latter modified; Husserl's emphasis). *Hua* I, 80, 81.

5. Respectively, Husserl, *Cartesian Meditations,* §15, p. 37; *Paris Lectures,* 15; *Inhaltsübersicht im Urtext,* 190—in English, "The *ego,* plunged into phenomenological meditation, is the transcendental spectator of its own life and its own being, which are themselves turned toward the world" (*Hua* I, 197). Commenting on the sequence "Obviously one may say *I,* as naturally instituted *I,* [I] am also and always transcendental *I,* but I know this only by first carrying out the phenomenological reduction" (*Hua* I, 75), R. Ingarden has emphasized the difficulty more than anyone else: ". . . the great problem of identity is found here, the problem of the very identification of these two *I*s. What is this "also" worth in relation to this 'I = subject of transcendental consideration'? . . . But then the great difficulty exists, which to my knowledge no one has yet pointed out, [namely] *how a pure constituting I and a natural constituted I can be at the same moment one and the same thing* [*ein und dasselbe*], when the properties that are attributed to them are mutually exclusive, and cannot coexist together in the unity of *a single* object?" (*Bermerkungen* . . . , in *Hua,* I, 213)

6. *Nietzsche,* trans. Frank A. Capuzzi, 4 vols. (New York: Harper and Row, 1982), IV, 107. German text at *Nietzsche* (Pfullingen, 1961) II, 154. For information about the Heideggerian interpretation of Descartes see "Heidegger et la situation métaphysique de Descartes," *Bulletin cartésien* IV, *Archives de Philosophie* 38, no. 2 (1975).

7. *Nietzsche,* 106 (German text, 153). This expression appears in an almost identical form, ". . . Descartes' *cogito me cogitare rem . . . ,*" in *Sein und Zeit,* §82, p. 433, l. 14. May we locate the Cartesian texts that directly or indirectly confirm this? In addition to AT VII, 599, ll. 3–7 (to be discussed later), we mention two passages in the *Meditations:* ". . . *cum cogitem me videre . . . ,*" ". . . *quamvia concipiam me esse rem cogitantem . . .*" (AT VII, 33, ll. 12–14; 44, l. 24); and finally, from the *Conversation with Burman, "Conscium esse est quidem cogitare et reflectare supra suam cogitationem . . . ad cogitationes suas reflectare, et sic cogitationis suae conscia* [*anima*] *esse*" (AT V, 149, l. 17). For a summary of this topic see J.-L. Marion, *Sur la théologie blanche de Descartes* (Paris, 1981; 1991), 391.

8. *Critique of Pure Reason,* B131–2 (and see A123 and A382).

9. Ibid., A346 = B404.

10. Ibid., B155. [In this translation, the pair *I, i* is used to render the original *Je, je.*]—The *Opus Postumum* may be regarded as developing the aporia of a representative *ego cogito* with the formula, contradictory in its terms, which ceaselessly recurs there: "Consciousness of self (*apperceptio*) is the subject's act of making itself an object, and is purely logical (*sum*) without the determination of an object (*apprehensio simplex*). . . . Consciousness of myself, that is, to represent myself who thinks. Subject, at the same time as object, as object of thought" (*Ak. A.* XXII, 89 = Kant, *Opus postumum,* Fr. trans. F. Marty [Paris, 1986], 157). Again, "I think (*cogito*). I am conscious of myself (*sum*). I, the *subject,* make myself *object* (XXII, 95; Fr. trans., 162); "I am the object of my own representation, that is, I am conscious of myself . . ." (XXII, 98; Fr. trans., 165). Would it not be better to choose between two hypotheses: either I am conscious of myself [*moi*] as a represented object, and this *moi* in no way coincides with the *Je,* or I am conscious of a me [*moi*] equivalent to the *Je,* and this is not a represented object?—It may be that the alternative between consciousness and *ego* constructed by Sartre can only repeat the Husserlian, but also Kantian, aporia ("La transcendence de l'ego. Esquisse d'une description phénoménologique," in *Recherches philosophiques* [1936; revised, Paris: S. LeBon, 1981]).—This interpretation has found partisans among the most qualified of commentators on Descartes; thus, M. Gueroult consistently thinks of the *cogito* in terms of representation: ". . . knowledge of my nature, such as understanding legitimately represents it to me . . ." (*Descartes selon l'ordre des raisons* [Paris, 1953] I, 82; and see 75; 86–87; 87, n. 105; 95; etc.). Moreover, against P. Thevenaz's phenomenological interpretation, in "La question du point de départ radical chez Descartes et chez Husserl" (in *Problèmes actuels de la phénoménologie,* Acts of the Colloque international de Phénoménologie, 1951 [Brussels, 1952]), M. Gueroult recovers, under the pretext of distinguishing Descartes from Gassendi, the position which Descartes condemns in his response to Fr. Bourdin (Gueroult, 62). The primary and nearly the only textual argument here advanced consists in a short sequence from the *Praefatio ad lectorem:* ". . . the human mind, when directed towards itself, does not perceive itself to be anything other than a thinking thing [*mens humana in se conversa non percipiat aliud se esse quam rem cogitantem*]" (AT VII, 7, l. 20–8, l. 1); but this evidence implies (1) neither that *percipere* is equivalent to *reflectare;* (2) nor that the *res cogitans* is reduced to *intellectus;* (3) nor, above all, that this is a formulation of the *cogito, ergo sum* as such. He is thus led to conclude by repeating literally the Heideggerian interpretation: ". . . *cogito* as reflected knowledge: *mens in se conversa*" (Gueroult, 64); ". . . reflection on my first reflection" (94).

11. Seventh Responses: AT VII, 559, ll. 3–10; CSM II, 382 (my emphasis).

Clerselier's translation is ". . . *elle pense qu'elle pense* . . . ," in F. Alquié, ed., *Descartes, oeuvres philosophiques* (Paris, 1967) II, 1070.

12. Michel Henry, "Phénoménologie hylétique et phénoménologie materielle," in *Philosophie,* no. 15 (Paris, 1987) and in *Phénoménologie matérielle,* (Paris, 1990), ch. 1. This magisterial presentation picks up in a precise manner much earlier themes: "Immanence is the primitive mode by which the revelation of transcendence itself is accomplished and, as such, the primitive essence of receptivity" (*L'essence de la manifestation* [Paris, 1963], I, §30, 278, 288).

13. *Généalogie de la psychanalyse* (Paris, 1985), 35 (see p. 21); the phenomenological commentary on *videre videor* begins on p. 24 and governs the whole of chs. I to III. These chapters develop a position in fact already essentially gained in 1963: "Thus the actuality of form made manifest in the *cogito,* that is, on the plane of pure thought itself and precisely as the affectivity of that thought, is in a significant way recognized by Descartes, and at the same time denied by him . . ." (*L'essence de la manifestation,* IV, §57, II, 642ff.). More recently, see "Descartes et la question de la technique," in *Le Discours et sa méthode,* ed. N. Grimaldi and J.-L. Marion (Paris, 1987), 285–301. See also "The Soul According to Descartes," essay 4 of this book.

14. To Plempius for Fromondus, 3 October 1637: "He supposes that I think that animals see just as we do, i.e. sensing or thinking they see, which is said to have been Epicurus' view. . . . But . . . I explain quite explicitly that my view is that animals do not see as we do when we are aware that we see. . . . [supponit me putare bruta videre plane ut nos, hoc est sentiendo sive cogitando se videre, quae creditur fuisse opinio Epicuri . . . cum tamen . . . satis expresse ostendam me non putare bruta videre sicut nos, dum sentimus nos videre. . . .]" (AT I, 413, ll. 14–20; CSMK, 61–62)

15. For example, AT VII, 28, l. 22; VII, 34, l. 21; ". . . that mode of thinking which I call 'sensory perception' . . . [*isto cogitandi modo, quem sensum appello*]" (AT VII, 74, l. 8); ". . . faculties for certain special modes of thinking, namely imagination and sensory perception . . . [*specialibus quibusdam modis cogitandi, puta facultates imaginandi et sentiendi*]" (AT VII, 78, ll. 21–23); etc.

16. *Généalogie de la psychanalyse,* 31. This formula should appear less surprising when, in addition to its intrinsic phenomenological relevance, it accords with certain statements by authoritative commentators who are in agreement here even though elsewhere their viewpoints diverge. One is F. Alquié, who, in the course of denying all "reflexive redoubling," emphasizes that "the *cogito*'s evidentness therefore rests upon such an intimate presence of consciousness to itself that no reflection, no doubt, no separation, no logical subtlety can prevail against it" (*La découverte métaphysique de l'homme chez Descartes* [Paris, 1950], 189). Another is J.-M. Beyssade, who comments as follows on the *videre videor* (AT VII, 29, l. 14) which M. Henry singles out: "What is indubitable in thought is pure appearance insofar as it wards off all . . . distance between two terms . . . ," to the extent that it ". . . identifies thought with perception" (*La philosophie première de Descartes* [Paris, 1971], 234, 235; see 252 and 253). Another is J.-L. Nancy, who firmly emphasizes that "Descartes denies nothing so obstinately as the introduction of thought about thought, or reflexivity, into the *cogito,*" thus stigmatizing the standard misunderstanding which has governed the subsequent fate of his metaphyics: "And the entire history of the *cogito,* including Spinoza, Kant, Fichte, Hegel, Nietzsche, Husserl, and Lacan [omitting Heidegger!], has been nothing but a history of various, indeed antithetical, ways of denouncing, avoiding, reflecting, suspending, or mediating the *im*mediacy of the *cogito*" (*Ego sum* [Paris, 1979], 34 and n. 8). In the purely phenomenological field, M. Henry may be said to accomplish what M. Merleau-Ponty was only able to sketch: to think the *cogito sum* as

". . . the absolute contact of the I with the I . . ." (*Phénoménologie de la perception* [Paris, 1945], 342).

17. *Généalogie de la psychanalyse,* 58: ". . . the clouding of the *videor* by the *videre* and its progressive neglect . . . ;" pp. 61, 70, 82, 106, etc.

18. Respectively, to Mersenne, 28 January 1641: AT III, 295, ll. 24–27; CSMK, 172; and to Regius, May 1641: AT III, 372, ll. 13–16; CSMK, 182. See also ". . . as I agreed before, we never will anything of which we have no understanding at all . . . [*quamvis nihil unquam velimus, de quo non aliquid aliquo modo intelligamus, ut jam ante concessi*]" (to Hyperaspistes, August 1641: AT III, 432, ll. 5–7; CSMK, 195—a text all the more remarkable because its concern is to *distinguish* will and understanding, not to confuse them!); or ". . . I have never said that all our thoughts are in our power, but only that if there is anything absolutely in our power, it is our thoughts [*Discourse,* AT VI, 25, ll. 23–24; CSM I, 123], that is to say, those which come from our will and free choice [je n'ai jamais dit que toutes nos pensées fussent en notre pouvoir; mais seulement que, s'il y a quelque chose absolument en notre pouvoir, ce sont nos pensées, à savoir celles qui viennent de la volonté et du libre arbitre]" (to Mersenne, 3 December 1640: AT III, 249, ll. 4–8; CSMK, 160). Therefore, it is legitimate to speak, in both cases, of a reversibility of will and perception, both in the case of perception of volitions and in that of the volition to master thoughts.

19. The rapprochement between generosity and Aristotle's μεγαλοψυχία is obvious; that makes the divergences all the more significant. We may begin with this one: the λεγαλοψύχος is not amazed and does not admire: οὐσ θαυμαστιχος ουσὲν γὰϱ μεγα ἀυτῷ εστὶν (*Nicomachean Ethics* IV, 8, 1125 a2–3). In Martin Ostwald's translation (Indianapolis: Bobbs-Merrill, 1962), "He is not given to admiration, for nothing is great to him" (p. 98).

20. In fact Descartes hesitates on this point: the emotions interior to the soul "differ from these passions, which always depend on some movement of the spirits" (a. 147), but this does not keep them from being "often joined with the passions which are like them" (ibid.). It remains true that esteem and scorn can occur either "without passion" (a. 150) or with a "movement of the spirits" (a. 149; the same ambiguity recurs in aa. 160 and 161).

21. See to Elisabeth, 1 September 1645: "there is no [passion] which does not represent to us the good to which it tends [*il n'y en a aucun qui ne nous représente le bien auquel elle tend*]" (AT IV, 285, ll. 24–25; CSMK, 264). It is here especially that generosity is distinguished from μεγαλοψυχια: generosity recognizes as (non-) object only *its* good use and *its* own will, whereas μεγαλοψυχία admits τα εχτος αγαθά (*Nicomachean Ethics* IV, 1123 b17 and 20), or, according to St. Thomas Aquinas, *res exteriores* (*Summa Theologica* IIa, IIae, q. 129, a. 1, c), *res exterius existentes* (ibid, a. 2, c.), *res humanus exteriores* (ibid, a. 3, c). Paradoxically, here it is Descartes who seems exempt from the essence of representation, by freeing himself from objectivity, and Aristotle who submits to it; is this mere appearance?—*Bonne volonté:* a. 154: AT XI, 446, l. 22 and 447, l. 3; a. 187: AT XI, 470, l. 5; a. 192: AT XI, 473, ll. 10–11; CSM I, 384, 395, 397, respectively.

22. See *Passions de l'Ame,* a. 83: ". . . to distinguish among loves by the esteem one has for what one loves in comparison with oneself [*distinguer l'amour, par l'estime qu'on fait de ce qu'on aime à comparaison de soi-même*]"; a. 204: "For seeing that one is esteemed by others is a reason for esteeming oneself [*Car c'est un sujet pour s'estimer, que de voir qu'on est estimé par les autres*]." We observe that the μεγαλοψύχος is also said to know—ἐπιστήμονι ἔοιχεν (*Nicomachean Ethics* IV, 4, 1122 a34). "A magnifi-

cent man is like a skilled artist: he has the capacity to observe what is suitable and to spend large sums with good taste" (Ostwald translation, 90).

23. To Christine, 20 November 1647: AT V, 85, ll. 1–3; CSMK, 325–326. Moreover, the *Discours de la Méthode* already understood esteem as an imprecise mode of *cogitatio:* AT VI, 24, ll. 12–17, and 74, ll. 18–19; CSM I, 123 and 149).

24. To Mersenne, 15 April 1630: AT I, 145, ll. 21–24; CSMK, 23.

25. To Elisabeth, 6 October 1645: AT IV, 305, ll. 4–5; CSMK, 268.

26. To Christine, 20 November 1647: AT V, 85, ll. 6–12; CSMK, 326.

27. Respectively, to Chanut, 1 November 1646: AT IV, 536, ll. 27–28; CSMK, 299; to Elisabeth, 1 September 1645: AT IV, 284, ll. 25–27; CSMK, 264.

28. To Elisabeth, 1 September 1645: AT IV, 284, ll. 24–25; CSMK, 264; see "*vrai usage*": AT IV, 286, l. 25; CSMK, 265.

29. To Elisabeth, 15 September 1645: AT IV, 293, ll. 6–7; CSMK, 266. No doubt this text advises the moderation, for reasons at once moral and social, of solitary survival ("*subsister seul*"), but then the point is precisely that Descartes would not have had to issue this warning if the *ego* could not already claim such an autarchy on its own. Therefore the latter is acquired.

30. *Passions de l'Ame,* a. 152, and to Christine, 20 November 1647: AT V, 85, ll. 14–16; CSMK, 326. On this thesis, its other formulations, and its ambiguity, see Marion, *Sur la théologie blanche de Descartes,* sec. 17, 411–426.

31. Respectively, to Christine, 20 November 1647: AT V, 84, ll. 21–22; CSMK, 325 (and cf. "*en cette vie,*" *Passions de l'Ame,* a. 212); to Elisabeth, 1 September 1645: AT IV, 287, ll. 5–6; CSMK, 265.

32. This study owes much to discussions with M. Henry, to remarks by J.-M. Beyssade and S. Voss, and to the impetus provided by my master F. Alguié (discussion with him echoed in Alquié, *Le Cartésianisme de Malebranche* [Paris, 1974], p. 365) and, later, G. Rodis-Lewis in her article "Le dernier fruit de la métaphysique cartésienne: la générosité," *Les Etudes Philosophiques* (January/March 1987, 43–54). A further discussion of my thesis by D. Kambouchner appears in "Bulletin Cartésien XIX," *Archives de Philosophie,* 1991, no. 54/1, 61–70.

6

Did Caterus Misunderstand Descartes's Ontological Proof?

Willis Doney

Did Caterus misunderstand Descartes's proof of God's existence in the Fifth Meditation? The question is complex, for, in the First Objections appended to the *Meditations*, Caterus makes a number of claims about that proof. I shall be concerned with his attempt to locate and formulate Descartes's argument, an argument which he takes to be the "crux of the matter" (AT VII, 97; CSM II, 70),[1] though I also have something to say about his claim that the proof in the Fifth Meditation is the same as an argument criticized by Aquinas; that is (though Aquinas in the passage Caterus quotes and Caterus himself do not name Anselm), Aquinas's version of Anselm's proof in *Proslogion* II. In reply to Caterus, Descartes makes it clear that, in his opinion, Caterus misunderstands his proof (AT VII, 115; CSM II, 82–83). After giving a reason for saying that the argument criticized by Aquinas is indeed fallacious, he goes on to specify what his argument in the Fifth Meditation is, and the argument he states is markedly different from that attributed to him by Caterus. Who is right, Caterus or Descartes?

I argue that, in a sense and with of course qualifications, both are right on the ground that there are two arguments concluding 'God exists' stated or clearly implied in the Fifth Meditation. The argument that Caterus formulates is like one of these arguments, and the argument Descartes states in his Reply is like the other. I conclude with some remarks about the question: which of these arguments should be said to be, using Caterus's expression, the "crux of the matter"?

My attempt to adjudicate between Caterus and Descartes is based on the thesis that two arguments concluding 'God exists' are stated or implied in the Fifth Meditation. To support that thesis, I shall comment at some length on two passages in the Fifth Meditation, which I have called A and B; and I shall extract from them two arguments, A* and B*.

A* is to be found in the sentences in the Fifth Meditation in which the question of God's existence is first raised. I have marked the places in this passage in which I find three premises A1, A2, and A3:

> But if [A1] the mere fact that I can produce from my thought the idea of something entails that everything which I clearly and distinctly perceive to belong to that thing really does belong to it, is not this a possible basis for another argument to prove the existence of God? Certainly, [A2] the idea of God, or a supremely perfect being, is one which I find within me just as surely as the idea of any shape or number. And [A3] my understanding that it belongs to his nature that he always exists is no less clear and distinct than is the case when I prove of any shape or number that some property belongs to its nature. Hence, even if it turned out that not everything on which I have meditated in these past days is true, I ought still to regard the existence of God as having at least the same level of certainty as I have hitherto attributed to the truths of mathematics. (AT VII, 65–66; CSM II, 45)

The French translation differs from the Latin in a number of respects, and we cannot be sure whether the changes are Descartes's or the translator's. At A3 the first edition has *ad ejus naturam pertinere ut existat actu,* and the second *ut semper existat.* The translator appears to have compromised with *une actuelle et éternelle existence.* More significantly, for our purposes, *une preuve démonstrative* is added in the translation. It can be conjectured that this is Descartes's addition and that it is added to make it clear that, appearances perhaps to the contrary, an argument concluding 'God exists' is indeed being stated in this passage. Also of possible significance is *qui ne regardent que le nombres et les figures.* This may have been added by Descartes to reinforce a point made earlier that the entities referred to in mathematical demonstrations need not be assumed to exist *hors de ma pensée* (AT VII, 64; AT IX–1, 51) and to suggest here the point that a demonstration of God's existence, being similar to mathematical demonstrations, does not presuppose the existence of God and so is not question-begging.

In the rhetorical question at the outset, Descartes states a principle that he implies is involved in some way both in mathematical demonstrations and in his proof of God's existence.

> If I can produce an idea of something from my thought, everything I perceive clearly and distinctly to belong to that thing really belongs to it.

In view of Descartes's discussion of the role of general propositions in inferences like the *cogito,*[2] a question can be raised as to whether this principle is intended to be a premise of the argument that is to be stated. Bearing that point in mind, there will be, I believe, no harm here in representing it as a first premise. In the First and Second Replies, Descartes sharpens his use of the terms *res* and *natura*[3] and, according to ostensible precisions of this principle there, the first premise can be stated:

> A*1. If I can produce an idea of something from my thought, everything I perceive clearly and distinctly to belong to the nature of that thing really belongs to the thing.

Removing the comparison with mathematical entities from the beginning of the next sentence, we get:

> A*2. I find in me the idea of God, or a supremely perfect being.

A connection is made here between the terms "God" and "supremely perfect being"; and, in presentations of his proof, Descartes seems to use these expressions as interchangeable equivalents, moving freely from 'A supremely perfect being exists' to 'God exists' and conversely without pause or reason.[4] A question to be raised about this passage is whether the addition of "or a supremely perfect being" is supposed to be an integral or essential part of the argument. Or could the argument be stated without this addition? Reformulations ostensibly of the argument here in the First and Second Replies do not have this or any similar expression. But, as this may constitute a change, I shall leave the premise in the logically not very satisfactory state in which it is presented.

Again removing the comparison with ideas of mathematical entities in what follows and making the harmless assumption that, for Descartes, to understand something clearly and distinctly and to perceive something clearly and distinctly come to the same and, neglecting the problem of reference just raised regarding "this nature," we can state a third premise:

> A*3. I perceive clearly and distinctly that actual and eternal existence pertains to this nature.

For our purposes, I believe Descartes' various qualifications of the sense or kind of existence that is supposed to pertain to God are of no consequence, and I have used 'actual and eternal existence' as in the French translation.

In the final part of A, where Descartes is evidently stating a conclusion, the conclusion is not, as one might perhaps expect, 'Actual and eternal existence pertains to God', or 'God exists actually and eternally' or simply 'God exists', but rather a complex statement[5] about the certainty of God's existence. Yet a conclusion about God's (actual and eternal) existence appears to be clearly implied in A, for a proposition to that effect follows logically from the premises that are stated there. I shall therefore take a conclusion implied in A to be:

> A*4. Therefore, actual and eternal existence pertains to God.

And this can be supposed to be a complicated way of saying 'God (actually and eternally) exists'.

There are two objections that can be raised to what I have said so far. (1) It can be objected that I have in fact misrepresented the conclusion drawn in A. The conclusion is 'It is to some degree certain that God exists' and not a proposition that is equivalent to or that entails 'God exists'. And it can be argued that such a proposition is clearly not implied in this passage on the ground that Descartes does not believe that the argument stated here can be used to prove with metaphysical certainty that God exists. My answer to this objection comes in two parts. First, I did not say that the conclusion 'God exists' is stated in A but rather that it is clearly implied; and the reason that I gave seems to me to be a very strong one, namely, that that conclusion appears clearly to follow from premises stated in A. Second, the argument to show that 'God exists' is not clearly implied contains a fairly obvious contradiction. The reason given, namely, that according to Descartes the argument stated there cannot be used to prove with metaphysical certainty that God exists, seems to be when made explicit: according to Descartes, the argument *for God's existence* stated there cannot be used to prove with metaphysical certainty that God exists. Given this reason, it is plainly presupposed that there *is* an argument concluding 'God exists' in A. Yet it is maintained that the conclusion 'God exists' is not stated or implied in A. If there is no better reason than this for saying that 'God exists' is not implied in A, it appears that my extraction of an argument concluding 'God exists' is justified. It is noteworthy that when Gueroult paraphrases A, the argument he states concludes 'God exists'.[6]

(2) A second objection takes a different tack. Granted that Descartes intends to present an argument concluding 'God exists' in A, it can be objected that the premises stated here are supposed to be only the beginning, or only a part, of the argument and that he thinks these premises need to be supplemented by premises stated in the ensuing discussion.[7] Now there is a sense of 'supplement' in which this is undoubtedly true. Immediately following A, Descartes observes, "At first sight, however, this is not transparently clear, but has some appearance of being a sophism"; and he proceeds to try to explain and defend what he has just said by raising and attempting to answer several objections. But it would be a mistake to attribute to him the view that an additional premise or premises are required to get from A*1, A*2, and A*3 to A*4. That view is too obviously confused, for, as I noted earlier, A* appears to be a valid argument and an additional premise or premises would be supernumerary. What Descartes can more plausibly be said to intend in the ensuing discussion is to attempt to answer objections that can be raised to the argument stated in A, though as I shall point out, that is not all that he in fact does. It may be that his answers to objections should be included under the umbrella "Descartes's proof." That is a complicated question.[8] But what is, I believe, clear is that Descartes thinks he states a valid argument in A and that the argument is in this sense complete. When he observes that what he says in A may appear to contain a sophism, he clearly implies that, appearances to the contrary, it does not.

In the ensuing discussion, arguments containing the premises 'God is a supremely perfect being' and 'Existence is a perfection' are suggested on two occasions by means of expressions contained in parentheses. Answering a first objection, Descartes observes,

> It is just as much of a contradiction to think of God (that is, a supremely perfect being) lacking existence (that is, lacking a perfection) as it is to think of a mountain without a valley. (AT VII, 66; CSM II, 46)

Tackling another objection, he says,

> I am not free to think of God without existence (that is, a supremely perfect being without a supreme perfection) as I am free to imagine a horse with or without wings. (AT VII, 67; CSM II, 46)

In neither passage is it suggested that the conclusion 'God exists' is supposed to follow directly from these premises alone. On the contrary, the conclusion that is being supported in the first passage seems to be 'Existence cannot be separated from the essence of God' and that can be taken to be a truncated version of A*3; and, in the second passage, he seems to be arguing that it is not just—in non-Cartesian terms—psychologically but logically impossible to think of God as not existing.[9]

It is in the course of answering a further objection or objections that we find an argument with the conclusion 'God exists' and with premises like 'God is supremely perfect' and 'Existence is a perfection'. In this passage (B), Descartes does not use the expression 'supremely perfect being', but 'first and supreme being' here seems clearly intended to be its equivalent. I have marked the parts of the passage from which three premises are extracted B1, B2, and B3. The place where I take Descartes to be stating a conclusion is B4:

> [B1] Now admittedly, it is not necessary that I ever light upon any thought of God; but whenever I do choose to think of the first and supreme being, and bring forth the idea of God from the treasure house of my mind as it were, [B2] it is necessary that I attribute all perfections to him, even if I do not at that time enumerate them or attend to them individually. And this necessity plainly guarantees that, [B3] when I later realize that existence is a perfection [*cum animadverto existentiam esse perfectionem*] [B4] I am correct in inferring [*recte concludam*] that the first and supreme being exists. (AT VII, 67–68; CSM II, 46–47)

In the French translation, there are two noteworthy changes from the Latin. In the translation *après que j'ai reconnu que l'existence est une perfection* is in parentheses; whereas, in the Latin *cum animadverto existentiam esse perfectionem* is not. The Latin *recte concludam* is replaced by *pour me faire conclure* or possibly *pour me faire conclure . . . véritablement.* Again, we do not know whether these changes are Descartes's. And I shall again allow myself a conjecture that they are and that they were made to remove the impression that an argument concluding 'God exists' is stated in this passage. But, since the question at issue is whether Caterus misunderstands Descartes and since it is the Latin that Caterus interprets, I shall refer to it in extracting B*.

At the beginning of B, Descartes moves from 'thought of God' to 'thinking of a first and supreme being', and he implies that the terms are interchangeable. From this, I take a first (implicit) premise to be:

B*1. God is a (or the) first and supreme being.

Though a question of reference can be raised at B2,[10] he seems to be asserting when he says, "It is necessary that I attribute all perfections to him . . ."

B*2. A first and supreme being necessarily has all perfections.

In the Latin, it is, I believe, clear that a premise of the argument stated in this passage is supposed to be

B*3. Existence is a perfection.

The conclusion is "I am correct in inferring that a (or the) first and supreme being exists." Since 'A first and supreme being exists' and 'God exists' are according to B*1 equivalent, a conclusion stated or clearly implied is

B*4. Hence, God exists.

Against my interpretation of B, there are two sorts of objections. (1) It can be objected that, though Descartes may seem to state an argument for God's existence in this passage, this is clearly not what he intends. For he leads us to believe that, in what follows A, he is explaining and defending an argument in A; and, in the explanation and defense of an argument concluding 'God exists', it would be logically odd, to say the least, to state a second and different argument concluding 'God exists'. If—the objection continues—we were to formulate an argument in accordance with Descartes's intentions, it would be something like this: 'God is a first and supreme being; All perfections belong to the nature of a first and supreme being; Existence is a perfection; Hence, existence pertains to the nature of God'. This is an auxiliary argument that could be used to support A*3, and it seems that this is what Descartes intends in B.

This objection contains a number of mistakes. Granted that Descartes did not intend to state an argument with the conclusion 'God exists' in the discussion that follows A, the fact is that he does. If we admit the presence of this argument, it is true that we have to accuse Descartes of a lapse and of some confusion in his thinking, but that is not a compelling reason for saying that the argument is not stated. In B, moreover, there is no explicit reference to the nature or essence of God, and it seems very implausible to take Descartes to be arguing in the way suggested in the formulation of the objection.[11] Finally, it is a mistake to suppose that, in B, Descartes is attempting to support A*3. The premise of the earlier argument that seems to be in question here is A*2, and part of what Descartes tries to show is that the idea of God is not factitious but rather, like the ideas of numbers and shapes, is (as he puts this in A2) "found" in him or is (as he says here) a "true idea" innate in him. A reason that he gives for this is that the idea is deductively fertile in the sense that properties can be discovered which a person may not be aware of when first considering the idea. An example given of such a property is existence; and, in the course of telling how that property can be discovered, he states an argument for God's existence, namely, B*.

(2). But it can then be objected that, if Descartes's intention in B is to support A*2, it follows that his intention in B is not to state a proof of God's existence. The objection is based on the questionable assumption that Descartes is single-minded and clear in his intentions here.[12] But, supposing that he does not intend to give a proof of God's existence in B, it does not follow that he does not state an argument with the conclusion 'God exists'. Philosophers state arguments for a variety of reasons one of which is of course to prove the conclusion. So a distinction must be drawn between stating an argument with the conclusion 'God exists' and stating an argument that is used or meant to prove God's existence. In B, Descartes certainly does the former though it is arguable that he does the latter. From neither of the contentions about Descartes's intentions in these objections does it follow that B* is not stated in B.

The question "Who is right, Caterus or Descartes?" can now be answered but not simply nor without qualifications. Though Caterus does not cite B and falters in his attempt to locate and state Descartes's argument, it is clear that he has an argument like B* in mind. Just before asserting, "This is the crux of the matter," he cites the statement Descartes makes in answering the first objection to A*, "It is just as much of a contradiction to think of God (that is, a supremely perfect being) lacking existence (that is, lacking a perfection) as it is to think of a mountain without a valley"; and reprehensibly he couples this statement with the last part of A in which Descartes asserts that the existence of God is at least to some extent certain. The argument that Caterus thinks is stated here seems to be: 'God is a supremely perfect being; Existence is a perfection; It is a contradiction to suppose that a supremely perfect being does not exist; Hence, God exists'. This argument is again suggested when he attempts to show that Descartes's argument is the same as the argument criticized by Aquinas, though again the argument is not stated as clearly as one might like: "God is a supremely perfect being; and a supremely perfect being includes existence, for otherwise it would not be a supremely perfect being."[13] The *reductio* suggested here comes to the same as the argument suggested earlier, and, as that is a near relation of B*, Caterus can be judged to be right in implying that such an argument is stated in the Fifth Meditation.

In his Reply Descartes gives the following account of his argument in the Fifth Meditation:

> My argument . . . was as follows: 'That which we clearly and distinctly understand to belong to the true and immutable nature, or essence, or form of something, can truly be asserted of that thing. But once we have made a sufficiently careful investigation of what God is, we clearly and distinctly understand that existence belongs to his true and immutable nature. Hence we can now truly assert of God that he does exist'. (AT VII, 115–116; CSM II, 83)

And this appears to be a reformulation of the argument in A. There are some differences. The plural "we" replaces the singular "I." The principle implied in the rhetorical question is explicitly a premise. The phrase 'supremely perfect being' disappears. 'Idea' is deleted and *natura* is qualified by 'true and immutable'. There is no equivalent of A2, but the point made there seems to be implied in the qualification of *natura.* The changes seem to be minor, and they can be explained on the ground that Descartes attempts here to provide his adversary with an argument "in form."[14] Granting that the argument is a syllogistic reformulation of the argument in A, it is clear that Descartes is also right in implying that the argument he formulates is stated in the Fifth Meditation. Where I believe both Caterus and Descartes go wrong is in implying that an argument like A* or B* is the only argument to be found there.

Two further matters need to be adjudicated. (1) Is Caterus right in noting similarities between the argument he finds in the Fifth Meditation and the argument criticized by Aquinas? Unfortunately for Caterus, he overstates his case when he claims that the arguments are the same. In Aquinas's formulation of Anselm's argument, the expression 'what is signified by a name' is used, and there is certainly nothing about the signification of a name in the Fifth Meditation. This point is scored in Descartes's Reply. But, granting Descartes that point, are the arguments similar in other respects? Though there are some differences, Caterus in fact detects some important similarities. The expressions 'something than which nothing greater can be thought' and 'supremely perfect being' play similar roles in the arguments, as do also the premises 'what is in the understanding and in reality is greater than what is in the understanding alone' and 'existence is a perfection'.[15] Though Caterus makes some mistakes in drawing the comparison, he is certainly not as wrong as it seems Descartes would have us believe.

(2) In a final point of adjudication, should we agree with Caterus that the "crux of the matter" is in B-like passages? Or should we say, as Descartes implies, that it is in A and the syllogism formulated in the First Replies? A number of commentators agree with Caterus, and their reason is apparent.[16] Viewed as an attempt to prove God's existence, A* seems to be defective, for what we need to know is how it can be shown that existence pertains to the nature of God. When Descartes states his syllogism for the third time in the Geometrical Exposition at the end of the Second Replies, the argument is patently nondemonstrative in a fairly clear sense of that term, namely, because the conclusion of the argument is said to be the same as, or logically equivalent to, one of the premises.[17] B* is not defective in this way; and, looking for a proof of God's existence, it seems that Caterus is justified in claiming to find something that might serve that purpose in B-like passages. Why, then, does Descartes locate his proof in A-like passages? That seems to me to be the most important and most difficult question about his a priori proof. I shall not venture an answer here. My attempt has been more modestly to see to what extent Caterus's interpretation of that proof can be defended.

Notes

An earlier version of this paper "Caterus aurait-il mal compris Descartes?" appeared in *Recherches sur le 17ème Siècle* 8 (1986): 19–28. This version also appears in *René Descartes: Critical Assessments,* ed. Georges J. D. Moyal, 4 vols. (London and New York: Routledge, 1991).

1. Caterus quotes Aquinas's version of the proof in *Summa Theologica,* Pars Prima, Q. II, Art. I.

2. Second Replies (AT VII, 140–141; CSM II, 100). See also *Conversation with Burman:* AT V, 147.

3. In the syllogistic formulation of his argument in the First and the Second Replies: AT VII, 115–116; CSM II, 83 and AT VII, 149–150; CSM II, 106–107. Also

in the "geometrical" formulation at the end of the Second Replies: AT VII, 166–167; CSM II, 117.

4. It seems that, for Descartes, these terms are interchangeable with no need of explanation or justification as in A2 and farther on: "For what is more self-evident than the fact that the supreme being exists, or that God [*summum ens esse, sive Deum*], to whose essence existence belongs, exists?" (AT VII, 69; CSM II, 47)

5. In the express conclusion, Descartes clearly implies that even if what he had concluded before were not known to be true, his conclusion would be *at least* as certain as mathematical truths. Does he imply that it would be *at most* as certain? That is of course the crucial question concerning the "independence" or "self-sufficiency" of his a priori proof.

6. Martial Gueroult, *Descartes selon l'ordre des raisons* (Paris: Aubier, 1953) I, 334–335.

7. There is a further difference between the Latin and the French translation. In the French translation, "*à la vérité . . .*" is conjoined with, and is part of the same sentence as, the last sentence of A; whereas, in the Latin, this is a new sentence. Perhaps this could be taken to support Etienne Gilson's interpretation (*Etudes sur le rôle de la pensée médiévale dans la formation du système cartésien* (Paris: Vrin, 1967), 171. Citing A and "*à la vérité . . . ,*" Gilson proceeds to cite the passage that follows and then speaks of "that argument." The problem for this interpretation is to specify what exactly *that* argument (in the singular) is.

8. I have made some points concerning this question in "L'Argument de Descartes à partir de la toute-puissance," *Recherches sur le 17ème Siècle,*" 7 (1985)

9. Another possible interpretation of this passage is that, contrary to an objection that conceptual truths based on ideas can be interpreted "hypothetically" and hence have no implication of existence, Descartes is concerned here to show that, in the case of the idea of God, we find an exception.

10. It seems more plausible to read this "It is necessary that I attribute to a first and sovereign being or God all sorts of perfections" than "It is necessary to attribute to the idea or the nature of a first and sovereign being or God all sorts of perfections."

11. In this section, after a statement of ostensibly one objection, Descartes includes, in fact, and tries to answer, two objections, namely, (1) that the idea of a being having all perfections is internally inconsistent (like the idea of a circle in which all quadrilaterals can be inscribed) and that (2) such an idea is "factitious."

12. See note 11.

13. The argument is taken to be the "minor premise" in Caterus's abortive efforts to recast the argument criticized by Aquinas and Descartes's as syllogisms.

14. It seems to me that the omission of 'a supremely perfect being' is not entirely due to the casting of the argument in syllogistic form. See my "L'Argument de Descartes à partir de la toute-puissance."

15. At AT VII, 98; CSM II, 71, Caterus points out these two important similarities.

16. See, for example, Jonathan Barnes, *The Ontological Argument* (London: 1972). Barnes cites B and extracts from it what he calls "the ontological argument" in the Fifth Meditation; of an earlier passage, he says, "this reads more like a report of an intuition than an argument. . . ." See also Gueroult, *Descartes selon l'ordre des raisons,* I, 334 ff.; who says of the syllogism in the First Replies *Car démontrer ou énoncer la condition qui rend valable une démonstration, ce n'est pas effectuer cette démonstration elle-même.*" On pp. 349–350, he locates the "demonstration proper" or "body of the proof" in an argument that is close to B*.

17. "To say that something is contained in the nature or concept of a thing *is the same as saying* that it is true of that thing . . . [emphasis added] But necessary existence is contained in the concept of God. . . . Therefore it may be truly affirmed of God that necessary existence belongs to him, or that he exists" (AT VII, 166–167; CSM II, 117). For an explication of the concept of a nondemonstration, see my "The Geometrical Presentation of Descartes's A Priori Proof" in *Descartes: Critical and Interpretive Essays,* ed. Michael Hooker (Baltimore: John Hopkins University Press, 1978), 1–25.

7

On the Idea of God: Incomprehensibility or Incompatibilities?

Jean-Marie Beyssade

TRANSLATED BY CHARLES PAUL

Here I would like to raise the question of the idea of God and its nature, because in the metaphysics of Descartes one thesis remains constant from his lost first draft, written in 1628–29, and because this thesis is paradoxical. The thesis is that the entire methodical structure of scientific knowledge depends on an assured knowledge of God. The paradox is that God is asserted to be incomprehensible.

The totality of Cartesian science is based on metaphysics, and two fundamental principles intersect within this metaphysics or first philosophy: one is called the *cogito* (I think, therefore I am; and I am a thinking substance); the other is called the *divine veracity* (God exists; and he cannot deceive me). To appreciate the function assigned to the idea of God one must understand "in what sense it can be said that, if one is ignorant of God, one cannot have any certain knowledge of any other thing."[1] Any other thing: neither mathematics nor physics nor metaphysics. Mathematics, whose reasoning had provided the model of certainty and evidence before metaphysical reflection, does not suffice to give the atheist geometer a true and certain science; but Descartes believes that he "has found how one can demonstrate metaphysical truths in a manner that is more evident than the demonstrations of geometry,"[2] how one can demonstrate the existence of God "in the same manner" as one demonstrates a property of the triangle, "or in a still more evident manner."[3] Physics, which is the trunk of the Cartesian tree, derives its scientific validity from its metaphysical roots: "this is how I have attempted to begin my studies; and I will tell you that I could not have discovered the foundations of physics if I had not sought them in this way."[4] Here order consists in passing from causes to effects, "without basing my reasons on any other principle than the infinite perfections of God;"[5] for "we will undoubtedly pursue the best method that can be used to discover the truth [*optimam philosophandi viam*] if, from our knowledge of his nature [*ex ipsius Dei cognitione*], we proceed to the explanation of the things he has created, and if we attempt to deduce it from the notions that naturally reside in our souls in such a way that we have a perfect knowledge [*science*] of it, that is, in such a way that we know the effects from the causes [*scientiam perfectissimam, quae est effectuum per causas*]."[6] Finally, in metaphysics—a discipline that is as fundamental for the physics which follows it as for the mathematics that preceded it—if the truth of the *cogito* is the first discovered therein, it appears as derived when retrospectively we connect it to the knowledge of God: "In some manner I had within me the notion of the infinite before [*priorem quodammodo*] I had the notion of the finite, that is, that of God before that of myself."[7] The common root of that triple dependence is to be sought in the general rule of the method: "the very thing that I just now took as a rule [and it matters little whether this *just now* refers to my past as a mathematician or to the *cogito,* which is my first assertion as a metaphysician], namely, that those things which we can very clearly and very distinctly perceive are all true, is guaranteed only because God is or exists, and is a perfect being, and because everything within us derives from him."[8] The evident, that is, the unique criterion of the universal method, namely, clarity and distinctness, therefore hangs on the divine veracity.

Now, by a paradox that is as old as Cartesian metaphysics itself, God is incomprehensible. This thesis appears as early as the letters to Mersenne of spring 1630 on the creation of the eternal truths—the first echo to reach us from the approach adopted in the previous year. "We cannot comprehend [*comprendre*] the greatness of God, even though we know it [*connaissions*]."[9] "Since God is a cause whose power exceeds the limits of human understanding, and since the necessity of these truths (the eternal truths of mathematics) does not exceed our knowledge," one must surmise "that they are something less than this incomprehensible power, and subject to it" (6 May). "I say that I know it, not that I conceive it or comprehend it, because one can know that God is infinite and all-powerful even though our mind, being finite, can neither conceive nor comprehend it" (27 May). Here incomprehensibility is linked to the greatness of God, and in particular to his power. It is, throughout Cartesian metaphysics, the characteristic of the infinite. "The infinite, *qua* infinite, is never truly comprehended, but it is nevertheless understood [*intelligi, entendu*]."[10] "In order to have a true idea of the infinite, it is in no way necessary that one comprehend it, inasmuch as incomprehensibility is itself contained in the formal reason of the infinite."[11] We seem driven to ask whether the method, in requiring divine veracity, may not require a foundation which in its incomprehensibility would violate that very method. In basing the truth of everything that is evident on the divine infinity, the method seems to introduce an element that is irreducible to what is evident, an element perhaps intrinsically obscure and confused. We may go further. If the Cartesian God is not just provisionally misunderstood at the beginning of the process, but if he also reveals himself at the end of it to be definitively incomprehensible, is there not a danger that this avowed incomprehensibility in reality conceals internal contradictions, incompatibilities? "An infinite and incomprehensible being," Descartes had written on 6 May 1630.[12] "An absolutely incomprehensible and contradictory being" is how the atheist critic will translate it, for example Baron d'Holbach in the eighteenth century.[13]

Incomprehensibility or inconsistencies—that is our question concerning the idea of God and the nature of God in the metaphysics of Descartes. The paradox can be extended in various directions. We shall develop only one of those directions. We raise the question how the idea of God is capable of satisfying the requirements of the method. The method is absolutely universal. It requires that every perception (or cognition or idea) without exception be clear and distinct if the corresponding proposition (or judgment or statement) is to be included in science. The idea of God must therefore be clear and distinct, and, if the judgment concerning God is the first one of the true science, this idea must be recognized as "the clearest and most distinct of all those present in my mind."[14] Is there no inconsistency between these two assertions, namely, that the idea of God is incomprehensible and that it is the clearest and most distinct of all ideas?

God, *qua* infinite, is incomprehensible. The idea of God is the clearest and most distinct idea of all. These two theses are both incontestably Cartesian. Are they incompatible? Is there an inconsistency here? We do not think so.

First we need to dig deeper into the correlation between (divine) incomprehensibility and distinctness or differentiation. In fact, from 1630 on, Descartes quite rigorously associates the knowledge of God and the recognition of his inconceivable infinity. The knowledge of God is doubly positive: we know at the same time *that* he exists and, with respect to a certain number of attributes (e.g., omnipotence, immutability, creator of existences and of essences), *what* he is. The recognition of his incomprehensibility is negative at first: the impossibility that we should embrace or encompass or master his nature. If clarity corresponds to presence, then incomprehensibility instead marks an absence, and this is why it seems connected to obscurity and confusion. This contrast is not false, but it is simplistic and one-sided. The truth is that starting with the letters of 1630, the divine incomprehensibility does not only have the negative function of limiting our knowledge of God by the recognition of something beyond which escapes our grasp. In a positive way it introduces into our idea of God the original and true knowledge of an incommensurable distance. Thanks to it God is not beyond the idea we have of him, like a hidden God, in which case our idea of him would not display him as he is. To the contrary, his greatness is given directly as present, without any possible confusion with our own properties. Incomprehensibility is the positive manner in which the infinite reveals itself to a finite mind as it is, that is to say, as incomparable. By a reversal illustrated in the comparison made between God and a king, what at first seems to be a principle of confusion is shown to be a principle of distinctness.[15] "We cannot comprehend the greatness of God, even though we know it": the phrase "even though," introducing a subordinate clause, contrasts what we know (which is positive, or clear) with what seems negative and obscure (namely, what we cannot comprehend). "But this very fact, that we judge it to be incomprehensible, makes us esteem it the more": the phrase "this very fact" marks the reversal, from a subordinate clause indicating opposition into an explanation indicating assimilation. The failure to reduce (by means of dominating through comprehension) is actually a success; it is the way a finite mind recognizes and esteems the more what in fact can never be esteemed too much, since it is absolute greatness. "Just as a king possesses greater majesty when he is less familiarly known by his subjects": thus distance is a mark of majesty, and to decrease familiarity is not to decrease knowledge, but to disclose to a subject the true knowledge of his unequal relation to his king. On the condition, to be sure, that the distant king is not a king who is hidden or unknown: "provided, however, that this does not make them think that they are without a king, and provided that they know him sufficiently well not to have any doubts about it." The phrase "provided that" leads us back again to the subordinated opposition of the "even though" between knowledge that is sufficient to dispel doubt (presence, or clarity) and noncomprehension (absence, such as distance and distinctness).

This equilibrium is maintained in the great systematic expositions, notably in the Third Meditation.[16] "It is useless to object that I do not comprehend the infinite, or [*vel*] that there are an infinity of other [*alia*] attributes within God that I can neither comprehend nor even perhaps reach by thought in any way at all." Here incomprehensibility seems to function as a barrier between two categories of attributes, the ones that I perceive clearly and distinctly and the rest. The first ones ensure knowledge that is sufficient to dispel doubt: "everything real and true that my mind conceives clearly and distinctly and that contains in itself some perfection is entirely contained and enclosed in that idea." Here clarity of presence extends to conception (the Latin only gives *percipio*), and, it seems at first, to comprehension as well. The other category of attributes ensure distance and majesty. I can neither comprehend them nor perhaps, for certain of them, have any other species of idea of them: this is pure absence or obscurity, which surrounds my knowledge with a black line, like the curtain behind which the king withdraws. "For it is of the nature of infinity that my finite and limited nature cannot comprehend it." The axiom which makes of incomprehensibility the true relation between the infinite and the finite can be counted on to bring us back from opposition (*alia*) to an explanation indicating assimilation.

"And it is sufficient that I conceive this well [*me hoc ipsum intelligere*], and that [*ac*] I judge that all things that I conceive clearly and in which I know there to be some perfection, and perhaps also an infinity of others [*atque etiam forte alia innumera*] of which I am ignorant, are in God formally or eminently, in order for [*ut*] the idea I have of him to be the most true, the most clear, and the most distinct of all those existing in my mind." Two conditions must be met in order that the idea of God attains the maximum of clarity and distinctness. It is sufficient that I perceive thoroughly the link between (positive) infinity and incomprehensibility: *hoc ipsum,* "this very thing," was precisely the reversal of 1630. But this is not the only condition: it is also necessary that I endow God with predicates; and in an attenuated form the *ac* takes up again the phrase "provided that" of 1630. These predicates are of two kinds. One kind are unknown—innumerable *alia* which escape me entirely. The other kind, the first ones named, correspond to perfections recognized and identified by me; they constitute the positive element without which there could be no clarity.

A commentary for the benefit of Clerselier, of 23 April, 1649, fixes the doctrine once and for all. It refers quite specifically to our phrase "and it is sufficient that I understand this very thing well," which I have labeled the *reversal.* Descartes clarifies: "Yes, it is sufficient that I understand this very thing well, namely that God is not comprehended by me, in order that I understand [*intelligam*] God according to the truth of the thing [*juxta rei veritatem*] and such as he is [*qualis est*]."[17] And so incomprehensibility is not an obstacle or a limit to our intellectual understanding of God; on the contrary, it reveals God in his truth, in his real and positive transcendence. This incomprehensibility does not reveal a regrettable and provisional failure of my limited mind, but instead a necessary incommensurability between the infinite and any finite mind, even one more perfect than my own, even the mind of an angel. The truth of my idea is ensured *thanks to* this lack of comprehension, this intellectual understanding of the incomprehensibility, and not *in spite of* it. Must we say, with Alquié, that our intellectual understanding of God consists "simply in the apprehension of his incomprehensible character"?[18] To do so would be to forget the necessity of the other element, namely, the presence which is required by clarity. The letter to Clerselier restores to it all the amplitude of the subordinate clause; it revives the overly discreet *ac* to its true value, namely, "provided that." "Provided that in addition [*modo praeterea*] I judge that there are in him all the perfections that I know clearly [*clare intelligo*] and moreover [*et insuper*] many others which I cannot comprehend." Incomprehensibility is not devoid of perfections; it is superadded to them: the fact that these two terms are externally related, which is implied by the subordinate phrase (*modo,* "provided that"), is accentuated by *praeterea,* "in addition." And among the required perfections two species are recorded anew: those of which I have a clear intellection and those, much more numerous (*multo plures*), which I cannot comprehend. Does this mean that I comprehend the first kind? One might think so, and assimilate my perception of them to a conception, and even a comprehension. Only the second kind, the *alia,* would then be incomprehensible.

But this would be a mistake. This error must be corrected in order to present Descartes's doctrine in its perfect coherence. The end of the Third Meditation is instructive here. For in fact it discusses, not the divine perfections of which I am ignorant (no doubt there are an infinity of them), but those I know. God exists, therefore, "this same God, I say, the idea of which is within me, that is to say the one who possesses all those exalted perfections [*illas perfectiones*] which I can, as for myself, not comprehend, but in one manner or another [*quocunque modo*] reach [*attingere*] by thought."[19] In the strict sense of the word my thought can never comprehend a single divine perfection. But there are a certain number of them which I can reach and, so to speak, touch by thought, in contrast to an infinity of others of which I am completely ignorant. The perfections to which I can attain are those of which I find marks within myself, such as my knowledge, my free will, my power. I comprehend those perfections within myself from the inside, intimately—even my freedom, which is often said to be infinite.[20] They are like traces which allow me to form the idea of a divine (omniscient) understanding, a divine will, a divine omnipotence.[21] I am able to form a concept or a conception of each of them, and I should then conceive them in God as infinite or as indefinite, the two adjectives, usually contrasted, here being equivalent, not distinct from one another.[22] But we must not allow this legitimate conception to become transformed erroneously into a comprehension, something that would correspond to a drift toward the univocal. It is precisely because all the intelligible perfections are united in God that each of them is, properly speaking, infinite, and none of them can be truly comprehended by me, but only reached by thought or conceived or, still better, understood (*entendu*).

Let us take up the train of thought as the Second Replies explicates it. It is necessary to begin with those "attributes of God of which we recognize some trace within ourselves": we comprehend them within ourselves, and, were no distance or distinctness to be added to their presence and clarity, we would be content to transfer them, in amplified form, into God, which would ensure the strict univocity of the attributes by turning God into a man writ large.[23] "But in addition [*praeterea*] we understand [*intelligimus, concevons*] in God an absolute immensity, simplicity, and unity which embraces and contains all his other attributes, and of which we find no instance either in ourselves or elsewhere."[24] This absolute unity, which is one of the most exalted of the divine perfections, is intelligible but neither comprehensible nor even conceivable. It ensures the absolute inseparability of the divine perfections, which is the same thing as the absolute simplicity of God, or what Spinoza was to call, by contrast with that which is merely infinite in its own kind, the absolutely infinite.[25] This unity, which is not comprehensible by a finite mind, is itself comprehensive. *Non tam capere quam . . . capi:* this divine unity is not comprehended, "grasped together," by finite minds; instead, it grasps them.[26] And—what is a different matter—it grasps or comprehends, embraces, *complectentem,* all the divine attributes.[27] Undoubtedly God comprehends himself; that is, he has an adequate concept of all his properties, both those we know and those of which we are ignorant.[28] But it is different for us. First of all, there are attributes of which we have no idea: these are the *alia,* perhaps innumerable, which are as profoundly unknown as, for Spinoza, all the attributes except for extension and thought are unknown. For Descartes, only revelation is capable eventually of rendering them accessible to us. Then there are attributes of which there are traces within us (e.g., knowledge, will, and power). We may now return to them without risk of univocity.[29] For their union with the other attributes, in other words, their connection with the absolute unity on which they depend, deprives them of any possibility of being comprehended. They are nonetheless conceivable, for their relation to our own perfections precludes our speaking of a simple equivocity. What we have here is analogy in the most traditional sense, since the clarity of presence (which alone leads to identity, to comprehension, to univocity) is qualified by distance as distinctness (which distance alone leads to otherness, to ignorance, to equivocity). The infinite is intelligible for the very reason that it is not comprehensible.

Let us conclude by investigating how the idea of God works in relation to the unique and universal method, whose general rule requires clarity and distinctness. We discover that these characteristics, whose conjunction defines the evident, undergo two successive transformations in the course of the operation carried out by metaphysics. Before that operation, clarity and distinctness had been separated, after the example of mathematics, which had served in the *Rules for the Direction of the Mind* and in Part II of the *Discourse on Method* both as their prototype and as their model. For an object presented to the view of the mind and made subject to its command, clarity signifies presence (the presence of a spectacle to a spectator, *ob-versari,* something which is there to see);[30] and distinctness signifies difference (the difference between two objects next to each other, which are distinguished through *juxta-posing* them, as in the case of a polygon with 1,000 sides next to one with 999 sides).

The procedure of the *cogito* constitutes the first subversion: although the same general rule of evidence, namely, the rule of clarity and distinctness, is derived by reflection on this first truth, the prototype and model has changed, and with it the meaning of the criterion. For a mind which itself makes the discovery of itself, and gradually makes itself better known and more familiar to itself, clarity signifies presence to oneself (the consciousness of a subject which senses and experiences itself, *in se con-versus*);[31] and distinctness signifies exclusion (by means of doubt I make myself distinct, in that I reject through denial everything I face, so that I may grasp myself on each occasion as the subject of that exclusion).[32] Note well that nothing in the rule has changed—neither its universality nor its univocity. The new example takes up within itself the previous ones, and deepens them; it leaves the mathematically evident with all of its brilliance, and simply lays claim to being still more evident, on the basis of the very criteria of the older prototype, which is not so much lowered in class as surpassed in class, and whose criteria have not so much changed as they have manifested what remained implicit in them, yet to be perceived.

The same operation is redoubled in the passage from the *cogito* to God. For the infinite, the intellectual grasp of which emerges as soon as I comprehend my finitude, clarity signifies the implicit presence of the being (an immediately given reality, a perfect unity prior to all limitation and fragmentation);

and distinctness signifies transcendence (separation by distance, by incomprehensibility, which eliminates all confusion by establishing an insurmountable dissimilarity).

Of course, at each passage it is possible to reject the new model, to reduce rationality to the previous model, to consider the shift in foundation as foreign to the method. But what is characteristic of the Cartesian enterprise is that its methodic procedures remain univocal, and in this sense the idea of God must occupy the first place according to the very order of the true science.[33] That is why this idea must be maximally evident according to the method itself.

It is therefore not sufficient to set in opposition God, who is incomprehensible, and the idea of God, which is clear and distinct. It is not sufficient to distinguish the properties of the idea from those of its object: the idea of red is not red, the idea of a sphere is not spherical, and the idea of obscurity may not be obscure, but clear and distinct.[34] Certainly this difference between the idea and its object is important. In the case under consideration, God is infinite but the idea of God is not infinite: it is, on the contrary, finite and suited to the small capacity of our minds (*finita et ad modulum ingenii nostri accommodata*).[35] Conversely, if the idea of God is the most clear and the most distinct of all, it would be absurd to speak of God as being clear and distinct: this characteristic pertains to an idea, not to its object. But incomprehensibility, which pertains to the nature of God, or to the nature of the infinite, is also a characteristic of his idea. *Idea . . . infiniti, ut sit vera, nullo modo debet comprehendi:* it is emphatically the idea of God, and not God himself, that is spoken of (*pace* the overzealous translation of Clerselier, not reviewed here by Descartes); and it is this idea which, if it is to be true, must not in any way be comprehended.[36] A characteristic of the object, in this case God or the infinite, which is incomprehensible, is therefore introduced into the idea of the object: this idea, first of all (and then perhaps many other ideas, later on), cannot in any way be comprehended. But it is precisely in the case of this idea that this characteristic is eminently positive. It establishes the true relation—once it is noticed, the difference is incommensurable and impossible to miss—between the Being which it represents on the one hand and any knowable object and my knowing mind on the other hand. It is because God is incomprehensible that the idea of him is also incomprehensible; and it is not *even though* this idea is incomprehensible, but rather *because* it is incomprehensible that it *is* the most clear and the most distinct of all.[37]

Notes

1. *Principles of Philosophy* I, a. 13, developing Meditation III: AT VII, 36, ll. 28–29; in CSM II, 25: "for if I do not know this, it seems that I can never be quite certain about anything else."

2. To Mersenne, 15 April 1630: AT I, 144, ll. 14–17; *Descartes: Oeuvres philosophiques,* ed. Ferdinand Alquié, 3 vols. (Paris: Garnier, 1963–73) I, 259 and n. 1 (henceforth abbreviated FA).

3. *Discourse on Method* IV: AT VI, 36, ll. 24 and 27–28, developed in Meditation V: AT VII, 65, ll. 28–29; AT IX, 52; FA II, 472 and n. 2; in HR I, 104: "in the same manner . . . or even more evidently still."

4. To Mersenne, 15 April 1630: AT I, 144, ll. 8–11, developed in the letter to Mersenne of 28 January 1641: AT III, 297–298; FA II, 316–317.

5. *Discourse* V: AT VI, 43, ll. 6–8; FA I, 615 and n. 2; in HR I, 108: "without resting my reasons on any other principle than the infinite perfections of God."

6. *Principles* I, a. 24 (on the difference between the Latin and the French, see FA III, 106, n. 1).

7. Meditation III: AT VII, 45, ll. 27–29; AT IX, 36; in CSM II, 31: "my perception of the infinite, that is God, is in some way prior to my perception of the finite, that is myself."

8. *Discourse* IV: AT VI, 38, ll. 16–21; FA I, 611 and n. 1; in HR I, 105: "that which I have just taken as a rule, that is to say, that all the things that we very clearly and very distinctly conceive of are true, is certain only because God is or exists."

9. To Mersenne, 15 April, 6 May, and 27 May 1630: respectively, AT I, 145, ll. 21–22; 150, ll. 18–22; 152, ll. 9–13; respectively, FA I, 260 and n. 4; 265 and n. 3; 267.

10. First Responses: AT VII, 112, ll. 21–23; AT IX, 89; FA II, 531; in CSM II, 81 (and n. 3): "the infinite, *qua* infinite, can in no way be grasped. But it can still be understood."

11. Fifth Responses: AT VII, 368, ll. 2–4; FA II, 811 and n. 2; in CSM II, 253: "for the idea of the infinite, if it is to be a true idea, cannot be grasped at all, since the impossibility of being grasped is contained in the formal definition of the infinite."

12. To Mersenne, 6 May 1630: AT I, 150, ll. 6–7; FA I, 265.

13. *Le bon sens du Curé J. Meslier,* ch. 40, a work published anonymously in 1772 by d'Holbach, its author.

14. Meditation III: AT VII, 46, ll. 27–28; AT IX, 37; HR I, 166; CSM II, 32.

15. To Mersenne, 15 April 1630: AT I, 145, ll. 21–28; FA I, 260.

16. Meditation III: AT VII, 46, ll. 16–28; AT IX, 36–37; HR I, 166; CSM II, 32 and n. 1. On the relation between this passage and the end of the Third Meditation: AT VII, 52, ll. 2–6; AT IX, 41; HR I, 171; CSM II, 35, a passage which will be examined later, see J.-L. Marion, "Descartes et l'ontothéologie," *Bulletin de la Societé Française de Philosophie* (24 April 1982), 143; discussed by J.-M. Beyssade in *Bulletin cartésien* XIII, *Archives de Philosophie* 47, no. 3 (July–September 1984): 47; taken up again in *Sur le prisme métaphysique de Descartes* (Presses Universitaires de France: Epiméthée, 1986), 119–120 and n. 54. It seems to us that the first passage conjoins *comprehendere* and *attingere* ("*nec* comprehendere *nec* attingere"), while the second one opposes them ("*non* comprehendere *sed* attingere"); but this is because the first passage does not deal with the idea of God in general; it deals only with the *alia,* the unknown perfections ("which I can *neither* comprehend *nor* even reach"), whereas the second one deals with the known perfections ("which I can *certainly* reach in thought *but not* comprehend").

17. To Clerselier, 23 April 1649: AT V, 356, ll. 22–27; FA III, 924 and n. 2.

18. F. Alquié, *La découverte métaphysique de l'homme chez Descartes* (Presses Universitaires de France, 1960 and 1966), ch. 10, 216 and n. 2, a formula developed by H. Gouhier in a remarkable commentary to which we owe a great deal, *La pensée métaphysique de Descartes* (Paris: Vrin, 1962), ch. 8, ii, 212 and n. 28.

19. Meditation III: AT VII, 52, ll. 2–6; AT IX, 41; HR I, 171; in CSM II, 35: "God, a God, I say, the very same being the idea of whom is within me, that is, the

possessor of all the perfections which I cannot grasp, but can somehow reach in my thought."

20. *Principles* I, a. 41: AT VIII, 20, ll. 25, 28–29; HR I, 235.

21. Second Responses: AT VII, 137; AT IX, 108; FA II, 560 and n. 1; CSM II, 98–99. We comment on this passage later.

22. *Indefinitae, sive infinitae,* Second Responses: AT VII, 137, ll. 24–25; CSM II, 99, l. 1: "indefinite (or infinite)." Cf. Conversation with Burman: AT V, 154; *Descartes' Conversation with Burman,* ed. John Cottingham (Oxford, 1976), 14–15.

23. To Regius, 24 May 1640: AT III, 64; FA II, 244 and n. 1.

24. Second Responses: AT VII, 137: ll. 15–18; AT IX, 108; FA II, 560 and n. 2; CSM II, 98–99; the relevant passage is AT VII, 137, l. 8–138, l. 1.

25. Meditation III: AT VII, 50, ll. 16–19; AT IX, 40; HR I, 169–170; CSM II, 34.

26. First Responses: AT VII, 114, l. 7; AT IX, 90; in CSM II, 82: "not so much to take hold of them as to surrender to them."

27. Second Responses: AT VII, 137, l. 17; AT IX, 108; in CSM II, 98: "which embraces all other attributes."

28. On adequate concepts, cf. Second, Third (no. 11), and Fifth Responses: respectively, AT VII, 140, ll. 3–4; 189, ll. 17–18; and 365, ll. 3–4. The debate of the Fourth Responses (AT VII, 220) is continued in the Conversation with Burman: AT V, 151–152; *Descartes' Conversation,* 10–11.

29. *Univoce,* Second Responses: AT VII, 137, l. 22; in CSM II, 98: "in the same sense." On the relation between Cartesianism and analogy, see Gouhier, *La pensée métaphysique,* ch. 8, ii and iii; and J.-L. Marion, *Sur la théologie blanche de Descartes* (Paris: Presses Universitaires de France, 1981).

30. *Obversari,* Third Meditation: AT VII, 35, ll. 21–22; in HR I, 158: "were presented to my mind"; in CSM II, 24: "appeared before my mind."

31. *In se conversa,* preface, *Meditations:* AT VII, 7–8; in HR I, 137: "reflecting on itself"; in CSM II, 7: "when directed towards itself."

32. *Principles* I, 60: AT VIII, 29, l. 2, *excludere;* in HR I, 244: "shut off from itself."

33. Marion, *Sur le prisme métaphysique de Descartes,* seems to us to be completely right in speaking, not of irrationality, but of "another rationality" (p. 243). But he believes that this metaphysical rationality must be "shielded from the method's domain of application" (p. 242, and again pp. 324–325, n. 29); we are not sure that this is necessary.

34. Second Responses: AT VII, 147, ll. 18–27; AT IX, 115; FA II, 573 and n. 1; CSM II, 105.

35. First Response: AT VII, 114, ll. 14–17; AT IX, 90; FA II, 533; in CSM II, 82: "knowledge of the finite kind just described, which corresponds to the small capacity of our minds."

36. Fifth Responses: AT VII, 368, ll. 2–3; Clerselier's translation in FA II, 811 and n. 2.

37. I am deeply indebted to Charles Paul and Stephen Voss for many linguistic and philosophical emendations. The remaining mistakes are mine.

II

CARTESIAN METAPHYSICS: THE MIND'S CAPACITIES AND RELATIONS TO THE BODY

8

The Role of the Intellect in Descartes's Case for the Incorporeity of the Mind

Marleen Rozemond

Descartes held that the mind, the subject of mental states, is an incorporeal substance. He held that most mental states, for instance sense-perception and imagination, involve states of the body as well. Purely intellectual activity, however, does not. Why he held this view of pure intellection is a relatively neglected question in Descartes scholarship. Still, Margaret Wilson has addressed it. She claims that this view was very unusual at the time, and explains Descartes's adherence to the view in terms of his scientific preoccupations. Descartes thought that all physical phenomena could be explained mechanistically, but was confronted with the difficulty of providing such explanations for human intelligence.

I will propose a rather different picture. First, Descartes's view of intellection as an activity of the mind alone was not unusual; the view was common among Aristotelian Scholastics. Furthermore, Descartes thought this view counted in favor of the immortality of the soul, and saw this as an advantage of the view.[1] Wilson correctly points out that Descartes thought that mechanistic explanation of intellectual activity is impossible. Her account is misleading, however, because it does not connect the issue of the immortality of the soul and the immateriality of intellection.

Aquinas and other Scholastics had relied on the immateriality of intellectual activity to argue that the soul is an incorporeal substance. I will argue that Descartes's most important argument for the incorporeity of the soul also relies on claims about the intellect, and not about sensation and imagination. In Descartes's terms the conclusion of that argument is that mind and body are really distinct. I will call this argument the *Real Distinction Argument.* I will contend that the complete immateriality of the intellect, which distinguishes it from sensation and imagination, plays a role in that argument.

On the other hand, Descartes differed from Aristotelian Scholastics in that he held that the soul is *only* the principle of thought. The Aristotelians thought it was also the principle of nutrition, growth, locomotion, and sensation; Descartes thought that these operations (except for a part or aspect of sensation) could be accounted for mechanistically.[2] According to Descartes this point of difference with the Aristotelian Scholastics meant that he had a better case than they did for the incorporeity of the soul. This and other aspects of my interpretation help us understand Descartes's confidence in this much criticized argument.

On various occasions Descartes draws a contrast between the intellect on one hand, and sensation and imagination on the other hand. The following passages are examples:

> . . . When the mind understands, it in some way turns towards itself and inspects one of the ideas which are in itself; but when it imagines, it turns towards the body and intuits something in the body which conforms to an idea understood by the mind or perceived by the senses. (AT VII, 73)
>
> I have also often distinctly shown that the mind can operate independently of the brain; for certainly the brain can be of no use to pure intellection, but only to imagination or sensing. (AT VII, 358)[3]

Wilson argues that this contrast shows that Descartes's dualism differs rather dramatically from the modern version of Cartesian dualism.[4] The main point of the latter view is that "mental events *are not identical* with events in the body (brain, or whatever)." This point is compatible with the idea that "*every* type of mental occurrence, from twinges of pain to metaphysical reflection, has a *corresponding* or *correlated* type of physical occurrence." According to Wilson Descartes thought that acts of intellection are not even *parallelled* by any physical acts.[5]

Wilson wonders why Descartes held this version of dualism. She suggests that the Real Distinction Argument does not support it and that Descartes was an odd man out with this form of dualism in the seventeenth century. For instance, Hobbes, Leibniz, and Spinoza all accepted materialism or parallelism. Wilson rules out a concern with personal immortality on the ground that Leibniz and Spinoza were more concerned with this issue but did not adhere to Descartes's view of the intellect. Instead, she suggests, Descartes was *motivated* by his "universalist pretensions" in physics and the observation that he had no account of the human intellect. A *reason* for his view that intellection is completely immaterial may be that he was committed to mechanistic explanations in physics and that he thought that such explanations could not account for human intellectual activity.[6]

Wilson is right in claiming that for Descartes acts of intellection are not accompanied by correlated physical events. But it is important to see that Descartes's *point* in the passages in question is not to deny that there are physical events that parallel intellection. Rather his point is that intellection, unlike sensation and imagination, is *independent* of the body.[7] Intellection is an operation of the mind alone in which the body does not take part. In the second passage quoted earlier this is exactly what Descartes says. I will call the view that intellection is an operation of the mind alone the *Independence*

Thesis. It is important that the independence of the intellect is Descartes's point, because this idea was used in Aristotelian Scholasticism to argue that the soul is an incorporeal substance. The argument in question was used by Aquinas, whose views were a central component of Jesuit teaching, and by Suarez, Eustache, and the Coimbra commentators; Descartes must have been familiar with this argument. I will contend that the Independence Thesis played a role in the Real Distinction Argument.[8,9]

The question now is why Descartes held the Independence Thesis. It is not surprising, however, that he held it when one considers that it was a widely accepted view among Aristotelian Scholastics. They also believed that intellection is an activity of the soul alone. They thought that intellection differs in this respect from sensation and imagination. Whereas the soul alone is the subject of intellection, the body or the body–soul composite is the subject of sensation and imagination.[10] Descartes also thought that sensation and imagination differ from intellection in that they require a body.[11] So Descartes was not an odd man out with respect to his Aristotelian predecessors for holding the Independence Thesis. Consequently Descartes's adherence to this view is not as urgently in need of an explanation as it would be if he were unusual in holding the Independence Thesis, and it is unlikely that Descartes's scientific preoccupations moved him to adopt it. It may have seemed natural to Descartes to think that the human capacity for intellection can only be exercised by an incorporeal entity (which may, however, be joined to a body).

Wilson rules out the possibility that a concern with personal immortality explains why Descartes held that intellectual activity is completely immaterial. But a concern with the immortality of the human soul does in fact emerge in the *Discourse on Method* when Descartes discusses the fact that certain human capacities require reason.[12] Descartes describes there how various functions of the human body can be explained mechanistically. Next he claims that animals cannot be distinguished from machines, but that human beings can, because no machine could have our linguistic abilities or be capable of as many different activities as we are. In this way also, he continues, human beings can be distinguished from animals, since animals do not have these abilities either. The fact that they do not shows that animals do not have reason at all. He concludes with the observation that it is very important to see that the souls of animals are radically different from our souls. For if one clearly sees this difference,

> one understands much better the reasons that prove that our soul is of a nature entirely independent of the body, and that, consequently, it is not subject to dying with it. Furthermore, since one does not see any other causes that destroy it, one is naturally brought to judge that it is immortal. (AT VI, 59–60)[13]

Descartes makes clear in this discussion that he thinks that mechanistic explanation cannot account for our capacity for language and for the wide variety of our abilities. But he also contends that mechanistic explanation does cover all functions common to animals and human beings, and he is more concerned to make the latter point. As a comment by Arnauld suggests, Descartes was out of step at the time more because he extended the scope of mechanistic explanation as far as he did than because he thought it did not include intellectual operations. Arnauld foresees resistance to the application of such explanation to animal behavior.[14]

Furthermore, Descartes *uses* the idea that mechanistic explanation covers all animal behavior in support of the immortality of the human soul. This idea, in combination with the idea that mechanistic explanation does not cover certain human abilities, shows that our soul is radically different from the soul of animals. This difference counts in favor of the immortality of our soul, he says, because it allows us to see better that our soul is completely independent of the body.

Why does Descartes think that the scope of mechanistic science as he sees it supports the immortality of the soul? There are two reasons. First, it was thought that if animals and human beings had the same kind of soul there was a problem for the immortality of the human soul, since animals were not thought to have immortal souls.[15] In Descartes's view the only ground for thinking that animals have souls would be that their behavior shows that they have reason. But, he argued, animal behavior does not show this, and all of it can be explained mechanistically. So there is no reason, he thinks, to ascribe souls to animals, and he believed that animals do not have souls at all. Consequently we need not doubt the immortality of our souls on the ground that animals have souls like ours.

Second, Descartes meant to supplant the Aristotelian conception of the soul according to which it is the principle of a variety of functions of living beings, which include nutrition, growth, motion, sensation, imagination, and intellection. On the Aristotelian view plants, animals, and human beings all have souls. The human soul is the principle of all the functions mentioned earlier, and shares them all, except for intellection, with the souls of animals. The functions humans and animals have in common take place in a body and are performed by the ensouled body. Intellection is an operation of the soul alone, and distinguishes our soul from the souls of animals.

The idea that in intellection the soul operates independently of the body (the Independence Thesis) was used by Aquinas and others, including Descartes's immediate predecessors Eustache, Suarez, and the Jesuits of Coimbra, to argue that the soul is not merely the form of the body, but an incorporeal, spiritual entity independent of the body, which can exist without it; that is, it was used to argue that the human soul is an incorporeal substance.[16] The idea that the soul is a substance independent from the body was important for the view that the decay of the body did not necessitate the death of the soul, and was used to argue that the soul is immortal.[17]

Consequently, for Aristotelian Scholastics the human soul is an unusual entity. On the one hand, it is the form of the body. As such it is united to and dependent on the body; it is a component of a hylomorphic substance. On the other hand, it is an incorporeal substance. These two aspects of the human soul are in tension with each other, as Aquinas saw very clearly.[18] Other Aristotelians thought that they are incompatible. Medieval Aristotelians attributed the idea that intellection is not an operation of the body to Aristotle.[19] From the idea that intellection is not an operation of the body Averroes and others had concluded that intellection is not an operation of the soul—that is, of the form of the body—but of a separate intellect. They thought that on this conception of intellection its subject cannot be the form of the body, but must be a separate thing. Aquinas, on the other hand, made use of the Independence Thesis to defend the Christian belief in the afterlife. He attempted to reconcile this aspect of the human soul with its function as form of the body in rendering the human being a unified entity.

Descartes's view of the scope of mechanistic science meant that all operations traditionally ascribed to the soul, except for intellectual ones, could be accounted for mechanistically and did not require a soul. It is clear then how Descartes's view of the scope of mechanistic science is supposed to bring out the difference between the souls of animals and human souls, and strengthen the case for the independence of the human soul from the body. For all operations shared by animals and human beings fell within the scope of mechanistic explanation, so that animal souls were reduced to the configuration of the parts of their bodies. On the Aristotelian view, these operations indicated the dependence of the soul on the body, since the soul needed to be united to a body to form a hylomorphic whole which could then exercise these operations of which it is the principle. Descartes restricted the human soul to the principle of intellectual operations, which were precisely the ones that were thought to show that the soul is a substance that can exist without the body. He eliminated the functions of the soul that made it dependent on the body.[20] In effect he eliminated the aspect of the soul that made it the form of the body, and on his picture the soul was just a spiritual substance.

The confinement of the soul to the principle of intellectual operations is also part of the Real Distinction Argument. Descartes introduces his conception of the soul at the beginning of the Second Meditation. There he considers the traditional functions of the soul: nutrition, movement, sensation, and thought, and rejects all of them but one, retaining only thought as belonging to his essence. At that point thought only includes intellection. This is clear from the fact that Descartes proceeds to use the claim that thought alone belongs to him to conclude that he is a mind, intelligence, intellect, or reason (*mens, sive animus, sive intellectus, sive ratio*).[21] All of these terms were used to refer to the intellectual part of the soul. Descartes does not include other mental operations as thoughts until later in the Second Meditation.

Whereas to a later reader this characterization of the soul as intellectual is striking because it leaves out sensation and imagination—other kinds of thoughts—to Descartes's contemporaries it must have been striking because it leaves out nutrition, locomotion, sensation, and imagination. In the Second Meditation the point of Descartes's claim that the soul is intellectual is clearly the exclusion of these traditional functions of the soul.

The discussion in the *Discourse* suggests that for Descartes this confinement of the essence of the soul was very important for proving its incorporeity. Descartes emphasized on a number of occasions the fact that thought constitutes the *entire* (*totus*) essence or nature of the soul. This phrase is intended to exclude other traditional functions of the soul.[22] In the letter to De Launay of 22 July 1641, Descartes seems to express the view that once one sees that the essence of the soul consists in thought and the essence of the body consists in extension, it is pretty obvious that they are really distinct.[23] Descartes himself may have regarded this view of the essence of the soul (and the body) as his most important contribution to the argument that the soul is an incorporeal substance.[24]

What have we learned about Descartes's reasons and motives for holding the Independence Thesis? The fact that the Thesis was held by the Aristotelian Scholastics does not touch Wilson's claim that Descartes's commitment to mechanistic science gave him a *reason* for holding the Thesis. But this fact makes it unlikely that Descartes was actually *motivated* by this reason, or by his "universalistic pretensions" in physics, to adopt the Thesis. Nor does the discussion in the *Discourse* show that he was.[25]

On the other hand, this passage in the *Discourse* does show that Descartes saw his efforts in mechanistic science as contributing to our hope of immortality. They resulted in a restriction of the soul to a principle of intellectual operations, which he regarded as supporting his claim that the soul is an incorporeal substance, independent from the body. This claim in turn supports belief in our immortality, as Descartes makes clear. From Wilson's discussion one gets the impression that Descartes felt forced to hold that pure intellection is completely immaterial, because he could not account for it mechanistically, and that he would have been better pleased if he felt that pure intellection could be explained mechanistically. But the discussion in the *Discourse* suggests in fact that Descartes had a stake in believing that intellectual operations are independent of the body given that such a belief supports the immortality of the soul.[26] This role of the immateriality of the intellect may not actually have moved Descartes to adhere to it. But it would have moved him to resist the idea that intellection can be accounted for mechanistically.

Now we can see one point that helps us understand Descartes's confidence in the Real Distinction Argument. Descartes saw his restriction of the soul to intellection as important for the incorporeity of the soul. A later reader can easily overlook this point, since for later thinkers a mind or soul needs to be postulated at most to account for thought. For us there is no question about whether functions other than thought require a soul. Thus the question of the incorporeity of the soul only depends on whether thought requires an incorporeal substance. But Descartes believed that most of the work was done by the time he had confined the essence of the soul to thought and the essence of body to extension.

I think part of the explanation for Descartes's attitude is that he was more concerned with supplanting Aristotelian Scholasticism than with defeating materialism. Descartes admitted that accomplishing the former was his purpose in the *Meditations*.[27] The *Principles of Philosophy* were meant to replace Aristotelian textbooks. The restriction of the soul to intellection was directed in the first instance against Aristotelianism rather than materialism. And the reader of the Third and Fifth Replies cannot fail to be struck by the impression that Descartes did not take materialism very seriously. For instance, he did not seem to see a need to argue against the view that thought is motion, which was the form of materialism then current.[28] Since the Aristotelian Scholastics thought that intellection was incorporeal, Descartes may not have felt as great a need to argue for its incorporeity as we might expect.

Let us turn now to the relationship between the Independence Thesis and the Real Distinction Argument. The Independence Thesis was used by Scholastics to prove that the soul is an incorporeal substance. Descartes argues for the incorporeity of the soul in the Real Distinction Argument. I think that his argument also relies on the Independence Thesis. This interpretation requires that the argument relies only on claims about intellection, and not about sensation and imagination, since the Thesis applies to intellection but not to the other two operations. I will presently defend this idea. Next I will discuss the role of the Independence Thesis in the Real Distinction Argument.

The Real Distinction Argument proceeds roughly as follows. Descartes develops a clear and distinct conception of the mind as a complete thinking and unextended thing or substance in the Second Meditation. In the Second, Fifth, and Sixth Meditations, he develops a conception of body as an extended substance. In the Sixth Meditation he uses these conceptions to conclude that the mind is an incorporeal substance, really distinct from the body. He does so by validating the clear and distinct conceptions of mind and body via God. I think that the validation of clear and distinct perceptions is the only role God plays in the argument.

This interpretation is controversial; it is in competition with an interpretation according to which the mere validation of clear and distinct perceptions is not enough and God plays a bigger role.[29] It would take too long to give an adequate defense of my view. Descartes himself describes the argument in terms that agree with my interpretation in the Synopsis and the Fourth Replies.[30] What I have to say in the sequel does count in favor of my interpretation insofar as I address a particular objection that arises against it. According to this objection there is a question as to how Descartes comes by such a full perception of the mind as would merely need validation in order to result in the real distinction. Thus Steven Wagner has objected that the concept of thought neither rules out extension nor includes possible nonextension, and that the concept of the mind as only thinking is not enough to show the possibility of an unextended mind.[31] I will argue that the argument is less vulnerable to this objection if it relies only on intellection, and not on sensation and imagination.

I will defend the claim that the Real Distinction Argument relies on the nature of intellection in two stages. (1) In the Real Distinction Argument Descartes is concerned to argue that the soul is an incorporeal substance rather than that intellection is an incorporeal operation. He relies on the nature of the activity of the soul to establish its incorporeity. (2) The activity he relies on is intellection. I will now discuss (1). In doing so I will assume (2) for expository purposes. I will then defend (2).

(1) One might think that the Real Distinction Argument is supposed to support the immateriality of intellection.[32] But in fact the Independence Thesis should come in at the other end of the argument. The Thesis cannot be its conclusion but should be expected to be *used* in the argument. For the Real Distinction Argument aims to establish substance dualism: the conclusion of the argument is that the *mind* is an incorporeal *substance.*

The importance of the point that the Real Distinction Argument aims to establish substance dualism is clear in the Sixth Replies. The objectors had claimed that Descartes had failed to show that thought is not motion.[33] Descartes's reply is revealing about what he takes his task to be.

> When someone notices that he is thinking, and he understands what motion is, it is impossible that he believes that "he is mistaken and is not thinking but merely moving." Since the idea or notion that he has of thought is quite different from his idea of corporeal motion, he necessarily understands the one as different from the other. But because of his habit of attributing to one and the same subject many different properties between which no connection is known, it can happen that he doubts, or even affirms, that he is one and the same being who thinks and who moves. It must be noticed that there are two ways in which those things of which we have different ideas can be taken for one and the same thing: either by a unity and identity of nature, or only by a unity of composition. (AT VII, 422–423)

So Descartes claims that it is quite impossible for anyone to confuse thought and motion, and does not seem to worry about this kind of confusion. After dealing with it very briefly he points out what mistake a person might indeed make: someone might think that thought and motion belong to the same subject. Descartes then launches into a discussion of the difference between unity of composition and unity of nature and argues that the mind and body form a unity of composition.

So Descartes does not think that he needs to show that thought is not motion. Since materialists in Descartes's time held that thought is motion, it would seem then that Descartes did not think he needed to argue that thought is incorporeal. He does see a need to argue that the *thing* that thinks is really distinct from the *thing* that moves. Consequently we should not expect the Real Distinction Argument to show that *intellection* is an incorporeal activity but that the *mind* is an incorporeal *thing.*[34] Descartes should base this conclusion on the nature of intellection rather than the other way around, given his views about the way we know substances. For he thinks we do not know substances directly, but via their properties.[35]

(2) I will now turn to the claim that the argument relies on intellection, and not on sensation and imagination. Descartes describes the mind in the Second Meditation as a thing that "doubts, understands, affirms, denies, is willing, is unwilling, imagines and senses."[36] It is usually thought that this conception of

the mind constitutes the basis for the Real Distinction Argument. However, immediately after that argument Descartes writes:

> Moreover, I find in me faculties for certain special modes of thinking, namely the faculties of imagining and sensing. I can clearly and distinctly understand myself as a whole without them; but not vice versa them without me, that is, without an intelligent substance in which they are: for they include some intellection in their formal concept, hence I perceive that they are distinguished from me as modes from a thing. (AT VII, 78)

Descartes says that imagination and sensation belong to him *after* he proposes the Real Distinction Argument. This fact suggests that the argument does not rely on claims about sensation and imagination. Furthermore, Descartes makes clear here that sensation and imagination do not belong to the essence of the mind; he says that he can clearly and distinctly understand himself without them. But the Real Distinction Argument relies on the conception of the essence of the mind, so that is an additional indication that sensation and imagination are not included in the argument. Moreover, Descartes says that imagination and sensation are modes of the mind because they include intellection. Thus it seems that the argument for the real distinction relies on a conception of the mind as a thing that engages in intellection.

Given Descartes's position in the history of philosophy and science, the Real Distinction Argument should be expected to rely only on intellection and not on imagination and sensation. Considerations later urged against the corporeity of the mind often turn on qualia such as those occurring in sensations of secondary qualities. Centuries of successful science have relied on the idea that secondary qualities as they appear to us do not characterize the physical world. The phenomenological nature of our sensations of colors, flavors, and the like is taken as a reason to think that these sensations and the subjects that have them are not a part of the physical world.

Of course for Descartes it would not have been a good strategy to rely on this argument. He could not look back on a tradition of the exile of secondary qualities from the physical world. On the contrary, he was one of the founders of this view. One of his purposes in the *Meditations* and elsewhere was to replace the Aristotelian conception of the world and substitute his own. Part of this substitution consisted in eliminating secondary qualities from the physical world to make it safe for his mechanistic, mathematical conception of science.

Descartes sought to confine secondary qualities to the mind. This meant a change in the conceptions of sensation and imagination (as well as the passions). His Aristotelian predecessors had regarded the representations, or "species," that give these acts of the soul content as inhering in the body or the soul–body composite. For Descartes's purposes these species, or "ideas," needed to be located in the mind. For on the scholastic view, the mind is the intellectual part of the soul that operates by itself and not in a corporeal organ. Thus in terms of the historical context he needed to *argue* that sensation and imagination (or a part or aspect of these operations) are modes of the mind. This view of sensation and imagination would have been more controversial than the view that the soul is an incorporeal substance.

For the Aristotelian Scholastics the soul was the principle of sensation and imagination. Some thought that they are operations of the body, others that they are operations of the soul–body composite. Consequently these operations would have made a poor foundation for the real distinction without substantial argument for the view that they belong to the mind; that is, the part of the soul that does not operate in the body. For Descartes's readers these operations indicated the dependence of the soul on the body rather than its independence, as the real distinction requires.

In fact Descartes's own comments suggest that he thought that sensation and imagination would constitute an obstacle to recognizing the real distinction. In the Sixth Meditation he claims that through inner sensation we know that we are not united to our body as a pilot to his ship; for if we were, then we would perceive damage to and needs of our bodies intellectually. So Descartes thinks that the nature of sensation shows that we are closely united to our bodies. Earlier in the Sixth Meditation he had argued, although tentatively, for the same conclusion on the basis of the nature of imagination.[37]

This is not to say that Descartes thought it impossible to establish the real distinction on the basis of sensation and imagination. In the Third Replies he seems to rely on intellection and volition as well as sensation and imagination.[38] But in the *Meditations* he clearly relies only on intellection. The reasons cited earlier suggest at least that Descartes thought that consideration of the nature of sensation and imagination does not lead so easily to recognition of the real distinction of mind and body. This view distinguishes Descartes from later proponents of versions of the Real Distinction Argument, who tend to regard sensations as making the most convincing case.

The passage from the Third Replies might suggest an objection to the present interpretation of the Real Distinction Argument. One might claim that the passage suggests that the argument relies on the attribute of thought which underlies the various kinds of modes of the mind, rather than on intellection which is just one of these modes. For there Descartes claims in support of the real distinction that thought and extension, which are the attributes of mind and body, differ completely. The argument in the *Meditations,* one might argue, should be understood in this way as well.

Here I can only outline my response to this point, which I do not regard as incompatible with my interpretation. For in my view intellection, or, as Descartes sometimes says, pure intellection, is not just a mode of the mind on a par with other kinds of thought. Its relation to the attribute of thought is different: intellection constitutes the attribute of thought. This point is expressed by Descartes's statement that sensation and imagination include intellection in their formal concept,[39] and by his use of the term "pure intellection." Sensation and imagination contain an intellectual component: this is their relation to the attribute of thought. These operations contain an additional component, which comes in some way from the body.[40] They are impure forms of intellection. The operation of pure intellection is a pure manifestation of the attribute of thought, which is the essence of the mind: Descartes also uses the term "pure mind" to refer to this operation.[41,42] Since pure intellection is a pure manifestation of the attribute of thought, reliance on it to demonstrate the real distinction between mind and body amounts to relying on the attribute of thought. Furthermore, since sensation and imagination are impure manifestations of this attribute due to a corporeal element, they are less suited to showing the real distinction.

I have argued that the Real Distinction Argument relies only on intellection, and not on sensation and imagination. For Descartes as for his predecessors, intellection was distinguished from these two other operations by virtue of the Independence Thesis. Consequently it seems likely that this Thesis plays some role in the argument. I will now explain how the Thesis is important for the argument.

Descartes claims that the argument relies on the fact that he has a conception of the mind as a thinking *thing* (*res*), or, more explicitly, as a *complete* thinking thing. A *res* or complete thing is a substance or a thing that subsists or exists *per se,* an *ens per se,* that is, a thing that exists through itself or in its own right.[43] I will argue that the Independence Thesis contributes to the plausibility of Descartes's claim that he has developed a conception of the mind as a thinking, complete thing.

When Descartes introduces the notion of a complete thing as important for the Real Distinction Argument in the First and Fourth Replies, he does not explain how he sees that his conception of the mind as a thinking, unextended thing is a conception of it as a complete thing. Descartes does provide an explanation in the letter to Gibieuf: we see that our conception of the mind as a thinking, unextended thing is complete (that is, as he explains to Arnauld, we see that it is a conception of a complete thing) because we can *deny* extension of the mind.[44] This explanation raises two questions: (1) Why does the deniability of extension show that the mind is complete as thinking and unextended, and (2) how does Descartes know that he can deny extension to the mind?

(1) The answer to the first question depends on Descartes's conception of substance. He thinks that each substance has a principal attribute which constitutes its nature, and that its other properties are modes of the substance (or transcendental attributes like existence and duration). A mode cannot be conceived without the attribute of the substance of which it is a mode. Thus sensation and imagination cannot be conceived without thought (or intellection); motion, shape, and size cannot be conceived without extension.[45] On this view the fact that we can deny extension of a thinking thing shows that thought is not a mode of extension. Descartes thinks that there is no other property that is presupposed by thought or intellection, and thus it follows that thought is not a mode, but a principal attribute.[46] In this way Descartes arrives at the conception of the mind as a complete, thinking thing.[47]

(2) I think that the widespread acceptance of the Independence Thesis explains Descartes's confidence that extension can be denied of a thinking

thing. More importantly, given Descartes's conception of the various cognitive faculties, the claim that thought does not presuppose extension is more plausible if it is based on a consideration of intellection rather than sensation or imagination. For the latter faculties a problem arises with this claim which brings out the importance of the Independence Thesis. This problem is best elucidated by discussing Descartes's comparisons between imagination and intellection, for the Independence Thesis usually comes up in those comparisons. It is clear that Descartes thought the relevant difference between imagination and intellection also obtains between sensation and intellection.[48]

Descartes thinks that imagination differs from pure intellection in that in the former operation we are aware of images. The phenomenological nature of these images suggests that they may be extended. Thus he speaks of considering the three sides of a triangle as if present to the mind in imagination.[49] This conception of imagination suggests that it depends on an extended image. Descartes seems to think so; he argues, albeit tentatively, from this feature of imagination to the existence of our body at the beginning of the Sixth Meditation. He writes to Gassendi that imagination requires an image that is corporeal, that is, a "true body," a *verum corpus*.[50] But then it would seem that imagination presupposes extension and that its subject must be extended. Thus imagination is unsuitable as a ground for the claim that thought does not presuppose extension, and thus it is unsuitable as a basis for the Real Distinction Argument.

Descartes wants to say that imagination requires both a mind and a body. But this account presupposes the real distinction; it presupposes that there is a mind and a body. The fact that imagination requires a corporeal image could equally well be accounted for by a view on which the subject of imagination is one thing that is both extended and thinking.

So the phenomenology of imagination suggests a dependence on the body. This problem does not arise for pure intellection, since it does not involve images. This point could not be enough to establish that pure intellection is independent of body in every way, but it is the sort of dependence at issue when Descartes discusses the Independence Thesis. At any rate, my purpose here is not to consider Descartes's arguments for the Independence Thesis. The point is that the fact that images are involved in imagination suggests dependence on the body. Thus imagistic content is an obstacle to establishing the claim that thought does not presuppose extension.[51] In this way the importance of the Independence Thesis becomes clear. For the fact that pure intellection does not involve images and lacks this dependence on the body is important for the claim that thought does not presuppose extension.[52]

Descartes's conception of the intellect and his efforts on behalf of the incorporeity of the soul are best understood in the context of his relationship with Aristotelian Scholastics. His conception of the intellect as independent of the body is not surprising given that they adhered to it as well. Furthermore, he followed them in relying on this conception to argue that the soul is an incorporeal substance. For Descartes the point that the soul is only the principle of thought and not of operations that depend on the body is an important point in favor of its incorporeity. This aspect of Descartes's conception of the soul distinguishes him from the Aristotelians. Unlike them, Descartes thought that mechanistic explanations could account for all functions of human beings except thought. I have argued that Descartes saw his view of the scope of mechanistic science as welcome support for the incorporeity of the soul, and that he would have been reluctant to give it up.

My interpretation of the Real Distinction Argument contributes to understanding Descartes's confidence in it in the following ways. (1) I think that Descartes was more preoccupied with the Aristotelian Scholastics than with materialism. Consequently the incorporeity of intellection would have struck him as less in need of argument than we might expect. But he regarded his claim that thought alone constitutes the essence of the soul as an important contribution to the case for its incorporeity. (2) Seeing the argument as relying on intellection removes an obstacle to the claim that thought does not presuppose extension. For intellection does not, according to Descartes, include the kinds of images that one finds in sensation and imagination and that do suggest a dependence on extension.

I think it is fair to say that Descartes does not say enough to establish that thought does not require a corporeal substance. This is not to say that his strategy is doomed to fail; the question whether it could be successful is beyond the scope of this essay. But I think that on Descartes's conception the soul is a better candidate for incorporeal substance than it is on the Aristotelian conception, since it is not the principle of functions that can only be exercised in a body. And the scholastic conception of the soul strikes me as ultimately incoherent because it is both a form of the body and an incorporeal substance, whereas on Descartes's conception it it just an incorporeal substance.[53]

Notes

1. Descartes wrote that the incorporeity of the soul gives us hope of an afterlife (AT VII, 13). (Translations are my own, but have benefited from consultation of those found in CSM and CSMK.)

2. For Descartes the soul was identical with the mind, whereas for the Aristotelians the mind was the intellectual part of the soul. (When I use the terms "Aristotelians" and "Scholastics" I refer to Aristotelian Scholastics.)

3. See also AT VII, 385, 387, and AT II, 598; CSMK, 140.

4. Margaret D. Wilson, *Descartes* (London, Henley and Boston: Routledge and Kegan Paul, 1978).

5. Ibid., 180.

6. Ibid., 181–183.

7. I think Wilson might agree with my claim about Descartes's point in the passages in question (cf. ibid., 180–181; Wilson, "Cartesian Dualism," in *Descartes, Critical and Interpretative Essays,* ed. Michael Hooker [Baltimore and London: Johns Hopkins University Press, 1978], 199–201). Her claim that Descartes did not accept parallelism for intellection is not intended to be a claim about Descartes's point in

these passages, but rather a claim about the difference between Descartes's dualism and modern "Cartesian" dualism. Wilson herself does not clearly distinguish, however, between the idea of nonparallelism and the idea that the intellect is independent of the body. But it is important for understanding Descartes to focus on the latter idea.

8. References to scholastic sources are to be understood as follows:

Aquinas, *Summa Theologica;* referred to by part, question, and article; abbreviated "ST."

Eustache de Saint Paul, *Summa Philosophica Quadripartita* (Paris: Carolus Chastellain, 1609); referred to by part and page for the first and second editions.

Works by the Jesuits of Coimbra: (a) *Commentarii in Tres Libros de Anima Aristotelis* (Coimbra, 1598); referred to by book, chapter, question, and article; abbreviated "Coimbra (a)."

(b) *De Anima Separata* (Coimbra, 1598); referred to by disputation and article; abbreviated "Coimbra (b)."

Suarez, *De Anima,* in *Opera Omnia* (Paris: Vives, 1856); referred to by book, chapter, and section.

9. It is necessary to point out the following difference between Descartes and the Aristotelian Scholastics. I will focus on Aquinas, but what I say here applies to Eustache, Suarez, and the Coimbra commentators as well. Aquinas thought that the intellect is independent of the body in the sense that the soul alone is the subject of inherence of the operation of intellection. On the other hand, he thought human intellection depends on the body, because it depends in two ways on the activity of the imagination—which he regarded as a corporeal faculty in that it acts in the body. (1) Intellectual ideas, *species* as they were called, are derived from sense experience through the imagination (cf. ST 1a, 84.6, 85.1). (2) Human beings cannot understand without forming images, which inhere in a bodily organ; intellectual activity is always accompanied by imagination (ST 1a, 84.7, 86.1). The distinction between these two roles of imagination is particularly clear at ST 1a, 85.1 ad 5.

Descartes did not think that intellection depends on imagination in either of these ways. Thus he thought that intellection is independent from the body in a stronger sense. One might think that this stronger sense of independence plays a role in the Real Distinction Argument, but I do not think that this is the case. For my reasons, see my dissertation, "Descartes's Conception of the Mind" (UCLA, 1989), 218–223; and n. 52 in the present essay.

10. Aquinas, ST 1a, 77.8; Coimbra (b), III, I; Suarez, *De Anima* II, III, 2–3 and VI, III, 2; Eustache, *Summa Philosophica* III, 286–287. Ockham, on the other hand, held that the sensitive soul is the subject of sense perception. Cf. *Reportatio* IV, qu. 9, Gedeon Gal and Rega Wood with Romauld Green, eds., *Opera Theologica* (St. Bonaventure, NY: Franciscan Institute, 1984) VII, 162.

11. Cf. *Principles of Philosophy* I, a. 48. I will not try to specify the sense in which Descartes thought sensation and imagination require a body. This issue is addressed at length by Paul Hoffman in "Cartesian Passions and Cartesian Dualism," *Pacific Philosophical Quarterly* 71 (1990):310–333. Also see Wilson, *Descartes,* 200–201.

12. AT VI, 55–60.

13. Although Descartes speaks of souls of animals here, he thought, of course, that animals do not have souls (cf. AT VII, 229–231).

14. AT VII, 204–205. In his reply Descartes refers to the *Discourse on Method* (AT VII, 229–230).

15. See Gilson's discussion of these issues in his *Discours de la méthode, texte et commentaire* (Paris: Vrin, 1925), 420–438.

16. Aquinas, ST 1a, 75.2; Eustache, *Summa Philosophica* III, 413–414; Coimbra (a), 2,1,1,6 and 2,1,2,2; and Coimbra (b), I, 3. Suarez used a different version of the same argument. He argued that the soul is spiritual on the basis of the spirituality of some of its operations (*De Anima* I, IX).

17. Cf. Suarez, *De Anima* I, X; Eustache, *Summa Philosophica* III, 413–414; Coimbra (b), I, 3. Aquinas argues that the soul is incorruptible (ST 1a, 75.6).

18. Mary C. Fitzpatrick and John J. Wellmuth, trans., *On Spiritual Creatures,* (Milwaukee, Wisconsin: Marquette University Press), 33. Aquinas made ingenious, although in my view ultimately unsuccessful, attempts to reconcile the two aspects of the human soul.

19. Relevant texts are *De Anima* III, 4, 429a, 18–28; 5, 430a, 10–25. I do not mean to make a claim about Aristotle's views here. The point concerns the interpretation of Aristotle by medieval Aristotelians. For a discussion of Averroes's treatment of this issue see the introduction by Beatrice Zedler to her translation of Aquinas's *On the Unity of the Intellect against the Averroists* (Milwaukee, Wisconsin: Marquette University Press, 1968). As she points out, there was yet a third position according to which only the agent intellect is separate.

20. As I have pointed out, the Aristotelian Scholastics thought that in a sense the soul depends on the body for intellectual activity as well. But Descartes did not agree (cf. n. 9).

21. AT VII, 27.

22. See, for instance, the Second Meditation (AT VII, 27): "I am, I exist—that is certain. But for how long? For as long as I think. For it could be that if I ceased to have any thought, I would totally [*totus*] cease to exist." In the Sixth Meditation he writes that he can understand himself clearly and distinctly as a whole (*totum*) without sensation and imagination (AT VII, 78). Again in the Replies to Gassendi he says that the whole (*tota*) nature of the mind consists in the fact that it thinks (AT VII, 358).

The passage in the Sixth Meditation suggests that in this context "thought" is not supposed to include sensation and imagination. The term is clearly supposed to refer to the nature of the mind, which Descartes distinguishes from the various modes of thought (see his letter to Arnauld of 29 July 1648: AT V, 221; CSMK, 357). I discuss these issues later.

23. AT III, 420–421; CSMK, 188. See also the Fourth Replies (AT VII, 226), where he claims that when one conceives of substances through different concepts one always thinks they are really distinct

24. The argument relies in addition on a set of metaphysical premises some of which Descartes regarded as obvious. If one accepts the idea that for Descartes his claim about the essence of the mind and body is particularly important as opposed to other premises, it becomes intelligible, I think, why statements of the argument are generally so frustratingly short.

25. Wilson thinks that the passage shows that Descartes reflected seriously on the possibility of a mechanistic account of human behavior (Wilson, *Descartes,* 184–185; "Cartesian Dualism," 204). Jeanne Russier claims that Descartes's appeal to the human capacities there discussed was actually not an unusual move in defense of the spirituality of the human soul. She refers to Silhon and Boucher. I have been unable to lay hands on either of the works she cites (Jeanne Russier, *Sagesse Cartésienne et Religion* [Paris: Presses Universitaires de France, 1958], 48). Russier's claim, if correct, raises questions about how seriously we must assume Descartes considered the possibility of mechanistic explanations for all human behavior.

26. Cf. also Descartes to Plempius for Fromondus, 3 October 1637: AT I, 413–415; CSMK, 61–63.

27. To Mersenne, 28 January 1641: AT III, 298; CSMK, 173.

28. See Emily Michael and Fred S. Michael, "Two Early Modern Concepts of Mind: Reflecting Substance vs. Thinking Substance," *Journal of the History of Philosophy* 27 (January 1989): 29–48, esp. p. 35.

29. For a discussion of versions of my interpretation and its rival see Steven J. Wagner, "Descartes's Arguments for Mind-Body Distinctness," *Philosophy and Phenomenological Research* 43 (1983): 499–517.

30. AT VII, 13, 226.

31. Wagner, "Descartes's Arguments," p. 508.

32. Wilson has pointed out that intellection, but not sensation and imagination, is involved in the Real Distinction Argument (*Descartes,* 201). She considers the question whether the Real Distinction Argument supports Descartes's conception of the intellect, and suggests that it does not (*Descartes,* 181; "Cartesian Dualism," 201). On the other hand, in "Cartesian Dualism," 206–207, she considers the possibility that the Real Distinction Argument *relies on* the immateriality of the intellect.

33. AT VII, 413.

34. The discussion of the mind in the Second Meditation should be read accordingly. Descartes introduces the idea that he thinks, in the narrow sense of intellection, after eliminating other properties of himself on the ground that they require a body. But he seems to assume, or seems to think it is clear, that thought does not require a body. For he does not discuss the possibility that thought requires a body, as he does in the cases of sensation and imagination later on in the Second Meditation.

35. AT VII, 222; *Principles* I, a. 52. In fact this point should not be surprising. For it is usually thought that the incorporeity of the mind is derived from the nature of thought. Once it is seen that the argument relies on intellection, the incorporeity of the mind should be expected to be derived from the nature of intellection. This point is worth making, however, given its importance for my interpretation, and given the fact that Wilson does not clarify the place of the nature of intellection in the argument.

An exchange between Gassendi and Descartes is interesting in this context. Gassendi had written that in order to show that the mind is different from the body Descartes had to come up with an operation that the mind performs independently of the body (AT VII, 269). Descartes replied that he had shown that the mind does perform such an operation, namely pure intellection (AT VII, 358). This reply supports the view that Descartes thought the operation of intellection shows the real distinction.

On the other hand, Descartes's reply might be thought to cause a problem for my view that the Independence Thesis plays a role in the Real Distinction Argument. For Descartes seems to present the independence of the intellect from the body as support for the incorporeity of the mind *in addition to* the Real Distinction Argument. In a letter of 1638 Descartes gave yet a different picture of the relationship between the two ideas: there Descartes claimed that the possibility of the mind thinking without the body is a *consequence* of the real distinction, which he there derives from the Real Distinction Argument (AT II, 38; CSMK, 99).

So Descartes expresses different views of the relationship between the Independence Thesis on one hand and the real distinction and Real Distinction Argument on the other hand. Descartes may have been unclear about these issues. His comments are very brief, however, and he may have had particular points in mind which would turn out to be compatible. Thus they might not be in conflict with my particular account of the role of the Independence Thesis in the Real Distinction Argument.

36. AT VII, 28.

37. AT VII, 81 and 73, respectively. Descartes writes in the Fourth Replies: "I do not deny, however, that the close union of the mind with the body, which we experience constantly through the senses, is the reason why we do not notice the real distinction between mind and body without attentive meditation" (AT VII, 228–229).

38. AT VII, 176. This passage cannot be used to argue that the Real Distinction Argument in the *Meditations* relies also on imagination and sensation. For the dialectic is very different in the two passages. As we saw, in the *Meditations* Descartes first gives the Real Distinction Argument, and then claims that sensation and imagination belong to the mind. In the Third Replies he first claims that intellection, volition, sensation, and imagination belong to the same substance. Then he claims that these thoughts have nothing in common with corporeal modes and uses this observation to support the real distinction of mind and body.

39. AT VII, 78.

40. Cf. AT VII, 73.

41. AT III, 395; CSMK, 186.

42. Versions of the view that the attribute of thought should be identified with intellection can be found in Martial Gueroult, *Descartes selon l'ordre des raisons* (Paris: Aubier, 1953), I, 63–67, 76–81, and in Robert McRae, "Descartes' Definition of Thought," in *Cartesian Studies,* ed. R. J. Butler (New York: Bobbs-Merrill, 1972), 55–70. They have different views about what the attribute of thought amounts to and in what sense sensation and imagination include intellection. My view is closer to Gueroult's: I think that the intellectual element consists in consciousness.

43. AT VII, 222, 224, 226.

44. 19 January 1642; AT III, 475–477; CSMK, 202–203. It is not clear that Descartes always saw deniability as the ground for completeness. For Descartes suggests in the Fourth Replies as well that what belongs to the body can be denied of the mind, but he presents this as a point *in addition to* the perception of the mind as a complete thing, not as a point *supporting* it (AT VII, 225).

45. *Principles* I, a. 61; AT VII, 78–79.

46. See *Principles* I, a. 53.

47. This point is what the thought experiment of the Second Meditation is supposed to establish (cf. AT VII, 223; AT VIII-2, 350). For discussion of this point see my dissertation, "Descartes's Conception of the Mind," 89–101.

48. Cf. for instance AT II, 598; CSMK, 139–140; AT VII, 78; and AT VII, 358.

49. AT VII, 72.

50. Ibid., 387.

51. Two ideas should be distinguished. (1) The view that the imagistic content of imagination constitutes an obstacle to *establishing* the incorporeity of the mind on the basis of consideration of imagination. This view concerns the question whether imagination can be used to establish the real distinction, and it strikes me as plausible. (2) The view that the imagistic content of imagination shows a dependence on the body, once the incorporeity of the mind is established. I find (2) less plausible, and it is not clear what philosophical ground Descartes had for holding it, especially given his view that in sensation the body causes ideas to occur in the mind in accordance with correlations established by God.

52. We are in a position now to answer the question raised in n. 9, whether the

Real Distinction Argument relies on Descartes's view that intellection is independent from imagination. The answer to this question is negative, for the following reason. The independence of the intellect from the body comes into the argument via the idea that thought does not presuppose extension, in the sense that it does not require an extended substance as a subject of inherence. But this idea is compatible with the view that intellection requires imagination in the ways in which Aquinas and others thought it does.

53. This paper has benefited from presentation at the University of Southern California Graduate Student Conference, at the Descartes conference in celebration of the 350th anniversary of the *Discourse* in San Jose, and at the University of California at Irvine. I am grateful to Marilyn Adams, Robert M. Adams, Philip Clark, Keith DeRose, Andrew Hsu, Jeremy Hyman, Alan Nelson, Derk Pereboom, Thomas Prendergast, who commented at San Jose, and Stephen Voss for helpful comments on earlier drafts.

9

Mind–Body Interaction in Descartes

Stephen I. Wagner

Recently, the problem of mind–body interaction has reemerged as a topic of debate among commentators on Descartes. The problem is surely not a new one. Any number of thinkers, from his contemporaries onward, have maintained that Descartes's account of his two substances rules out the possibility of the interaction that he attempted to defend. Often, however, the ground for asserting this impossibility has been left less than explicit. Recent discussion has attempted to clarify the issue by asking whether we can specify grounds within Descartes's philosophy which are sufficient to rule out mind–body interaction. It is this question that I want to address. And while the results we reach may seem outdated to our contemporary minds, perhaps a clearer understanding of Descartes's treatment of the problem will help to shed some light on more general discussions of dualism and its tenability.

There are three elements of Descartes's thinking which might seem to create problems for mind–body interaction—his insistence that mind and body are absolutely distinct substances, his own restrictions on possible causal relations, and his views on the freedom of the will. Recent work has focused on the first two of these issues and I, also, will restrict my discussion in this way. My central goal is to suggest that an essential element of Descartes's worldview has been overlooked in this recent discussion, and to show that once it is taken into account many of the apparent difficulties about Cartesian interaction can be resolved.

The place to start our consideration of the first issue is with Descartes's own claim that the heterogeneity of mind and body was *not,* in itself, an obstacle to their interaction. Responding to doubts about the possibility of interaction, Descartes says,

> . . . the whole problem contained in such questions arises simply from a supposition that is false and cannot in any way be proved, namely that, if the soul and body are two substances whose nature is different, this prevents them from being able to act on each other. (AT IX-1, 213; CSM II, 275)

On the other hand, he sometimes seems to qualify this assertion radically. For instance, in the *Principles of Philosophy* he says,

> Now we understand very well how the different size, shape and motion of the particles of one body can produce various local motions in another body. But there is no way of understanding how these same attributes (size, shape and motion) can produce something else whose nature is quite different from their own. . . . (AT VIII-1, 322; CSM I, 285)

Certainly, reconciling these two statements requires some work on the part of commentators. A recent analysis by Mark Bedau is most important for our purposes.[1]

Bedau has argued convincingly that these two passages show Descartes's view to be the following: We can assert *that* mind and body interact without knowing *how* they interact. Bedau claims that there is nothing inherently problematic in such a view. As he says,

> All causal explanations . . . must eventually stop at a fundamental claim or law that itself is not explained. In electromagnetic dynamics, the explanation might stop at the fundamental claim that electromagnetic fields just *can,* by their nature, exert a force on ferrous matter. Or the explanation might stop with the claims that oppositely charged particles just *do* attract one another and that electrons and nuclei just *are* held together by the "weak" force. What brings the explanation to a stop might be simply the limits of our understanding. Or, it might be that there is nothing more, nothing "deeper" about the phenomenon in question for us to understand.[2]

But Bedau concludes by explaining that, even if we allow Descartes an option such as this, a serious gap in his worldview remains:

> Up to now I have been arguing (what Descartes argues) that nothing *prevents* something conscious and nonextended from interacting with something nonconscious and extended. The point I want to make now is that nothing in what Descartes has told us about mind and body can *explain* their ability to interact. Although Cartesian interaction is *conceivable,* it is still not *explainable.*[3]

And finally, he describes what remains to be provided—namely, some property of the two Cartesian substances which makes their interaction explainable:

> Now, if mind and body can interact, this too must hold in virtue of something about them that enables them to interact. It is not that there must be some underlying, "deeper" fact about minds and bodies that explains their ability to interact. They might interact simply in virtue of being the kinds of things that they are. The point is this: if minds and bodies can interact simply because of being the kinds of things that they are, then they must not be merely what Descartes thought they were. Their respective consciousness and extendedness is insufficient to account for their ability to interact . . . [T]heir natures must include more than what Cartesian interaction allows.[4]

Bedau's challenge here is a most reasonable one. Our first step, then, in clarifying Descartes's position is to see that his thinking about mind and body *does* in fact offer the explanatory element which Bedau is demanding.

To start, it is crucial to remind ourselves that the interaction we are considering is not simply between mind and body understood as *essences,* but between mind and body insofar as they *exist.* We must, then, clarify the significance of the term "existence," as Descartes employs it. It will be easiest to do this first as it applies to physical things. In his article "The Metaphysics and Physics of Force in Descartes,"[5] Martial Gueroult tells us,

> The principle of existence is neither extension nor motion construed geometrically, but God the Creator. The existence and endurance of things is due to the presence in them of a creative *force* which makes them exist and conserves them in existence, that is, in duration. Hence it is clear that while the modes and essence of existing things are referred solely to extension and motion, the existence with which physics deals, the forces which animate these and the laws which govern them, should be referred to God, who is the principle of the forces by which these things exist, endure and change.[6]

Gueroult points us here, in a very straightforward way, to a partial answer to the problem posed by Bedau. There is nothing in the *essence* of body which can account for its ability to interact with mind and to cause ideas. The "nature" of body is indeed simply extension along with its modes. But a body that exists cannot be exhaustively described simply by reference to its modes of extension. What is also required is reference to the force which keeps it in existence. Insofar as bodies *exist,* they *must* be referred to God as the cause of their own existence and as the very ground of their own capacity to effect causal change. Indeed, Gueroult points us to a virtual *identification* of the existence of physical things with the force in them:

> In reality, force, duration and existence are one and the same thing [*conatus*] under three different aspects, and the three notions are identified in the instantaneous action in virtue of which corporeal substance exists and endures, that is, possesses the force which puts it into existence and duration.[7]

It is through reference to this force that we find the "something more"—perhaps the something "deeper"—which makes their ability to interact not only "conceivable," but, as Bedau urged, "explainable."

It will help to look one step further at Gueroult's analysis. His central concern in this article is with the implications of this perspective for the development of a mathematical physics, and he goes on to explain,

> Consequently, we can see that physics must rest on two quite different foundations: on extended substance and motion geometrically defined as a mode, which allows us to use mathematics in *giving an account of modes in terms of their substance;* and on God as the sole power capable of creating matter, in short as the *cause* of the existence of extended substance and its modes, which allows us to *give an account of effects in terms of their causes,* that is, motions, no longer in terms of extension alone but in terms of forces.[8]

Descartes's introduction of a dynamic element, then, is not incompatible with the development of a mathematical physics, but it does leave such an account radically incomplete. And we can see the error in R. C. Richardson's claim that the form of causation proper to bodies is mechanical causation "which is ultimately a function of their extension."[9] Rather we should say that while the laws governing the realm of bodily interactions are expressible through mathematics, the causation underlying these laws is ultimately a function of God's creative power. And while a mechanical, kinematic account of *res extensa* can be given in terms of extension, it is not fundamental.

Finally, we can look at the demand this places on us in formulating the concepts of physics:

> Hence, it is understandable that when it comes to formulating precisely the concepts appropriate to physics, Descartes expressly urges us to "distinguish carefully" between the *modes* of extension and the *forces* which, determining the appearance or disappearance of these modes as existing things, directly express the Divine creative will. Consequently, the various concepts cannot be conceived in a completely clear and distinct way solely by means of the notions of extension and motion which allow their manifestation to be expressed adequately; they also require the metaphysically certain—yet clear and distinct—concepts of the Divine immutable will and continuous creation.[10]

Surely, if the principles and concepts of physics—those describing interactions *within* the realm of extended things—cannot be adequately formulated without reference to these forces, much less so can the concepts of metaphysics, which refer us to the deepest level of explanation and causation. We must expect, then, that the explanations of mind–body interaction will also be radically incomplete apart from reference to these forces.

Gueroult's insights, then, focus us on the importance of a comment Descartes made to More:

> I said that God was extended in virtue of His power, because that power manifests itself, or can manifest itself, by acting on extended substance. (AT V, 403; CSMK, 381)

Our discussion pushes us to the view that their manifestation of God's power constitutes the very existence of physical things. And it raises a question about Descartes's discussion of the existence of physical things in the *Meditations:* Is his Sixth-Meditation claim that physical things exist in fact a claim that they possess a force or power? Gueroult himself does not address this issue directly, but he suggests that Descartes introduced the dynamic picture of the physical world only when he realized that the kinematic view would not serve the needs of his physics. I think, though, that if we look carefully at Descartes's Sixth-Meditation proof we can see the dynamic perspective already present in Descartes's thinking.

After establishing the real distinction between mind and body, as well as the distinction between himself as a thinking thing and the modes of sensing and imagining which belong to him, Descartes says,

> Now there is in me a passive faculty of sensory perception, that is, a faculty for receiving and recognizing the ideas of sensible objects; but I could not make use of it unless there was also an active faculty, either in me or in

> something else, which produced or brought about these ideas. But this faculty cannot be in me, since clearly it presupposes no intellectual act on my part, and the ideas in question are produced without my cooperation and often even against my will. So the only alternative is that it is in another substance distinct from me—a substance which contains either formally or eminently all the reality which exists objectively in the ideas produced by this faculty (as I have just noted). This substance is either a body, that is, a corporeal nature, in which case it will contain formally <and in fact> everything which is to be found objectively <or representatively> in the ideas; or else it is God, or some creature more noble than a body, in which case it will contain eminently whatever is to be found in the ideas. But since God is not a deceiver, it is quite clear that he does not transmit the ideas to me either directly from himself, or indirectly, via some creature which contains the objective reality of the ideas not formally but only eminently. For God has given me no faculty at all for recognizing any such source for these ideas; on the contrary, he has given me a great propensity to believe that they are produced by corporeal things. So I do not see how God could be understood to be anything but a deceiver if the ideas were transmitted from a source other than corporeal things. It follows that corporeal things exist. (AT VII, 79–80; CSM II, 55; I use diamond brackets to indicate additions in the 1647 French translation.)

We can see in this passage that Descartes seems to appeal, on both a conceptual and experiential level, to the notion of a force present in material things. First, he reasons that in order for his passive faculty of sense perception to have these ideas, there must be an "active faculty" capable of producing them. He then looks at the two active faculties he is aware of in himself—his understanding and his will—to see if they can be the source of these ideas. It is not fully clear how he grounds his claim that the faculty of producing these ideas "presupposes no intellectual act on my part." Perhaps he means it to be derived conceptually from the real distinction he has previously established, or perhaps it is meant as an experiential claim—I experience these ideas without acting (intellectually) at all. But his claim regarding the role of his will in their production seems clearly an experiential one—"the ideas in question are produced without my cooperation and often even against my will." The crucial point here is that Descartes is discussing the source of these ideas in terms of the locus of the causal power involved in producing the ideas in him. He finds that this power is not in himself; and his central ground for this claim seems to be that he experiences a power which is not his own and which both imposes these ideas on him and pushes him to assent to the belief that the ideas are produced by corporeal things; indeed, God has given him "a great propensity" in this direction. Thus, it appears that Descartes's final claim—that God would be a deceiver unless corporeal things exist—should be taken to signify the conclusion that this power is in fact in the corporeal things themselves. Perhaps, then, we can say that the dynamic picture of *res extensa* is already part and parcel of Descartes's Sixth-Meditation proof.

To facilitate our later discussion of Descartes's causal theory, we should follow out this perspective a bit further, in order to gain some insight into Descartes's use of the notion of objective reality in this proof. If the existence of corporeal objects denotes the force or power in them, the representative character of our ideas of them is most significant, with regard to this proof, insofar as it is in fact a representation of that power. So when Descartes says that some other substance must contain "either formally or eminently all the reality which exists objectively in the ideas produced by this faculty," it would seem that the reality which is found objectively in our ideas is a representation of the formal existence of the cause of the ideas, that is, a representation of its actual power. But in order for an idea to provide a representation of a power, it must itself provide awareness of some "image" of that power. So we can understand the crucial significance of Descartes's claim that his ideas push his will to assent to the existence of physical things out there as causes of these ideas—in so doing they provide a direct awareness of power. That is, insofar as they effect this inclination of his will, these ideas can be said to manifest a power of their own. Once again, we see that the experiential level is crucial. And we seem to find Descartes committed to two claims about the objective reality of his ideas of corporeal things: (1) it is the representation, via an idea, of some external power or force; (2) our awareness of the objective reality of an idea is provided by the power of the idea to compel the assent of our will.

We can clarify this a bit further by using Descartes's Third-Meditation example of a stone. Suppose I have an idea of a stone and I am asking whether there is an actual stone which exists as the cause of my idea. What I have to determine is whether there is something out there which possesses the power to produce this idea in me. And the representative features of my idea might seem to be relevant in two ways. First, the "picture image" of the stone might help me to identify features of the purported object my question is about. But this picture image cannot help me to answer the relevant question. The only way that the idea can represent the stone's *existence* is by providing a representation of the power in the stone to cause my idea—and Descartes is telling us that it does this through the power of the idea to compel our assent. Then, once I can establish that the power represented is indeed in the stone, I will have established that the stone in fact exists. Thus, the crucial sense in which my idea "represents"—that is, has objective reality—is that it manifests a power whose cause must be in the stone. In this way the idea can help me establish that the stone itself exists, that is, possesses the power which is represented in my idea.

We can find another indication that the representative nature of our ideas in the "picture image" sense cannot be central to the Sixth-Meditation proof. In the proof, Descartes says that if the cause of his idea is a body, it will contain "formally and in fact everything which is to be found objectively or representatively in the ideas." But immediately after concluding the proof, Descartes denies that the body must contain everything contained in my picture image of the stone: he says that corporeal things "may not all exist in a way that exactly corresponds with my sensory grasp of them, for in many cases the grasp of the senses is very obscure and confused." It would seem, then, that the thing must contain all that my idea represents in some other sense of representation—and our analysis has provided what seems like a suitable alternative.

Following Gueroult's perspective, then, has led to some interesting results regarding the presence of a dynamic account of *res extensa* in the Sixth Meditation; and we seem to have located Descartes's ground for his claim that existing bodies can affect minds. It remains for us to investigate briefly whether Descartes's conception of mind can point us in a similar direction regarding the ground of mind–body interaction.

We have seen that Gueroult's equation between force and existence appears to be reflected in Descartes's Sixth-Meditation proof. And this equation, it would seem, should also hold for the minds that God creates and conserves. Indeed, the realm of mind is more clearly a realm of power. Descartes makes this clear when he explains to More how he conceives of incorporeal substances:

> I conceive them as powers or forces, which although they can act upon extended substances, are not themselves extended. (AT V, 270; CSMK, 361)

If, then, our equation between force and existence is central for Descartes, we should expect to find this reflected in his proof of the existence of mind in the Second Meditation. And if we use our perspective toward the Sixth-Meditation proof as background, we can draw out some suggestive analogies between that proof and the discovery of our own existence in the *cogito*.

If we take a mirror image of the Sixth-Meditation proof, we come up with the following analogies with regard to the *cogito*. First, coming to know our own existence must mean coming to know our own force or power, and this power must be made available to us in the *cogito*—that is, the proof of our own existence would be achieved through an experiential awareness of our own power. Second, this awareness would involve experiencing an idea which pushes our will to assent to the presence of a power in us to cause this idea. Third, the assent-compelling power which this idea manifests—its objective reality—would be the significant sense in which the idea represents the existence of our mind, just as a similar power represents the existence of corporeal things in the Sixth Meditation. Without going into details, my suggestion would be that our analysis points us to a reading of the *cogito* very much in line with my generative account,[11] which argues that the apprehension of the thinker's existence in the Second Meditation should be understood as the experiential discovery of the power of our mind to generate representations. In fact, I think that these parallels can be directly extended to the Third-Meditation proof of God's existence. While such an account is well beyond the scope of this paper, the possibility that the direction I have outlined can provide a parallel in structure between the three existence proofs in the *Meditations* is an intriguing one—and perhaps provides a strong motivation for pursuing further the readings I have proposed.

For our present purposes, the value of our perspective toward the *cogito* is that it provides the other side of the ground for mind–body interaction that

Bedau demanded. The "explanation" of the ability of minds and bodies to interact is the knowledge provided by the discoveries of the *Meditations* that, insofar as they exist, both minds and bodies possess power. We will return in our conclusion to a further consideration of the adequacy of this explanation.

We can turn, at last, to the second element in Descartes's thinking which has been seen as creating problems for his defense of mind–body interaction. In a number of places, Descartes makes statements which require that there be a likeness between an effect and its cause. The central statements assert that a cause must contain at least as much reality as it brings about in its effect. For example, he says in the Third Meditation,

> Now it is manifest by the natural light that there must be at least as much <reality> in the efficient and total cause as in the effect of that cause. (AT VII, 40; CSM II, 28)

Claims like this do not seem to rule out interaction between mind and body; since these are both finite substances, they possess the same degree of reality. Recently, however, a number of commentators have insisted that Descartes's statements about causality in fact require a stricter likeness between cause and effect. Daisie Radner points to Descartes's own explanation of his view in the Third Meditation:

> For where, I ask, could the effect get its reality from, if not from the cause? And how could the cause give it to the effect unless it possessed it? (AT VII, 40; CSM II, 28)

Radner goes on to interpret the implications of this passage:

> The reason why the cause must have as least as much reality as the effect is that the reality of the effect must pre-exist in the cause. And the reason why the reality must pre-exist in the cause is that the cause communicates the reality to the effect. The communication principle puts a stronger restriction on the causal relation than the "at least as much" principle. The mere fact that one thing is at least as perfect as another is not enough to ensure that one can be the cause of the other. It must also be shown that some reality or perfection possessed by the first can be communicated to the second.[12]

Radner, then, sees Descartes's causal theory as committing him to the view that the reality of an effect must preexist in and be communicated by the cause. And she takes this one step further. In the Second Replies, Descartes grounds his "at least as much reality" principle in the "common notion" that "Nothing comes from nothing."[13] Radner explains,

> What is produced in the effect must first exist in the cause. If the cause produced something in the effect which it did not first possess in itself and communicate to the effect, that thing would be produced from nothing. Thus to say that the cause must contain in itself at least as much reality as the effect is to say that the cause must contain in itself at least that which it brings about in the effect. In order that the cause may contain in itself what

> it brings about in the effect, the cause and effect must have something in common, viz., the ability to possess the same sort of modification.[14]

In her view, then, Descartes's causal principles entail that a cause be able to possess the same sort of modification as it brings about in its effect. And on this reading, causal interaction between mind and body would indeed be ruled out, since the essential difference between them makes impossible their possession of the same modifications.

Following Bedau, we can dub this stricter reading of Descartes's causal principle the "category" interpretation, in contrast to the weaker "degree" reading. There have been a number of objections to this category reading of Descartes's causal principles. For instance, Bedau himself asserts that, since Descartes explicitly defended the view that mind and body do interact, "it is implausible on the face of it that Descartes accepted the category interpretation."[15] The arguments offered in these responses, however, have not provided the clarification of the relevant passages which is needed to resolve the debate. I think we will find that the perspective set out earlier in this essay will go a long way toward this end.

The best place to look for such clarification of Descartes's theory of causality is in his use of his causal principle in the Third Meditation. Radner focuses on the second causal proof, in which Descartes says,

> . . . there must be at least as much in the cause as in the effect. And therefore whatever kind of cause is eventually proposed, since I am a thinking thing and have within me some idea of God, it must be admitted that what caused me is itself a thinking thing and possesses the idea of all the perfections which I attribute to God. (AT VII, 49; CSM II, 34)

She interprets his reasoning as follows:

> The conclusion Descartes draws here would never follow from the "at least as much principle" alone. One also needs the communication principle or at least the pre-existence principle interpreted as a likeness principle. Descartes is not merely saying that the cause of my existence must be at least as high on the ontological scale. He is saying that it must have what I have: since I am a thinking being, my cause must be a thinking being, and since I have the idea of God, my cause must have the idea of God's perfections.[16]

Radner assumes in her reading that Descartes believes the modes of thought he possesses must preexist in and be communicated to him by some cause that possesses them in itself. But there is another perspective possible, one grounded in the distinction between forces and modes to which Gueroult has directed us.

The direct connection between our previous discussion and this Third Meditation causal argument is that Descartes is here asking for the cause of his own *existence* as a thinker. If we invoke Gueroult's identification of force with existence, and if we insist on consistency in Descartes's use of terms, his Third-Meditation argument translates into a question about the cause of his own *force* or *power* as a thinker. From this perspective, his causal principle entails that what must preexist in and be communicated by this cause would not be the same modifications of thought, but rather something more fundamental which underlies the possession of these modifications—namely, the power to give rise to these modifications. And if, as I've suggested, we take the reality of my mind to denote my power to generate representations, Descartes is telling us that the cause sufficient to explain my possession of this power must itself be a reality, that is, a power, of a similar or higher kind—a power at least sufficient to generate any and all of the ideas which I am capable of generating. The idea of God is central here because it is the idea which will help to prove His existence. But the cause of my existence must "have what I have" in the most basic sense—the sense we have described.

We can take this one step further by carrying this perspective over to Descartes's first causal proof in the Third Meditation. Here the discussion indeed revolves around my ideas themselves—the very modifications of my thinking mind. In this proof, Descartes argues that each of his ideas demands a cause which possesses at least as much formal reality as the objective reality possessed by the idea. The category interpretation might well take this to be a demand that the cause of my idea of a stone possess the same qualities (e.g., shape, extension, color, etc.)-which characterize my idea. Or perhaps it would insist that the cause possess the actual mental state which *is* my idea of the stone. But, on the line I am pressing, this would be a misreading of "objective reality" and "formal reality"—indeed of "reality" itself, as Descartes is using the term. As our look at the Sixth Meditation has shown, what is most significantly contained in our idea of the stone is the power of the idea to effect an inclination of our will. This is a reflection of the power in the stone to cause our idea—its formal reality. What must preexist in the cause of my idea and be communicated, then, is once again the power of this thing itself rather than its modifications as such.

To conclude our discussion of Descartes's causal theory, we can look at two final passages in the light of the perspective we have offered. Radner says,

> If the body causes sensations then it must contain them "in a similar or in some higher form." Sensation cannot exist in a "similar" form in the body, for the body is extended and unthinking. And whatever sensation "in some higher form" may be, it certainly is not figure and motion. So the action of body upon mind is in conflict with the principle of pre-existence. A similar argument against the mind's causation of motion in the body would complete the problem of interaction.[17]

We see here that Radner ignores Gueroult's and Descartes's caution to distinguish between forces and modes. The body is not only extended and unthinking—it *exists,* hence it possesses power. It is in this form that the body "contains" sensations. Similarly, the mind, by virtue of *its* power, can be understood to be capable of causing motion in bodies.

And finally, we can address an assumption which seems to have been operative throughout our discussion. The category interpretation sees Descartes as requiring a communication of modes in causal interaction. I have been arguing that it is the *power* of minds and bodies, rather than their modes, which is the ground of their interaction, assuming without argument that this perspective makes more plausible a transference or communication between bodies and between minds and bodies. It might help to see that Descartes seems to hold just such a view:

> You observe correctly that a *motion, being a mode of a body, cannot pass from one body to another.* But that is not what I wrote; indeed, I think that motion, considered as a mode, continually changes. . . . But when I said that the same amount of motion always remained in matter, I meant this about the force which impels its parts, which is applied at different times to different parts of matter in accordance with the laws set out in articles 45 and following of the Second Part [of the *Principles*]. So there is no need for you to worry about the transmigration of rest from one possessor to another, since not even motion, considered as a mode which is the contrary of rest, transmigrates in that fashion. (AT V, 404–405; CSMK, 382)

If Descartes takes it as apparent that the forces in bodies can be applied at different times to different parts of matter, there would seem to be no reason to rule out such application to minds as well.

I have argued that the notion of force or power is central to Descartes's conception of the existence of both mind and body. And I have also argued that, when seen in the light of this element of his dualism, Descartes's claims about the distinctness of mind and body and his thinking about causality do not rule out the assertion that mind and body can interact. But it is well to remind ourselves of the limits both of Descartes's claims and of the defense I have offered.

As Bedau insisted, Descartes wants to maintain *that* mind and body interact without knowing *how* they interact. And as Bedau also pointed out, Descartes must here be making a claim about the limits of our understanding. On the one hand, we can know clearly and distinctly that mind has the power to think, and perhaps we know how it does so—that is, by the generation of ideas. On the other hand, through our mathematical physics we can give a clear and distinct account of the laws describing bodily motions, and Descartes seems to take this as a conception of how such changes come about. All of this, however, comes down to conceiving minds and bodies as two distinct things. But, as Descartes says to Elisabeth,

> it does not seem to me that the human mind is capable of conceiving at the same time the distinction and the union between body and soul, because for this it is necessary to conceive them as a single thing and at the same time to conceive them as two things; and this is absurd. (AT III, 693; CSMK, 227)

Conceiving of the two substances as one thing must mean seeing them as part of a single, interactive existing order, in which the power of existing minds operates to cause changes in bodies and vice versa. And it is here that our understanding, at least in part, fails us. The *Meditations* has shown us that minds and bodies possess power, making their interaction at least explainable. And it has also shown us that this power derives from and depends each moment on God's conserving activity. But beyond that we seem unable to go—we have reached the fundamental level of explanation. Whether this is a satisfactory philosophical result remains a topic for debate. Yet our discussions shows, I would maintain, that Descartes's assertion of the interaction between mind and body is not ruled out by his thinking—and it helps us to see more clearly where any dissatisfactions with his dualism must lie.[18]

Notes

1. Mark Bedau, "Cartesian Interaction," *Midwest Studies in Philosophy* 10 (1986): 483–502.

2. Ibid., 492.

3. Ibid., 495.

4. Ibid., 496.

5. In S. Gaukroger, ed., *Descartes: Philosophy, Mathematics & Physics* (New Jersey: Barnes and Noble Books, 1980), 196–229.

6. Ibid., 196.

7. Ibid., 197. In this statement, Gueroult seems to suggest that we need to distinguish the different "aspects" under which a thing is considered, and also says that the three notions are "identified" within the act of existing and enduring. My concern is to argue that the thinker of the *Meditations* directly grounds claims about the existence of mind and body in the discovery of the force in them—this is the sense of the "virtual identification" of force and existence which I have asserted.

8. Ibid., 200–201.

9. R.C. Richardson, "The 'Scandal' of Cartesian Interactionism," *Mind* 91 (1982): 24.

10. Gueroult in *Descartes,* ed. Gaukroger, 196–197.

11. "Descartes' Cogito: A Generative View," *History of Philosophy Quarterly* 1 (1984): 167–180, also discussed in "Descartes' Wax: Discovering the Nature of Mind" (unpublished). In these papers I argue against the view held by some commentators that Cartesian self-awareness is nonrepresentational. And I argue for the claim that a discovery of the power of mind grounds the claim of its existence. My analyses of the Second and Sixth Meditations suggest that Descartes was committed to a nonoccasionalist model of mind–body interaction, insofar as the thinker of the *Meditations* identifies a power in mind and in bodies, which a nondeceiving God would not misrepresent. Whether that view is maintained to the very end of the *Meditations,* and whether it is consistent with other aspects of Descartes's thought, are questions that I do not consider.

12. Daisie Radner, "Is There a Problem of Cartesian Interaction?" *Journal of the History of Philosophy* 23 (1985): 41.

13. AT VII, 135; CSM II, 97.

14. Daisie Radner, "Descartes' Notion of the Union of Mind and Body," *Journal of the History of Philosophy* 9 (1971): 161.

15. Bedau, "Cartesian Interaction," 484.

16. Radner, "Is There a Problem of Cartesian Interaction?," 42.

17. Ibid.

18. I would like to thank Stephen Voss and an anonymous reviewer for helpful suggestions in revising an earlier version of this paper.

10
Simplicity and the Seat of the Soul

Stephen Voss

Between 1637 and 1641 Descartes discussed, sometimes directly, sometimes tangentially, which part of the body might qualify as "the seat of the soul" (*le siège de l'âme*)—the part of the body to which the soul was directly or most specifically or most intimately united, and which could thereby mediate causal relations in both directions between the soul and the rest of the body.

Descartes's discussions appear in three kinds of context. In the first two, his focus is on other questions entirely—the cause of the heartbeat and a problem of theodicy. But in spite of their diversity, a single thread runs through all three discussions—the premise that the soul is simple or indivisible. We can gain important insights into Descartes's system if we examine the principles which he found it natural to rely as he staked out a position on the seat of the soul.

The insights come in three varieties—textual, rhetorical, and philosophical. First, it is possible to identify and clarify the chief principle Descartes relies on, particularly in light of the contrast with philosophers who, in correspondence and in the Replies to the *Meditations,* drew different conclusions from similar premises. Second, this study is capable of unearthing reasons why Descartes has seemed historically so much more convincing than his rivals. Third, Descartes's argument contains hitherto unnoticed materials for philosophically evaluating his supposed Achilles' heel—his doctrine of the interaction of soul and body. The perplexity is easy to state: on the one hand, enormous numbers of critics find the doctrine of interaction between Cartesian souls and bodies philosophically objectionable; on the other hand, vanishingly few of them succeed in articulating what is objectionable about it. Hume's old questions are yet unanswered:

> Matter and motion, 'tis commonly said in the schools, however vary'd, are still matter and motion, and produce only a difference in the position and situation of objects. Divide a body as often as you please, 'tis still body. Place it in any figure, nothing ever results but figure, or the relation of parts. Move it in any manner, you still find motion or a change of relation. 'Tis absurd to imagine, that motion in a circle, for instance, shou'd be nothing but merely motion in a circle; while motion in another direction, as in an

> ellipse, shou'd also be a passion or moral reflexion: That the shocking of two globular particles shou'd become a sensation of pain, and that the meeting of two triangular ones shou'd afford a pleasure. Now as these different shocks, and variations, and mixtures are the only changes, of which matter is suceptible, and as these never afford us any idea of thought or perception, 'tis concluded to be impossible, that thought can ever be caus'd by matter.
>
> Few have been able to withstand the seeming evidence of this argument; and yet nothing in the world is more easy than to refute it. We need only reflect on what has been prov'd at large, that we are never sensible of any connexion betwixt causes and effects, and that 'tis only by our experience of their constant conjunction, we can arrive at any knowledge of this relation. Now as all objects, which are not contrary, are susceptible of a constant conjunction, and as no real objects are contrary; I have inferr'd from these principles, that to consider the matter *a priori,* any thing may produce any thing, and that we shall never discover a reason, why any object may or may not be the cause of any other, however great, or however little the resemblance may be betwixt them.[1]

Simplicity and the Beating of the Heart

Descartes first used the doctrine that the soul is simple in a letter to Plemp of 15 February 1638. Vopiscus Fortunatus Plempius (1601–61), a physician and philosopher at Louvain, corresponded with the philosopher during 1637–38 about the beating of the heart. Descartes held that it was due to violent expansion of incoming blood caused by the heat of the heart, while Plemp defended Galen's ancient doctrine, writing that "the heart is in fact moved by a faculty" of the soul.

In response, Descartes commented on a curious objection Plemp had leveled against the Cartesian theory—"if one removes an animal's heart and cuts it up, each piece continues to beat for some time, even though there is no more blood entering or leaving."[2] Descartes responded that a little blood, doubtless still heated from contact with the heart, always remains in the dissected parts, and then offered this counterargument:

> This very objection seems to me to have much more strength against the common opinion of so many others who believe that the movement of the heart proceeds from a faculty of the soul: for how, I ask, will that [motion] depend on the human soul—that [motion], I repeat, which is even found in the divided parts of the heart? For it is *de fide* that the rational soul is indivisible, and that it has no other soul, neither sensitive nor vegetative, to which it is adjoined.[3]

Descartes moves explicitly from the premise that the soul is indivisible to the conclusion that the soul cannot act directly upon the dissected parts of the heart. The principle he relies on is this.

> The Simplicity Principle: If the soul is simple, or indivisible, it can interact directly with only one object at once.

If Descartes had applied the Simplicity Principle only in this letter to Plemp, it might deserve relegation to the pigeonhole for academic trivia. But he also applies the Principle when he attacks a central metaphysical problem in the Sixth Meditation, and again when he wants to identify the seat of the soul. It then becomes striking and significant that when Descartes has much bigger fish to fry, he is happy to rest a great deal of weight on a principle he had first employed several years earlier in an apparent throwaway line written to a Flemish physician.

Simplicity and Theodicy

Descartes argues in the Sixth Meditation that soul and body are not only really distinct but also intimately united, for pain, hunger, and thirst teach me "that I am not merely present in my body as a pilot in his ship, but that I am very closely joined and, as it were, intermingled with it, so that I and the body form a unit [*je compose comme un seul tout avec lui*]. If this were not so, I, who am nothing but a thinking thing, would not feel pain when the body was hurt, but would perceive the damage purely by the intellect. . . ."[4] So, while there is a real distinction between soul and body, "the soul is truly joined to the whole body."[5]

The next clause in the characteristic Cartesian dualism is developed in the course of an attack on a problem of theodicy: how can a perfect God allow bodily sensations, like the thirst of a person afflicted with dropsy, to deceive the soul about what is harmful to the compound of soul and body? "The first observation I make at this point," Descartes says, is that mind and body are not merely very different from each other, but are in one crucial respect contrary in nature: "the body is by nature always divisible, while the mind is utterly indivisible [*Nempe imprimus hic adverto magnam esse differentiam inter mentem & corpus, in eo quod corpus ex natura sua sit semper divisible, mens autem plane indivisibilis*]."[6]

Two features of this observation call for immediate attention. First, Descartes uses it as an initial premise in a complex *argument;* we shall need to be clear about its role within this argument. Second, he regards the observation as a central metaphysical truth: "This one argument [he means his observation] would be enough to show me that the mind is completely different from the body, even if I did not already know as much from other considerations." In fact, the observation is not only philosophically sufficient to establish the real distinction; according to a perhaps surprising remark in the Seventh Replies, it is rhetorically necessary as well:

> I cannot refrain from pointing out here that this doctrine of the divisibility of thinking substance seems to me exceedingly dangerous and entirely at variance with the Christian religion. For as long as anyone accepts it he will never be persuaded by the force of reasoning to acknowledge the real distinction between the human soul and the body.[7]

Descartes's second observation is that "the mind is not immediately affected [*immediate affici*] by all parts of the body, but only by the brain, or perhaps just by one small part of the brain . . . ," elsewhere identified as the pineal gland. "Every time this part of the brain is in a given state, it presents the same signals to the mind, even though the other parts of the body may be in a different condition at the time."

We must now ask a crucial question: What is the role of Descartes's first observation, that while the body is divisible, the mind is "utterly indivisible," within the overall argument? Why is this observation needed at all? The only plausible answer, I suggest, is that it is presented as support for the second observation, that one small part of the brain is what directly mediates causation from body to mind. While Descartes argues that his second observation "is established by countless observations," he also means to defend it theoretically with his first observation.

After observing that whenever a part of a body is moved by a distant part it can always be similarly moved by any intervening part, Descartes presents a fourth and final observation, drawing the conclusion that constitutes his theodicy:

> My final observation is that any given movement occurring in the part of the brain that immediately affects the mind produces just one corresponding sensation; and hence the best system that could be devised is that it should produce the one sensation which, of all possible sensations, is most especially and most frequently conducive to the preservation of the healthy man. And experience shows that the sensations which nature has given us are all of this kind; and so there is absolutely nothing to be found in them that does not bear witness to the power and goodness of God.

Martial Gueroult offers this account of the problematic of Descartes's argument:

> It is the very difficulty of the problem which in reality constitutes the essential proof of God's innocence. The divine omnipotence cannot alter the data of the problem which it sets itself . . . : to unite strictly in their reciprocal action two radically incompatible beings, the indivisible and the divisible.[8]

We must be grateful to Gueroult for his striking vision of a Cartesian God at work on a problem in "metaphysical geometry," a problem constituted by terms that God is constrained by his own eternal decree to observe. Philosophical interest and dramatic tension in this context both derive essentially from the image of a God who is subject to restrictions when it comes to creating human nature. Still, the radical incompatibility Gueroult mentions calls for a second look.

The simple and the composite are, indeed, incompatible in a perfectly clear sense: simplicity and compositeness cannot be truly predicated of any one thing. But such incompatibility has no direct bearing on God's problem. Does Gueroult mean to imply that the simple and the composite are incompatible in the sense that no union between them that enables direct causal relations is possible? But that clearly cannot be the restriction that specifies

God's problem, since he solved his problem precisely by creating such a union between soul and body.

The question which exercises Descartes is not how there could be a union between things whose natures are incompatible. It is rather the question why a perfect God did not unite soul and body in such a way that each part of the body could directly signal the soul when it is damaged. Within this complex argument, it is only Descartes's first observation that can help answer that question. Given the Simplicity Principle, it has straightforward implications concerning the constraints which God observed in creating human beings. The Principle enunciated in the letter to Plemp is sufficient to take us directly from that observation to the conclusion that the soul cannot be affected directly by all the parts of the body. I suggest that this principle is the necessary fulcrum of Descartes's Sixth Meditation argument.

In this context Descartes uses the Simplicity Principle to reason about the conditions under which the body might affect the soul. Earlier, when he wrote to Plemp, he had used the same principle to reason about the conditions under which the soul might affect the body. Descartes has now applied the same principle to consider direct causation in each direction.

It will therefore come as no surprise to see him apply the principle directly to the question of the seat of the soul—which directly mediates causation in both directions between body and soul. Descartes finished editing the *Meditations* in April 1640, and it was not until he wrote to Mersenne on 30 July of that year that he dealt directly with the question of the seat of the soul by relying explicitly on the Principle—that is, by giving as a premise the simplicity of the soul, as he had in the two passages examined earlier. But all the pieces were now in place.

We shall examine Descartes's application of the Simplicity Principle to that question later. First, however, I want to call attention to certain apparent liabilities of the Principle within Descartes's philosophy.

Internal Difficulties for Simplicity

The Simplicity Principle is so strong that it conflicts with doctrines which a naive or enthusiastic Cartesian might espouse in a variety of areas. We might label the conjunction of such doctrines and this Principle "exuberant Cartesianism," by contrast with the "circumspect Cartesianism" we have come to expect from Descartes himself. In particular, the Principle poses a threat to Cartesian theology, entails an abridgement of Cartesian physics, and clashes with other principles Descartes deploys in thinking about the seat of the soul. Descartes's adherence to the Principle helps explain some of the limitations of Cartesian theory, some of the areas that the natural light seems forever incapable of illuminating. Such *specific* and *local* conflicts within exuberant Cartesianism, I suggest, are a central cause of the *general* and *global* feeling which Hume decried, that Descartes's account of mind–body interaction is paradoxical or incomprehensible.

(1) First, the Simplicity Principle threatens Cartesian theology. For God is also an indivisible mind or soul, although infinite and perfect. In fact, God's very perfection implies his indivisibility, for "being divisible is an imperfection."[9] That is why, when Henry More proclaimed that God was spatially extended, Descartes leveled this reproach at him: "You also imagine some divine extension which goes further than the extension of bodies; and thus you suppose God has parts side by side and is divisible, and attribute to him all the essence of a corporeal thing."[10]

But then does God's indivisibility prevent him from acting directly on more than one thing? Descartes shrank from that inference in his correspondence with More: "I think," he confessed, "that God is everywhere in virtue of his power. . . ."[11] And it is certainly hard to see how God could carry out his moment-by-moment preservation—his "continual creation"—of all the other substances in the universe if he were so restricted. If the simplicity of God does not prevent direct action on two things at once, why must the simplicity of a human soul prevent it?

I see no way to resolve this perplexity. But I think that part of the explanation for its occurrence within Descartes's writings is found in the fact that Descartes—like Bacon and Hobbes, unlike Pascal, Malebranche, and Spinoza—evinces in his writings little intrinsic interest in developing a satisfactory theology. And it is not surprising that when he discusses the indivisible soul's relation to the heart and the pineal gland—issues that may seem to have no direct connection with the unique case in which indivisibility is a consequence of perfection—he may have his eye on the imperfect human soul alone. It is entirely characteristic that Descartes should have completed the remark to More just quoted in this manner: "I think that God is everywhere in virtue of his power; yet in virtue of his essence he has no relation to place at all. But since in God there is no distinction between essence and power, I think it is better to argue in such cases about our own mind or about angels, which are more on the scale of our own perception. . . ." Nevertheless, Descartes *is* interested in those bits of theology that he regards as necessary to sustain his epistemology and his physics. If the Simplicity Principle were taken seriously in theology, how would it complicate the claims that God preserves Descartes's own soul, and the parts of matter in the extended universe?[12]

(2) The Simplicity Principle imposes specific restrictions on Cartesian physics. To see this, consider the nature of the movement of the pineal gland, when it is due to the action of the soul. According to the Simplicity Principle, when the soul acts on the pineal gland it does not do so by acting upon the gland's components. Therefore, the resulting movement of the gland is not explicable in terms of the movements of its parts. For this reason, the soul's action upon the pineal gland constitutes an exception to a principle which Descartes relies on throughout his physics. Descartes is a *microreductionist* in physics: he holds that *what it is* for a physical thing to undergo some change or have some feature *just is* for its parts (and perhaps the parts of other causally relevant physical things) to undergo the appropriate changes or have the right

features.[13] In particular, the movement of a physical thing is explainable in terms of movements in its microscopic parts, which have themselves been pushed or pulled by other microscopic things. Consider in particular one of the tiny parts of the undivided pineal gland. In this case, and in this case alone, its motion is explained by the motion of the whole of which it is a part, and not vice versa. For the soul does not cause movement in the pineal gland by causing movement in its microscopic parts. In this case alone, the microreductionist principle in physics fails. In the light of the ideal of explanation that underwrites Cartesian physics, this motion of the components of the pineal gland is, while not inconceivable, deeply inexplicable.

(3) The Simplicity Principle comports poorly with another of Descartes's arguments that the pineal gland is the seat of the soul, which runs as follows. The pineal gland is the only organ in the brain that is single and not double. The seat of the soul cannot be a double organ. For if it were, the soul would have two thoughts, or have two objects represented to it, when using double sense-organs. So the double impressions (*espèces, images, impressions*) that are generated by the eyes or ears must be united into a single impression, in a single bodily organ, before arriving at the soul.[14]

I admit that I find it hard to feel the force of this argument, because it is hard to make sense of the untoward consequence that Descartes fears if double impressions were to be transmitted unfused to the soul. Would the soul have two identical sensory images to consider? Would two copies of an identical proposition seek acceptance? A plausible reading of the argument would help answer the vexed question of the nature of sensory thoughts in Descartes, but unfortunately none seems forthcoming.

Whatever this argument's proper interpretation, though, it clearly demands that we imagine what would happen if two distinct bodily organs were simultaneously to affect the soul. And according to the Simplicity Principle, that sort of thing would not merely have untoward consequences; it is a metaphysical impossibility. The present argument not only fails to bridle directly at this supposition; it intimates that we can understand a violation of the Principle with such distinctness that we can be sure, for example, that if two corporeal impressions were to be transmitted to the soul at once, the soul would come up with two thoughts and not do its own fusing and come up with but a single thought. Although the two arguments converge on a single quite specific conclusion, namely, that the seat of the soul must be identified with a single bodily organ, their respective premises cast doubt on each other.

Simplicity and the Seat of the Soul

Let us turn from heartbeat and theodicy to Descartes's explicit participation in the controversy over the seat of the soul. Taking for granted interaction between soul and body and the simplicity of the soul, he posed the question in these terms: where does the soul "exercise its principal functions" that involve interaction with the body—memory, imagination, sense perception, and acts of will with the body as terminus?

Descartes consistently identified the pineal gland as the seat of the soul—partly because it was mobile, durable, protected from outside influence, and accessible to the nerves. Such reasons will not concern us here. But early in 1640 he wrote two letters in which he gave as a reason for singling out the pineal gland the fact that it is the only part of the brain that is not double.[15] One letter went to the physician Lazare Meyssonnier; the other went to Mersenne. In April Mersenne forwarded copies of both letters to Christophe Villiers, a physician of Sens.

Villiers's own view was that the principal seat and instrument of the soul was to be found in certain tiny bodies in the brain which he called "spirits of generation." One variety of spirits of generation were deployed throughout the brain in order to prepare "influencing and roving spirits" to transmit indirectly the soul's influence through the body. He called a second variety of spirits of generation "fixed spirits," since their habitat was the cerebellum. It was the spirits that are fixed there that immediately carried out the operations of the soul. Villiers's view is captured in the letter he wrote to Mersenne for Descartes at the end of April 1640.

> . . . I do not want to insist . . . against this excellent philosopher [Descartes] that it is impossible for [the principal functions of the soul, e.g. reason, memory, and fantasy] to be carried out by means of [the pineal gland], since our soul is *tota in toto* and *tota in qualibet parte.* But . . . it seems to me that it would have to use some instrument not subject to change and alteration. Now to say that the parts of the brain are all double except for this one, and that the soul would rather use this very mobile and small [part] than two—this argument does not seem necessary to me, in connection with a subtle and penetrating spirit like our soul. And since we also clearly see and know that the soul uses animal spirits, which cannot reside in such a small gland, it is necessary to look for another part or instrument to make them, retain them, and distribute them—all of which things depend on this soul being seated in some place. . . .
>
> But what place? . . . I say that the parts of the body—the brain and so on—are not primarily and intrinsically the principal residence and instrument of the soul; at best, they serve it accidentally, insofar as they are, as it were, matrices preserving until death the spirit of generation and first seed. So we can say that this spirit, when interred in matter, nevertheless contains that matter rather than being contained in it, since it has made those parts and not vice versa. For if we consider the motion of seed in generating and conceiving us, we may easily see that these spirits have made and formed the parts where they must lodge during our lifetime and not vice versa; even matter serves the seminal spirit only as a vehicle and a covering. . . . So the fixed spirits of the brain form and forge in their likeness these influencing spirits to help them carry out all operations performed there. . . . It is also believable that . . . it is in the cerebellum, which is single like the pineal gland, that the above-mentioned operations must be carried out. . . . You should draw the conclusion that it is not the pineal gland that is the principal

instrument of the soul in carrying out its principal functions, but rather the fixed spirit in the cerebellum, helped out by the influencing spirit which it has made, and by that same cerebellum which it has made.[16]

Descartes responded to Villiers, in a letter to Mersenne of 30 July 1640, that while the soul can indeed *use* double parts of the body, and the myriad animal spirits, it cannot *act immediately* on such a multitude. In terminology that Descartes uses here for the first time, he argues that the soul is "immediately joined or united [*immédiatement jointe ou unie*]" to a single part of the body, the pineal gland:

> When he [Villiers] says that the soul can definitely use double parts, I agree with him; and that it also uses spirits, which cannot all reside in this gland. For I do not imagine that the soul is so embraced by [the gland] that it does not extend its actions much further. But it is one thing to use, and another to be immediately joined or united; and our soul not being double, but one and indivisible, it seems to me that the part of the body to which [the soul] is most immediately united must also be one and not divided into two similar [parts], and I find no such [part] in all the brain except for this gland. For, as for the cerebellum, it is one only superficially and nominally; and it is certain that even its vermiform process, which has the greatest semblance of being only one body, is divisible into two halves; and that the spinal cord is composed of four parts, of which two come from the two halves of the brain and two from the two halves of the cerebellum; and the septum lucidum also, which separates the two anterior ventricles, is double.[17]

Descartes's argument rests on a breathtakingly definite and robust conception of the simplicity of the soul. As he had done in considering heartbeat and theodicy, he again relies explicitly and consistently on the premise that the soul is "not . . . double, but one and indivisible," using his conception of simplicity to generate powerful conditions on the seat of the soul. For example, the fact that the cerebellum is constituted of distinguishable parts tells Descartes that the soul would not be able to induce movement in it except by independently moving those parts. But that would violate the Simplicity Principle; therefore, the cerebellum could not possibly serve as the seat of the soul. At first glance, the simplicity of the soul seems a vacuous and jejune idea. But in the hands of someone whose principles are as clearly defined as Descartes's, the idea acquires a remarkable capacity to determine a priori which sort of bodily part can serve as liaison with the soul.

Descartes writes in a similar vein to Mersenne on 24 December of the same year:

> And inasmuch as [the pineal gland] is the only solid part in all the brain which is singular [*unique*], it must of necessity be true that it is the seat of the common sense, i.e. of thought and consequently of the soul; for the one cannot be separated from the other. Otherwise we should have to admit that the soul is not immediately united [*immédiatement unie*] to any solid part of the body, but only to the animal spirits which are in its concavities and which continually enter and leave them like the waters of a stream—which would be considered too absurd.[18]

Again Descartes speaks with surprising confidence: the seat of the soul must be *unique,* and, whatever Villiers may think, it would be *absurde* to imagine the soul interacting directly with the animal spirits.

There is a specific reason why Descartes's view of the seat of the soul should been more persuasive than that of his opponent. As the long excerpt from his letter shows, Villiers linked his account with an animistic conception of the fixed spirits: he thought they worked collectively as purposive agents, even helping to form other bodily parts. It is easy even now to feel the attractiveness of the linkage: once particles within the brain were endowed with properties akin to those of the soul, it was natural to see fewer difficulties in the proposition that the soul could act directly on a multiplicity of them at once. But Descartes thought it superstitious and scientifically useless to attribute such qualities to corporeal particles. Most of his readers were prepared to agree on that score. But when they did, the thought that the soul interacts directly with a multiplicity of particles would have become infected, in their minds, with the same aura of superstition. And so, at a brief but decisive moment in intellectual history, Descartes's own genuinely remarkable view came to seem the reasonable one—that the soul should interact directly with a single part of the brain whose nature was entirely contrary to that of the soul. By the time readers of Descartes began to recoil from direct interaction between Cartesian souls and Cartesian bodily parts, they had accepted his mechanistic view of those parts, and in the bargain rejected as intellectual live options not only an animistic view of bodily parts but also any account of a multiple seat of the soul.

At the opposite end of the spectrum from Villiers's animism stands the radical empiricism of Pierre Gassendi, the author of the Fifth Objections to the *Meditations.* When Gassendi wishes to examine Descartes's conception of simple substances, his style is to begin with the idea of an observable physical point, refine it by the use of imagination to obtain the idea of a geometrical point, and use that idea as a model to investigate the Cartesian conception. In his view, even such an abstraction as a geometrical point is suspect, no matter how useful it might become in a Cartesian or a Newtonian idealized physics: only confusion can result from failure to distinguish sensible physical points from putatively imaginable mathematical points. It is not surprising that the idea of a Cartesian soul—a "metaphysical point," as Leibniz was to put it—is entirely beyond his grasp. How could anything modeled after a geometrical point be capable of what the Cartesian soul is capable of? It is from such a stance that Gassendi remonstrates with Descartes.

> . . . you still have to explain how that "joining and, as it were, intermingling" or "confusion" can apply to you if you are incorporeal, unextended and indivisible. If you are no larger than a point, how are you joined to the entire body, which is so large? How can you be joined even to the brain, or a tiny part of it, since . . . no matter how small it is, it still has size or extension? If you wholly lack parts, how are you intermingled or "as it were intermingled" with the particles of this region? For there can be no intermingling between things unless the parts of each of them can be intermingled.

> Moreover, since all compounding, conjunction or union takes place between the component parts, must there not be some relationship between these parts? Yet what relationship can possibly be understood to exist between corporeal and incorporeal parts?

Gassendi's dispute with Descartes is deeper than Villiers's. I began this section by formulating Descartes's question—a question that was hypothetical: On the assumption that the soul is simple and that it interacts with the body, where does it exercise its principal functions that involve interaction? But Gassendi challenges the very hypothesis: if the soul is simple it is pointless to ask where its seat in the body might be, because a simple thing cannot interact with a body. For not only can a simple thing not be joined with a body; it cannot even undergo alteration. In fact, Gassendi continues, a soul conceived on the model of a geometrical point could not even feel pain. His target is precisely Descartes's reliance in the Sixth Meditation on hunger and pain to derive his doctrine of soul–body union. Here is Gassendi's argument:

> Pain involves being acted upon and cannot be understood as occurring except as a result of something pushing in and separating the components and thus interfering with their continuity. . . . Again, since pain either is an alteration, or involves an alteration, how can something be altered if it has no more parts than a point, and hence cannot change or alter its nature without being reduced to nothing? I may add that pain comes from the foot and the arm and other regions at the same time, and hence surely you would have to have various parts enabling you to receive pain in various ways if you are not to have a confused sensation which seems to come from only one part. In a word, the general difficulty still remains of how the corporeal can communicate with the incorporeal and of what relationship may be established between the two.[19]

Neither Descartes nor Gassendi has any wish to deny the common sense deliverance that I can feel pain in different parts of my body. But while Descartes holds that my soul's simplicity—that is, my simplicity—must be communicated to the gland that mediates these feelings so that it possesses a bodily analogue of that simplicity, Gassendi holds to the contrary that if I am to have those feelings the body's compositeness must be communicated to me. Thus emerges what we might call *Gassendi's Principle:* If the soul interacts with the body, the soul cannot be simple.

Descartes replies that Gassendi's objection is tenable only if his model is, and that his model for the simplicity of the soul and for the union of two substances is derived from imagination. Since it is impossible to form an adequate idea of the soul with an image derived from the senses, imagination is not a suitable faculty for investigating the soul's simplicity or its union with the physical.[20]

The reply clarifies a fundamental distinction between Descartes's and Gassendi's principles: the essentially different epistemological routes they hold to be proper in arriving at a conception of simplicity. Descartes tells Princess Elisabeth in general that "the soul can be conceived only by the pure intellect,"[21] and what emerges in particular from the reply to Gassendi is that the implications of the soul's simplicity are not derivable from the implications that might follow from any kind of bodily simplicity that might be conceived with the aid of imagination.

All the same, as Steven J. Wagner has suggested in correspondence, it is surely worthwhile to ponder Descartes's position that the Simplicity Principle is either derived or derivable from a rationalist epistemology. For that matter it is worthwhile pondering Gassendi's view that his own principle is derivable from his epistemology. Perhaps it is different "childhood prejudices" that underwrite each philosopher's understanding of the way in which a thing without parts would have to resemble a point. The merits of such "prejudices" are what matter philosophically. The pattern of their acceptance in the seventeenth century is what matters historically.

The depth of Gassendi's dispute with Descartes provides a specific explanation of why people who read the Fifth Objections and Replies might have found the Simplicity Principle persuasive. Not everyone will side with Descartes against Gassendi that the soul is simple; this dispute becomes one of the enduring fundamental disagreements between rationalists and empiricists, as Kant signals when he makes it the focus of the Second Paralogism.[22] Not everyone will agree that intellect is a better route than imagination to a conception of the soul's simplicity. But those who do agree will find no reason forthcoming from Gassendi to disagree with any of the corollaries that Descartes derives from the doctrine that the soul is simple. For those people, Gassendi leaves the field entirely to Descartes when it comes to determining what the simplicity of the soul might involve.

History smiled upon Descartes in these disputes and many others, partly because of his own rhetorical genius—his consistently displayed conviction of the correctness of even the most specific corollaries of his views; his skill in insinuating charges of prejudice, superstition, and scientific fruitlessness against opposing views; his exploitation of the lacunae in those views. In particular, it came to seem natural to derive, from reason rather than from senses and imagination, a quite specific conception of the soul as a simple substance.[23]

Nevertheless, that very simplicity, given content by the Simplicity Principle, did much to constitute a nearly insuperable barrier to the soul's participation in the natural world. For the occasionalists, indeed, the barrier was actually insuperable; for many others, causation between soul and world was undeniable and yet beyond the reach of science or philosophy to decipher. All of Hume's protests, with their own rhetorical genius, were too little and too late to prevent soul–body interaction from taking its place, along with the nature of God and mathematical infinity, as a paradigm of the paradoxically unintelligible. When people thought about God or infinity or interaction, they thought they could be sure that something real was out there—but the natural play of their minds with what they thought they knew generated paralogism and confusion. Indeed, this essay has disclosed quite specific reasons to think that if the Simplicity Principle is one thing that Descartes thought he knew, its ramifications for his own conception of God, mind, and the natural world begin to reveal how tenuous that claim to knowledge was.[24]

Notes

1. David Hume, *Treatise of Human Nature,* ed. L. A. Selby-Bigge (Oxford: Clarendon Press, 1888), I, iv, v, 246–247.
2. Plemp to Descartes, January 1638: AT I, 497.
3. To Plemp, 15 February 1638: AT I, 523; CSMK, 80–81.
4. Sixth Meditation (French version): AT IX, 64; CSM II, 56.
5. *Passions of the Soul,* a. 30: AT XI, 351; CSM I, 339.
6. Sixth Meditation: AT VII, 85–86; CSM II, 59. The entire argument, from which I quote in the next four paragraphs, appears at AT VII, 85–89; CSM II, 59–61.
7. Seventh Replies: AT VII, 520; CSM II, 354.
8. Martial Gueroult, *Descartes selon l'ordre des raisons* (Paris: Aubier, 1953) II, 198.
9. *Principles of Philosophy* I, a. 23.
10. To More, 5 February 1649: AT V, 274; CSMK, 364. See earlier in the same letter: AT V, 269–270; CSMK, 361; and *Principles* I, a. 23.
11. To More, 15 April 1649: AT V, 343; CSMK, 373.
12. See *The World,* ch. 7: AT XI, 37–38; CSM I, 93, and Third Meditation: AT VII, 48–52; CSM II, 33–36.
13. Texts like these make the case. *Dioptrics,* Discourses 2 and 10: AT VI, 94–95 and 226–227; to Plemp, 20 December 1637: AT I, 476–477; CSMK, 76–77; to Morin, 13 July 1638: AT II, 199–200; CSMK, 107; to Mersenne, 30 July 1640: AT III, 131; *Principles* I, a. 24; II, aa. 20, 23, 25, and 36; IV, aa. 200–204; to [Newcastle], 23 November 1646: AT IV, 569–570; CSMK, 302; to More, 5 February 1649: AT V, 268–269; CSMK, 360–361.
14. The argument is presented in to Meyssonnier, 29 January 1640: AT III, 19–20; CSMK, 143; to Mersenne, 24 December 1640: AT III, 264; CSMK, 162; and *Passions of the Soul,* a. 32: AT XI, 352–353; CSM I, 340. Descartes also argues from the fact that the pineal gland is not a double organ in to Mersenne, 1 April 1640: AT III, 48; CSMK, 145–146, but he does not make clear whether he has in mind the present argument or the one from the Simplicity Principle to be discussed later.
15. To Meyssonnier, 29 January 1640: AT III, 19–20; CSMK, 143; and to Mersenne, 1 April 1640: AT III, 48; CSMK, 145–146.
16. Villiers to Mersenne for Descartes, end of April 1640: *Correspondance du P. Marin Mersenne,* ed. Cornelis de Waard (Paris: CNRS, 1965) 9, 293–297.
17. To Mersenne, 30 July 1640: AT III, 123–124; partially in CSMK, 149.
18. To Mersenne, 24 December 1640: AT III, 264; CSMK, 162.
19. Gassendi, Fifth Objections: AT VII, 343–345; CSM II, 238–239.
20. Fifth Replies: AT VII, 390–391; CSM II, 266–267.
21. To Elisabeth, 28 June 1643: AT III, 691; CSMK, 227.
22. See not only both the first and second edition versions of the Second Paralogism but also both versions of the Transcendental Deduction in the *Critique of Pure Reason.*
23. The Simplicity Principle expresses only one aspect of Descartes's doctrine of

the simplicity of the soul. That doctrine also has implications for the question of immortality, the possibility of struggle within the soul, the traditional doctrine of faculties in the soul, and the doctrine of the real distinction between soul and body, all of which fall outside the scope of this essay. See also Steven J. Wagner, "Descartes's Arguments for Mind–Body Distinctness," *Philosophy and Phenomenological Research* 43 (1983): 499–517; and "Descartes on the Parts of the Soul," *Philosophy and Phenomenological Research* 45 (1984): 51–70.

24. My sincere thanks to Edwin Curley, Marjorie Grene, Pamela Kraus, Vere Chappell, and Steven J. Wagner.

11

Ingenium, Memory Art, and the Unity of Imaginative Knowing in the Early Descartes

Dennis L. Sepper

On the face of things, Descartes and imagination have as much to do with one another as *res cogitans* and *res extensa.* Imagination, after all, is unreliable and even deceptive. Yet in a few of his early writings imagination plays a positive role; the best-known of these is the *Regulae ad directionem ingenii* (abandoned ca. 1628–29),[1] which from Rule 12 on expressly develops a cognitive method of imaginatively figuring problems. In his scientific work and even in his mature philosophical writings Descartes frequently resorted to images.[2] Are such "facts" about imagination in Descartes isolated and aberrant, or do they reveal something deeply ingrained in his thought? What is the ultimate status of imagination in Descartes?[3]

In this essay I propose to take the first few steps toward understanding the problematics of imagination in Descartes. I will show that in writings preceding the *Regulae* Descartes conceived imagination as the chief faculty in the work of cognition, indeed the chief faculty for unifying knowledge. In this light the *Regulae* will appear not simply as an early formulation of the principles of method,[4] but as the tension-filled outcome of an attempt to think through the heuristic and cognitive competencies of imagination on the basis of a human psychology strongly correlated with human physiology. Although the inadequacies of this attempt ultimately led to the cognitive demotion of imagination, there are nevertheless reasons for thinking that the early framework, shaped by the primacy of imagination, was not so much rejected as transformed in Descartes's mature work.

The Unified Knowing of Imagination: On the Way to the *Regulae*

In his very first complete work, the *Compendium musicae* (1618), Descartes remarks that the rhythmic division of a song

> is marked by percussion or beat, as they call it, which occurs in order to aid our imagination; by means of which we might more easily be able to perceive all the parts of the song and enjoy [them] by means of the proportion that must be in them. Such proportion is most often observed in the parts of a song so that it might aid our apprehension thus, that while we are hearing the last [part] we still remember the time of the first one and of the rest of the song; this happens, [e.g.] if the whole song consists of 8 or 16 or 32 or 64 etc. parts, i.e., when all the divisions proceed in double proportion. For then, when we hear the first two members, we conceive them as one; when [we hear] the third member, we further conjoin that with the first ones, so that there occurs triple proportion; thereafter, when we hear the fourth, we join that with the third so that we conceive [them] as one; thereupon we again conjoin the two first with the latter two so that we conceive these four simultaneously as one. And thus our imagination proceeds all the way to the end, where at last it conceives the entire song as one thing fused out of many equal members.[5]

The imagination portrayed here is an active power of synthesizing the parts of a song into a whole, a synthesis that is made pleasing (and possible) by the proportions that obtain between the parts. It functions at every moment of the song, and works by a recursive process: A is heard, then B, and immediately B is conjoined to A; C is heard, and conjoined to AB; then comes D, which is conjoined to C, and then CD is conjoined to AB, and so forth.[6] Although Descartes does not provide a similar account of imagination's operation with musical tone, he might easily have done so, since the progression of tones is based on proportions, and the pleasures and displeasures taken in the melody depend on tone as well as on rhythm.

This passage shows that in late 1618 Descartes thought of imagination as a cognitive power that allows us to construe (construct) proper musical sense by means of a series of proportions. This imaginative work fuses the past with the present, and, presumably, also with the future, since a well-constructed system of proportions allows extrapolation from what is already given. This, of course, suggests that imagination functions as a kind of short-term memory. Moreover, the passage treats conceiving (*concipere*) as an act of the imagination.[7] It would be just a small step to argue that imagination works similarly outside the musical realm, that it might well be responsible for the sequential or discursive synthesis of conception and meaning for senses other than sound, especially in light of the long philosophical tradition that understood sensation as based on ratios.[8]

Developments along these lines can be found in occasional notes from the period 1619–21, preserved by Leibniz and finally published in 1859.[9] Many of these private cogitations, as they are called, reflect a hierarchical metaphysics and epistemology of resemblance. Lower things are understood as bringing the searcher after truth into touch with higher things through similitude; the most powerful instrument of this upward progress is imagination. One of the cogitations suggests that there are in fact two "species" of imagination, one corporeal, the other intellectual, and that the latter is ordinarily put to better use by poets than by philosophers:

> As imagination makes use of figures to conceive of bodies, so intellect makes use of certain sensible bodies to figure spiritual things, such as wind and light: by which, philosophizing more profoundly, we can draw our mind by cognition to the heights. It may seem remarkable that there are more weighty judgments in the writings of poets than of philosophers. The reason is that poets write with enthusiasm and the force of imagination: there are within us, as in flintstone, sparks of the sciences which are educed through reason by philosophers but which are struck forth by poets through imagination. (AT X, 217)

Four notes later there appear specific examples of the kinds of images higher or poetic imagination employs: "Sensible things help us to conceive Olympian things [*Olympicis*]. Wind signifies spirit; movement in time, life; light, knowledge; heat, love; instantaneous activity, creation. Every corporeal form acts through harmony." Three notes further on the epistemological primacy of sense-knowledge is affirmed for natural philosophy: "Knowledge of natural things [comes] only through their resemblance to things falling under the senses. Indeed, we esteem the person to have philosophized more truly who discovers the greater resemblance between what is being investigated and what is known by the senses."

These private cogitations not only illuminate the realm revealed to the young Descartes in his three famous dreams of the night of 10–11 November 1619;[10] they also point to the centrality of images and imagination in his conception of knowledge. In essence, the synthetic-cognitive imagination of the *Compendium musicae* has been elevated to a place among the highest human cognitive faculties, and the proportions that were operative in song have been extended to encompass the cosmos as a network of forms and analogies operating within and according to a grand harmony.

It is perhaps not surprising, then, that imagination also figures prominently in the physical and mathematical writings of the early 1620s. The imagination-words in the mathematical writings are used to indicate visualizing complex or dynamic geometrical constructions, conceiving potentially infinite processes and their limits, postulating a unit to provide a measuring standard where none is given, and so on. In the physical (or, to use Isaac Beeckman's term, *physico-mathematical*) writings imagination designates the very act of applying mathematical concepts to physical situations.[11] But if we look beyond the usage of words to the basis of Descartes's practice, we can see that imagination is pervasive in his early mathematics and, by extension, his physics, too, that it is in fact foundational for them.

Descartes's mathematics has its center of gravity in the study of proportionalities. For example, the mathematical compass, the invention of which he proudly announced to Beeckman in 1619, was designed to find any number of mean proportionals between two given magnitudes, and the work leading up to the *Géométrie* of 1637 was in essence the intensive exploration of how to manipulate and preserve determinate proportionalities of whatever complexity. Thus the private cogitations having to do with the epistemology and ontology of analogical relationship represent reflections on the ultimate foundations underlying the existence and the universal significance of proportion.[12]

Consider the private cogitation quoted earlier, beginning "As imagination makes use of figures." There is a body that is sensed and perceived as such (or perhaps remembered); thereupon the imagination uses figures to try to conceive or understand it. This is a lower, corporeal imagination: given a corporeal body, or given some impression in the mind that can ultimately be traced back to such a body (as in memory), we can schematize or figure it (say, by considering just its outline, its length, its color, etc.). With the higher imagination, which is identified as a work of intellect, we take corporeal things (not just their schemas) or the total (and not schematized) impression of the thing and use that in turn as a projection or figure of some spiritual (Olympian) truth. Both the lower and the higher figuration depend on the existence of analogies, especially the kind of rigorously determinate analogy that allows things to be represented algebraically and geometrically. Moreover, just as lower imagination is constituted so as to conceive corporeal things, the higher, intellectual imagination is constituted to use corporeal things to conceive things of the spirit. It should not be surprising, then, that proportionality, in the guise of the science of order and measure, should be fundamental to all disciplinary knowing, that is, to *mathesis,* when Descartes turns his attention to the universal use and functions of the power of knowing in the *Regulae.*[13] Since the cosmos is governed by proportions, and since proportions can be perfectly and perspicuously displayed in drawn or imagined figures, that is, in the protocorporeal form of geometry, such imaginative, mathematical-mathetical activity truly deserves to be called *mathesis universalis.*

In summary, imagination is both corporeal and spiritual; it therefore serves not just as the foundation of physics and mathematics but also as the agent of all intelligent perception and the chief faculty for rising to spiritual truths. It should not be surprising, then, that imagination also served as the core of an early Cartesian reflection on the method and the unity of the sciences, in another of the *cogitationes privatae,* which proposes two approaches to a "true art of memory."

> On reading through Schenckel's profitable trifles (in the book *De arte memoria*)[14] I readily thought that everything I have discovered had been embraced by imagination. It occurs by the leading back [*reductio*] of things to causes: when all those things are finally led back to a single one, there will be no need of memory for any science. For whoever understands causes, will easily form anew in the brain the altogether vanished phantasms by the impression of the cause. This is the true art of memory and it is plain contrary to the art of that sorry fellow [Schenckel]. Not because his [art] lacks effect, but because it requires the whole space[15] that ought to be occupied by better things and consists in an order that is not right; the [right] order is that the images be formed from one another as interdependent. He omits this (whether advisedly I do not know), which is the key to the whole mystery.

> I have excogitated another mode: If from the images of not unconnected things there are learned in addition [*addiscantur*] new images common to all, or at least if out of all of them at the same time there comes to be one image, not only would there be a relation to the closest, but also to the others: so that should the fifth relate to the first by means of a spear thrown on the ground, the middle one [would be related] by stairs from which they descend, the second one by an arrow projected at it, and the third by some similar rationale, in accordance with the reason of signification either real or fictitious.[16] (AT X, 230)

Both Paolo Rossi and Frances Yates quote this passage in their books on the art of memory;[17] Rossi in particular uses it to show that the memory art was instrumental in shaping Descartes's conception of method. It would be going too far afield to give an account of what was involved in this art and its long tradition going back to ancient Greece and Rome. It must suffice to remark that it was based on putting images in places (thus it was also called *local memory*). One chose a familiar space, say a Roman basilica or a theater, and then located within it, in an easily reproducible order, vivid and significant images that could be re-collected in sequence whenever one needed. The images could be direct or merely mnemonic, either conventional or personal.[18] Schenckel's treatise is a by no means nonstandard account of the memory art, based on the physiology of the brain and on human psychology as these were understood in the Middle Ages and the Renaissance. The techniques it teaches are supposed to be applicable to anything that needs remembering, including all sciences.

Yates remarks that the first, causal approach that Descartes offers as an alternative to Schenckel is innovative, whereas the mnemonic devices employed in the second are quite traditional. The first almost eliminates the need for memory: one impresses the cause in imagination, and this produces the entire sequence of all the related images or phantasms. The mind in possession of causes is therefore in virtual possession of all the phantasms that derive from them. On the other hand, the second alternative depends on finding an image that is common to all others, so that one need not go outside the realm of images (to causes). In this second mode the images all stand in a determinate relationship to one another that can be recalled to mind by symbols like the hurled spear (for the most distant relation of first to fifth) and the stairs (which bring us from the first to the middle level). This conception of ordering phantasms could easily be translated into terms of sequences ordered by proportion.

The Theory of Imagination and *Ingenium* in the *Regulae*

Both the art of memory and the *Regulae*'s art of problem-solving appeal to the physiology of the brain and the functioning of mind. Schenckel claimed that his art was based on an understanding of the material composition of the organs of memory and of the brain locations of the internal senses: the common sense, *imaginatio, phantasia,* and *memoria.*[19] Descartes, using these same terms, gives in Rule 12 a hypothetical psychophysiology that provides the foundation for the technique of mathematical representation and manipulation explained in the subsequent rules.

As part of his hypothesis Descartes says that there is a crucial organ of imagination in the brain, the *phantasia.*[20] It is the place where images occur, whether they derive from the senses, from memory, or from the activity of the intellect. When the knowing power, the *vis cognoscens,* applies itself, along with imagination, to the so-called common sense, it is said to see, touch, and so forth; when it applies itself to *phantasia* already occupied with existing images it is said to remember; when it applies itself to the *phantasia* to make new figures it is said to imagine or conceive; when the knowing power acts on its own it is said to understand (*intelligere*) (AT X, 415–416). It is clear from this description that the knowing power, if it is not acting by itself, always acts in and through the *phantasia.*[21]

How the knowing power acts by itself Descartes says (AT X, 416) he will explain "in its appropriate place"; in the existing text of the *Regulae* he does not make good on the promise. But one sentence later he defines a key term of the *Regulae* by remarking that the knowing power "is properly called *ingenium* when it either forms new ideas in the *phantasia* or applies itself to those already made." That is, *ingenium* strictly speaking is the knowing power acting in *phantasia,* regardless of whether the ideas or figures found there are made by the knowing power itself—what a few sentences earlier is called imagining or conceiving—or derive from sensation or memory. Put somewhat more concisely, *ingenium* is the power of making and attending to images as images. In this light the *Regulae ad directionem ingenii* is a set of rules for the direction of imagination. We could read the words of Rule 1 accordingly: "The goal of our studies ought to be the direction of the imagination to producing solid and true judgments about all things that occur to it."

This is not so surprising given what we have seen of Descartes's writings before the *Regulae.* An examination of the earlier uses of '*ingenium*' in his writings would show that although it often is equivalent to 'spirit' it sometimes carries the connotation of a corporeal basis and almost invariably suggests the particular native endowment (especially the cognitive abilities) of the individual.[22] What is new in the *Regulae,* in comparison with these writings of 1618–21, is the conceptual and psychophysiological correlation of imagination and *ingenium.*[23] As Norman Kemp Smith suggested, this *ingenium* is "our total mind–body equipment."[24] It is because of the reliable interconnection between our body and our various cognitive and motive faculties that human sensing, imaging, acting, and thinking are concretely possible; and even though there is variation from individual to individual in the exact constitution of the *ingenium,* there are nevertheless invariants that hold between individuals, and it is possible to sharpen and improve these faculties through practice and proper direction. It makes perfect sense for someone who has become aware of this to offer guidelines for improving the use of *ingenium.*

Memory, Method, and the Function of Simple Natures

Throughout the *Regulae* Descartes makes provision for a specific shortcoming of human *ingenium,* the weakness of memory (e.g., AT X, 387–388, 408–409). No more than two things are to be considered at a time (AT X, 452, 454), and simple marks are to be used to keep track of what is not currently under direct consideration (AT X, 455). Because most knowledge must be arrived at by a discursive process rather than through intuitive self-evidence, deduction "in some way borrows its certainty from memory" (AT X, 370); since there are natural defects in memory the method aims at overcoming them with the natural strengths of *ingenium,* in particular by analyzing questions into elementary steps that are intuitively evident and that can be surveyed continuously and uninterruptedly in an ever more rapid sweep of thought that itself approximates a simple intuition (AT X, 388; cf. 455). The geometric apparatus of the second part serves this end by teaching us to strip away everything inessential so that we may use the simplest possible representations of the problem; by choosing one element as the unit and then representing all the other parts of the problem in proportion to this unit we can have a network of manipulable parts that all stand in a determinate relationship to one another; by applying the rules of manipulation we can then "solve" for an unknown that is constructed out of all the other parts. This technique of representing problems by rectangles, lines, points, and diagrams described in Rules 12 ff. is essentially a rigorous art of producing and processing phantasms; it is predicated on the notion that whenever a problem can be given a directly or indirectly visible instantiation it ought to be presented to the senses and imagination (e.g., when reasoning about a line one needs at least to imagine it or even to draw it; see AT X, 416–417, 440–441, and 443). These elements make the art of the *Regulae* a mathematized version of the Aristotelian-Scholastic theory that thinking requires a phantasm (see the final section), and at the same time Descartes's ironic memory art: ironic, in that it reduces dependence on memory to a minimum.

There is also external evidence that the *Regulae* was conceived first in analogy to the art of memory. In October 1628 Descartes visited Isaac Beeckman and described to him a technique of problem-solving that Beeckman punctiliously recorded in his journal as "a certain specimen of Descartes's algebra." The specimen uses up to three-dimensional figures, and as the complexity of problems increases and can no longer be represented in three dimensions they are to be represented by three-dimensional figures imagined as being made of a series of materials (wood, stone, iron, gold, etc.). What this means is that in late 1628 Descartes was explicitly combining a geometrical "algebra" of lines, figures, and solids with imagery techniques drawn from the memory art—techniques intended to produce vivid images that embody all relations that needed to be recalled. In contrast, the *Regulae* as it stands uses only the first two geometrical dimensions and promises techniques for reducing higher dimensional problems to the first two. This not only simplifies the technique of problem-solving, it is also a further accommodation to the limitations of human *ingenium,* especially of memory.[25]

The cognitive exploitation of images thus retains a developing central importance, from the early notes about memory and the resemblance of higher and lower things, to the final draft of the *Regulae.* Descartes's first inkling of the general significance of imagination seems to have been his recognition of the poet's ability to "read" spiritual truths using corporeal things. This ability is not limited to poets, however, for the private cogitations had suggested that all human beings carry within them the sparks of the sciences, which can be educed in different ways (AT X, 217). The *Regulae* continues this theme of divine sparks, of seeds of thinking and truth in human beings *qua* human (e.g., AT X, 374 and 376), and it even thematizes the analogy of seeing in explicating human access to them. One might express the implicit development in Descartes's thinking thus: Although poets have in a preeminent way the power of recognizing, of seeing or intuiting,[26] likeness and unlikeness, everyone is capable of instantaneously recognizing the similarities and dissimilarities of simple things. Insofar as objects are complex, they can be analyzed into elements and relations that anyone can ascertain by virtue of intrinsic and evident simplicity. This of course is what the *Regulae* teaches in its central doctrines of simple natures and the mathematics of geometrical symbolization and manipulation. These doctrines are in effect elaborations of the logic of the two methods of the Schenckel note, that of using causes to generate sequences of images and using images to symbolize the order of things. How both methods could have been intended to function in harmony is revealed by a closer look at the techniques of the *Regulae.*

According to Rule 4, the *Regulae*'s chief aim is to present the science of order and measure. Rule 6 explicates this by presenting "the chief secret" and "most useful rule" of the *Regulae*'s art: "To distinguish the simplest things from the involved and to follow them out in order, it is necessary, in each and every series of things in which we have deduced certain truths directly from others, to observe which is most simple, and in what way all the rest are more, or less, or equally removed from this one" (AT X, 381). It is here that Descartes introduces the "pure and simple natures." He remarks that the project of the *Regulae* does not consider the solitary natures of things but instead compares them to one another; in this sense, everything can be considered as either *absolutum* or *respectivum* (absolute or respective). Absolute things are those that *contain* the pure and simple nature in question, "like everything which is considered as if independent, cause, simple, universal, one, equal, similar, straight, or others of this kind." Respective, on the other hand, is what "participates [in] this same nature or at least [in] something from it, according to which it can be referred to the absolute and deduced from it through some series"; in addition, there are involved in this concept things called 'respects', "such as whatever is said to be dependent, effect, composite, particular, many, unequal, dissimilar, oblique, etc." (a list in strict parallel to the one explaining 'absolute').

> These respective things, the further they are removed from the absolute, the more respects of this kind subordinated to one another they contain; in this rule we advise that all these are to be distinguished, and their mutual nexus among themselves and the natural order are to be observed so that we might arrive from the last one to that which is maximally absolute by going through all the others.
>
> And the secret of the whole art consists in this, that we diligently note what is maximally absolute in everything. For certain things under some one consideration are more absolute than others, but seen [*spectata*] otherwise they are more respective. (AT X, 382)

Although the interpretation of this and related passages requires no little exegesis, the main outlines seem clear enough. Knowledge comes through comparing things to one another rather than through considering their natures as such. Still, natures are taken account of in this sense: a thing either wholly contains some nature and in that case is called absolute, or it merely participates in the nature or some portion of the nature and then is called respective. 'Absolute' and 'respective' are thus answers to the question, "In what manner does the object of our interest contain/participate in a nature in view of which we are considering the object?" That is, the nature, by being contained or participated in, gives us a perspective or axis along which we judge to what degree the thing participates in that nature. This provides us with a principle of ordering things with respect to the nature, in view of it. A king may be wholly independent in a political sense, and thus absolute; a prince would participate in independence, less so than the king, but more than a minor vassal; a serf participates minimally, or perhaps not at all. If it is possible to find a unit of measurement these things can be not just ordered but also measured. Independence does not come in units, but a nature like extension does.[27] The further removed the object is from things that wholly contain the nature, the more involvements, or relations, or respects (*respectus*) the object will have—presumably to other objects that participate in the same nature in different ways, or that participate in other natures as well. What makes a vassal a vassal and not a king is that his relations to the king, other vassals, and serfs are differentiated and mediated in various ways and to various degrees; moreover, this has consequences for the degree to which his actions can be viewed as causes or effects (which are natures different from 'independence'). The example Descartes gives at the end of Rule 6 for practicing this art of seriation is simpler but makes a similar point about the increasing complexity of relations: the proportions that hold between any two elements in the number series 3, 6, 12, 24, 48, and so on, are various and variously complex, yet the basic relation between each member and the following is the proportion 1:2, and all other proportions can be expressed in some more or less complicated relation to this basic one.

Note, however, that "3" is treated as the absolute member of the series; one might say that it contains the "nature 3" wholly, purely, simply, whereas the other numbers participate in "3" in a derivative, respective way. But is "3" a nature? One might speculate that "3" in some way derives from the unit. Yet in terms of the method of Rule 6 it does not matter whether "3" is genuinely absolute, but only that it is the closest to absolute in the series. Indeed, as Rule 6 presents them, the natures are methodological rather than ontological; they are recognized *in the things under consideration* rather than as though they had an absolute existence in themselves. As far as the method is concerned, one can form a series, even if none of the things being considered wholly contains a nature, by ordering the series from that which participates most to that which participates least. Thus Rule 13 can argue that it is sensible to begin analyzing a problem from a limited set of data, be they true or false (AT X, 431); in any set of things to be compared one looks for a common perspective, a "nature," that can be treated as though it is absolute. It is not necessary that the nature in view be genuinely pure and simple, nor even that it be really present in the objects under consideration. Rule 14, in introducing the concept "dimension" (which includes things like weight, speed of motion, and division of time into smaller units), points out that "there can be infinitely many different dimensions in the same subject, and these add nothing further to the dimensioned thing but are understood in the same manner whether they have a real foundation in these subjects or have been excogitated out of the judgment of our mind" (AT X, 448). From the point of view of seeking knowledge, natures and dimensions are both artifacts of the method, end points relative to the problem being attacked, imaginative projections of what the things being ordered have in common.

This brings us back to a theme struck in the Schenckel note. The second method proposed forming a new image common to other images and using mnemonically suggestive images to preserve the proportional distances between the things being remembered. Rule 6 enunciates a principle of degrees of participation in natures that generalizes this technique but also allies it with causality. The nature is a *principle of resemblance* that plays the role of the common image, but it is *causal* in that it is participated in differently by different things; and, as the second part of the *Regulae* teaches, this participation can be newly *represented* under the aspect of order and measure by appropriate geometrical line segments, quadrilaterals, and other symbols that are proportioned to one another according to the terms of the problem. The geometry and geometrical manipulations (as well as the associated algebraic notation) preserve in schematic form the proportional relations that hold between the things in question as viewed in accordance with certain natures real or fictitious. What this amounts to is a formalization of the ontology and epistemology of resemblances to which Descartes held in his private cogitations of 1619–21. Wind can symbolize spirit, movement can symbolize time because despite their differences the pairs of things have something in common; they either participate in the same thing or the networks of relations that each is part of are analogously proportioned.

But what is the *ontological* status of these common things, these natures? Rule 8, pointing ahead to Rule 12's longer discussion, divides them into the "maximally simple natures" and the "complex or composite" and remarks that the simple ones are "either spiritual, or corporeal, or pertaining to both"[28] (AT X, 399). Descartes is therefore beginning to consider the nature of simple natures and their relations to one another. On the one hand this looks like a violation of Rule 6, which foregoes the examination of natures as such; on the other hand it could be seen as an effort to generalize the method to include natures themselves, to extend the analogy of conceiving ordinary things in view of natures to the question of the foundational principles of all natures, relations, and kinds. But these foundational principles go beyond the limits of a method adapted to the powers and limitations of human *ingenium,* a method employing seriation and imaginative representation of elements seen in their analogical relationships; and the emergence of natures that are not at all corporeal puts the adequacy of a method based on resemblance in jeopardy. Rule 12 grants that there are things neither corporeal nor similar to the corporeal (AT X, 416); how does one treat these methodically? Only the promised but undelivered inquiry into the knowing power acting on its own (AT X, 416) could answer this. Is it not plausible that at precisely this juncture Descartes came to a more radical, Cartesian understanding of the corporeal and the spiritual, which undermined the hope for a universal method based on ontological resemblance?

Le Monde and the Imaginative Replication of the World in Mature Cartesian Science

Although the *Regulae* was born of imagination, the faculty of imaging, it ends by reducing the manifold relations in complex problems to a manageable, representative mathematical form and manipulating these relations so that a solution might be found, with natures providing the initial orientation that allows the problems to be determinately defined. If cognitive imagination is based on the metaphor of seeing by means of an image, the task of the *Regulae* can be understood as turning this power to discursive purposes. Recalling again the private cogitation about the poet's ability to recognize in a glance what the plodding philosopher struggles to approach, it is as though the philosopher is being taught how to recognize what things have in common and the poet how to reduce the leaps of imagination to a stepwise progression. The power of using images is joined to the power of discursivity; in the vocabulary of the internal senses, the phantasm is to be the product not just of imagination but also of another traditional internal sense, the *vis cogitativa* (cogitation).[29] In the case of things representable by lines and figures (all corporeal and corporeal/spiritual things), one can simplify discursive thought by means of geometrical and symbolic manipulations that express relations (in particular of an unknown) with perfect exactitude in terms of other things. Nor does one need to keep all the relations of things in mind while doing this; in fact it obstructs the process of solution if one attends to more than two things at once. But this means that cogitation no longer needs to attend to images as images; it uses them simply as markers, as placeholders, which stand for or refer to a content but are manipulated in abstraction from that content. The technique of the second half of the *Regulae* thus begins to weaken the foundation in *direct* intuition of the first half. All one needs for exactness are the intuitable relations of geometry; resemblance, in particular resemblance based on participation in the same natures, no longer has a thoroughgoing methodological role to play.

By the time he wrote the opening chapters of *Le Monde* Descartes had fully accepted that in general there need be no resemblance whatsoever between representing symbols and the things represented; in language, after all, the sounds uttered in no way resemble what they bring to mind (AT XI, 4–5). The critique of resemblance was based in psychophysiology, or more precisely, in a separation of the issues of physics and physiology from those of psychology. It was no longer an impressed image that was transmitted to the brain but rather simply motion. The halfway house of the *Regulae* is thereby abandoned. Rule 12 had at least postulated the existence of some kind of genuine analogy between the impression of a shape in wax and the action of *phantasia* on *vis cognoscens*. The new, post-*Regulae* psychophysiology rejects any imagined, or even intelligible, link between the realms of body and thought. Instead, the pineal gland serves as the virtual vanishing point where there takes place a complex and mysterious coordination of corporeal motions with the acts and passions of the soul.[30]

Yet even in *Le Monde* the imagination still plays an interesting and curious role that provides an ontological basis for purely corporeal knowledge. When in chapter 6 Descartes begins constructing "a completely new" world, that is, when out of the elements of the first five chapters he begins presenting a theory of the whole cosmos and its workings, he does so "in imaginary spaces" that can be extended indefinitely in every direction. "Now since we are taking the liberty of feigning this matter to our phantasy, let us attribute to it, if you please, a nature in which there is nothing at all that anyone could not know as perfectly as possible" (AT XI, 33). Accordingly, we imagine, or think, this world as devoid of ordinary qualities except matter's extension, divisibility, and capacity for any conceivable motion.

What is new here? Descartes has given up on the direct cognitive relevance of images; but on the other hand, indirectly, the whole space "created" by imagination participates in the same nature and behavior as real space, provided that imaginers limit themselves to what anyone can know with perfect certainty. The fundamental laws governing activity in this space do not derive from imagination but from the intellect. However, such laws, if they are obeyed, guarantee that space, whether it is the externally existent one (what Descartes calls "this true world") or the space of the imagination, will inevitably produce a cosmos or a replica of the cosmos that is veridical:

> For God has so marvelously established these Laws, that even if we suppose that He created nothing more than what I have said [viz., the space in imagination that is indefinitely extendable and divisible and that bears no qualities but those that are known with certainty], and even if He puts no order or proportion in it but makes of it the most confused and most disordered Chaos that the Poets could describe: they are sufficient to make the

> parts of this Chaos untangle themselves, and dispose themselves in such good order that they will have the form of a most perfect World, and in which one will be able to see not only Light, but also all the other things, both general and particular, that appear in this true World. (AT XI, 34–35)

Thus, if the imagination conforms itself and the space it makes to the fundamental laws of motion and divisibility discovered by intellect, it will dynamically reproduce the order and measure of the actual world. In imagination so conceived one no longer seeks out the analogies and proportions contained by individual images or sets or images, but rather observes intellectively given (and presumably intellectively enforced) laws governing the motions of imagined matter, which laws have governed real motions and given rise to cosmic order. From the methodical, step-by-step imaginative problem-solving of the *Regulae* Descartes has advanced to a dynamically continuous imaginative production of a space and matter that are no mere representations of external reality but participants in the very same spatiality and lawfulness that characterize the externally real.

By deemphasizing images, and by more sharply separating the competencies of intellect and imagination through a rigorous distinction between what is extended (corporeal nature) and what is known (spiritual nature), Descartes "solves" the problem of what grounds and justifies the use of imagination. The elimination of the arbitrariness that was associated with traditional memory art has come about through the imaginative duplication of space. Although this introduces a rift between the physiological and physical processes of sensation and the consciousness of images, a kind of certainty in the imaginative realm is guaranteed by combining the imaginative projection of a space-matter just like that which God made with the laws that only intellect can infallibly know.

Ingenium and the Tradition of Embodied Intelligence

In the *Regulae, ingenium,* the embodied power that treats of images, is the focal point of cognition. Yet, on the other hand, the *Regulae* clearly affirms that the knowing power can act on its own (then it is called 'intellect') (AT X, 416), that truth and falsity are properly in the intellect (396), that there are simple natures that cannot be represented by anything corporeal, like cognition, doubt, ignorance, and volition (419). It would appear, then, that the direction of *ingenium* cannot provide us with a comprehensive or universal method for knowing. It almost seems that the *Regulae* has in fact achieved the perspective of the later Descartes. When intellect, the knowing power acting on its own, is paired with the organ *phantasia* interpreted as the first avatar of the pineal gland, we seem to have a rehearsal of his mature philosophy. There is much to be said for this, but I prefer to see the *Regulae* as a halfway house. True, Descartes makes a sharp distinction between the knowing power and the body, but the analogy he uses ("this power through which we properly know things is no less distinct from the whole body than the blood is from the bone, or the hand from the eye" [AT X, 415]) suggests that this is something less than the full-blown real distinction between *res cogitans* and *res extensa*.[31] In a curious locution of Rule 16, we are told that we can contemplate dimensions depicted in *phantasia* "by an intuition either of the eye or of the mind" (AT X, 454), although intuition would seem to be the act of intellect par excellence and thus properly of mind. In Rule 12 Descartes represents colors by figures in a manner that could suggest at least an implicit reduction of secondary qualities to primary, but he also says that the receptive membranes of the sense organs take on shapes "from sound, odor, and flavor" (AT X, 413). Besides the organ of *phantasia* there is also an organ for *sensus communis,* rather than the single organ (the pineal gland) of the later psychophysiology. In these and other respects it is doubtful that the mature position has been entirely achieved.

Is there any way of gaining more precision about the ways in which the *Regulae* stands between the earlier and the later Descartes? It might help to restate what we now understand about the trajectory of Descartes's work in the decade of the 1620s. The epistemological and methodological notes and passages early in the decade put a premium on imaginative cognition, and although intellect was terminologically distinguished from imagination it did not play a fully independent role. Intellect figures spiritual things by using bodies, and imagination-using poets accomplished this better than discursive philosophers. Descartes hoped to bring the virtues of imaginative insight to the plodding and often obtuse discursivity of reasoning by showing that ratios (i.e., proportionalities) were the basis of all knowing and reasoning (Latin *ratio*), and he found a technique adaptable to his goals in the image-making and -manipulation of the memory art.

Then at some point in the decade he must have realized that it was necessary to give a specific account of how imagination works in human beings and on what it is based. The psychophysiological hypothesis of Rule 12 seems to be a rather primitive attempt to bring his notion of imagination in line with medieval and early modern psychology and physiology, which understood *imaginatio, phantasia, sensus communis, vis cogitativa,* and *memoria* as internal senses, and which located these faculties in different parts (viz., the concavities or ventricles) of the brain.[32] These internal senses had been intended to resolve some of the problems posed by Aristotle's writings on soul and its functions, in particular to make sense of his dictum that there is no thought without a phantasm (*De Anima* 431 a16–17) and of the analogy he posited between sensation and intellection (e.g., *De Anima* 429 a13–19). Traditional Aristotelianism had reserved the power of knowing per se to the intellectual part of the human being but had also attributed certain cognitive powers to sense, imagination, and other pre-intellectual powers. The medical (or Galenic) tradition required that all faculties participating in cognition, the external and internal senses, be located in bodily organs and that the process from sensation to knowledge follow a well-defined organic progression. In

High Scholasticism, particularly in its Thomist form, understanding was conceived as originating in the senses and leading to the production of a phantasm from which an intelligible species was educed by the action of agent intellect and impressed in passive intellect, neither of which, in contrast to the internal senses, had a bodily organ. The mutual reinforcement of the two traditions, Aristotelian and medical, gave the theory an authoritative aspect even outside Scholasticism, so that some version of it can be found in virtually every thinker who attends to the question of knowledge.[33]

Descartes in the *Regulae* simplified the scheme of the internal senses by reducing memory to a function of imagination and retaining only the common sense and *phantasia/imaginatio.*[34] Sensation was to be understood as a direct transmission of an integral impression from objects in the world to the sense organs, on to the common sense, then to *phantasia,* and finally (although here the notion of "impression" was analogical rather than literal) to the knowing power (AT X, 414–415). One can easily imagine that this simplified scheme led Descartes to wonder further (1) about the physical nature and mechanism of this process of impression in the external world (a question anticipating concerns of *Le Monde*), (2) about the transmission of these impressions within the body (anticipating *l'Homme*), and (3) about precisely how and where the intellect intervenes in this process and about how and when it can act on its own (anticipating fundamental epistemological and metaphysical concerns of his later philosophy).

The shift in the *Regulae* to a technical use of '*ingenium*' represents an increasingly comprehensive concern with embodied intelligence, with the totality of the mind–body equipment, yet also a continuing conviction about the cognitive primacy of imagination owing to its ability to exploit the proportions in things. Although from the viewpoint of his mature philosophy this may seem odd, it is not so at all if we look backwards rather than forwards. After all, the entire philosophic tradition of Western Christianity had allowed that soul and body have radically different natures, which are yet joined in human beings, and precisely the faculties and organs governing the production of phantasms had been accepted as a bridge between the two. This tradition had maintained that certain proportions were maintained between the thing in the world, the sense organ in act, the phantasm, and the intelligible species; and it had even by and large supported the notion that some kind of analogy holds between finite creatures and the infinite God.[35] In this light, it is possible to interpret the *Regulae* as the crucial turning point in Descartes's philosophical career, where he was thinking through to its ultimate consequences the traditional conception of human knowing by attempting to integrate as thoroughly as possible what was known and said about physics, anatomy, physiology, psychology, and mathematics.[36]

My larger contention is that the failure of the project of the *Regulae* nevertheless set the terms in which Descartes thought out his later philosophy, that the early theory of imagination left a lasting mark, and therefore that we need to consider Descartes's philosophical career as being fundamentally driven by the problems of philosophical psychology and anthropology. Whether this contention proves to be true in all important respects is something that only future research can clarify. In conclusion I pose a question leading in this direction. In thinking about the mature philosophy of Descartes, in which the *res extensa* is radically distinguished from the *res cogitans,* in which the first truth beyond skepticism is *cogito, ergo sum,* in which therefore it is crucial that we understand the nature of thinking, *cogitatio:* have we paid sufficient attention to the ways and means by which the later notion of thinking is rooted in Descartes's understanding of the internal sense *vis cogitativa?* The internal senses were at the very center of Descartes's earliest work, and he thought his way through this philosophical and scientific tradition as no one before him; it seems likely, then, that we will not fully grasp his later conception of mind unless we follow him along this way.

Notes

1. Since there is no direct evidence of when Descartes began the *Regulae* or why and when he stopped, dating it is necessarily speculative. Most scholars agree that he left off around 1628, but the are split on the issue of the beginning date. Theorists who argue for an extended period of composition argue for late 1619, whereas others believe that the whole work was composed in a relatively short period. I begin this essay by looking at early works of Descartes other than the *Regulae,* so the question of whether the latter, or part of it, should be counted among the earliest works does not immediately arise. But the logic of the argument I present about imagination in the early Descartes suggests to me that Descartes began the *Regulae* later rather than earlier, in any case not before 1621. In addition, I present here fairly solid evidence that Descartes had not settled on the final form of the last, mathematical rules as of October 1628, and thus that it is likely he continued working on it at least into 1629.

2. On the abundance of suggestive images in the later writings, see Geneviève Rodis-Lewis, "From Metaphysics to Physics," essay 16 of this book.

3. There exists a relatively small body of literature that highlights the importance of the imagination in Descartes. In the first part of this century the focus was on the role of imagination in his mathematics (e.g., Emile Boutroux, Léon Brunschvicg, and Jacob Klein; a recent, profound reevocation of this theme is found in David Rapport Lachterman, *The Ethics of Geometry: A Genealogy of Modernity* [New York: Routledge, Chapman & Hall, 1989], esp. 67–91); more recently the focus has been on the importance of imagination to finite human being, at least in the early Descartes (e.g., Lüder Gäbe, *Descartes' Selbstkritik: Untersuchungen zur Philosophie des jungen Descartes* [Hamburg: F. Meiner, 1972], and Josef Simon, *Wahrheit als Freiheit: Zur Entwicklung der Wahrheitsfrage in der neueren Philosophie* [Berlin: de Gruyter, 1978], esp. 121–149; this approach was adumbrated already in Boutroux), or on imagination as an indicator throughout Descartes's career of the development and evolution of his philosophy (Véronique Fóti, "The Cartesian Imagination," *Philosophy and Phenomenological Research* 46 [1986]: 631–642). The present work will take a new tack by showing the intimate relation between imagination and *ingenium,* arguing that imagination was central to the early Descartes, and claiming that the abandoned doctrine left important traces in his later work.

4. For examples of this approach, see Norman Kemp Smith, *Studies in the Carte-*

sian Philosophy (London: Macmillan, 1902), e.g., 19; and L. J. Beck, *The Method of Descartes: A Study of the Regulae* (Oxford: Clarendon Press, 1952).

5. AT X, 94.

6. Descartes asserts that there are only two kinds of time in music, double and triple; and so although C can be joined to AB immediately to transform a double into a triple time, D cannot be joined immediately to ABC, since that would produce an impermissible quadruple time.

7. This close relationship between *concipere* and *imaginari* is preserved in the *Regulae,* where in Rule 12 the act of forming new images in the organ of imagination is called "*imaginari vel concipere*" (AT X, 416).

8. This doctrine has its roots in Pythagoreanism but is also present in Platonism and Aristotelianism. See David Summers, *The Judgment of Sense: Renaissance Naturalism and the Rise of Aesthetics* (Cambridge: Cambridge University Press, 1987), 54–70, esp. 65–69.

9. Under the heading "*Cogitationes privatae,*" in *Oeuvres inédites de Descartes, précédées d'une introduction sur la méthode,* ed. Aléxandre Foucher de Careil, 2 vols. (Paris: Auguste Durand, 1859–60), I: 1–57; reprinted with corrections in AT X, 213–248. Leibniz apparently made a partial copy in 1676 of a notebook that Descartes kept in those two or three years.

10. See especially Henri Gouhier, *Les premières pensées de Descartes: Contribution à l'histoire de l'anti-renaissance,* 2d ed. (Paris: Vrin, 1979), 42–103, esp. 84–85. The dreams are narrated by Descartes's biographer Adrien Baillet on the basis of a section of the no longer extant notebook, mentioned in n. 9, under the title "*Olympica,*" a narrative that from Baillet we know began: "10 November 1619, when full of enthusiasm I was discovering the foundations of a wonderful science" (see AT X, 179–188).

11. For examples of these mathematical and physical uses see AT X, 67–78, e.g. 73 and 75; 232–233; 271. Cf. Dennis L. Sepper, "Descartes and the Eclipse of Imagination, 1618–30," *Journal of the History of Philosophy* 27 (1989): 379–403, esp. 383–384. One reason we might expect imagination to be important to Descartes at this period is Beeckman's demand that the solutions of physico-mathematical problems be picturable; see Klaas van Berkel, *Isaac Beeckman (1588–1637) en de mechanisering van het wereldbeeld,* Nieuwe Nederlandse Bijdragen tot de Geschiedenis der Geneeskunde en der Natuurwetenschappen, no. 9 (Amsterdam: Rodopi, 1983), 155–216, 317–318.

12. Jules Vuillemin, *Mathématique et métaphysiques chez Descartes* (Paris: Presses Universitaires de France, 1960), esp. 112–127, interprets the *Géométrie* as a generalized theory of proportions and Descartes's metaphysics as an analogical extension. Timothy Lenoir, "Descartes and the Geometrization of Thought: The Methodological Background of Descartes's *Géométrie,*" *Historia Mathematica* 6 (1979): 355–379, says that for Descartes "all relations consist in proportions between the items compared" (p. 373) and places this view against a background of Ramist theory of logic and method. John Schuster, "Descartes' *Mathesis Universalis,* 1619–28," in *Descartes: Philosophy, Mathematics and Physics,* ed. Stephen Gaukroger (Sussex: Harvester Press, and Totowa, N.J.: Barnes and Noble, 1980), 41–96, emphasizes the central importance of proportionality in the development of the theory of universal mathematics (see esp. 49–55, 68–69, and 78–79).

13. Rule 4 presents *mathesis universalis* as the general science in which order and measure are examined, and "it is of no matter whether this measure is to be sought in numbers, or figures, or stars, or sounds, or any other object whatever" (p. 378). Since the theory representing the elements of problems and their relations developed in Rules 14 ff. employs proportionalized line segments and plane figures, items that are

measurable par excellence, it might appear that the science of proportions is only part of *mathesis universalis,* viz., the part having to do with measure, and that order is independent of the domain of proportionality. Rule 14 (pp. 451–452), however, makes it clear that measure is a kind of indirect ordering based on a unit, and that by appropriate representation measure can be reduced to an inspection of order. These and related passages of course require unpacking and are susceptible of differing emphases, but I believe that they would support the contention that order itself already contains the elements of the theory of proportion that are made explicit and exact in the doctrine of measure.

14. Adam and Tannery identify this "profitable trifle" as Lambert Thomas Schenckel's *De memoria* (1595) (AT X, 251). According to Rossi, this work was reprinted in Schenckel's 1610 omnibus collection *Gazophylacium* of memory treatises; see Paolo Rossi, *Clavis Universalis: Arti della memoria e logica combinatoria da Lullo a Leibniz,* 2d ed. (Bologna: Il Mulino, 1983), 149. I have consulted [Johann] Lambertus Schenckelius Dusilvius, *Gazophylacium artis memoriae,* published in *Variorum de arte memoriae, tractatus sex,* 2 vols. in 1 (Frankfurt and Leipzig: J. H. Ellinger, 1678) I, 1–182.

15. 'Space' is the translation of Frances A. Yates, *The Art of Memory* (Chicago: University of Chicago Press, 1966), 373. The word is actually *chartam,* meaning paper, sheet, or tablet. Schenckel's art employs the "space" of the imagination, not external, material aids.

16. The last clause reads: "*et tertia simili aliquâ ratione in rationem significationis vel verae vel fictitiae.*"

17. Rossi, *Clavis Universalis,* 175; and Yates, *The Art of Memory,* 373–374.

18. Yates repeatedly makes the point that in most versions of the art vividness required creating the images for oneself, although Medieval and Renaissance proponents often provided conventionalized symbols and emblems. By direct image I mean, for example, the image of Socrates talking, used to remember what he said to Glaucon; by mnemonic I mean, for example, the image of Socrates used to stand for wisdom.

19. Schenckel, *Gazophylacium* I, 1–3. There is no single, authoritative list of inner senses for the Middle Ages and the Renaissance, but four or five are commonly given; usually added to common sense, imagination, and memory is the *aestimativa* (in animals) or *cogitativa* (in human beings). *Phantasia* and *imaginatio* sometimes refer to the same faculty, whereas in other authors (e.g., Schenckel) the latter designates the power of image retention while the former indicates powers of dividing and recombining these images (which is usually one of the functions of the *vis cogitativa*). For an introduction to the tradition of the psychology and anatomy of the internal senses, see E. Ruth Harvey, *The Inward Wits* (London: Warburg Institute, 1975); Harry Austryn Wolfson, "The Internal Senses in Latin, Arabic, and Hebrew Philosophic Texts," *Harvard Theological Review* 28 (1935): 69–133; Katharine Park, "The Organic Soul," *The Cambridge History of Renaissance Philosophy,* ed. Charles B. Schmitt and Quentin Skinner (Cambridge: Cambridge University Press, 1988), 464–484; and Summers, *The Judgment of Sense.*

20. *Imaginatio,* too, is used to refer to the organ, although it is also the preferred term for indicating the activity of imagining.

21. That Descartes describes the knowing power as applying itself to the common sense, albeit along with imagination, suggests that the knowing power is more deeply involved with the body than would seem to be the case in his later psychophysiology, where the pineal gland is the point of joining between the realm of body, apparently

governed by purely mechanical principles, and the autonomous realm of soul. Thus the *phantasia* would be a precursor of the pineal gland but not identical in scope and function. In determining their exact relationship it would be important to examine especially those places in the later Descartes where the pineal gland attends to memories and to the figures produced on its surface by the animal spirits (e.g., AT III, 45 and 359, and *Passions of the Soul,* aa. 42 and 136; I thank Stephen Voss for calling the relevance of these and other passages to my attention).

A phrase in a recent translation of Rule 12 is misleading about the relationship of the knowing power and *phantasia* to the common sense. "It [the knowing power] is one single power, whether it receives figures from the 'common' sense at the same time as does the corporeal imagination, . . ." renders "*vnicamque esse, quae vel accipit figuras à sensu communi simul cum phantasiâ*" (AT X, 415, ll. 16–18); see CSM I, 42. The translation implies that the *phantasia* and the knowing power are simultaneously but more or less separately receiving images from the common sense. This reading might be justified if "*simul cum phantasiâ*" were read as the elliptical subjunctive clause "*simul cum phantasia,*" but the unambiguously ablative "*cum imaginatione*" at the end of the same AT page (X, 415, l. 27–416, l. 1) undermines the plausibility of such emendation. Haldane and Ross rendered the phrase with perfect literalness: "it is a single agency, whether it receives impressions from the common sense simultaneously with the fancy"; see HR I, 38. The Latin suggests an instrumental relationship, that is, that the knowing power applies itself to the common sense by means of *phantasia.*

22. For substantiation of the points just made about *ingenium,* see, for example, AT X, 214, 215, and 217 (from the *Cogitationes privatae*), the occurrences of the word in Descartes's letters to Beeckman of 1618–19 (pp. 151–169), and the letter of 1628 to an unknown recipient in which Descartes evaluates the writing and character of his friend Guez de Balzac (AT X, 5–11).

23. Rule 12 is the first indication of Descartes's interest in anatomy and physiology, but it scarcely goes beyond standard Medieval and Renaissance discussions. The first express evidence of Descartes's independent anatomical studies comes in early 1630 (to Mersenne, 15 April 1630; AT I, 137). He must have made prodigious progress, since he was offered a chair in theory of medicine at the university of Bologna in late 1632; see Vincenzo Busacchi, "La chiamata di Cartesio alla cattedra eminente di teorica della medicina nello studio di Bologna nel 1633," *Pagine di storia della medicina* 11, no. 2 (1967): 9–13.

24. Norman Kemp Smith, *New Studies in the Philosophy of Descartes: Descartes as Pioneer* (London: Macmillan & Co., 1952), 151.

25. For additional evidence of Descartes's early interest in memory and the memory art, see Baillet's account of the *Studium bonae mentis,* AT X, 200–201.

26. The cognitive role of the image helps us understand the often-noted primacy of the visual in Descartes, and I must agree with Marion's contention that the central meaning of *intuitus* in the *Regulae* is best conveyed in translation by a term with the implication of seeing. See René Descartes, *Règles utiles et claires pour la direction de l'esprit en la recherche de la vérité,* trans. and ed. Jean-Luc Marion (mathematical notes by Pierre Costabel), Archives internationales d'histoire des idées, 88 (The Hague: Nijhoff, 1977), 295–302.

27. This difference between the orderable and the measurable is explicated at the end of Rule 14; see n. 13.

28. It is perhaps a sign of a transformation in Descartes's thinking that Rule 12 refers to these as "either purely intellectual, or purely material, or common" (AT X, 419).

29. The *Regulae* itself makes this terminological connection. The statement of Rule 7 (echoing Rule 3 [AT X, 369] and Rule 11 [407–408]) characterizes deduction as a survey "in a continuous and in no way interrupted motion of cogitation." But a few lines further on the motion is called one of imagination (pp. 387–388). In Rule 11 it is also called a motion of *ingenium* (p. 407).

30. Contrary to Marion, I believe it is here in *Le Monde,* and not in the *Regulae,* that Descartes introduces a code in need of epistemological deciphering. See J.-L. Marion, *Sur la théologie blanche de Descartes* (Paris: Presses Universitaire de France, 1981), 231–346.

31. Descartes uses a very similar locution in the sixth set of replies to objections against the *Meditations:* "So, for example, we do not have the same idea of figure and motion; just as we do not have the same [idea] of intellection and volition; nor also of bones and flesh, nor of thought [*cogitationis*] and *res extensa*" (AT VII, 423). The similarity does not by itself establish that the *Regulae* passage belongs to the later conceptual framework; it may simply establish this as an enduring Cartesian trope. Moreover, the later passage presents an alternation of systematically contrasting ideas: two qualities of extension, two acts of thinking, two extended substances, and finally the two fundamental kinds of substance, *res cogitans* and *res extensa;* whereas the passage from the *Regulae* merely compares the difference between the knowing power and the whole (human) body to two sets of corporeal things, without any clear systematic tendency. Once again, the *Regulae* appears to be a kind of halfway house.

32. See references at n. 19.

33. Thus it is probably vain to seek *the* source of Descartes's psychophysiological understanding: he probably got it from many (and all) sources.

34. Wolfson pointed out that Eustache de Saint Paul had somewhat earlier proposed a similar reduction of all internal senses to *phantasia;* see "The Internal Senses," 126.

35. Thus a theory of imagination based on proportionalities that stretch from the corporeal to the spiritual inevitably leads, in a Christian context, to the problem of the analogicity between God and His creatures, which is one of the central questions of Marion, *Sur la théologie blanche de Descartes.* Here I wish to note as well that whereas Marion in his analysis of the *Regulae* argues that its theoretical background is a not fully explicit reaction to Aristotelian metaphysics, I am arguing for an analogous background, and foreground, in traditional theories of soul and its process of knowing; see J.-L. Marion, *Sur l'ontologie grise de Descartes: Science cartésienne et savoir aristotelicien dans les Regulae,* 2d ed. (Paris: Vrin, 1981).

36. For further considerations see Sepper, "Descartes and the Eclipse of Imagination," 397–403. And in this last note I wish to thank Stephen Voss for his consistently illuminating comments on earlier drafts of this essay; they have greatly improved it, not least by saving me from many an error (though I am sure I have persisted in a few).

12

Descartes on the Perception of Primary Qualities

Margaret D. Wilson

Throughout his writings Descartes contrasts "sensations" of color, sound, taste, and so on with ideas of size, shape, position, and motion. The former are merely "confused" ideas, which fail to "resemble" any quality existing in physical reality: they must be "attributed to sense." In the *Principles of Philosophy,* for instance, he remarks of color:

> . . . when we think we perceive colors in objects although we do not know what this might be, that we call by the name of color, and we cannot understand any similarity between the color which we suppose to be in objects and what we experience to be in sense, yet, because we do not notice this . . . , it is easy to allow ourselves to fall into the error of judging that that which we call color in objects is something entirely similar to the color we sense, and thus supposing what we in no way perceived is clearly perceived by us. (I, a. 70: AT VIII-1, 34; CSM I, 218)[1]

When Descartes denies that confused ideas or sensations "resemble" or are similar to qualities in physical objects, part of what he has in mind is that sensations (of sound, color, and so on) do not present to us "images" of variations of motion and figure; but such variations are all that is really present in the external world, are what account for the different confused sensations in us.[2]

Ideas of size, shape, motion, and position, however, "are not otherwise understood or sensed by us than they are or at least can be in bodies." Thus, he writes in *Principles* I, a. 69:

> We know [*cognoscere*] in a quite different way what size, or shape, or motion . . . , or position, or duration, or number, and the like are in a body that we see, which [qualities] I have already said are clearly perceived, than we know what color, or pain, or odor, or taste, or any other of those things are, which I've said must be attributed to the senses. (AT VIII-1, 33–34; CSM I, 217–218)

And at the end of the *Principles* he defends his mechanistic explanatory framework in the following terms:

> . . . who has ever doubted that bodies move and have various sizes and shapes, and that their various different motions correspond to these differences in size and shape; or who doubts that when bodies collide bigger bodies are divided into many smaller ones and change their shapes? We detect these facts not just with one sense but several—sight, touch and hearing; and they can also be distinctly imagined and understood by us. But the same cannot be said of the other characteristics like color, sound and the rest, each of which is perceived not by several senses but by one alone; for the images of them which we have in our thought are always confused, and we do not know what they really are. (IV, a. 200: AT VIII-1, 323–324; CSM I, 286)[3]

Ideas of size, shape, position, and motion, which apply exclusively to body, together with a small number of other ideas (such as number and duration) that apply equally to mental and corporeal substance, thus constitute the total repertoire of "clear and distinct" knowledge of bodies. As Descartes explains in the Third Meditation, in discounting the "objective reality" of sensation, there is very little in the ideas of corporeal objects which he perceives clearly and distinctly:

> [I do clearly and distinctly perceive in corporeal things] size or extension in length, breadth, or depth; shape which results from the boundary of this extension; position, which the different figured things [*figurata*] maintain with respect to each other; and motion, or the change of these positions; to which can be added substance, duration and number. . . . (AT VII, 43; CSM II, 30)

We know that Locke, in his famous account of the "primary/secondary quality distinction" in chapter 8 of Book II of the *Essay,* combines the *denial* that ideas of colors, sounds, tastes, and the like "resemble" qualities in objects, with the affirmation that ideas of such "primary qualities" as size, shape, and motion "*are Resemblances* of them, and their patterns do really exist in the objects themselves. . . ."[4] His discussion makes clear that he intends to maintain that *particular sense ideas of primary qualities* "resemble" the concretely realized qualities of particular objects that are sensed:

> A piece of *Manna* of a sensible Bulk, is able to produce in us the *Idea* of a round or square Figure; and, by being removed from one place to another, the *Idea* of Motion. This *Idea* of Motion represents it, as it really is in the *Manna* moving: A Circle or Square are the same, whether in *Idea* or Existence; in the Mind, or in the *Manna*. . . .[5]

Occasional remarks of Descartes's suggest that he holds a somewhat similar, simplistic view about sensory perception of primary qualities of bodies: for example, the statement about detecting differences of size and shape, and so on by "more than one sense."[6] I believe, however, that systematic consideration of the Cartesian texts establishes that he in fact holds a far more complex and qualified view about our perception of bodily shapes, sizes, locations, and motions.

Briefly, my claims will be these. First, when Descartes writes (in the

Meditations and *Principles*) of our ability to apprehend such qualities clearly and/or distinctly, he normally has in mind qualities understood *generally or abstractly*—as opposed to the specific, fully determinate qualities of actual bodies around us. Although it may be "stimulated" by sense, such apprehension is *intellectual* (possibly with assistance from imagination). Second, insofar as Descartes does acknowledge that we are able to apprehend reliably the size, position, shape, motion, and distance (from us) of actual bodies, he insists that we do not do so strictly *by sense.* (Although *this* kind of primary quality perception is also "intellectual," there are reasons to doubt that it can broadly be characterized as "distinct.") *Both* aspects of his position on primary quality perception bear on the interpretation of certain passages that suggest an extreme antiempiricism, a virtual nihilism about sense perception, such as the following from *Principles* II, a. 3:

> Perceptions of the senses do not teach [us] what really is in things. . . . Perceptions of the senses . . . do not teach us, except occasionally and by accident [*nisi interdum & ex accidenti*] what exists in [external bodies] themselves [*qualia in seipsis existant*]. (AT VIII-1, 41–42; CSM I, 224)

Certain expressions in passages already quoted should make us wary of attributing to Descartes the claim that, with regard at least to "primary qualities," we do perceive by sense particular qualities as they exist in bodies around us (say the size and shape of a chair across the room). Consider the cautious formulation from *Principles* I, a. 70: "are not otherwise sensed or understood by us than they are or at least can be in bodies." Descartes is surely not asserting that shapes and sizes and motions are in bodies *as* we (concretely and determinately) sense them; he is rather indicating that we apprehend these qualities as real in the sense that we understand clearly what extension, shape, and so on *are* (and perhaps what triangularity and so on are), and see that they are qualities that bodies can really have. The same point applies to the proof of the existence of bodies in the Sixth Meditation. This argument concludes with the observation that while corporeal things

> do not all perhaps exist just as I comprehend them by sense, . . . at least all those things are in them which I clearly and distinctly understand, that is to say, all things which, viewed generally [*generaliter spectata*], are comprehended in the object of pure Mathematics. (AT VII, 80; CSM II, 55)

The phrase "speaking generally" quite evidently excludes the apprehension of particular qualities as realized in actual things; for Descartes goes on to remark,

> So far as concerns the rest, however, which are either only particulars [*tantum particularia sunt*], as for example, that the sun is of such a size and shape, &c., or which are less clearly understood, such as light, sound, pain and the like, it is certain that although they are very doubtful and uncertain, nevertheless this same fact, that God is not deceptive, and that consequently he has not brought about that any falsity occurs in my opinions unless there also is in me some other faculty deriving from God for correcting it, presents

> to me a sure hope of attaining the truth even in these matters. (AT VII, 80; CSM II, 55–56)

I will consider later what "truth" Descartes has in mind in the last clause. The point I am concerned with at the moment is just this: it is as qualities considered generally or abstractly, not as particular qualities of actual things at a particular time, that the ideas in question are accepted as "distinct."

Even passages in which Descartes seems at first to be saying, precisely, that we perceive the particular figures of actual bodies affecting our senses much more distinctly than their colors, and so on, tend not to sustain such a reading very well on close inspection. For example, the following passage from *Principles* I, a. 69, which appears first to be conveying such a position, takes on a more ambiguous aspect when reconsidered in light of the possibility that Descartes only has in mind qualities understood generally or abstractly:

> . . . we know in a very different way what size is in a body which is seen, or figure or movement . . . , or situation, or duration, or number, and the like, which as already said are clearly perceived, than what color is in the same body, or pain [*sic*], odor, taste, or any other of those things which I have said are to be attributed to the senses. For although in seeing any body we are not more certain that it exists in that it appears figured than from its appearance of being colored: nevertheless we much more evidently know what being figured is in it, than what being colored is. (AT VIII-1, 33–34; CSM I, 217–218)

At first sight Descartes may seem to be saying here that we do have a clear knowledge, through sense perception, of the particular shapes and so on of the things around us. But what he actually says we know clearly with respect to a given body is just "what being figured is in it." Even the existence of a body is said to be apprehended just "from the fact that it appears figured [*quatenus apparet figuratum*]"—or colored for that matter; there is no commitment whatsoever to the view that a particular body's shape is reliably presented to us in a particular sense perception.[7]

The curious phrasing of the passage in the *Principles* concerned with establishing the existence of a physical world conveys even more clearly an emphasis on grasp of the general features of matter, a downplaying of the significance of any particular sensory given:

> . . . inasmuch as we perceive, or rather stimulated by sense we apprehend clearly and distinctly a matter which is extended in length, breadth, and depth, the various parts of which have various shapes and motions, and give rise to the sensations we have of colors, odors, pains etc. (II, a. 1: AT VIII-1, 40; CSM I, 223)

And it is with respect to this matter in general that Descartes here introduces a very rare *positive* use of the notion of resemblance between idea and physical reality:

> . . . we clearly apprehend this matter as different from God, or ourselves, or our mind, and appear to discern very plainly that the idea of it is due to

> objects outside of ourselves to which it is altogether similar. (AT VIII-1, 41; CSM I, 223)[8]

The phrase "stimulated by sense, we apprehend . . ." suggests, it seems to me, that Descartes is consciously avoiding committing himself to the view that we perceive by sense the true qualities of the physical world; it thus fits in with the claim previously cited that the senses do not tell us, "except occasionally and accidentally," what things are like in themselves.

What then, are the "truths" about particularities of sense that Descartes has in mind in the passage recently quoted from the Sixth Meditation? The claims that he goes on to make in the following paragraphs of this Meditation are closely similar to those he endorses in other works; and they allow to the senses an *extremely* minimal role in conveying information to us. Besides testifying to the fact of our own embodiment, the senses "teach" us (1) that there are bodies around ours; (2) that some of these are beneficial to us, and others harmful; and finally (3):

> . . . from the fact that I sense very different colors, sounds, odors, tastes, heat, hardness and the like, I rightly infer that there are in the bodies from which these various sensory perceptions come, certain variations corresponding to them [i.e., to the different sensations], though perhaps not similar to them. (AT VII, 81; CSM II, 56)

The beliefs that I have *mistakenly* supposed that my senses reliably taught me include not only the views that there are empty spaces; or that there are in bodies the heat, colors, and tastes that I perceive through my senses (or exact resemblances of these "ideas"); but also "that stars and towers and other distant bodies have the same size and shape which they present to my senses" (AT VII, 82; CSM II, 57). In short, the nature God has given us, as a composite of mind and body,

> . . . does not appear to teach us . . . to draw any conclusions from these perceptions of the senses about things located outside us without a prior examination by the understanding. For to know the truth about such matters seems to pertain to the mind alone, not to the composite. (AT VII, 82–83; CSM II, 57)

Thus the internal qualitative differences within our sensory manifold inform us reliably *only* about corresponding "variations" in the physical world (a theme of the *Dioptrics* and *Principles* also). Beyond this, and their pragmatic role in preserving the mind–body union, the senses provide *stimulation* to distinct perception of those *general or abstract* features of physical reality which are also presented in imagination and understanding.

The final sentence of the last passage raises a question, however. Does "the truth about such matters" encompass also truths about the particular (primary) qualities of actual bodies which Descartes has mentioned a little earlier: that the sun is of such and such a size and shape, for instance? Does Descartes really mean to hold that "the mind alone" can apprehend such qualities? In a way, I think he does. But to explain the meaning of this suggestion I need to introduce additional texts.

There are important parts of Descartes's treatments of "primary quality" perception that are not at all covered by the reading I have so far developed. These include, particularly, the impressive discussion of distance perception and related issues in the Sixth Discourse of the *Dioptrics,* and a fairly well-known but rather anomalous discussion of "levels of sense" that occurs in Descartes's Replies to the Sixth Objections to the *Meditations.* In both of these passages Descartes evidently takes for granted that human beings routinely determine with reasonable accuracy the size, shape, and location (at least) of particular objects presented to them by the senses.

At the beginning of the Sixth Discourse of the *Dioptrics*—"Of Vision"—Descartes observes that "all the qualities that we apprehend in the objects of sight can be reduced to six principal ones, which are: light, color, position, distance, size, and shape" (AT VI, 130; CSM I, 167). His purpose in the chapter is to explain "what enables our mind to know," or be "informed of" or to "perceive" these qualities. He comments that light and color "alone properly belong to the sense of sight": our perception of light depends on the "force" of the movements at the base of the optic nerves in the brain; whereas the perception of color depends on the nature of the movements (AT VI, 130–131; CSM I, 167). He further discusses the physiology of these perceptions—noting, for instance, how aspects of the structure of the optic nerves inevitably limit the range of colors, and distinctness of outline, that can be perceived under certain circumstances. All of these comments accord well enough with the view that we have very limited powers to apprehend the particular qualities of bodies: for the perceptions of brightness and color he is discussing may easily be understood as essentially *mere* discriminations of variations or differences among external stimuli.

The case is a bit different with respect to his discussion of position, distance, size, and shape, however. He does emphasize quite strongly that it is "easy to be mistaken" in distance perception (AT VI, 147; CSM I, 175; cf. AT VI, 144; CSM I, 173). And (anticipating several comments in the *Meditations*), he particularly stresses the illusions characteristic of our perception of extremely distant objects. But it certainly *appears* that throughout this discussion Descartes is assuming that we do with some reliability (and not merely "accidentally," as the *Principles* has it) visually determine the actual qualities of specific bodies—at least insofar as we are concerned with position, distance, size, and shape—when the conditions of observation are not unfavorable. His point, it seems, is not that we cannot do this, but rather that understanding *how* we do it will make plain why there are such definite limitations on the reliability of vision, and also show that "images" do not play the central and literal role that one might tend to ascribe to them. I will give some indication of the character of his treatment.

Descartes notes that neither the perception of distance nor the perception of position can be fully explained by postulating images emitted from objects.[9]

The perception of an object's position, for instance, depends on the position of our own eyes or head, as registered in the inmost parts of the brain: the appropriate "movements" in the brain, by virtue of an "institution of nature," in effect notify the mind of where we are looking, and hence where the different parts of the object are situated in relation to us. Thus we must not be surprised "that the objects can be seen in their true position, even though the picture that they imprint on the eye has a quite opposite one," or that only one object is seen despite there being two retinal images (AT VI, 135–137; CSM I, 169–170).

Size perception, he says, is determined in part by our beliefs about how far away the objects are "compared with the size of the images that they imprint on the back of the eye; and not absolutely by the size of these images . . . ," as the phenomenon of size constancy demonstrates (AT VI, 140; CSM I, 172). Finally,

> . . . it is also obvious that shape is judged by the knowledge, or opinion, that we have of the position of various parts of the objects, and not by the resemblance of the pictures in the eye; for these pictures usually contain only ovals and diamond-shapes, yet they cause us to see circles and squares. (AT VI, 140–141; CSM I, 172)

I said that it *appears* clear that Descartes is assuming that at least in favored cases we apprehend by vision the qualities of actual bodies. The reason for this qualification is not that the text leaves much room for doubt that we do apprehend such qualities in favorable cases: it is rather that there is room for arguing about whether he means to imply that we apprehend them by the *sense* of sight. Throughout the discussion of our perception of these qualities—particularly distance, size, and shape—Descartes makes frequent references to "judgment," and some references to "implicit reasoning." For example, we "judge" the distance of an object in part by distinctness of outline and strength of light, in part by its known size, in part by the fact that some other objects may be seen as interposed between it and ourselves, and in part by comparison of shapes and colors, among other factors (AT VI, 138–140; CSM I, 172). In a particularly famous passage he even holds that convergence of our eyes helps us determine distance, by virtue of an implicit reasoning "quite similar to that used by surveyors" (AT VI, 138; CSM I, 170).[10] Is it possible that when Descartes, in other works, rejects the senses as a source of knowledge of the actual qualities of bodies, in contrast to the legitimate claims of intellect, he is using "sense" in a peculiar and restricted way, that abstracts from much of what we would normally consider sense perception? If so, his dismissal of sense perception as a source of knowledge of particular qualities of things would not, after all, rule out the reliable apprehension of the determinate (primary) qualities of objects before us in *what we normally think of as sense perception.* Perhaps, in insisting on the extreme limitations of "the senses," Descartes only means to indicate that the normal ways of acquiring knowledge of particular bodies and their qualities, traditionally considered "sensory," ought to be reclassified as largely "intellectual"—not that they should be broadly dismissed.

This hypothesis derives strong support from a passage in the Sixth Replies. Descartes is responding to a suggestion that sensory errors are corrected by other sensory data, not by "the understanding." (For example, the sense of touch corrects the erroneous belief derived from vision that a stick placed in water becomes bent.) In rejecting this suggestion he finds it necessary to distinguish "three degrees" [*gradus*] of sense. One is the strictly physiological, shared by humans and brutes: "and this can be nothing but the motion of the particles of the [sense] organs, and the change of figure and position resulting from this motion" (AT VII, 436–437; CSM II, 294). In human beings, however, such motions in the body "immediately result" in changes in the mind that is united to it; the second level comprises "all" of these:

> The second [level] includes all that immediately results in the mind because it is united to a corporeal organ affected in this way, and such are the perceptions of pain, pleasure, thirst, hunger, color, sound, taste, odor, heat, cold and the like, which arise from the union and as it were the intermingling of mind and body, as I have explained in the Sixth Meditation. (Sixth Replies: AT VII, 437; CSM II, 294–295)

A little later Descartes makes the observation that I am most concerned to emphasize here, namely: "*Nothing else should be ascribed to sense, if we want to distinguish it accurately from the intellect* [. . . *nihil aliud ad sensum esset referendum, si accurate illum ab intellectu distinguere vellemus*]" (AT VII, 437; CSM II, 295). He eventually concludes this passage with the remark that,

> we have to have some reason to believe the judgment based on touch concerning this matter, rather than that based on vision; which reason, since it was not in us from infancy, must be attributed not to sense, but only to the understanding. (AT VII, 439; CSM II, 296)

But this suggestion that a learned preference for the testimony of touch—*not* formed "from early infancy and without any consideration" (AT VII, 438; CSM II, 295)—must be ascribed to a supersensory faculty, obscures the point Descartes first makes in drawing the distinction between the second and third "levels of sense." For he draws this distinction in a way that ascribes the perception of certain qualities *within* one sense (vision) to the understanding, *even when the perception does date from early infancy.*

The third grade of sense, he begins, "includes all those judgments which, on the occasion of motions in the organs of the body, we have been accustomed to make since our earliest youth about things outside us" (AT VII, 437; CSM II, 295). In considering an example of visual perception—seeing a stick—he distinguishes the elements of sense, properly so called, from the third level of sense, which is the level at which judgment occurs. In seeing the stick, I perceive light or color reflected from it: these sensations alone belong to the second level.

> For although from this sensation of color that affects me, I judge that the stick located outside me is colored, and also from the extension of this color [*ex istius coloris extensione*], its boundary, and its position in relation to the parts of the brain, I reason out [*ratiociner*] the size, figure, and distance of this stick: although this is commonly attributed to the senses, and for this reason I have here referred it to the third grade of sensing, nevertheless it manifestly depends on the understanding alone. But I have demonstrated in the *Dioptrics* that size, distance and figure can only be perceived by reasoning out [*ratiocinationem*] one from the others. (AT VII, 437–438; CSM II, 295)

This passage may help to explain Descartes's cagey references to "sense or understanding" in his discussion of the distinct ideas of bodies. It further suggests that his extremely derogatory comments elsewhere about the cognitive role about "sense" or "sense perception" need to be interpreted with care. For it opens the possibility that in such passages he is restricting his reference to what he here calls the "second level" of sense, rather than employing the broad common usage. If so, the antiempiricistic implications of such passages may be considerably less drastic, in relation to ordinary beliefs, than at first appears.

I will not attempt to pursue this possibility further here. Rather, I will close with some further observations relating to the interpretation of the Sixth Replies passage, and its relation to the *Dioptrics* and other works.

One thing that quickly emerges from Descartes's further remarks in the Sixth Replies is that he does not intend to equate the intellectuality of the judgments here at issue with *reliability.* (Here as elsewhere in Descartes an association with earliest infancy connotes unreliability or prejudice.)

> . . . when we say *the certainty of the understanding is much greater than the certainty of the senses,* this means only that now that we are adults the judgments we make as the result of any new observations are more certain than those which we made from earliest infancy and without any consideration; which is true without doubt. (AT VII, 438; CSM II, 295)

From this comment it seems quite clear that whatever the significance of the intellectual aspects of the "third level of sense," and whatever Descartes's reasons may be for distinguishing the second and third levels in this way at this place, the "distinctness" elsewhere attributed to ideas of size, shape, and position is not directly a function of their intellectuality understood in *this* way.[11]

There are a number of other things that seem to me quite confusing about this passage, considered in conjunction with the part of *Dioptrics* to which Descartes here alludes. Let me briefly indicate the most important.

First, the neat distinction between sense and judgment put forward in the Replies just does not square that well with the discussion of our perception of position, distance, size, and shape in the *Dioptrics.* For instance, in the latter work (as we saw) the head's or the eyes' position is said to figure in the perception of position by virtue of the "natural institution" of a relation between body state and mind; "natural institution" is also appealed to in explaining the effect of the shape of the eye on the perception of distance. In other words, the direct results of embodiment are not restricted to sensations like color and light (AT VI, 134–137; CSM I, 169–170).[12]

Second, there is certainly room for confusion about what exactly Descartes thinks is directly and prejudgmentally given in sense, even if one restricts one's consideration to the Sixth Replies, and does not worry too much for the moment about the issue of conscious awareness. He seems to want to say that only color and light are available on the "second level of sense," yet he simultaneously clearly implies that *in some sense* shape, size, and position are too ("the extension of the color, the boundary, the position"). And of course the picture is further muddled when one notes that in the *Dioptrics* there seems to be no particular distinction drawn, with respect to aids for judging something's distance, between "knowing its size," "the distinctness of its shape and color," and "changes in the shape of the body of the eye."

The issue of conscious awareness complicates these problems further. In the *Dioptrics* Descartes does not take a definite position on the extent to which we are conscious of the various physical and mental states that he thinks underlie our perception of distance, and the other qualities under discussion.[13] But he does tend to write as if all these perceptions rested on something quite like ordinary discursive reasoning, presumably accessible to consciousness:

> [A]s to the manner in which we see the size and shape of objects, I need not say anything in particular, inasmuch as it is all included in the manner in which we see the distance and the position of their parts. That is, their size is estimated according to the knowledge, or the opinion, that we have of their distance, compared with the size of the images that they imprint on the back of the eye. . . . And it is also obvious that shape is judged by the knowledge, or opinion that we have of the position of various parts of the objects. . . . (*Dioptrics*, Discourse 6: AT VI, 140; CSM I, 172)

And, in any case, it seems obvious that in Descartes's metaphysical scheme the "surveyor-like" reasoning said to be involved in distance perception *must* be ascribed to the realm of mind, not body. Yet Descartes's official doctrine concerning the mind is that we must be "in some manner conscious" of everything that is in it. But is it even remotely plausible to suppose that we are conscious, even potentially, of the effect of the eyes' convergence on normal distance judgments—let alone of the retinal images that we are said to "compare" with our "knowledge or opinion" of the relative distances of things?

It must be acknowledged that Descartes confronts this issue with some directness in the Sixth Replies. "I demonstrated in the *Dioptrics*," he writes,

> that size, distance, and shape can be perceived only by reasoning out one from the others. The only difference is that those things which we now judge for the first time because of some new observation, we attribute to the intellect; but those which we have judged, or even inferred by reasoning, from our earliest years, in exactly the same way as now, concerning the

> things that affect our senses, we attribute to sense. This is because we carry out the reasoning and judging [*ratiocinamur & judicamus*] concerning the latter at great speed on account of habit, or rather we remember the judgments we have long made about similar things; and so we do not distinguish these operations from simple sense perception. (AT VII, 438; CSM II, 295)

So apparently Descartes does mean to hold that most of the factors that go into our judgments of distance are in principle accessible to consciousness: we are not aware of them most of the time simply because of a lack of attention born of familiarity.[14]

This position is open to various obvious challenges. It seems perfectly in order to argue against it that we are not in fact able to become conscious of many of the "reasonings" or "judgments" that Descartes claims underlie our outer "perceptions." Further, there is the painfully obvious question of how the human ability to home in on a distant object relates, on the one hand, to distance perception as Descartes interprets it, and, on the other hand, to the ability of *animals* to do the same thing. Without making an issue about "consciousness," it's still hard to deny that in some sense my dog "knows" where the ball fell as well as I do: after all, he runs directly to it, just as I do. Now according to Descartes subhuman animals have no reasoning ability at all. It would seem to follow that, on Cartesian theory, either I do not rely for such physical acts on distance and position perceptions as Descartes explains them, or that the explanation of my dog's ability is *totally* disanalogous to the explanation of mine. Both positions are, it seem to me, extremely implausible.[15]

As I have noted, Descartes does in the *Dioptrics* connect perception of position and distance with the natural institution of brute correlations between body and mind, as well as with imagination, judgment, and reasoning. And although the former aspect of his discussion there may be (as I've said) somewhat in conflict with the Sixth Replies passage, one may still feel that it is on the right track, in so far as it at least mutes an otherwise overly intellectualistic conception of perceptual processes. But it should be noted that even this aspect of his treatment is of no help in connection with the problem of animal abilities: for animals no more have mind–body unions than they have the ability to reason, on the Cartesian view.

It is perhaps also worth observing in this context (though obvious, from the point of view of contemporary psychology) that Descartes's attempt to drive the sense/intellect wedge at the point that he does in the Sixth Replies runs afoul of the fact that perceptions of colors and sounds are themselves not really reducible to the passive reception of atomistic sensations. Descartes, as I've mentioned, appeals to the phenomenon now known as size constancy in arguing that perceived size is not a direct function of the size of the retinal image. Color constancy, however, is an equally powerful and pervasive phenomenon; and color perception also depends on many factors like background, juxtaposition, and so on (as well as on one's conceptual repertoire).[16]

It would be childish, of course, to belabor the observational and theoretical limitations of a perceptual theorist working at the dawn of modern science. The nature and limitations of Descartes's claims about sense perception are nevertheless worth taking seriously in view of their close interconnections with interpretive and critical problems that arise with respect to his broader philosophical position. In conclusion I want particularly to stress the following points.

First, Descartes does, in the *Dioptrics* and Sixth Replies passages, construe the perception of position, distance, size, and shape as involving strong intellectual elements (if not as *wholly* intellectual, as the Replies passage almost suggests); and he holds that they differ in this fundamental respect from ordinary perceptions of color, sound, heat and cold, taste, and the like, which are said to consist just in having "sensations" that "arise from the mind–body union."[17]

Second, this position leaves room for uncertainty about what he means when he speaks elsewhere of the near-uselessness of sense perceptions in informing us of particular qualities of bodies, in so far as it opens the possibility of a quite restricted understanding of 'sense perception' in these contexts.

Third, Descartes (unlike Locke) *pervasively* distinguishes the ideas of size, shape, position, and motion from simple ideas of sense—though (as I have argued) there are two different ways of understanding Descartes's position on this point. The ideas in question are either, it seems, distinct abstract or general ideas with their source in the intellect, or (if one has in mind the shapes and so on of particular bodies "presented to sense") complicated constructs based to some degree on a rather opaquely specified sensory given. In the *Meditations* and the *Principles* Descartes for the most part has in mind the former when he discusses the contract between the confused and the distinct "ideas of body."[18]

Fourth, the intellectual constructions of the "third degree of sense" are not in any direct way connected with certainty or (presumably) *distinctness* of perception. *All* distance perception, for instance, involves intellectuality in this sense, but *such* intellectuality is consistent with judgments about the distance of things being at least as liable to error as judgments of other sorts.

Finally, the treatments of perception in the *Dioptrics* and the Sixth Replies, impressive as they may be in some respects, are far from presenting a coherent and consistent position, that can settle difficulties found in Descartes's remarks on the subject elsewhere.[19] If anything, they make it *harder* to be sure how Descartes thinks of the relation between sense experience on the one hand, and the intellect, certainty, the mind–body union and so forth on the other hand. In particular, they raise additional complications for already difficult interpretive questions concerning Descartes's view of the cognitive role of the senses.[20]

Notes

1. I use the standard abbreviations for the Adam and Tannery edition (AT) and the Cottingham, Stoothoff, Murdoch translation (CSM). Translations are substantially my own, however.

2. This point is clear from passages such as the following:

> . . . if the sense of hearing brought to our thought the true image of its object, it would have to be the case that, instead of making us conceive sound, it made us conceive the movement of the parts of Air which tremble against our ears at the time. (*Treatise on Light:* AT XI, 5; CSM I, 82)

> . . . colors are nothing else, in bodies we call colored, than the diverse ways in which these bodies receive light and reflect it against our eyes. (*Dioptrics,* Discourse 1: AT VI, 85; CSM I, 153)

3. The emphasis placed here on the distinction between the common and special sensibles is unusual in Descartes's writings. Presumably it is at least partly explained by the fact that the passage is concerned to establish that Descartes has not employed any principle not accepted by Aristotle and "other philosophers of every age."

4. John Locke, *An Essay Concerning Human Understanding,* ed. Peter H. Nidditch (Oxford: Clarendon Press, 1975), bk. II, ch. 8, sec. 15, p. 137.

5. Ibid., sec. 18, p. 138.

6. The term 'primary quality' is not used by Descartes, so far as I know. It it not used always the same way by those seventeenth-century writers in whose works it does occur—e.g., Galileo, Boyle, and Locke. Locke himself does not maintain one constant view of what the primary qualities are (i.e., which qualities are primary qualities). In this essay I use the term to designate what Descartes takes to be the qualities that are "really in" body uniquely: that is, size, shape, distance, position, motion. (I do not, however, discuss in detail his treatments of our perception of each of these qualities individually.)

7. Compare *Principles* IV, a. 198, where the *caption* seems to indicate that the message will be that we know only size, shape, and motion in bodies through the senses; but where the text does not endorse any view about apprehending particular quality–instances by sense (AT VIII-1, 321–322; CSM I, 284–285).

8. Comparing different passages from the *Principles,* the *Meditations* (V and VI), the Replies, the *Notae in Programma,* and so on gives rise to a lot of questions about just how, and to what extent, Descartes conceives of our ideas of bodies as "due to" bodies. I discuss some of these issues in detail in "Descartes on the Origin of Sensation," *Philosophical Topics* 19 (1991), pp. 293–323.

9. Position ("*situation*") Descartes defines as "the direction towards which each part of an object is placed in relation to our body . . ." (AT VI, 134; CSM I, 169).

10. "As if by a natural geometry" is the famous phrase—although Descartes does not in fact use it directly of visual perception in this passage. Rather it is embedded in the ongoing analogy of the blind man discriminating the qualities—in this case the location—of a thing by the use of sticks in his hands.

In my opinion the "natural geometry" phrase has been widely overemphasized and overread. (On this point see Celia Rose Curtis Wolf, *The Retreat from Realism: Philosophical Theories of Vision from Descartes to Berkeley* [Ann Arbor: University Microfilms International, 1987], 223–226. A revised version of this dissertation appears in the *Journal of the History of Philosophy* monograph series under the title *Descartes on Seeing: Epistemology and Visual Perception* [Southern Illinois University Press, 1993].)

11. See Gary Hatfield, "The Senses and the Fleshless Eye: the *Meditations* as Cognitive Exercises," in *Essays on Descartes' Meditations,* ed. Amélie Rorty (Berkeley: University of California Press, 1986), 59. Hatfield indicates that the "third level" is really constituted just by the judgments of our early years, with those of mature adulthood counting as a "fourth level." Relative certitude is limited to the latter. It is

important to note, though, that Descartes goes on to stress that the judgments of childhood involve "exactly the same" processes as those we make now. Also, it seems to me open to question whether even the maturest judgments about particular features of things around us are meant to count as "distinct."

12. Wolf, *Retreat from Realism* (212–213), points out that one should not take at face value Descartes's indication in the Sixth Replies that he is there only reiterating what he said in the *Dioptrics*. Wolf discusses in detail changes in Descartes's accounts of position, distance, and so forth through various works.

13. He does indicate that we ordinarily change the shape of our eyes without reflecting on it (AT VI, 137; CSM I, 170).

14. Ronald Arbini seems to take it as self-evident that the processes in question could not be conscious, and to use this point in challenging a representationalist interpretation of Descartes that in effect makes mental sense data or ideas the basis of all knowledge of external things; see his "Did Descartes have a Philosophical Theory of Sense Perception?," *Journal of the History of Philosophy* 21 (1983): 321. He is too hasty, I think, in asssuming Descartes would accept his premises—evident as they may seem today.

In "The Sensory Core and the Medieval Foundations of Early Modern Perceptual Theory" (*Isis* 70 [1979]: 377) Gary Hatfield and William Epstein stress that, in virtue of Descartes's equation of the mental and the conscious, events at the "second level of sense" must be regarded as conscious. They are inexplicit, though, about whether the judgments based on these sensory items must themselves be accessible to consciousness.

15. A similar point is raised by Wolf, *Retreat from Realism,* 231. My present phrasing of the worry owes something to an objection by Jean-Marie Beyssade to an earlier version, though I am by no means sure I have fully met this objection.

16. I have talked with people who think that the phenomenon of color constancy (that something that looks a certain color under normal lighting will continue more or less to look that color under radically different lighting) is sufficient to suggest that colors, like shape are "objective." I am not sure, however, why they consider this fact more impressive, in this connection, than the simple fact that things retain "their" colors from time to time under *normal* lighting. Perhaps there is a tendency to conflate the idea that a perception may involve complex cognitive processes—and hence is not a "mere sensation"—with the idea that it is not "just in the mind."

In "The Case of the Colorblind Painter" Oliver Sacks and Robert Wasserman discuss the problem of understanding color "judgments," comparing it in passing with "a *much simpler*" form of visual "judgment the judgment or perception of depth (stereopsis) . . ." (emphasis added) (*New York Review of Books* 34, no. 18 [19 November 1987]: 31).

17. As Peter Markie has pointed out (see n. 20), the distinction between the second and third levels of sense does not correspond well with the *Meditations* distinction between what the senses "teach us" and the determinations of intellect. That we are embodied, that there are bodies around ours, and so on, though "taught by sense," are still *judgments*. I believe that this observation invites a further distinction between mere inferences to external causes of an idea, and the reasoning or judgment involved in the actual construction of a specific quality perception—say, of the distance of a thing.

18. In his discussion of the "Molyneux Problem" (*Essay,* bk. II, ch. 9, secs. 8–10, Nidditch, 145–146) Locke himself acknowledges that the "*ideas we receive by sensation, are often* in grown People *alter'd by the Judgment,* without our taking notice of it" (p. 145). Thus, upon receiving the "idea" of a variously colored or shaded plane circle,

we come habitually to form by judgment the "perception of a convex Figure, and an uniform Colour. . . ." Like Descartes before him, Locke explains that the judgment is unnoticed because formed so quickly and so habitually: the result, he says, is that "we take that for the Perception of our Sensation, which is an *Idea* formed by our Judgment . . ." (p. 146). The implications of this concession for the doctrine of simple ideas developed through bk II, ch. 8 are severe; but my interest in Locke is here restricted to the statements of these early sections.

19. Although I believe that Descartes's writings on perception have important interconnections with his more properly "philosophical" views, I am unable to agree with Arbini's claim (in "Did Descartes have a Philosophical Theory of Sense Perception?") that the *Dioptrics* and related texts provide "a clear coherent account of sense perception" which can be shown to provide solutions for problems set forth in the *Meditations* (pp. 317–318; 328ff.).

Incidentally, Arbini is mistaken in taking me to have held in my book *Descartes* (London: Routledge and Kegan Paul, 1978) that Descartes "was somehow committed to one or another form of perceptual representationalism" (p. 317). The passage he cites (without quoting the relevant part) in fact has more or less the opposite significance: After raising the question whether the Sixth Meditation provides grounds for ascribing to Descartes any "theory of sense perception at all, in the ordinary philosophical sense," I comment, "It would certainly be misleading to call him either a causal realist or a representative realist, as far as the evidence of the Sixth Meditation goes . . ." (*Descartes,* 203). My reasons for raising the question there were similar to those developed in greater detail in this essay, having to do with the highly depreciatory cast of many of Descartes's remarks about the cognitive role of the senses.

20. Earlier versions of this paper were presented at colloquia at the University of California at San Diego, the University of Cincinnati, the Instituto de Investigaciones Filosóficas of the Autonomous University of Mexico, and St. Mary's College, Maryland, as well as at the San José Conference. Of the many helpful comments made on these occasions I would like to single out for special thanks some remarks by Philip Kitcher and written criticisms by Peter Markie, both of which have substantially influenced the present version.

13

Language and Machine in the Philosophy of Descartes

Jean-Pierre Sèris

TRANSLATED BY STEPHEN VOSS

Descartes offers forthright answers to two questions still being asked today: (1) Can machines fully imitate the functioning and behavior of living things? (2) Can machines think? He answers the first affirmatively and the second negatively. His mechanism will thus be at once hyperbolic and elliptical in the eyes of a reader at the end of the twentieth century, for whom there may still be, if not doubts, at least disputes over these matters. Descartes's two categorical answers are each rooted in the principle of the substantial distinction between body and soul—that is to say, in a metaphysical argument. Given this fact, the nature of the machinery a man of his time might have in mind is irrelevant here, and the modest development of seventeenth-century mechanization ought not to invalidate the perhaps exaggerated boldness of the positive answer to (1), any more than it explains or, a fortiori, justifies the negative answer to (2). All these things, commonplace though they be, deserve to be recalled, at a time when it is precisely the performances of machines which leads our contemporaries to pose such problems, and when the cell machinery of bacteria is currently compared to a factory.

On the other hand, there is one point in Descartes's argument which, far from surprising today's reader, may wrongly be underestimated and taken for granted: the link Descartes sets up between the problematic of language and that of the two questions we are considering. Insofar as there exists a Cartesian theory of language, it is knitted in a quite curious way to the theory of machines. Descartes is the first philosopher, to our knowledge, who systematically derives profit for his reflection on machines (in general what can a machine do?) from reflection on language (what is it to speak?), even if he is convinced, or just because he is convinced, of their definitive disparity. He is also, we believe, the first philosopher who exhibits the essential character of human language by opposing it to a mechanical communication or a transmission of encoded differences. Even though the machines he invokes as models for the organs of living bodies are mere shadows of our automata, mechanics in its wider extension is for him something like automatic translation. By contrast, human speech is a nonmechanizable performance, because it depends, not on a "mechanical and corporeal principle,"[1] but on the function of the soul, which is to think.[2] This essay attempts to state precisely and to interpret Descartes's teaching about the mutual light that language and machine are capable of casting on one another.

Let us begin with what is most obvious, and see how Descartes confronts language and machine with the explicit intention of establishing between them an unbridgeable gulf. In the *Discourse on Method* he asserts that there are "two very certain means" of distinguishing true men from anthropoid machines intentionally designed to throw us off the track: "the first is that they could never use words, or put together other signs, as we do in order to declare our thoughts to others" (AT VI, 56; CSM I, 139–140). Putting together words or other signs that indicate that one is thinking what one says cannot be the effect of a natural movement that a machine can imitate: even before he shows that animals (animal-machines) lack speech, Descartes believes he can show that machines cannot possess speech. We observe that there is, besides speech arranged "differently so as to give a response appropriate to the meaning of everything said in [their] presence" and so as to "put together a discourse by which [they] could make their thoughts understood," a second means of avoiding any confusion or mistake: these machines "would inevitably fail in other [things], which would reveal that they were acting not through understanding but only through the composition of their organs." Two means appear again in the letter to X of March 1638: "one is that these automata never respond appropriately, except by chance, either by words or by signs, to what they are asked . . ." (AT II, 40; CSMK, 99). Why *two* means? Why *two* indicators? The second, derived from the topical, adaptive, pertinent character of human action in contrast to the preregulated (we would say "programmed") acts of automata, arises, we believe, within the problematic of this page of the *Discourse,* conveyed by the letter to X, because what is at issue here is a problematic of reason, one that may be both practical and theoretical.

Speech may nonetheless count as the single criterion when our concern is no longer to detect the presence of reason in a being on the basis of its behavior, but to disclose the presence of thought in an otherwise corporeal being. Thus we read in the letter to the Marquis of Newcastle of 23 November 1646, "In fact, none of our external actions can show anyone who examines them that our body is not just a self-moving machine but contains a soul with thoughts, with the exception of spoken words, or other signs that have reference to particular topics without expressing any passion" (AT IV, 574; CSMK, 303). In the end, in the letter to Henry More of 5 February 1649, Descartes may appear less dogmatic: "But in my opinion the main reason which suggests that the beasts lack thought is the following. . . . It has never yet been observed that any brute animal reached the stage of using a true language, that is to say, of indicating by word or sign something pertaining to pure thought and not to natural impulse."[3] And yet there is in fact no other argument, for he immediately adds, "Language is the only certain sign of thought hidden in a body [*haec enim loquela unicum est cogitationis in corpore latentis signum certum*]." Moving from the question of possibility "What can a machine do?" to the question of fact "Can animals think?," Descartes recognizes that it cannot be shown that they lack thought, "since the human mind does not reach into their hearts" (AT V, 276–277; CSMK, 365). In the Sixth Replies he mocks those who "speak [of animals] as though they understood them, and saw everything that happened in their hearts" (AT VII, 426; CSM II, 288). Nor can the souls of other men be penetrated any more readily, so that we may be present at their intimate or private thoughts. It is, then, the use of speech which assures me that other men can think. The *loquela,* the properly human performance and use of language, is the unique certain indicator of the presence of thought in the body. But, inversely, the absence of that *loquela* or of performances analogous to our own in animals cannot be regarded as "a certain sign" that they do *not* have thinking souls. All we can say is that so long as we meet no animals who speak as men do, the "persuasive" arguments in favor of the Cartesian thesis retain all of their force. Confirming again that the human use of speech is the only certain indicator of thought, Descartes concludes that "we can take language as the true difference between men and beasts."[4]

Three distinct points make of this *loquela* the only true discriminant. They are developed in the word-by-word commentary which the letter to the Marquis of Newcastle gives of the definition of the human use of language. They can be formulated as follows:

(1) Indifference of sensible mode of realization, whether by voice or gesture, whether audible or visible. Mutes express their thoughts by gestures as well as we do by voice. Furthermore, they "invent" such signs.

(2) Pragmatic relevance in conversation: the fact that subjects produce statements "that have reference to particular topics" (AT IV, 574; CSMK, 303), or that they "respond . . . in an appropriate way to what is asked" (AT II, 40; CSMK, 99), or that they "give an appropriately meaningful answer to whatever is said" in the presence of the speaker (AT VI, 56–57; CSM I, 140). Appropriateness as a quality of discourse is defined as relevance in relation to what is said, and not only in relation to what is done; it is a characteristic of the subject in the situation of linguistic communication, the interlocutor in the relation of dialogue.

> We can certainly conceive of a machine so constructed that it utters words, and even utters words which correspond to bodily actions causing a change in its organs (e.g., if you touch it in one spot it asks what you want of it, if you touch it in another it cries out that you are hurting it, and so on). But it is not conceivable that such a machine should produce different arrangements of words so as to give an appropriately meaningful answer to whatever is said in its presence, as the dullest of men can do. (AT VI, 56–57; CSM I, 140)

"Madmen," "fools," and those who are "stupid and insane"[5] do as well. In connection with the wonders and the limitations of simulated appropriateness, this false, artificial appropriateness which rests on predetermined causal links, the reader is referred to the celebrated page of the *Treatise on Man* at which a Diana, a Neptune, and a sea monster make successive appearances (AT XI, 130–131; CSM I, 100–101).

(3) Independence in relation to the passions. "Natural movements which express passions . . . can be imitated by machines as well as by animals" (AT VI, 58; CSM I, 140–141). In fact, Descartes is well aware that certain animals can be taught sentences "by artifice": "if a magpie is taught to say hello to its mistress when it sees her coming, this can be by making the utterance of this word the expression of one of its passions; that is, it will be an expression of hope that she has something to eat if it has been accustomed to receive some delicacy when it has said that word" (AT IV, 574; CSMK, 303). In this case of "operant conditioning," gained by reinforcement of the appropriate response, the utterance of "Hello!" by the magpie upon its mistress's arrival is in fact an effect, and for us alone an indication, of the corporeal movements constituting hunger. The training introduces supplementary middle terms of its choice—this is its "artifice"—in the chain of corporeal movements or that of the mechanism of the passions. It does not modify the purely deterministic nature of this transmission. Human speech, by contrast, may and does emancipate itself from this determinism.

The three traits given as characteristics of the human use of language are united in that they certify the nonautomatic, nonpreregulated character of the production of statements, at the level of the choice of perceivable signs, of their arrangement, and of the execution of the act of speaking. Beyond these apparently negative traits lurks the positive nature of thought.

Although Descartes uses the same terms, *exprimer, témoigner,* and *signifier,* both to evoke the link of gesture or cry with passion and to express that of word with thought,[6] these words have their proper meaning only in the second case. In the first, they are to be taken either figuratively or, more accurately, as an anthropomorphic façon de parler. It is only in relation to man, as observer or accessory, that the automatic exteriorization of an inner movement by a movement perceivable by the senses can count as indicator. Intrinsically, it simply causes the intervention of a mechanical transmission of movement from one place to another. The theory of human speech requires entirely different resources. It is in reality in its very performance an indication that a man is thinking; but it is also an expression of his thought. In speech, the thought gets said. The words have a meaning, which is a thought. "When we learn a language, we connect the letters or the pronunciation of certain words, which are material things, with their meanings, which are thoughts, so that when we later hear the same words, we conceive the same things, and when we conceive the same things, we remember the same words" (AT IV, 604; CSMK, 307). Descartes's characterization of authentic language as an exclusively human fact is a reflection of the theory of the substantial union of soul and body. Learning a language causes us to experience the establishment or institution of a lasting and reciprocal link between sounds or letters, "material things," and thoughts. Between word and thought, as between body and soul, there can be no mechanical coupling (since thought is not a corporeal movement and the soul is not a machine) and no instrumental, mediate, and revocable relation (AT VI, 59; CSM I, 141; and AT VII, 81; CSM II, 56). This is why the *learning* of a language, and not only the *invention* of a spoken or written tongue, is evoked by Descartes not only as a model but as providing a proof of the possibility of instituting, artificially or naturally, a lasting link between terms that are *toto coelo* different. In the same way "certain motions of the heart [are] naturally connected . . . with certain thoughts, which they in no way resemble" (AT IV, 603–604; CSMK, 307).

Speech is not just a distinctive sign of man. It is the most direct experience and the most immediate proof of the substantial union which constitutes him, insofar as it allows communication only between beings who have learned the meanings of words which they can understand and pronounce. Descartes was already aware of this consequence when he wrote in the Fourth Discourse of the *Dioptrics,* "We should, however, recall that our minds can be stimulated by many things other than images—by signs and words, for example, which in no way resemble the things they signify" (AT VI, 112; CSM I, 165). Within one dimension of the difference, we see that the word, a material thing, signifies in that it arouses a thought, which in no way resembles it, in the mind of speaker and hearer.

However, article 197 of Part IV of the *Principles of Philosophy* articulates a second dimension of the difference, perpendicular to the first one. This second dimension involves writing and the pen that writes. This is not simply the difference or dissimilarity between the word and the thought it signifies. To prove that movements made in the body are sufficient to make the soul have all sorts of thoughts, "without it being necessary that [those movements] contain anything which resembles what they make it conceive," Descartes points out that "words spoken by voice or written on paper make [the soul] conceive all the things they signify, and then give it different passions" (AT IX–2, 315–316; CSM I, 284). He continues,

> With the same paper, pen and ink, if the tip of the pen is pushed across the paper in a certain way it will form letters which excite in the mind of the reader thoughts of battles, storms and violence, and passions of indignation and sorrow; but if the movements of the pen are just slightly different they will produce quite different thoughts of tranquillity, peace, and pleasure, and quite opposite passions of love and joy. (AT IX, 316; CSM I, 284)

This time the point is to show that differences between ideas are preserved, or transcribed, or expressed, as is said in Rule XII,[7] in spite of the non-resemblance between word and idea just mentioned. This difference involves not two but four terms: the difference between A_1 and A_2 is transcribed by the difference between B_1 and B_2. This is a recurrent Cartesian theme. It appears to us to imply the idea of an encoding. In Rule XII "the infinite multiplicity of figures is sufficient for the expression of all the differences in perceptible things" (AT X, 413; CSM I, 41). We might also recall the Eighth Discourse of the *Meteorology* (AT VI, 325–344) and the theory of colors given in the context of the explanation of the phenomena of the rainbow. In Rule XII the example of the pen appears again, but without involving the meaning of written words: the example is employed only to show that the shape received by the external sense may be transported instantly into the common sense without the movement of matter and without the loss of what distinguishes it from other shapes:

> When an external sense organ is stimulated by an object, the figure which it receives is conveyed at one and the same moment to another part of the body known as the 'common' sense, without any entity really passing from the one to the other. In exactly the same way I understand that while I am writing, at the very moment when individual letters are traced on the paper, not only does the point of the pen move, but the slightest motion of this part cannot but be transmitted simultaneously to the whole pen. All these various motions are traced out in the air by the tip of the quill, even though I do not conceive of anything real passing from one end to the other.[8]

The blind man's stick in the First and Fourth Discourses of the *Dioptrics* plays the same role as faithful transmitter of differences: the bodies he touches, "causing his stick to move in different ways according to the different qualities in them, . . . move the nerves in his hand in the same way, and then the regions in his brain where these nerves originate. This is what occasions his soul to have sensory perception of just as many different qualities in these bodies as there are differences in the movements caused by them in his brain" (AT VI, 84 and 114; CSM I, 153 and 166).

The terms *differentiis exprimendis* ("expression of differences"), *designari* without *transmigrare,* and *potentiam . . . communicatur nuda* ("communication of bare power")[9] present both a quantitative aspect and a "linguistic" aspect. It is necessary first of all that the range of varieties at the origin, whether discrete or continuous, have at a minimum the same extension as that deployed at the end. Even more than the frequency of his recourse to the example of writing, and that of writing instruments themselves, it is the fact that relevant differential traits are immediately and without residue transcribable which in our view justifies the use of the vocabulary of representation.

We find this philosophy of representation at work in the *Treatise on Man,* in particular in these lines on natural inclinations:

> . . . as for animal spirits, they may be more or less abundant, their parts more or less coarse, more or less agitated and more or less uniform at one time than another; and it is by means of these four differences that all the different humors or natural inclinations within us (at least insofar as they do not depend on the constitution of the brain or on particular affections of the soul) are represented in this machine. (AT XI, 166)

Another very characteristic example, that of the explanation of taste: the little filaments in the nerves of the tongue "may be moved in four different ways by the particles of salt, acid, water, and eau de vie or brandy, whose sizes and figures I have just explained to you, and thus . . . they can make the soul sense four different kinds of taste" (AT XI, 145–146). Finally, in connection with shapes traced on the inner surface of the brain and the pineal gland, Descartes gives the following account, which leads him at the same time to reveal the extension which his physics of external senses and even of inner sense gives to the "encoding":

> Note that by 'figures' I mean not only things which somehow represent the position of the edges and surfaces of objects, but also anything which, as I said above, can give the soul occasion to perceive movement, size, distance, colours, sounds, smells and other such qualities. And I also include anything that can make the soul feel pleasure, pain, hunger, thirst, joy, sadness, and other such passions.[10]

This physics of communication is connected with a metaphysics of communication of the substances in the union, by means of a scheme closely analogous to that of a punched card: "Now I maintain that when God unites a rational soul to this machine (in a way that I intend to explain later) he will place its principal seat in the brain, and will make its nature such that the soul will have different sensations corresponding to the different ways in which the entrances to the pores in the internal surface of the brain are opened by means of the nerves."[11] However, from the start, and in principle, the communicational aspect of the physics of the animal-machine owes nothing to the union: it concerns only the functions of the body. Descartes makes this clear in the letter to More of 5 February 1649: "I do not deny life to animals, . . . and I do not even deny *sensation,* in so far as it depends on a bodily organ" (AT V, 278; CSMK, 366). There is a code of the senses, antecedent to that of the sensations of the soul united to the body. In the same way, there is a purely mechanical use of the scheme of the "punched card," if we may be permitted this anachronism,[12] for example in the explanation of memory, prior to the institution by God of a link between shapes (conveyed by an array of pores capable of being opened or closed) and sensations.

Does this physics of communication make the machine the locus for a study of information? The idea of the machine as vehicle of information has been generously attributed to Descartes, from very different points of view, by several French authors, from G. G. Granger to J. Vuillemin, from D. Dubarle to J.-L. Marion.[13] It is certainly true that Descartes represents mechanics not only as the diversification of movements on impact (AT XI, 37; CSM I, 92–93), but also as the instantaneous communication of differences at a distance, by encodings and automatic translations which save or preserve diversity. There is nothing surprising in the fact that he chose to give his *World* the form of a *Treatise on Light.* And what is his "mechanism" but the decoding of the world of physical phenomena according to a grid or an alphabet or a sieve which restores its effects (*Principles* IV, aa. 204 and 205)? All the more reason why the descriptions of the animal-machine or the machine of the living body as receiving, translating, and sorting sensory data transmitted to the common sense should suggest to the contemporary reader that the Cartesian automaton, like a cybernetic automaton, is in informational communication with its environment.

The term "information" would nevertheless be very inadequate and inopportune as a designation of what the Cartesian machine transmits from one point to another. First, because what it transmits, in the course of transforming it, is shape, size, movement, as geometrically defined, and—Descartes insists—nothing else; next, because the concept of information belongs to a completely different scientific, technological, and intellectual universe; and further, because the concept of information is inseparable from the evaluation of probabilities, a notion of which Descartes was ignorant and which his epistemological choices precluded: the "difference" or "diversity" which the Cartesian mechanism encodes is not that of improbability.[14] Finally, there is nothing more anti-Cartesian than the ambiguity of the word "information," which dresses up a mathematized physical magnitude with a name that evokes the production and reception of messages by a subject who bestows their entire value on them. The Cartesian automaton is not a center of decision, in a position to react on the external world and on its modifications.[15] Only the soul united to a body "perceives" these modifications which are imprinted on the body to which it is joined, in order to make a decision on its own. But then we are no longer in the realm of the animal-machine.

It is precisely at this point that Descartes develops what might be called his theory of *signals,* for example in the Sixth Meditation. We follow the Latin text, which is much more explicit. A signal has, first of all, a utilitarian and not a directly cognitive function: sense perceptions are given to me only *ad menti significandum quaenam composito, cujus pars est, commoda sint vel incommoda,* not to enable it to know the essence of external bodies, *de qua . . . nihil nisi valde obscure et confuse significant* (AT VII, 83; CSM II, 57–58). We know that this is what generates for Descartes the difficult problem of false signals, the problem of the man with dropsy: the dryness of the throat, *quae sitis sensum menti inferre solet,* impels him to drink and so to do harm to himself (AT VII, 84–85; CSM II, 58). Descartes remarks again that it is *respiciendo ad compositum* that there can be false signals or errors of nature. The Cartesian solution of this problem clarifies for us the nature of signals:

> . . . since any given movement occurring in the part of the brain from which the mind immediately receives impressions produces just one corresponding sensation [*non nisi unum aliquem sensum illi infert*], one cannot wish or imagine anything better than that this movement should produce the one sensation which, of all the sensations it is capable of causing [*quam si eum inferat qui, ex omnibus quos inferre potest*], is the most especially and most frequently conducive to the preservation of the human body when it is completely healthy. (AT VII, 87, and IX, 69–70; CSM II, 60)

According to the same principle, "when the nerves in the foot are set in motion in a violent and unusual manner, this motion, by way of the spinal cord, reaches the inner part of the brain, and there gives the mind its signal for having a certain sensation, namely pain . . . [*ibi menti signum dat ad aliquid sentiendum, nempe dolorem tamquam in pede existentem*]" (AT VII, 88; CSM II, 60). We have seen that the term-by-term correspondence instituted by God between the shapes or "ideas" "traced in spirits on the surface of the [pineal] gland" (AT XI, 176; CSM I, 106) and the sensations in the mind has all the properties of a lexicon. But the movement occurring in the brain is not only the sensible or symbolic equivalent of the sensation in the mind; it also has the power of causally determining whether it appears. It is the union of these two functions which authorizes us in seeing in the *signum* a *signal.*

There can be a sign or even a signal only for a mind. The words of the magpie which we mentioned a little while ago can *speak* of hunger only for the mistress who supplies the delicacy, just as the clock "tells the time" only for the mind capable of reading it. Descartes, who conceived the mechanism to which animal and machine are reduced as a communication of encoded differences, could not, we hold, develop this idea, because he restricts linguistic communication to interhuman relationships, and, as we shall see more clearly, because he restricts signs to a purely instrumental status.

Let us now ask whether there are for Descartes mechanical aspects of language—"true language [*vera loquela*]" (AT V, 278; CSMK, 366). Let us return to the letter to Mersenne of 20 November 1629. Learning a language is not reducible to acquiring a lexicon: "There are only two things to learn in any language, the meaning of the words and the grammar" (AT I, 76; CSMK, 10). If words effectively acquire meaning only through being learned by a composite of soul and body, and through the vigilance of the mind who conceives the thoughts to which the words correspond, whatever the (acquired) spontaneity of that association, grammar poses an apparently different problem when we go on to ask under what conditions it can be learned. "There are no men so dull-witted and stupid—and this includes even madmen—that they are incapable of arranging various words together and forming an utterance from them in order to make their thoughts understood; whereas there is no other animal, however perfect and well-endowed it may be, that can do the like," we read in the *Discourse* (AT VI, 57; CSM I, 140). "To arrange" words "in different ways, to respond to the meaning of everything said in its presence," is not within the scope of beasts; it is within the scope of the insane, the stupid, the dull,[16] who are souls united to bodies. Descartes speaks here of composing topical sentences, and of expressing the subject's thought. He does not speak only of grammatically correct sentences. What is to be said of them? Could a machine produce them? In the terms of the *Discourse,* if we employ what Descartes has said previously about reason in its practical use, we are led to ask whether reason—the "universal instrument which can be used in all kinds of situations" (AT VI, 57; CSM I, 140)—is indispensible in arranging grammatical statements, or whether "the particular disposition" of organs of a machine could suffice "for each particular action." It is on this subject that the letter of 1629 provides information about Descartes's thought. Indeed, grammar is very complex, even bizarre, in "common languages." It may be imagined that for Descartes the linguistic artifact suffers from the same ills as the repaired buildings, the "ancient cities which have gradually grown . . . into large towns," or the revised legislation of which he speaks at the beginning of Part II of the *Discourse.* An artificial language which is the work of a single person—like the "proposal for a new language" about which he responds to Mersenne—may, on the other hand, provide occasion for us to envisage a grammar free of these difficulties:

> If you make a language with only one pattern of conjugation, declension, and construction, and with no defective or irregular verbs introduced by corrupt usage, and if the nouns and verbs are inflected and the sentences constructed by affixes either before or after the primitive nouns, and all the affixes are listed in the dictionary, it would be no wonder if ordinary minds learned to write the language with a dictionary in less than six hours. . . . (AT I, 76; CSMK, 11)

Like "the work from the hand of a single master" (architect, engineer, or legislator) in the *Discourse,* the project Descartes considers here is not merely a simplification but a "reformulation" of grammar, which makes of its constituent, the rule, a uniformity without fault or exception. We confess that we do not see what would keep such a grammar from being mechanizable.

But Descartes does not even contemplate this possibility. He bars the ways that lead to it. He undertook the reform of his own thought, as he says clearly in the *Discourse,* with the aim of "building on a foundation which is all [his] own." The reformation of grammar, however, is an affair which necessarily involves others. He disputes its validity for three reasons, the last of which concerns the learning of grammar. (1) Considering the idea, at the end of the letter, that this new grammar should, as a universal grammar, be made common to all existing languages and of sufficient power to apply to all lexicons, he judges that its first drawback would be a clash of letters, or other sounds: cacaphony. (2) Within the slightly modified hypothesis according to which it would be applied to a new lexicon also created entirely anew, "no one would want to take the trouble" to learn it. (3) If anyone did want to, that would be materially impossible without speakers who could teach its use. Even though reformed, such a grammar would be composed, indeed, of rules best described as an arbitrary morphology and syntax, therefore requiring a period of learning, which would in turn require that there already be spoken words or books to read. So, according to Descartes, the very means proposed to facilitate the learning of the language would tend to render it impossible.

But cannot the new language be limited to a written one? Descartes examines the services which a universal dictionary of ideographic symbols might provide, a nonphonetic account of the "primitive words" which he explicitly considers as the semantic foundation common to all national languages. "Those who had the dictionary and knew its grammar could translate what was written into their own language. . . . But this would be no good except for reading mysteries and revelations" (AT I, 80; CSMK, 12). Far from being the silent crossroads where all the statements of Babel exchange their meaning without residue, this characteristic is devalued and disqualified, as maintaining around it and even within its propositions a low-grade mystery. It would barely be good enough to convey the "arcana" of which, as he says in the same letter, Descartes thinks very little. In short, a dead language, well fitted for inscribing just such sentences, in which meaning has vanished! Just as he stigmatizes the art of Lully in the *Discourse,* as being "of less use for learning things than . . . for speaking without judgment about matters of which one is ignorant" (AT VI, 17; CSM I, 119), so here he denounces the erosion of thought that would result from the rigidity of the language expressing it.

If the regularization of grammar is not enough to interest Descartes in the project of an artificial language, and if he is so hostile to the idea of a characteristic copied from common languages, the idea of a language that is, by contrast, universal not by artifice but in truth strikes him entirely otherwise. The establishment of this language "depends on true philosophy," because it presupposes the enumeration of all human thoughts and the discovery of the natural order of their composition. The last paragraph of the letter to Mersenne must be read in the light of the second part of Rule XII. Here we no longer have a characteristic of primitive words of common languages, hung together by the postulate of their effective synonymy, but instead an arithmetic of human thoughts.

> If someone were to explain correctly what are the simple ideas in the human imagination out of which all human thoughts are compounded, and if his explanation were generally received, I would dare to hope for a universal language very easy to learn, to speak, and to write. Its greatest advantage is that it would be an aid to judgment, representing all matters so clearly that it would be almost impossible to go wrong. (AT I, 81; CSMK, 13)

This language would have no grammar *stricto sensu,* if by grammar we understand, as we do now, a set of conventional rules of morphology and syntax: the natural order of thoughts would be the unique rule for the composition of complex terms (morphology), and syntax would only need to mold itself upon that. It would, without any risk of error, also govern the arrangement of well-formed consequences of well-formed statements. The analysis of signs, the composition of statements, and their entailments would be emancipated from subjection to restrictions of a purely grammatical type. If our "common languages," by contrast with arithmetic, have grammars, this is the measure of their divergence from the universal language. The characters would represent the very composition of the idea they signified; one could as well speak of "distinct words" as of "distinct ideas." Possessing terms of this nature, men would no longer give "their attention to words rather than to things,"[17] as they have always done till now. They would no longer give "their consent to terms which they did not understand, and which they were not much concerned to understand, either because they thought they had previously understood them or because it seemed to them that those who had taught them those terms knew their meaning, and they had learned it by the same means." Descartes wrote again to Mersenne: "Peasants could judge better about the truth of things than philosophers do now": they would do it, not by taking pen and paper, or computer keyboard, and saying the Leibnizian *Calculemus!,* but by saying *Voyons!* Not by algorithm. Not by calculating machine. It would only be necessary to intuit, in order to infer by deduction: "None of the errors to which men—men, I say, not the brutes—are liable is ever due to faulty inference. . . . Arithmetic and geometry prove to be much more certain than the other disciplines. . . . Where these sciences are concerned it scarcely seems possible for a *man* to err, except through inadvertence."[18]

Order as Descartes conceives it also excludes "those weapons of the schoolmen, probable syllogisms (*Scholasticorum aptissima bellis probabilium syllogismorum tormenta*]" (AT X, 363; CSM I, 11). "Those *chains* with which dialecticians suppose that they *regulate* human reason seem to me to be of little use here [*illa Dialecticorum vincula, quibus rationem humanam regere se putant*]" (AT X, 365; CSM I, 12). As Rule IV says again, one cannot set out to teach how intuition and deduction are to be carried out: "Nothing can be added to the clear light of reason which does not in some way dim it" (AT X, 372–373; CSM I, 16). The universal language, which we cannot hope to see in actual use, but which depends on a science capable of being found, is only the transparent instrument of the *mathesis universalis* presented in Rule IV: "This discipline should contain the primary rudiments of human reason and extend to the discovery of truths in any field whatever" (AT X, 374; CSM I, 17). A universal characteristic of this type would be no substitute for the judgment of the person using it. "It would be an aid to judgment" in no way means "it would replace judgment." It would not replace it. The mechanism of a calculus would not be proscribed, but it would be useless.

In this "ideal" use of the universal language, the instrumental value of the sign matters less than its perfect transparency, indeed its pure effacement before the very idea it transcribes. The sign, giving up its chance to be seen, in fact gives us the idea to be seen. Until now every language had to be an artifact, something made, an *institution,* as Géraud de Cordemoy said,[19] in the double sense of the arbitrary decision that posits it and the necessity to learn it. But in the language that true philosophy might "invent," artifice would take the nature of ideas as its model, so as to reveal their character. As a natural instrument it would be, in contrast with all other languages, preserved from the risk of ossification into second nature, that is, the risk of becoming mechanized and automatized. In opposition to the "symbol" used to communicate mysteries, it would be based on an analysis which distinguishes ideas "in such a way that they are clear and simple, which is in my view the greatest *secret* one can have for acquiring good science." The horizon of the thought of Descartes is the elision of the sign, to the point that the very thing it says about numbering makes us forget that there exist *systems* of numbering! This is the other side of the radical separation of machine and language in his thought.

In Part II of the *Discourse* Descartes differentiates his method from "three arts or sciences" which might seem needed as aids to it: logic, the analysis of the Ancients, and algebra. He criticizes logic because its syllogisms and "most of its other techniques are of less use for learning things than for explaining to others the things one already knows" (AT VI, 17; CSM I, 119). The mechanism of rules is interpreted as repetition and reproduction and not as being itself productive. Its extremely circumscribed pedagogic interest is, moreover, accompanied by a permanent and irreducible danger of surpassing the limits of what *can* be said with understanding; it is here that Descartes compares it to the art of Lully: effective mechanization, which is the historical trait salient to the latter, is the very figure of this danger. Furthermore, in scholastic logic the "mechanical" apparatus of valid inferences is constituted imperfectly; its functioning is perturbed by "harmful and superfluous" precepts (AT VI, 17; CSM I, 119).

As for the algebra of the Moderns, another science linked to a system of writing, its drawback derives from its subjection "to certain rules and certain symbols" which make of it "an obscure art which disturbs the mind rather than a science which cultivates it." Rule IV criticizes the "multiplicity of numbers and incomprehensible figures which overwhelm it" (AT X, 377; CSM I, 19). Symbolism and algorithm, signs and rules, far from giving way to a mechanization under the name of formalism, encumber, oppress, scatter, and bewilder: they are an obstacle to the mind's intuition. They are to be rejected, as "paths that are suspect and liable to error" (AT X, 370; CSM I, 15). The Cartesian path, the method, is free of these mechanical components or aspects. Its elimination of the risk of error, facility, heuristic efficacy, even its systematicity and exhaustiveness, accrue to it precisely because it separates off the mechanical play of signs, to the advantage of the order of ideas (AT X, 371–372; CSM I, 15–16). Descartes gives "rules" only in a sense which is extremely restricted and on the whole paradoxical: the Cartesian rule subjects the mind to no code of instructions, to no mechanical and symbolic instrument. Instead it goes much further: it teaches the mind that the exclusion of all such apparatus is the only way in which the mind can succeed in owing its direction only to itself.

We have attepted to locate, on both of the edges of the frontier separating them, the marks of the incompatibility of language and machine for Descartes. Descartes says that a machine, no matter how complicated, cannot acquire speech. Could a language be devised that was so regular that it could authorize the mechanical performance[20] of the production of grammatically well-formed statements? Descartes does not say. One cannot see why he would deny the possibility. It would not entail that human use of this language in appropriately spoken speech could be imitated by a machine. But Descartes does not say, probably because this question has no interest for him. What interests him instead is the performance of the act of thinking by the mind. What is spoken interests him only as an expression of that performance. In this way Descartes maintains the separation between machines (which encode and communicate differences, but which neither speak nor learn) and language, whose horizon is the grammarless language which would take no trouble to learn and permit the learning of everything of which the mind is capable—the language which would be the natural writing of thought. Human language, in the common tongues which are far from this horizon or limit, must be and can be learned, without exaggerated difficulties. They can be learned only by men, that is by substantial composites of soul and body. So machines (including those machines which are beasts) and language never meet: they belong to different domains of objects and to distinct orders of knowledge. This shows the point at which reference to Descartes, whether by cyberneticians or by linguists like Chomsky, rests on misunderstanding: these people all reason within the framework of an *episteme* in which, to the contrary, machine and language are inseparable. In devoting themselves to *Knowledge Engineering* or applied artificial intelligence, to *Computational Approaches of Learning* or cognitive sciences, to *Parallel Programming* or generative linguistics, our contemporaries are in fact exploring the field that Descartes excludes from his sight. The author of the *Meditations* makes indulgent fun, in the Sixth Replies, of those so opinionated in maintaining their prejudice (that everything occurs in beasts as in us) that they would rather strip themselves of their own thought than of this opinion when they have been shown that beasts are machines (AT VII, 427; CSM II, 288). Our *episteme* has its postulates, which are not, to be sure, simple "prejudices." The problem today becomes manifest when our contemporaries are shown that machines can "answer" questions, and even "learn" to do so: many of them have lost the sense that unless they abandon the opinion that these things take place in us and in machines in the same way, they will be forced to strip themselves of their own thought.

Notes

1. See *Passions of the Soul,* a. 8: AT XI, 333; CSM I, 331, and the letter to More of 5 February 1649: AT V, 278; CSMK, 366, for the "mechanical and corporeal principle." See *Discourse* V, passim; *Treatise on Man:* AT XI, 120; CSM I, 99; and *Passions of the Soul,* a. 2: AT XI, 328; CSM I, 328, for "functions of the body."

2. We question the validity of E. Gilson's amazing formula: "Since Descartes's man-machine can speak without its soul doing anything, there is no *a priori* impossibility that beasts should do it as well" (*Linguistique et Philosophie* [Paris, 1969], 111).

3. AT V, 278; CSMK, 366. Latin: *vera loquela uteretur. . . .*

4. AT V, 278; CSMK, 366. Latin: *eam loquelam. . . .*

5. Respectively, AT VI, 57 (CSM I, 140); AT IV, 574 (CSMK, 303); AT V, 278 (CSMK, 366).

6. Respectively, AT IV, 575 (CSMK, 303); AT VI, 58 and 57 (CSM I, 140); AT V, 278 (CSMK, 366). Latin: *nobis significant. . . .* See also AT I, 76 and 81; CSMK, 10 and 13.

7. AT X, 413; CSM I, 41. Latin: *omnibus rerum sensibilium differentiis exprimendis. . . .*

8. AT X, 414; CSM I, 41. Latin: *motuum diversitates . . . in aere designari. . . .*

9. Respectively, AT X, 413, 414, and 402; CSM I, 41 and 34.

10. AT XI, 176; CSM I, 106. See also *Principles of Philosophy* IV, a. 198.

11. AT XI, 143; CSM I, 102. Concerning memory, see AT XI, 178 (and fig. 30); CSM I, 107.

12. For a stimulating sketch of the history of punched cards, see P. Morrison and E. Morrison, eds., *Charles Babbage and his Calculating Engines* (New York, 1961), xxxiii–xxxv.

13. G. G. Granger, *La Raison* (Paris, 1970); J. Vuillemin, *Mathematiques et Métaphysique chez Descartes* (Paris, 1960), 31 and 34; D. Dubarle, "La notion cartésienne de quantité de mouvement," in *L'aventure de la science, Mélanges Alexandre Koyré* (Paris, 1964); and J.-L. Marion, *Sur l'ontologie grise de Descartes* (Paris, 1975), 119 and 123.

14. See Claude Shannon and Warren Weaver (*The Mathematical Theory of Communication*): information transmitted by a source is proportional to difficulty of precise prediction; that is, it may be defined as the measure of a message's unpredictability. The classical concept of probability therefore appears in Shannon's formula

$$I = \Sigma_i p_i \log p_i,$$

where the p_i are the probabilities of the different possible sequences of signals.

15. G. Canguilhem has demonstrated this in *La formation du concept de réflexe aux XVIIe et XVIIIe siècles* (Paris, 1955; revised, Paris, 1977).

16. The French terms are, respectively, *l'insensé, le stupide,* and *l'hébété.* On the precise meaning of these terms see M. Foucault, *Histoire de la Folie à l'âge classique* (new edition, Paris, 1972).

17. See AT X, 417–424; CSM I, 43–48; and *Principles* I, a. 74.

18. AT X, 365; CSM I, 12; and Leibniz, *Fragments et Opuscules,* ed. Couturat, 28.

19. Géraud de Cordemoy, *Discours physique de la parole* (Paris 1666). (New edition based on the edition of 1704: Paris, 1968), 15.

20. In the sense of S. Jevons, in his celebrated article "On the Mechanical Performance of Logical Inference," *Philosophical Transactions,* 1870.

Bibliography

Canguilhem, G. *La formation du concept de réflexe aux XVIIe et XVIIIe siècles.* Paris, 1955. Revised edition, Paris, 1977.

Chomsky, N. *Cartesian Linguistics.* New York, 1966.

Cooper, David E. "Innateness: Old and New." *Philosophical Review* 81 (October 1972): 465–483.

Cordemoy, Géraud de. *Six Discours sur la distinction et l'union du corps et de l'ame.* Paris, 1666. Paris: Clair-Girbal, 1958.

Costabel, P. *Démarches originales de Descartes savant.* Paris, 1982.

Drach, Margaret. "The Creative Aspect of Chomsky's Use of the Notion of Creativity." *Philosophical Review* 90 (January 1981).

Gunderson, Keith. "Descartes, La Mettrie, Language and Machines." *Philosophy* 39 (1964).

Heil, John. "Speechless Brutes." *Philosophy and Phenomenological Research* 42 (March 1982).

Hooker, M., ed. *Descartes: Critical and Interpretive Essays.* Baltimore: The Johns Hopkins University Press, 1978.

Leibniz, G. *Opuscles et Fragments.* Ed. Couturat. Paris, 1905.

Livet, P. "Le Traitement de l'information dans le *Traité des Passions*." *Revue philosophique* 103 (1978).

Nardi, A. "La luce e la favola del Mondo." *Annali dell'Instituto di Filosofia* 3 (Firenze, 1981).

Pariente, J.-C. *L'Analyse du langage à Port-Royal*. Paris, 1985.

Piatelli-Palmarini, M., ed. *Théories du Langage, Théories de l'Apprentissage*. Paris, 1979.

Rosenfield, L. C. *From Beast-Machine to Man-Machine*. New York: Oxford University Press, 1941.

Rodis-Lewis, G. *L'Anthropologie cartésienne*. Paris: Presses Universitaires de France, 1990.

Serres, M. "L'évidence, la vision et le tact." *Etudes philosophiques* (1968).

Stich, Stephen P. "What Every Speaker Knows." *Philosophical Review* 80 (October 1971).

Yolton, J. "Perceptual Cognition with Descartes." *Studia Cartesiana* 2 (Amsterdam, 1981).

III

CARTESIAN SCIENCE: ITS RHETORIC, PRINCIPLES, AND FRUITS

14

Whatever Should We Do with Cartesian Method?—Reclaiming Descartes for the History of Science

John A. Schuster

The Cult of Method in the History of Science and Cartesian Studies

Until relatively recently, interpretations of the Scientific Revolution have tended to be dominated by heroic tales of the discovery, perfection and application of the scientific method. Descartes, Bacon, Galileo, Harvey, Huygens and Newton were singularly successful in persuading posterity, historians of science included, that they contributed to the invention of a single, transferable and efficacious scientific method. The earliest systematic studies of the history and philosophy of science, the writings of d'Alembert, Priestley, Whewell and Comte, attempted to distill from the historical progress of science a sense of that method, so that its further perfection and wider application could insure the future growth of the sciences.[1] Earlier in this century, pioneer professional historians of science, such as George Sarton and Charles Singer, saw the elucidation of the scientific method as one of the chief functions of the study of the history of science.[2] Subsequently, a thriving subdiscipline of the history of science concerned itself with the history of methodological ideas in (supposed) relation to the larger course of the history of science,[3] and later Karl Popper, Imre Lakatos and their followers sought to revive the link between theorizing about the purported scientific method and rewriting a "method-centric" history of science.[4]

The treatment of Descartes's method by historians of science and historians of philosophy has been no exception to this pattern. The *Discours de la méthode* has been seen as one of the most important methodological treatises in the Western intellectual tradition, and Cartesian method has been viewed as doubly successful and significant within that tradition. First, Descartes's method has been taken to mark an early stage in that long maturation of the scientific method resulting from interaction between application of method in scientific work and critical reflection about method carried out by great methodologists, from Bacon and Descartes down to Popper and Lakatos.

Second, Descartes's considerable achievements in the sciences and in mathematics during a crucial stage of the Scientific Revolution of the seventeenth century have been taken to have depended upon his method.

The aim of much research on Cartesian method is serious, scholarly, "apologetic" exegesis: the analysis and explanation of how and why Descartes's well-omened methodological enterprise came to pass. Just as all Christian apologists believe in God, so apologists for Cartesian method agree on the basic aim of elucidating, historically and philosophically, what was in principle and in practice a triumph of an efficacious method. To be sure, differences over minor points of interpretation and emphasis have arisen. Just as Christian apologists differ over points of biblical exegesis, so, as I have argued elsewhere, apologists for Cartesian method fall into broad camps: there are naive literalists, sophisticated hermeneutical exegetes, and those whose belief takes a dry skeptical turn.[5]

This paper is motivated by some news which will probably be unwelcome among method cultists: we now have excellent grounds for being "atheists" about method. Although the message has not yet spread very widely, some historians, philosophers and sociologists of science have established that no doctrine of method, whether Descartes's or anybody else's, ever has guided and constituted the actualities of scientific practice—conceptual and material—in the literal ways that such methods proclaim for themselves.[6] From this perspective it follows that apologetic scholarship directed to Descartes's method is misguided, not so much in its separable scholarly detail, but certainly in its view of science, of method, and of their intertwined histories. And it further follows that insofar as biographical writing about Descartes is a function of the larger historiographies of method and of science, it too requires reformation.

As a historian of science of this peculiarly atheistical bent, my intention is to reclaim Descartes as a demystified object of study in my field. Since the cult of method and the apologetic Cartesian scholarship block that possibility, I seek the tools of demystification within those developments in the historiography of science and the related field of sociology of scientific knowledge just mentioned.

My argument will proceed as follows: First, we locate the grounds of modern "atheism" about method in the history of science in the writings of Koyré, Kuhn and Bachelard. Following a brief outline of the "core" of Descartes's methodological claims, we examine an example of demethodologized, "post-Kuhnian" analysis of Cartesian scientific practice. We then analyze method doctrines, Descartes's included, utilizing the previous example and demonstrating how the discursive structures of method theories guarantee their lack of efficacy *and* their creation of literary illusions of that very efficacy. With that model of discursive structure and dynamics in hand, we turn to the issue of some of the micropolitical and rhetorical functions of Cartesian-method discourse. The paper concludes with an account of Descartes's early career, premised upon our post-Kuhnian findings about the nature of method and its roles in the history of science.

Toward Methodological Atheism: Koyré, Bachelard and Kuhn on the History of Science

It is becoming increasingly clear to some historians and sociologists of science that the traditional belief in the existence of a single, transferable, efficacious scientific method is highly dubious. The work of Alexandre Koyré, Gaston Bachelard, and Thomas S. Kuhn especially pointed in this direction, although only lately have their insights been followed up in attempts to revise the "believer's" historiography of method.

Although Koyré firmly believed in scientific progress, he did not consider it the product of applying a general scientific method. Rather, for Koyré, progress depended on the adoption of appropriate metaphysical presuppositions and the pursuit of science within them. His classic example was Galileo's mechanics, which, he argued, owed nothing to any methodological achievement, but issued from Galileo's brilliance in working and arguing his case within the framework of a loosely Platonic, mathematical metaphysics. Similarly, Aristotelian physics had not failed for lack of a method, but largely because it had had the wrong conceptual presuppositions, ones too close to untutored commonsense about motion.[7] The point for Koyré was that a general, transferable method is neither necessary nor sufficient for the pursuit of science. "No science has ever started with a treatise on method and progressed by the application of such an abstractly derived method," Koyré intoned, commenting on the *Discours*, and at least some historians of science have tended, correctly, to agree.[8]

Bachelard's early work slightly pre-dated that of Koyré, and seems to have been subtly refracted in the thinking of both Koyré and Kuhn. In this process Bachelard's skepticism about method was not brought to the fore, and even with the wider dissemination of his writings over the past twenty years, the implications of his work for undermining the cult of method have not been sufficiently articulated. However, those implications are quite clear in the core of his work.

For Bachelard, each field of science consists in a set of interlinked, mathematicized concepts which interact dialectically with the instrumentalities through which the concepts are objectified and materialized.[9] To paraphrase Bachelard, the meaning of a concept must include the technical conditions of its material realization.[10] When a science is created, an artificial technical realm comes into being, in which phenomena are literally manufactured under the joint guidance of the system of mathematicized concepts and the instruments and experimental hardware in which those concepts have been realized. In an ironic jibe at positivist dogma, Bachelard termed any such realm of theoretically dominated artificial experience a "*phénoméno-technique,*" thus signifying that the phenomena of science are not discovered but made, not natural but artificial, being created and commanded in the light of theory and theory-loaded instruments. In Bachelard's view, therefore, each science is unique and self-contained; each has its own specific system of concepts and related instrumental armory. No single, transferable, general scientific method can explain the genesis of any science or its contents and dynamics.

Kuhn, too, can hardly be said to have focused on the demystification of method in his theoretical or historical writings. But, as with Koyré and Bachelard, there is in Kuhn a clear denial of the role traditionally ascribed to method, and that denial relates directly to the major premises of his position. In effect, Kuhn's approach vastly strengthened Koyré's assertion that grand set-piece doctrines of method are irrelevant to the practice of the sciences. The key point did not reside in Kuhn's conception of "scientific revolutions," but rather was implicit in his view of routine, "normal," "puzzle-solving" research within a "paradigm."

As is well known, a Kuhnian paradigm is that entire discipline-specific culture which at a given time governs cognition, action, and evaluation within a given mature field of scientific inquiry. For Kuhn a paradigm consists first of all in a "metaphysics," a set of deep conceptual presuppositions, which need not be of Koyré's Platonic type. A paradigm also contains the central concepts and law sketches of the field, and all the instrumental hardware and experimental procedures considered relevant to the posing and solving of problems within the paradigm. Kuhn stresses the theory-loading, or, more precisely, the paradigm-loading of the instruments and procedures. Standards and norms for the adequate use of instruments and procedures are also part of the paradigm, being inherent in the theoretical and craft training necessary to become proficient in paradigm-based research. One learns these and other parts of the paradigm through a course of practice on piecemeal, already solved problems—paradigms in the narrow sense (later designated "exemplars"), bearing some relation to Bachelard's *phénoméno-techniques*. There is also a negotiable pecking order of unsolved problems and their correspondingly negotiable degrees of "significance" or "anomalousness," which forms a resource for selecting, shaping, and evaluating courses of research and their results.[11]

Assuming that such paradigms, or anything like them, guide normal research in the various sciences, it then becomes highly unlikely that some single method guides the history of the sciences, individually or collectively. The elements making up a particular paradigm, and hence making possible a particular tradition of research, are unique to that field and are a sufficient basis for its practice. Moreover, if each field has such a unique and self-contained conceptual fabric and associated mode of practice, then it is irrelevant to our understanding of its cognitive dynamics to redescribe, gloss, or otherwise "account" for them by the use of heroic tales of method. This point also holds for *all* the sciences existing at any moment. Each has its own particular paradigm, and while neighboring or cognate fields might share certain paradigm elements in common, there is no reason to assume, as methodological accounts must, that there is some identity or long-term convergence among paradigms.

The radical antimethodism which can be extracted from Kuhn's position is illustrated in Figure 14.1. Any given field of science has at any given moment

CONCEPTS (C)	METAPHYSICS (M)	TOOLS (T)
STANDARDS (S)	AIMS (A)	EXEMPLARS (E)

Figure 14.1

its own paradigm, its own versions of the generic elements displayed in the matrix: (1) basic concepts and law sketches; (2) metaphysics; (3) tools and instrumentalities (including the theories and standards thereof); (4) standards of relevance and of adequacy for the selection of problems and for the formulation and evaluation of knowledge claims; (5) disciplinary goals of any internally or externally generated sort; and (6) concrete achievements, exemplars, instantiating laws, concepts, and standards.

At any given moment the domain of the sciences may then be presented as in Figure 14.2, where we have n *sui generis* fields, each with its own particular constellation of matrix elements, constituting for the time being its own paradigm. The sciences are thus many, not one. True, neighboring and cognate fields may share certain elements in common; concepts in one field may be taken up (under translation) as tools in another; or groups of fields may have emerged under the aegis of a common metaphysical umbrella. But none of this argues the identity or even the long-term convergence among paradigms.

In Kuhnian terms each field has its own "method(s)," inextricable from the contents and dynamics of its paradigm at that moment. But to speak of some putatively common, transferable, efficacious scientific method or epistemology—Baconian, Cartesian, Newtonian, Popperian—is merely to float above the lived, thought, and practiced life of each of the sciences, and fallaciously to substitute an externally prompted discourse for the dense cultures of the several paradigms. There are, in short, no unified and literally applicable methods. No method discourse corresponds to or maps onto any given domain of scientific practice, let alone a number of such domains.

Recent work in the sociology of scientific knowledge has deepened all these claims, by in effect unfreezing Kuhn's metaphor of routine puzzle solving, and suggesting that even in normal research there is a constant, subtle revision and negotiation of the elements in the paradigm.[12] This is because normal research always involves bids to make small, but significant, alterations in the prevailing disciplinary objects of inquiry. Such bids exert feedback effects on some of the elements of the paradigm—conceptual, instrumental, evaluative—if they are successful. So, normal science may be puzzle solving, but it is a peculiar version of that activity, because the pieces, the rules of assembly and the ultimate "picture" keep changing as the players play and negotiate.[13] And, if disciplinary method is inextricable from a particular paradigm, now it is also in flux, inextricable from the socio-cognitive dynamics of the field. Again, no general doctrine of method can command or describe this situation.

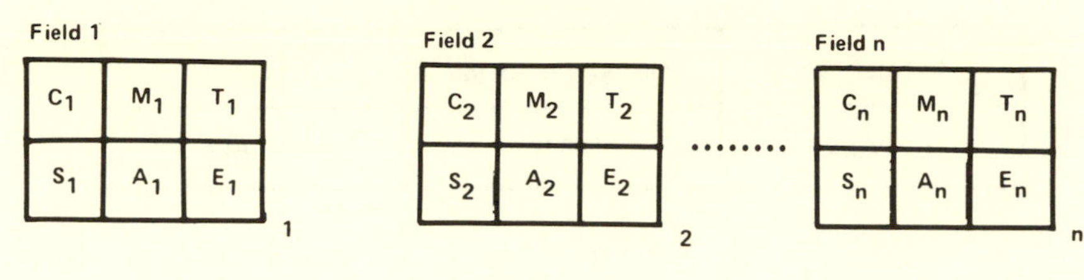

Figure 14.2

Indeed, the post-Kuhnian case against method does not stop here. Increasingly historians and sociologists of science are examining the social and political organization of normal fields and communities. If a field is not in the grip of a total and immobilizing consensus (until the next "revolution"), and if "significant" research is always a negotiated outcome subtly altering the state of disciplinary play, then a normal field must have a social and political life sufficient for the carrying out of these knowledge-making and knowledge-breaking maneuvers, and for keeping them, most of the time, within the accounted realm of the "nonrevolutionary" (hence, acceptable and "noncranky"). Accordingly, attention has shifted to the micro-sociology and micro-politics of scientific specialty groups to see how they manage, negotiate, refine, accept, and reject bids to modify the paradigm, that is, bids to have accomplished significant results. In this view the method of a discipline is not simply identified with its own particular paradigm, but further with the political and social structure and dynamics of the specialist community. The construction of scientific knowledge cannot be explained apart from the social processes in and through which that activity takes place.[14] So, again, no invocation of a general method can explain the manufacture and transformation of knowledge by paradigm-bearing and paradigm-negotiating communities, including the historically contingent sociopolitical structures of those communities. Method discourse abstracts from and floats above the proper cognitive and social complexity of scientific fields, and so it misses everything that now appears to be of importance in understanding the dynamics of the sciences.

The Koyré-Bachelard-Kuhn debunking of method offers both opportunities and pitfalls to the historian of science, including the historian of Cartesian science. Before we can explore these we need to establish what, in the remainder of this essay, will be meant by the term "Cartesian method."

Understanding the Core of Descartes's Method Discourse

The core of Descartes's method, his central methodological claims, is to be found in the *Discours* and in the *Regulae ad Directionem Ingenii,* where Descartes offers formal, systematized versions of his method. As I have argued elsewhere, this core of Descartes's method discourse, offered in Regulae II through XI and in the *Discours,* consists in three fundamental premises.[15]

(1) All rationally obtainable truths subsist in a network of deductive linkages, and this is the meaning of the unity of the sciences. (This will henceforth be termed Descartes's "latticework" vision of the unity of the sciences.)

(2) As rational beings, humans possess two divinely given faculties for the attainment of truth: the power of intuiting individual truths, and the power of deducing valid links between them.

(3) A single mind, exercising intuition and deduction, could in principle traverse the entire latticework; but some help is required in the form of practical hints or suggestions, heuristic rules, to aid in the preparation of inquiries, the ordering of inquiries, and the checking up after inquiries.

Therefore, there are two complementary moments or aspects within the statement of the rules of the method. First, there is a doctrine of truth. On the one hand, it informs us of what we presumably already know—that we can intuit and deduce truths. On the other hand, it adduces some negative heuristic advice from this fact: trust not in any authority, nor in unclear, indistinct belief, will or emotion; avoid precipitation and hasty judgment; go only as far as intuition and deduction reveal the truth. All this is essentially contained in rule 1 of the *Discours* and Regulae III and IV. Second, there is an open-ended set of heuristic rules, initially gathered from easy excursions around parts of the latticework of knowledge. These are contained in part in rules 2, 3, and 4 of the *Discours* and Regulae V to XI. We shall look at some of these later.

In the *Regulae,* as compared to the *Discours,* we meet an elaborate explication of the vision of the latticework of rational truths, an explication that is crucial in understanding Descartes's method claims about specific cases of scientific and mathematical practice. Descartes tells us in Regula VI that the logical chains of truths consist in "absolute" terms linked to a "series" of "relative" terms through a greater or smaller number of rationally specifiable "relations [*respectus*]." Absolute terms are the initial terms in particular deductive series, and they are themselves relative to a small set of what might be termed "absolutely absolute terms." Relative terms, properly so called, are those occurring further down deductive series. In some degree they "share the same nature" as their antecedents, the absolutes; but they also involve complex conditioning factors or "relations." Relatives are distanced from their absolute to the degree that they contain more "mutually dependent relations subordinated one to another."[16]

This sketch of the core will aid our later analysis of the discursive structure and function of Descartes's method discourse.

An Example of Post-Kuhnian Historiography of Science: Descartes's Construction of the Law of Refraction and its Methodological Fairy Tale

Koyré, Bachelard, Kuhn, and the post-Kuhnian sociologists of scientific knowledge offer historians of science the opportunity to reconstruct courses of scientific practice free from overriding fairy tales about the literal efficacy of scientific method. Certainly no progress can be made in understanding the natural philosophical career of Descartes and his place in the Scientific Revolution, unless we learn to explicate his science independently of his fable of method. We will examine an example of the distance between Cartesian method rhetoric and an arguably quite plausible reconstruction of one course of his scientific practice. This exercise in reconstruction will later serve as a building block for our attempt to grasp the structure and dynamics of Descartes's (or anyone else's) method discourse.

Our example concerns Descartes's discovery or construction of the law of refraction of light, Snel's law, and his attempt to explain the law by means of a mechanical theory of light. That theory states that light is a mechanical impulse of variable "force" transmitted instantaneously through continuous optical media. This greatest of Descartes's scientific achievements has long been the subject of mythical explanation, starting predictably with Descartes himself. In Regula VIII he gives an account of how both the law and the theory could have been discovered using the method, although he uses the subjunctive mood and does not actually claim to have done it this way.[17] In Descartes's story application of the method amounts to the sagacious posing of a series of heuristic questions for research against the background of the core method doctrines mentioned earlier. The answers to the questions unfold the best course of research to be followed, surely a sound sense of method as heuristic aid.

The first step is to see that the discovery of the law will depend on the relationship between the angle of incidence and the angle of refraction. At this point, Descartes observes, a mathematician must give up the search, for all he can do is assume some relation and work out the consequences. The method shows that the problem depends on knowledge of physics as well, for the relation of the two angles depends in some way on the manner in which light actually passes through media. But the answer to that question is seen to depend on the more general issue of "what is the action of light?", and the answer to that in turn supposedly depends on the answer to the ultimate question of "what is a natural power?" We must, by a "mental intuition," determine what this "absolute nature" is. (In fact, we know it will turn out to be mechanical action—impulse or pressure; but, God, literally, knows how we arrive at that intuition.) In any case, having intuited this basic "nature," we then proceed back down the chain of questions, "deducing" the more relative natures from the less relative ones. We may stall somewhere along this route, for example, in trying to deduce the nature of light from the nature of natural powers in general. In that case, we proceed by analogy; but, again, we know that we are not to worry, for the analogies can only be to other forms of mechanical action, and that narrows the field quite a bit. Ultimately this synthesis leads, through a theory of light, to the law of refraction. In the *Dioptrique* of 1637 Descartes presents a model for the theory of light: he talks of tennis balls rather than impulses, and he pretends to deduce the law of refraction from the central elements of the model and his principles of motion.

Leaving this story aside, what can the skeptical post-Kuhnian historian of science say about how Descartes may have come to construct the law of refraction and devise the model and the theory? My view of this is that he did it by being in the first instance a good practitioner of traditional geometrical optics, by working, that is, well within the paradigm of that field. The law was constructed by using data and principles available within the traditions of the field. The key principle used concerned the location of images of bodies seen under refraction. It assumed that the images of point sources could be determined on the basis of the behavior of one ray only. Interestingly, this assumption had been seriously threatened in the new theory of vision of Kepler, published in 1604, which Descartes had read, at least in parts. So, according to my reconstruction, in 1626–27 Descartes, using nothing better than the traditional (cooked) data and this very possibly obsolete principle, constructed the law in a trigonometric form somewhat different from that we use today. With the law to hand, he then moved to cover it with a mechanical theory.[18]

To understand how he constructed his mechanical theory, we have to recall first of all that since 1619 Descartes had been largely committed to a corpuscular-mechanical ontology, and that he had dabbled with a qualitative mechanical theory of light at that time. This early qualitative theory contained assumptions that would have hindered rather than facilitated the search for the law. What seems to have happened was this: having found the law by traditional means, Descartes acted in the light of his most basic scientific commitments, to wit, that the world is basically micromechanical, and that macroscopic mathematical regularities must bespeak underlying micromechanical causes. He therefore took the ray diagrams in which the law had first been discerned and he literally read into their parameters manifestations of underlying mechanical causes. (Back in 1619–20 he had done the same thing with hydrostatics diagrams from Stevin and optics diagrams from Kepler.) This permitted him to reformulate his old ideas about the mechanical cause of light and to mold his new ideas precisely to fit the diagrams. To cap it all off, he wrote the methodological "cover story" to Regula VIII.[19]

This case illustrates the redundancy of employing methodological stories in attempting to reconstruct courses of scientific practice according to the standards of our post-Kuhnian understanding of science. If we credit the post-Kuhnian story or anything like it, we see that the banalities of Descartes's method story batten on the prior existence of a dense local disciplinary culture of concepts, techniques, goals, and standards—in and through which Descartes worked. Needless to say, in a post-Kuhnian universe of historical discourse, the same points should apply to the reconstruction of every passage of scientific practice in which Descartes engaged.

The Structure of Method Discourses (Descartes's Included)

The sort of post-Kuhnian debunking of method just illustrated certainly helps liberate us from the myth of method in the history of science. However, it entails certain difficulties. For example, it suggests that methodologists must be cynics or fools: cynics for advocating doctrines of method which they know are ineffective; or fools for failing to grasp the wisdom of the post-Kuhnian critique of method. But this clearly will not do. It hardly suits historians of science weaned on Butterfield's *The Whig Interpretation of History* uncharitably to invent a new whiggish hagiography/demonology of their own discipline. So the question becomes "how can we understand the existence of honest and rational believers in method?" This problem first stimulated my own work on method, centering on the question of how it can possibly be that throughout the history of science, methodologists and their audiences have often genuinely believed in the efficacy of method doctrines which we post-Kuhnians "know" cannot have worked. In short, what is it about systematic method doctrines that sustains their plausibility to believers?

My answer, developed initially in an attempt to facilitate historical research on Descartes, is this:[20] All systematic method doctrines are examples of a determinate species of discourse. The species is characterized by the presence of a certain discursive structure common to all instances of the type. This structure is such that it necessarily defeats the ability of any methodology to accomplish what it literally announces itself to be able to accomplish. At the same time, this same discursive structure sustains a set of literary effects tending to create the illusion that the method in question can indeed accomplish what it claims to be able to do. In other words, all set-piece method doctrines have the same underlying discursive structure which explains their lack of efficacy as well as their ability to create the literary effect that they are efficacious.

Before we look at this structure and its characteristic effects, we must, however, remind ourselves of the fact that all method doctrines encountered in the Western tradition from Aristotle to Popper and beyond are structured around two intertwined metaphors: (1) to acquire knowledge is a matter of establishing a correct subjective grasp, or more typically, vision, of independently existing, objective objects of knowledge; (2) method, drawing on the literal Greek meaning of the term, is the subject's "way through" to the objects of knowledge, a set of prescriptions as to the path to be followed by the subject in the pursuit of knowledge. All particular method doctrines are attempts to explicate the key metaphors. Indeed, the history of method doctrines is in large measure the history of various and competing attempts to dress these notions in conceptual vestments deemed appropriate to each methodologist's perception of the context of debate and structure of sociocognitive relevances holding in his time and place.[21] Typically, a new doctrine is fabricated out of bits of older method doctrines, as well as pieces of neighboring varieties of discourse—theological, natural philosophical, ethical, mathematical, psychological, and so on.

Let us now turn to the generic structure of method discourses (Figure 14.3). Any and all systematic method doctrines consist of and operate on three interacting levels of discourse. Level I is that of explicit, "systematized" discourse

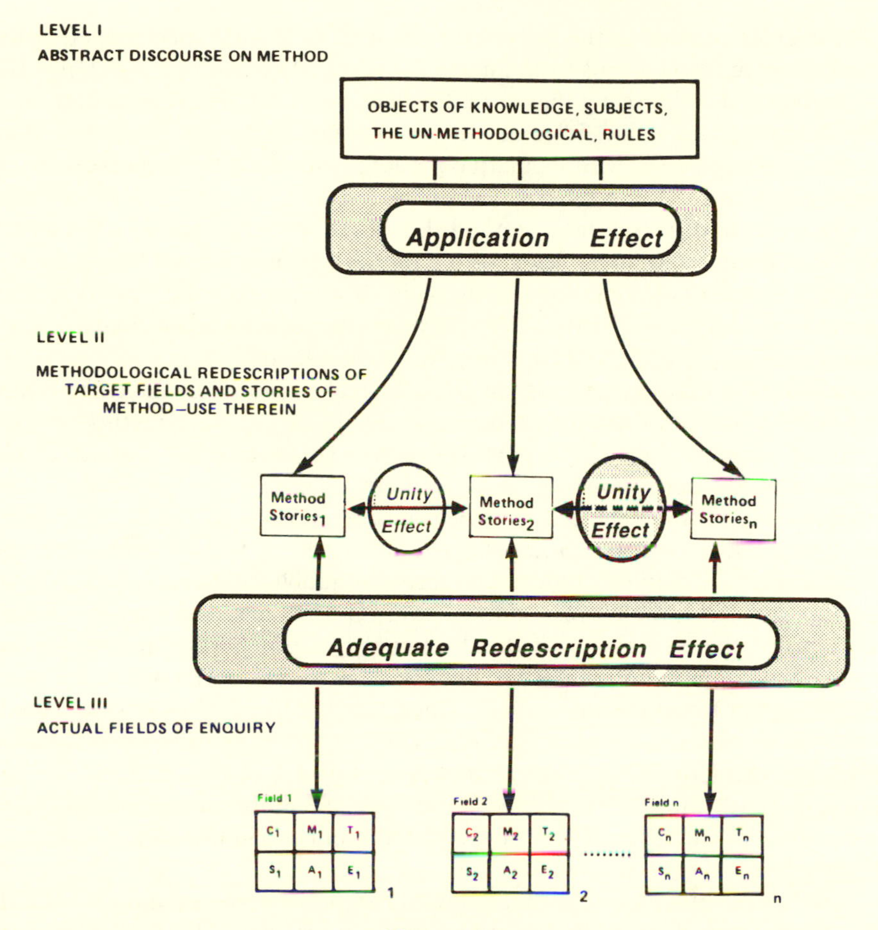

Figure 14.3

about the core of any given method doctrine. In any particular method doctrine Level I will consist in (1) generalized (nondiscipline specific) statements of the rules of that method, and (2) explicit, more or less systematized, abstract, and generalized discourse concerning the canonical themes, "knowing subjects" and "objects of knowledge," and how the rules help them to get together. There is typically present also (3) some discourse on the "pitfalls," "obstacles," and "sources of error" which can deflect a subject, mask or distort the objects, or lead to misapplication of the rules. Sometimes Level I is itself packaged within a metaphysical or even theological framework.

In Descartes's method we have already discussed this Level I core, as presented in the *Discours* and *Regulae*. It includes his teaching concerning intuition and deduction, the conception of the latticework with its intertwined concepts of absolutes, relatives, series, and relations, and, in addition, the statement of the rules of the method.[22]

Level III consists in the domain of scientific fields and specialties that the method in question claims to command. In Figure 14.3 this domain, Level III, is represented by inserting Figure 14.2, which, we recall, is a representation of the domain of scientific fields at any given time, each field viewed in post-Kuhnian perspective, with its unique paradigm signified by a matrix of paradigm contents.

In the case of Descartes's method, Level III should be thought to contain all the scientific traditions, fields, or disciplines because they all fall within the claimed scope of the method, along with all mathematical disciplines, and, indeed, all domains of rational inquiry, as opposed to those controlled by faith. We have already looked at one such target field, optics.

Level II consists of a set of "methodological versions" of the corresponding fields of inquiry represented on Level III. Here one finds methodological accounts or stories which purport to describe or capture the essence of the practice of the corresponding Level III fields. These stories or accounts are structured in terms of the elements provided by Level I, by the core discourse on "subjects," "objects," and rules characteristic of the particular method discourse in question. Such stories or accounts analytically proceed as follows: the "target" field, the corresponding Level III field, is redescribed or glossed in terms of the elements provided by Level I of this particular method discourse, and an account or story of practice is woven by reference to a subject (conceived in Level I terms) applying the rules within the glossed field. Hence Level II stories and accounts can only exist in so far as they are shaped by deployment of the conceptual resources of Level I of that method. In any given method, the stories on Level II are specific, episodic unfoldings of the conceptual resources provided on Level I as elements in the core discourse of the method.

In the case of Descartes's method we have just met one example of a Level II methodological story corresponding to the target field of optics. This story is couched in terms of the core methodological terms and rules available on Level I of Descartes's discourse on method.[23]

The Literary Effects of Method Discourses (Descartes's Included)

We can now attack the problem of explaining how method discourses, Descartes's included, succeed in creating literary effects of efficacy while in fact being structurally incapable of doing what they literally claim to be able to do. The first point to grasp is that the seduction of a historical actor is greatly facilitated if he or she is a member of a culture in which "scientific method" is generally believed to exist, in practice or in principle. Early Modern figures, such as Bacon and Descartes, moved in an intellectual culture permeated by this belief: the in-principle existence of efficacious methods of discovery and proof in mathematics and the sciences was largely unquestioned (except by some skeptics). The task was to devise and enforce *the* "correct" general method. In my view, the structural study of the dynamics of method discourse always must be joined to social historical and biographical enquiry into the expectations, aims, and discursive resources concerning method available to and/or enforced upon actors in their particular historical circumstances. Analytically speaking, there is the historical problem of explaining the construction or selection of a method by an actor, and then there is the general problem of explaining how a method discourse functions upon an actor, once he is "inside" it. In the case of Descartes, how and why he formulated his particular method is a historical problem; how his method could be sterile and yet appear not to be is a structural problem it shares with other method doctrines. How and why Descartes could believe in such a method is a function of both enquiries taken together.

Let us now examine the reasonable appearance of efficacy generated by method discourses. The key to the mythological operation of Descartes's or anybody else's method discourse resides in getting the audience, potential reasonable believers, operating on Level II. Recall our case study of Cartesian optical practice and its corresponding methodological tale. According to our new terminology, there is a Level III field of scientific practice and a corresponding Level II methodological account of this target field. Descartes's methodological tale about optics eviscerates and suppresses the specific content and dynamics of his practice in optics, the target field, while the tale itself is spun out of the Level I cloth of core discourse about rules, series, absolutes, relatives, and so on. In fact Descartes's method tale is inscribed by those two processes: (1) the suppression of the real content of optics; and (2) the fabular rendition of the core discourse as a Level II story to replace that content as the methodologically sound "essence" of the target field. However, although post-Kuhnian mythologists of method know all this, historical actors living in a culture of method most probably do not, for they, *ex hypothesi,* most likely have virtually no discursive resources for explicating and accounting for successful practice in a discipline other than those offered by some method discourse or other. Such a "believer" is likely to miss the slide between Level III and the method accounts on Level II; indeed, he might not even be aware of it since "method talk" is his preferred (or only) way of thematizing practice.[24] Once on Level II, however, he is likely to be impressed by the way the Level II account (1) "applies" the rules of the method (and generally articulates the core concepts of the method), while (2) (apparently) constituting an adequate account of what the disciplinary practice is about.

Therefore, when a reader or listener is confronted with a Level II redescription or story of rule-following, he is in danger of succumbing to two structurally produced literary effects characteristic of systematic method discourses. First, he may be taken in by the *adequate redescription effect,* producing the illusion that Level II redescriptions are in any sense adequate to Level III contents and practices. Second, he may be taken in by the *application effect,* producing the illusion that the application of the rules in the Level II story is (or could be) the application of the rules to the practice of the target field (Level III). These effects are structural in the sense that they are made possible and are sustained by the relationships among the three levels of discourse. That structural arrangement also explains, as we have seen, why a method discourse, such as Descartes's, must be inadequate and ineffective in real practice. In an appropriate cultural environment its upper two levels marginalize or displace the discursive thematizing of the Level III field as such, and pose in its place a desiccated phantom of its actual structure and practice. The phantom, the Level II account, is solidified and underwritten by its "obvious" congruence with the grandiose, self-proclaimedly authoritative core discourse on Level I.

These two literary effects are produced by the vertical relations holding among the levels of a method discourse. A third literary effect is created horizontally across Level II. This I term the *unity effect.* Although there is no space to elaborate here, it is obvious that a method discourse such as Descartes's can generate across Level II a range of redescriptions and stories, each one corresponding to a specific target field (see Figure 14.3). For example, I have elsewhere examined Level II method stories corresponding respectively to Descartes's practice of analytical mathematics and the corpuscular-mechanical explanation of magnetism.[25] Each Level II redescription or story will of course be couched in terms of Level I elements, and will involve an account of the application of the rules of the method to the redescribed field. Hence, within a given method discourse all such Level II accounts will appear to be similar. For example, Descartes's three Level II stories about optics, magnetism, and mathematics all involve tales of absolutes, relatives, series, and the rules. I have argued that this pleasing resemblance among Level II stories is productive of the unity effect, the illusion that the terms and rules of the method are applicable across some set of fields of inquiry. But, where a believer is impressed by the fact that all of Descartes's Level II stories articulate and use the same core method concepts and the same rules, a post-Kuhnian mythologist of method is unimpressed for two very good reasons. First, as we have seen, this unity is a unity in vacuity, for each Level II account floats loose of its target field (while appearing to appropriate it and grasp its essence). Second, the various Level II accounts often generate quite devastating equivocations. For example, I have shown that Descartes's use of the terms "absolutes" and "relatives" in his mathematics story bears no relation whatsoever to their respective denotations in the optics story.[26]

As in the case of the first two structural effects, the mechanism constituting this third effect also explains why the method cannot actually work in the ways it claims to work: Level II accounts are similar and the rules of the method gear into them *because* these accounts are woven out of Level I discourse; but for that very reason the Level II accounts cannot hope to be adequate glosses of the structure and dynamics of living, Level III fields; they eviscerate those fields in the interests of Level I and still equivocate among themselves.

In general, then, the three literary effects of any methodology relate to each other in this manner: In any method discourse the adequate redescription effect is fundamental, and it ultimately depends on the plausibility of

Level II stories within a cultural context according precedence to the Level I discourse as *the* way of thematizing scientific practice. The application effect depends on the adequate redescription effect, for it fosters the illusion that the application of the rules on Level II is the application of the rules in actual practice. The unity effect results from the iteration of the application effect across the spectrum of fields thought to be commanded by the method in question, and it is facilitated by the fact that Level II entities bear some analogical relations to each other, despite possible equivocations.

There is even a fourth literary effect of method, which I term the *progress effect*. Methodologists can proudly point to progress as the method is "extended"; that is, as new Level II accounts of new target domains are added. Methodologists can also label as progress the revising of existing Level II accounts of old domains in order to grasp and "explain" new developments in those already methodologized fields. "Progress" can also be discerned in the discovery and resolution of certain internal problems set in train by the very structure of the method discourse. Often this takes the form of adding to or revising the rules.

One can conclude that any believer seriously engaged in the business of prescriptive methodology will probably stumble into this hall of discursive effects. The believer will then happily expatiate on the unity, applicability, efficacy, and progress of this method; refine and explicate Level I, the Level II stories, and the rules; castigate other methodologists, and those who do not believe in methodology; and comment on all these matters at ever higher levels of metadiscourse. Like other believers, René Descartes got lost in this hall of discursive effects, only to be followed there by many of his loyal scholars. In order to write the scientific biography of Descartes and to understand his role in the Scientific Revolution, one must leave the hall of effects and subject it to the sort of critique begun here.

The Rhetorical Functions of Cartesian and Other Method Discourses

The skeptical historiographies of Koyré and Kuhn effectively debunk method as having no role in the dynamics of the sciences. We shall now see that our discursive model of method entails that methodologies can play some roles in the formation and negotiation of knowledge claims in science, although they cannot play the definitive roles they claim for themselves. Methods do not capture the (nonexistent) essences of their target fields; but they are certainly rather useful resources in the rhetorical combats and political struggles through which knowledge claims come into being, prosper, and/or die. This section explores these political and rhetorical functions of method and suggests some ways in which they apply to Descartes's work, in the interest of reclaiming him, and his method, for an historiography of science which neither merely debunks method, nor falls victim to its literary effects.

The work of Paul Feyerabend on the rhetorical and propaganda functions of Galileo's and Newton's methodological pronouncements began to point toward the political functions of method discourse in the life of the sciences.[27] His initiative has been extended in an emerging literature within the history and sociology of science that is beginning to capitalize on the post-Kuhnian challenge to explain what method discourse does in the sciences, if it does not and cannot do what had traditionally been claimed for it. Broadly speaking, this new work suggests that method discourses are often deployed as rhetorical weapons in those negotiations and struggles over the framing and evaluation of knowledge claims which go on at all levels of scientific activity, from the laboratory bench, through published texts, to disciplinary debate and its necessarily associated micro-politics of groups and institutions.[28]

Let us first consider what the "rhetorical" function of method discourse means at the level of the formulation of technical arguments and knowledge claims. Some historians of science and sociologists of scientific knowledge plausibly claim that technical scientific arguments, even in published form, are pieces of practical rather than formal reasoning, more akin to legal briefs than to chains of strictly valid inferences. The burden of a scientific argument is, typically, to promote some novel, or revised, claim about the "objects of inquiry" within a given field.[29] To that end various resources may be deployed: appeals are made to theory- and standard-laden data; claims are made about the objects, tools and techniques currently accepted in the field; and, implicitly, at least, field-specific standards of adequacy and relevance guide the assemblage of these resources into a "compelling" but not rigorous argument. Hence, scientific argument, as essentially persuasive argument, may rightly be termed rhetorical in the sense defined by students of "the new rhetoric," denoting the entire field of discursive structures and strategies used to render arguments persuasive in given situations.[30]

Now, all the various doctrines of scientific method, as well as the particular stories derivable from them, form a reservoir of discursive resources available to scientists in the formulation of such essentially rhetorical arguments. Hence, to this extent it is correct to say that methodological doctrines can be *partially* constitutive of knowledge claims in the sciences; that is, in terms of our model, Level I and II method discourse, especially Level II stories, can be deployed on Level III in the cut and thrust of scientific practice, and, hence, in that sense can be said to be partially constitutive of socially negotiated outcomes within the Level III matrices. Methods do not command, explain, or grasp the essence of Level III practice; but they can be deployed on that level as resources in the struggle to establish claims. Historians and sociologists of science have observed that all such rhetorical deployments of method discourses are highly flexible and context dependent, scientists sometimes giving different methodological accounts in different argumentative contexts, and sometimes even contradicting themselves by offering contradictory interpretations of their own methods or those of famous methodologists.[31]

Descartes certainly practiced such rhetorical deployments of method, mobilizing Level II accounts in order partly to constitute knowledge bids he was advancing on Level III. His methodological account in the *Regulae* of the discovery of the law of refraction and of its mechanistic explanation is just such a gambit. The story bears no relation to his "bench practice"; yet, it structures a presentation of his work and so is partly constitutive of it as a knowledge claim proffered to his audience. Moreover, Descartes's method story about his optical work served other subordinate functions in the overall interest of facilitating the acceptance of his claims. First, it occluded the dependence of his actual work on the traditional image principle made dubious by Kepler's findings. Second, it provided a (methodo-)logical connection between the geometrical-optical and mechanistic-explanatory stages in his work. Third, the vagueness of Descartes's methodological language about "natural powers," and his methodological reflections about "analogy"covered what I would contend was, in 1628, real hesitation and ambivalence about the best direction to take in articulating a mechanistic model of light.[32] The method story was a very valuable way of framing, constituting, and presenting his knowledge claims while finessing these secondary problems. When one additionally considers that Descartes probably believed that the work could have been done the way the story tells, the power and utility of the method become very clear. Descartes, one suspects, was probably getting the benefit of his own "just so" story (by virtue of the literary effects), just as his readers were (honestly, rather than cynically) intended to do.

All the foregoing points are based on our model of method discourse. Taken together, they also reinforce and articulate that model, because they allow us to see additional reasons why actors quite reasonably fall for the apparent efficacy and applicability of any method doctrine: for believers in a particular method, any deployment on Level III of its Level II stories will be highly privileged and impressive. These stories will probably be the only resources in play on Level III that label themselves as "methodological." Participants debating and negotiating claims on Level III will generate and hear these method stories as the only elements in the cluttered landscape of debate that are of a methodological character. Hence, believers will see method-talk "in action" as a crucial, or *the* crucial, element in the debate. This will lend more support to the truth of the Level II stories. The stories say "practice proceeds just thus and so," and here is "practice," that is, the social world of the laboratory, conference, published debate, and so on, in which method discourse is a crucial resource in the fray.[33]

Method claims on Level III need not be consensually accepted by all parties and can of course be contested. This can be understood in terms of the recent work in the sociology of science which further establishes that the evaluation and negotiation of knowledge claims is a social and political process, and that any and all of the tools or weapons used in constructing or evaluating a claim can be questioned.[34] The recourse to methodological discourse on Level III is simply one possible tactic in this knowledge-making/knowledge-breaking game, and so deployments of method discourse can become objects of contention within it. Hence, for a contestant like Descartes, not only did particular claims need to be woven out of the sturdy cloth of method discourse, but the method itself, the ultimate legitimating weapon, required support and justification. So, when Descartes presented his optics in terms of his method, he not only tried to legitimate the optics in the ways we have indicated; he was also legitimating the method by the "evidence" of concrete application and success. (The optics case illustrated a text on method, not vice versa.)

All this was particularly important, because the method in turn was going to have to bear the weight of legitimating any and all of his projects. Descartes, like others contending for scientific and natural philosophical preeminence, was not concerned simply with particular claims and arguments. He wanted to group together and package a certain family of results ranging over a spectrum of specialties, from mathematics to medicine. So, when Descartes grouped together otherwise widely disparate pieces of research as products of *his* method, he was staking out a series of political claims in the economy of the sciences. Not only was he endorsing his results individually, he was also linking them under the claim that they were all to be accepted as a piece, because they all fell within and followed from his method, the method. He was claiming methodological hegemony over these and other fields, positioning himself in relation to practitioners within and across those fields. The literary effects of method, especially those of unity and progress, probably provided him with a great deal of honestly held confidence about taking this posture.

In the final analysis the key issue for Descartes was the status of his system of mechanistic natural philosophy. Indeed, the central issue in the period of the so-called Scientific Revolution was precisely the clash of opposing systematic visions of natural philosophy, a clash which climaxed during the lifetime of Descartes.[35] His method functions on this peak level of struggle by supposedly underpinning his entire project in natural philosophy, underwriting, that is, his claim to preeminence in resolving the clash of natural philosophies of his day. This is intimated in the way the *Essais* of 1637, themselves appetizers for the system, are subordinated to the overarching tale of the method in the *Discours;* and in the way the metaphysical grounding for his natural philosophy is also offered as a triumph of method. Descartes even carried this method-rhetorical shaping of his claim to cognitive dominance to a higher, more personal, heroic, indeed Baroque level, when he claimed that his life as a natural philosopher, mathematician, and metaphysician had itself been shaped and lived, in order, according to the method.

But whether Descartes himself believed these wider claims, especially after he abandoned the *Regulae* in 1628–29, is another matter. Method discourses may systematically delude believers, but there may also be particular circumstances, social and biographical, in which actors cynically exploit the rhetorical power of a method discourse in which they have cause not to believe. Next, we will examine the possibility that Descartes's career in methodology conforms to a melodramatic plot in which the honest delusion of youth later gave way to cynical opportunism.

Rethinking Method and the Career of Descartes

The Original Inscription of Descartes's Method: Bricolage and Self-Deception

Our skeptical, post-Kuhnian view of method implies that the grand tradition of theorizing about method that extends from Bacon (indeed from Aristotle) to Popper is not a "whiggish" progression toward ever more clear insights into the "truth" about method. Each methodologist has operated with (and against) the available formal discourses on method; but each new methodology has been constructed by its author in the light of problems and goals which might relate to the tradition itself, to the perceived state of one or more of the contemporary sciences, or to other discourses believed to be relevant, such as natural theology, political theory, and moral philosophy. The perception and weighting of such concerns by a methodologist is a complex function of his biography, social location, institutional affiliations, and perceived interests. Moreover, it seems that a certain biographically and contextually conditioned bricolage of available cultural resources governs the manufacture of any particular "great" methodologist's brand of method.[36] The task of a new historiography of method is to abandon a heroic, "whig" history of spuriously efficacious methodological ideas in favor of a social and political history of theorizing about method, a history that also takes seriously the structure and literary effects of method discourses. By way of illustration, let me sketch some points about Descartes's early decisive experience as an understandably deluded *bricoleur* of method.

I have argued elsewhere in detail that the core of Descartes's method doctrine was constructed in late 1619 and early 1620; that his enthusiastically constructed method doctrine marked the third and final step in a series of youthfully overambitious and underarticulated enterprises, each one more grandiose and general than the previous one, each one inscribed partly by means of unjustifiable analogical extension of its predecessor. My argument was based on dating the earliest parts of *Regulae* from this period, on the basis of internal evidence and its relation to datable fragments of Descartes's mathematical and natural philosophical work.[37] I shall not enter into the details here, but merely sketch the story of Descartes's enthusiastic methodological bricolage.

In November 1618 Descartes met Isaac Beeckman and fell in with his dream of a natural philosophy that would be both corpuscular-mechanical and properly (rather than metaphorically) "mathematical," in the sense of depending on mathematical argument, analysis, and demonstration. They termed this project "physico-mathematics."Descartes and Beeckman were youthful, enthusiastic, and badly confused about the difference between aspiration and performance. They produced no convincing examples of this physico-mathematics, although in one or two special problem cases it is clear that they thought they had hit upon real instances of it. Wild aspiration masked a tissue of ad hoc ontology and post facto pseudo-geometrization. But what Descartes could see was that in principle physico-mathematics demanded a general way of mathematically stating and solving problems in physics.

In mid-1619 Descartes's dream of physico-mathematics, as well as his own recent researches in mathematics, were subsumed under an even more grandiose project of "universal mathematics." I have argued elsewhere that universal mathematics can be properly understood only if we correctly date and interpret that curious portion of Regula IV now termed rule IVB, and place it in the context of Descartes's recent mathematical researches.[38] Rule IVB was probably written as part of a projected treatise on universal mathematics; it predates the surrounding text of the *Regulae* which was composed shortly after November 1619 and deals, of course, with the method. Rule IVB tells us that universal mathematics embraces the axioms, principles, and methods common to all properly mathematical fields, that it is the science of "order" and "measure" wherever they appear in the various mathematical disciplines. "Measure" plausibly denotes here "quantity in general," the abstract object with which one deals after one has abstracted from the particular mathematical objects of the particular mathematical disciplines. "Order" seems to connote a concern with finding general schemas of analysis for problems, once they have been stated in abstract terms. All of this reflects neo-Platonically inspired ideas about a "general mathematics" that were current in the late sixteenth and early seventeenth centuries. I have argued that Descartes formulated rule IVB combining these available notions with a daring extrapolation of certain aspects of his mathematical and physico-mathematical researches of 1619.

At that time Descartes was very much interested in the proportional compass represented in Figure 14.4. In particular he was interested in its rough and ready practical use to solve problems. He focused not on the curves it drew (as he did later in the *Géométrie*), but rather on the way many problems in algebra or geometry could be modeled on the compass, provided the terms of the problems could be reduced to the finding of relations among proportional magnitudes. There were very real limits to the value of the compass in this respect; but Descartes ran directly over them in his haste to generalize.

It did not matter whether the problem was arithmetical, algebraical, or geometrical: one could abstract from the particular numerical, symbolic or figurate setting of the problem, translating the numbers of magnitudes into line lengths representable on the limbs and branches of the compass. Solving the problem so abstracted simply involved unfolding a set of proportions holding among these abstracted quantities. In other words, "quantity in general" was represented by limb lengths; "schemas of solution" could be examined by looking at the structure of relations among the quantities thus represented. Used in this way, the compass was a veritable exemplar for the idea that the various mathematical disciplines could be subordinated to a universal mathematics. When between March and November 1619 Descartes further realized that physico-mathematical problems, as well, would or should boil down to problems about structures of ratios and proportions holding among representative quantities, the dream of universal mathematics was born and rule IVB composed as part of the larger intended treatise. But it was only a

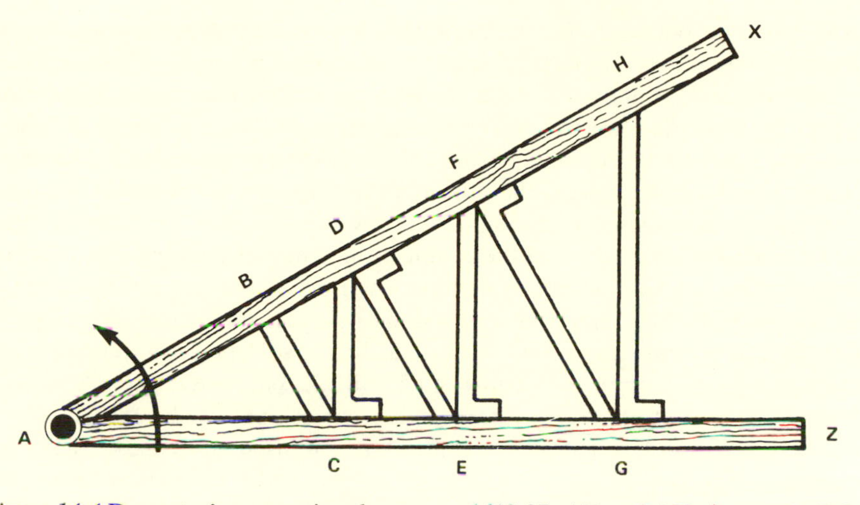

Figure 14.4 Descartes's proportional compass 1619-37: AZ and AX pivot at A. BC is fixed normal to AX. All the other rulers are movable (their extensions beyond AX, AZ are not shown). By similar right triangles: $\frac{AB}{AC} = \frac{AC}{AD} = \frac{AD}{AE} = \frac{AE}{AF} = \frac{AF}{AG} = \frac{AG}{AH}$.

dream; his techniques did not even work for all the algebraic problems he had attempted; and such treatment of physico-mathematical problems was, of course, a nonstarter. Yet he did have before him the successful special cases and the overblown grand idea. Soon, however, the whole undertaking was swamped by the grandiose vision of the method, which was, in fact, a vast analogical extrapolation of notions embodied in universal mathematics, notions themselves halfbaked and overextended.

We have in the *Regulae* some of the fossil traces of this process of extrapolation. Let us recall the peculiar portion of Regulae VI which elaborates the concepts of series, absolutes, relatives, and relations, notions which I have also argued served as the template for the elaboration of the heuristic rules of the method in Regulae VII through XI.[39] My contention is that the entire abstract and high-flown language of absolutes and relatives, of series and relations, *and* the portentous heuristic rules that go along with it, are nothing more than vast analogical extensions of a set of ideas fundamental to the as yet not fully constituted discipline of universal mathematics.

At the end of VI there is a little mathematical example about a series of numbers in a continued geometrical proportion. Such a series is, of course, typical of the sort of entities to be treated in universal mathematics, as I have unpacked it earlier. Descartes uses the series to illustrate some of the general heuristic rules, but although the example poses as an illustration, everything we have seen powerfully suggests that this is the sort of example in universal mathematics from which the central portions of the method discourse were analogically derived. Consider that for the methodological concept of the *absolute term,* we can read "defining ratio applied to an initial unit"; for *relative terms,* we can read "numbers subsequently generated in a continued geometrical proportion"; for the grandiose latticework of rational truths, we can read the orderly interlinked series of numbers in continued geometrical proportions; and, finally, for each of those heuristic rules of method "illustrated" by the series, we can read a concrete but fairly trivial piece of advice about the solution of problems arising about series of magnitudes in continued proportions. In other words, there is very good reason to think that what the overexcited young Descartes thought, wrongly, was true of universal mathematics, he daringly extended into the realm of all rational enquiry. The method discourse was not abstracted from successful practice in some genuine area of mathematics; it was produced by a megalomaniac performance of operations of analogical extension upon the terms of a discourse, universal mathematics, which itself could not do very much of what it was purported to do.

What we seem to have, therefore, in Descartes's path to his initial inscription of his method is a trail of somewhat confused and overenthusiastic bricolage. Bits of his own work are assembled with elements of culturally available discourse on "general mathematics," and then "method," in a series of analogical extensions and subsumptions of previous discourse, issuing in the manufacture of the method. And, as we know from our study of the enticing discursive dynamics of method discourses, Descartes was probably beginning to fall for the literary effects of his discourse. Yet, from Descartes's perspective his path to the method would have seemed a marvelous and triumphal progress. Recalled to study in 1619 by the vision of Beeckmanian physico-mathematics, he had, by mid-1619, merged that project with his work in mathematics to formulate the intoxicating dream of universal mathematics. Then, musing in the late autumn of 1619, he had seen how to conquer all rationally obtainable knowledge by generalizing his earlier revelations. No wonder, then, that on St. Martin's Eve 1619, Descartes, enthused by his skill in thus transforming one discourse into another, dreamed that the project he had glimpsed had been consecrated by God himself.

The Failure of the *Regulae,* The Birth of the System and the Problem of the Cynical *Discours de la méthode*

I have been suggesting all along that Descartes's project of method is crucial to understanding his career as a mathematician and natural philosopher, but not in the senses that he (or approving scholars) claim. Nowhere is this more apparent than in the decisive fifteen years following the methodological frenzies of 1619–20. Unless we maintain a cool, skeptical approach to method, we are likely to get hopelessly lost in Descartes's own mystifications, and so lose the key to reclaiming him as a realistically conceived actor in the history of science. To this end a proper, demystified understanding is required of Descartes's activities in the 1620s, in particular his attempt in the later portions of the *Regulae* to flesh out and partially redirect his method project of 1619.[40]

In 1620 Descartes was neither a builder of systems of natural philosophy nor a systematic metaphysician; he was—following Beeckman—a practicing, piecemeal mechanical philosopher and mathematician, as well as a self-appointed methodological prophet. We can understand how he was convinced that he possessed a method; that it subsumed universal mathematics; that it was efficacious; and that it could guide his researches in every field of rational inquiry.

By the time he settled in Paris in the mid 1620s, Descartes had produced a genuine mathematical triumph with his construction of all the "solid" problems of the Ancients, using only a circle and parabola (equivalent to a general construction for all cubic and quartic equations).[41] In Paris, sometime in 1626 or 1627 he produced his master stroke in physics: the construction of the law of refraction, followed by the development of a theory of lenses and the attempt to subsume the law under a mechanistic theory of light. Working in the circles around Marin Mersenne, he was very much a rising figure in the emerging community of French mathematical savants. Although these achievements had not been produced by application of the method, Descartes no doubt conceived the method to be relevant to his triumphs, and they in turn reinforced his belief in his method, according to the mechanisms already described.

Descartes also became enmeshed in the wider cultural life of the capital, which was then such a hothouse of political, religious, literary, and philosophical debate that some historians have been moved to speak of some sort of intellectual or religious/ideological "crisis" of the 1620s. Like his friend Mersenne, Descartes became convinced of the need to combat unorthodox philosophies of nature, those of alchemical, neo-Platonic or "Hermetic" inspiration, while avoiding the threat of a fashionable and corrosive skepticism. Eager to exploit his technical achievements in optics and mathematics, and to win public recognition for his personal methodological illuminations of 1619–20, Descartes entered the fray. As I have argued at length elsewhere, his tactics were modeled in part on those pursued by Mersenne: avoiding systematic natural philosophy or metaphysics, he would deploy, piecemeal, supposedly reliable bits of mathematical and natural philosophical knowledge in order to show, on the one hand, that unorthodox natural philosophies lack valid scientific foundations, while, on the other hand, showing that skepticism can be sidestepped, if not refuted, by the mere ostension of achievements whose practical efficacy could not reasonably be denied. Descartes, however, conceived that he had resources for these tasks far superior to those of Mersenne, for he had a method, and some outstanding results in mathematics and optics. Descartes's project took the form of returning to his universal mathematics of 1619, which he now tried to articulate in detail, under the guise of extending his 1619–20 text on method, roughly Regulae I to XI. Universal mathematics, carrying out Mersenne's tactics, would appear to grow out of the doctrine of method. Regulae VII to XI were written in Paris for this purpose.[42]

Taking up bits and pieces of his own theories of mechanistic optics and physiology, Descartes worked them into a sketch of a mechanistic theory of nervous function and sensation. Combining this with a reformulation of elements of scholastic discourse on psychology, he produced an idiosyncratic mechanistic account of perception and cognition, meant to underwrite universal mathematics and show how its logistical machinery was to work. The nub of this doctrine was that the spiritual or intellectual component of our human make-up is a *vis cognoscens,* a thinking power, which literally sees and inspects patterns and figures mechanically impressed in various brain loci. The *vis cognoscens* obviously is the conceptual resource out of which the "thinking substance" of the later metaphysics was fabricated, after the collapse of the *Regulae.*

A Mersennian mathematical science thus became possible in the following way: We limit ourselves to quantifiable, measurable properties, such as size, shape, weight (sic.), speed, density, and the like. Lines or figures representing the measures of quantities are directly impressible into appropriate brain loci. We then try to establish mathematical correlations among such empirically given and mechanically impressed measures of physical quantities. No skeptic can reasonably question the validity of such procedures, for the *vis cognoscens* has a direct validating vision of precisely what we are doing with and to these lines and figures. Unorthodox natural philosophies are also in trouble, for they clearly deal with fantasies; the only aspects of reality with which we can rationally and methodologically come to grips are measurable physical quantities. Number mysticism, immaterial agencies, occult causes, are epistemologically irrelevant, if not exactly shown not to exist.

The doctrine of the later Regulae was Mersennian in overall design and goal; but it was worked out in epistemological, psychological, physiological, and methodological detail undreamed of by Mersenne. There was only one thing wrong with this newly articulated universal mathematics—it did not work; and Descartes, I have demonstrated, realized this by late 1628, when he abruptly abandoned composition of the *Regulae* and moved to the United Provinces, there to work on the metaphysics and systematic mechanistic natural philosophy which could answer and transcend the difficulties on which the *Regulae* had foundered.

Close textual analysis shows that three related problems crippled the project of the later Regulae, opening new and unintended difficulties and creating the problematic in which the subsequent metaphysics and systematic corpuscular-mechanism were to move: (1) The newly articulated universal mathematics dealt with macroscopic "dimensions" directly known and certified. But Descartes's corpuscular-mechanical leanings in natural philosophy dealt with an invisible realm of microparticles. The answer was to elaborate a fully ontological doctrine of matter-extension which could licence macro-microscopic analogies, and ground a systematic corpuscular mechanism, but at the cost of giving up claims to proper mathematization, envisioned in the later Regulae. (2) Insistence that the world is known under geometrico-mechanical schemas focused the problem of the status and origin of non-geometrical perceptions. The solution was to extend and metaphysicalize the incipient systematic dualism of the later Regulae, so that one could, in the mature metaphysics, clearly distinguish between purely mental "ideas" and the corpuscular-mechanical states of affairs that sometimes occasion ideas, but which are not necessarily represented by them. (3) Not all mathematical operations and objects lend themselves to justification via the excessively simple procedures of imaginative representation, manipulation and inspection of line lengths advocated in the later Regulae. The text breaks off at precisely the point where this would have become clear to Descartes. The answer was to retreat from justification of mathematics by intuition of geometrical representations to a more abstract-relational view of the grounds of mathematical truth, and to erect a metaphysics that could supposedly guarantee intuitions that do not have to depend on imaginative representation, or geometrical presentation at all.

In sum, the very failure of the later Regulae structured problems and opportunities that Descartes then began to pursue through the elaboration of his mature metaphysics and systematic natural philosophy. The problem is that he was still to write the *Discours;* still to claim that the method guided his life and work; still to claim, indeed, that none of the messy history just outlined ever happened.

Nevertheless, these claims need not disarm (or impress) any cool, skeptical, post-Kuhnian mythologist of method. Virtually everything Descartes states in the *Discours* about the provenance, use, and development of the method, and its role in his career, is a fiction. It should be patently obvious by now that Descartes did not elicit his method by abstracting out and synthesizing the best aspects of scholastic logic, Greek geometrical analysis and algebra (his construction being more fraught and opportunistic);[43] that he did not develop his universal mathematics with logistic of line lengths in 1620, nor did he do it by applying his method;[44] that applying his method did not generate an ever enlarging collection of rules for mathematical analysis;[45] that, after 1618, the method in no way offered a full account of "everything that gives the rules of arithmetic their certainty";[46] and, finally, that the method, in 1619, did not dictate the course of his career, the preparatory years spent in lower studies before he was ready to assay metaphysics after 1628.[47]

We can, I think, conclude that until the collapse of the renewed project of universal mathematics in the later Regulae in 1628, Descartes was probably under the sway of his method discourse, generally believing, for the reasons already discussed, in its de facto or in principle relevance to his scientific and mathematical projects. After 1628, one cannot be so confident that Descartes was so firmly in the grip of the discursive dynamics of method, nor, accordingly, can one be so charitable about his likely beliefs and intentions. It would seem likely that when he used the method to articulate his autobiography in the *Discours,* he was largely covering the tracks of his abortive enterprise of the late 1620s and was cynically exploiting the method as a rhetorical device in the traditional perjorative sense. Similarly, in other contexts of crude methodological assertion, it becomes increasingly difficult to believe that Descartes genuinely believed what he was saying. And yet, the discursive mechanisms of method are such that no amount of experience must dissuade a believer; and the fact that Descartes was probably both a cynical manipulator of the method and the first of its many victims may explain the air of ambiguous ambivalence that seems to surround many of his later methodological pronouncements. He may have feared that the method did not work, and feared and resisted coming to grips with that suspicion. The psychology of a crisis of belief in a method may bear similarities to the better known contours of crises of religious belief, especially if method discourses are indeed powerful species of mythic speech.

Whatever one makes of these problems, it should at least be clear that the sorting out of Descartes's method discourse, the reconstruction of its genesis, and the identification of its discursive structure and dynamics, are all necessary conditions for our recovery (literary manufacture) of a historical rather than mythological Descartes. Although Descartes posed behind his method as a lone prophet of a new science, in reality—as an exponent of mechanism, practitioner of the mathematical sciences, and advocate of new values in natural philosophy—he was a figure highly symptomatic of the contextual forces in play and opportunities at hand at this crucial moment in the process of the Scientific Revolution. His method explains neither his manner of work, nor his achievements, nor the course of his symptomatic career. Rather, his absorption in method, his succumbing to its effects, and even his later suspected manipulation of it, are simply a part, an essential part, of that very contextual weave, a weave the method deceivingly claims to command and explain.

Notes

1. Cf. J. Priestley, *The History and Present State of Electricity with Original Experiments* (London, 1767), pp. v–vi; W. Whewell, *History of Inductive Sciences* (London, 1837), vol. I, p. 5; W. Whewell, *The Philosophy of the Inductive Sciences* (London, 1980), pp. 3–4.

2. C. Singer (ed.), *Studies in the History and Method of Science,* vol. I (Oxford, 1917–21), p. vi; G. Sarton, "Introduction to the History and Philosophy of Science," *Isis* 4 (1921–22), 23–31 at p. 25; G. Sarton, "The New Humanism," *Isis* 6 (1924), 9–34 at p. 26.

3. For example, A. C. Crombie, *Robert Grosseteste and the Origins of Experimental Science, 1100–1700* (Oxford, 1953); J. H. Randall, *The School of Padua and the Emergence of Modern Science* (Padua, 1961).

4. K. R. Popper, *The Logic of Scientific Discovery* (London, 1959); I. Lakatos, "Falsification and the Methodology of Scientific Research Programmes," in J. Worrall and G. Currie (eds.), *Imre Lakatos: Philosophical Papers,* vol. I (C.U.P., 1978), pp. 8–101.

5. J. A. Schuster, "Cartesian Method as Mythic Speech: A Diachronic and Structural Analysis," in *The Politics and Rhetoric of Scientific Method: Historical Studies,* ed. J. A. Schuster and R. Yeo (Dordrecht, 1986), 33–95, at p. 38–40.

6. J. A. Schuster and R. Yeo, "Introduction" to Schuster and Yeo (eds.) *The Politics and Rhetoric of Scientific Method: Historical Studies* (Dordrecht, 1986), pp. ix–xxxvii.

7. A. Koyré, *Études Galiléennes* (Paris: Hermann & Cie, 1939); Koyré, *Galileo Studies,* trans. J. Mepham (Hassocks, Sussex: Harvester, 1978); Koyré, *Metaphysics*

and Measurement: Essays in Scientific Revolution (London: Chapman & Hall, 1969); Koyré, "The Origins of Modern Science," *Diogenes* 16 (1959), 1–22.

8. Koyré, "The Origins of Modern Science."

9. Bachelard, *Le nouvel esprit scientifique,* 13th ed. (Paris: Presses Universitaires de France, 1975); Bachelard, *Le rationalisme appliqué* (Paris: Presses Universitaires de France, 1949); D. Lecourt, *Marxism and Epistemology: Bachelard, Canguilhem, Foucault,* trans. B. Brewster (London: New Left Books, 1975), 40–47, 60–70.

10. G. Bachelard, *La formation de l'esprit scientifique,* 9th ed. (Paris: Vrin, 1975), 61.

11. Presumably none of this surprises readers of T. S. Kuhn, *The Structure of Scientific Revolutions,* 2d ed. (Chicago: The University of Chicago Press, 1970), esp. the "Postscript"; Kuhn, *The Essential Tension: Selected Studies in Scientific Tradition and Change* (Chicago: The University of Chicago Press, 1977), ch. 13; J. R. Ravetz, *Scientific Knowledge and Its Social Problems* (Oxford: Clarendon Press, 1971), 71–240; B. Barnes, *T. S. Kuhn and Social Science* (London: Macmillan, 1982); Bachelard *La formation.*

12. Ravetz, *Scientific Knowledge;* M. Mulkay, *Science and the Sociology of Knowledge* (London, 1979); B. Latour and S. Woolgar, *Laboratory Life. The Social Construction of Scientific Facts* (London, 1979); K. Knorr-Cetina, *The Manufacture of Knowledge: An Essay on the Constructivist and Conventional Character of Knowledge and Cognition* (Oxford, 1981); H.Collins, *Changing Order* (London, 1985).

13. For early "derivations" of this position from the writings of Kuhn see Ravetz, *Scientific Knowledge,* and J. A. Schuster, "Kuhn and Lakatos Revisited," *British Journal for the History of Science* 12 (1979): 301–317.

14. These points are perhaps best brought out in full-scale contextualist studies in the history of science, for example, M. J. S. Rudwick, *The Great Devonian Controversy: The Shaping of Scientific Knowledge among Gentlemanly Specialists* (Chicago: The University of Chicago Press, 1985); S. Shapin and S. Schaffer, *Leviathan and the Air-Pump: Hobbes, Boyle and the Experimental Life* (Princeton, NJ: Princeton University Press, 1985); A. Desmond, *Archetypes and Ancestors: Paleontology in Victorian London, 1850–1875* (London: Blond & Briggs, 1982).

15. Cf. J. A. Schuster, "Cartesian Method," 40–47.

16. AT X, 382; CSM I, 21–22.

17. Regula VIII: AT X, 393, l. 22–396, l. 25; CSM I, 28–30.

18. J. A. Schuster, "Descartes and the Scientific Revolution—1618–34: An Interpretation" (Ph.D. diss., Princeton, 1977), 268–368.

19. Analogous remarks apply to that supposed case of application of the method, the discovery of the explanation of the formation and geometrical properties of the rainbow. This was indeed an exceedingly good piece of normal science, the solution to a classic puzzle in geometrical optics. But it was also highly traditional, conditioned by the aims, concepts, tools, and standards of the discipline. Descartes's recourse to a water-filled flask as a model rain drop was not novel, and even had it been, it could be interpreted as having been mediated by a very commonsensical, rather than methodological, rationale. Descartes's sole advantage over others was possession of an exact law of refraction, which now served as laws often do, as a tool in facilitating further research. An exact tool, a standard model, some sufficiently accurate data, and laborious calculation resolved the problem. To invoke the rules of the method here is to glide over the rich, tradition bound dynamics of the research.

20. J. A. Schuster, "Methodologies as Mythic Structures: A Preface to the Future

Historiography of Method," *Metascience: Annual Review of the Australasian Association for the History, Philosophy and Social Studies of Science* 1/2 (1984): 15–36; Schuster, "Cartesian Method."

21. See the section headed "Rethinking Method and the Career of Descartes."

22. Descartes also has a discourse on Level I concerning errors and pitfalls. See Schuster, "Cartesian Method," n. 119–p. 79.

23. Ibid, 62–65, 71–74. Here not only the case of optics is examined, but also those of analytical mathematics and magnetism (treated as a case study in corpuscular-mechanical explanation). The method stories corresponding to Descartes's Level I practice in these areas are discussed.

24. Even in his activities on Level III; see the section headed "The Rhetorical Functions of Cartesian and other Method Discourses."

25. Schuster, "Cartesian Method," 62–65, 71–74.

26. In the former case these terms denote respectively coordinates and algebraically expressed curves; in the latter case respectively corpuscular-mechanical ontological primitives and compounds.

27. P. K. Feyerabend, *Against Method* (London: New Left Books, 1975) and *Science in a Free Society* (London, 1978); cf. Schuster, "Cartesian Method," 36–37, 79–80.

28. Schuster and Yeo, "Introduction"; R. Yeo, "Scientific Method and the Rhetoric of Science in Britain, 1830–1917," in Schuster and Yeo's *Politics and Rhetoric,* 259–297.

29. See first page of this essay.

30. C. Perelman, *The New Rhetoric and the Humanities* (Dordrecht, 1979); C. Perelman and L. Olbrechts-Tyteca, *The New Rhetoric: A Treatise on Argumentation* (London, 1971); Ravetz, *Scientific Knowledge*; S. Yearley, "Textual Persuasion: The Role of Social Accounting in the Construction of Scientific Arguments," *Philosophy of the Social Sciences* 11 (1981): 409–435; W. Weimar, "Science as Rhetorical Transaction: Toward a Nonjustificational Conception of Rhetoric," *Philosophy and Rhetoric* 10 (1977): 1–29.

31. M. Mulkay and G. N. Gilbert, "Putting Philosophy to Work: Sir Karl Popper's Influence on Scientific Practice," *Philosophy of the Social Sciences* 11 (1981): 389–407; Feyerabend, *Against Method;* D. P. Miller, "Method and the 'Micropolitics' of Science: The Early Years of the Geological and Astronomical Societies of London," in Schuster and Yeo's *Politics and Rhetoric,* 227–257; H. E. LeGrand, "Steady as a Rock: Methodology and Moving Continents," in ibid., 97–138; P. Wood, "Methodology and Apologetics: Thomas Sprat's *History of the Royal Society,*" *British Journal for the History of Science* 13 (1980): 1–26; E. Richards and J. A. Schuster, "The Feminine Method as Myth and Accounting Resource: A Challenge to Gender Studies and Social Studies of Science," *Social Studies of Science* 19 (1989): 697–720.

32. Descartes was then probably playing with models of light involving bent arm balances and balls, as well as crude versions of his ontological model—mechanical disturbance in a medium; see Schuster, "Descartes and the Scientific Revolution," 346–352.

33. From all this we can derive two laws in the anthropology of method that help to explain why method-talk is deployed in certain ways in scientific debate. Consider a scientific community engaged in debate over two divergent knowledge claims:

(1) To the extent that all debaters share elements of the same method discourse, their debate will tend to take the form "to which claim does the method story attach," *not* "how can one credit stories generated in our method discourse?"

(2) If there are differences in preferred method discourse, debates about method will take center stage away from debate about the divergent claims per se. That is, debate about the claims will be carried on to a large extent by means of debate about which method is to be followed. In either case all sides will still share the method believer's view that the crucial element in debate is method.

34. P. Bourdieu, "The Specificity of the Scientific Field and the Social Conditions of the Progress of Reason," *Social Science Information* 6 (1975): 19–47; Latour and Woolgar, *Laboratory Life;* M. Callon, "Struggles and Negotiations to Define What is Problematical and What is Not: The Sociologic Translation," in *The Social Process of Scientific Investigation* (*Sociology of the Sciences Yearbook* IV), ed. K. D. Knorr et al. (Dordrecht, 1980), 197–219; S. Shapin, "The History of Science and its Sociological Reconstructions," *History of Science* 20 (1982): 157–211; M. Mulkay and G. N. Gilbert, "Putting Philosophy to Work: Sir Karl Popper's Influence on Scientific Practice," *Philosophy of the Social Sciences* 11 (1981): 389–407.

35. J. A. Schuster, "The Scientific Revolution," in *The Companion to the History of Modern Science,* ed. R. Olby et al. (London, 1990), 217–242.

36. See, e.g., R. Yeo, "William Whewell, Natural Theology and the Philosophy of Science in Mid-Nineteenth Century Britain," *Annals of Science* 36 (1979): 493–516; and Richards and Schuster, "The Feminine Method."

37. Details in J. A. Schuster, "Descartes' *Mathesis Universalis:* 1619–28" in *Descartes: Philosophy, Mathematics and Physics,* ed. S. Gaukroger (Brighton, 1980), 41–96, esp. 42–55; and Schuster, "Cartesian Method," 47–59.

38. Schuster, "Descartes' *Mathesis Universalis,*" 42–47; the delineation of portions 4B and 4A within Regula IV was owing to J.-P. Weber, *La constitution du texte des Regulae* (Paris, 1964), 5–7; rule IVB runs from AT X, 374, l. 16 to the end of Regula IV; rule IVA opens Regula IV at AT X, 371, l. 1 to 374, l. 15.

39. Schuster, "Cartesian Method," 44–47.

40. Material in the next eight paragraphs is dealt with in detail in Schuster, "Descartes' *Mathesis Universalis,*" 55–80.

41. Schuster, "Descartes and the Scientific Revolution," 127–149. Needless to say, this reconstruction of Descartes's discovery owes nothing to invoking the rules of his method.

42. Schuster, "Descartes' *Mathesis Universalis,*" 55–64.

43. AT VI, 18; CSM I, 119–120.

44. AT VI, 20; CSM I, 120–121.

45. AT VI, 20–21; CSM I, 121.

46. AT VI, 21; CSM I, 121.

47. AT VI, 21–22; CSM I, 121–122.

15

Method, Discourse, and the Act of Knowing

Evert van Leeuwen

In many respects the *Discourse on Method* contains the outline of modern philosophy. Only in the last seventy years has it become clear that the Cartesian method has an even richer source in the *Regulae ad directionem ingenii.* The *Discourse,* however, is still regarded as the popular work that gave Descartes's philosophy a widespread influence.[1]

Philosophically speaking, the *Discourse* even appears to determine the position of modern philosophy with respect to science. Just as in the Essays that are appended to the *Discourse,* science is now to stand on its own, so that it may grow and diversify in its own manner. The ways in which science is discovered and knowledge produced, the moral and ethical implications that follow from it, and the metaphysical questions that are raised, are no longer to be a part of true scientific reasoning. Mittelstrass therefore sees in the *Discourse* the root and defense of science's rationalistic monologue.[2] And Marion has implicitly criticized Descartes's love for science by developing the concepts of a "grey ontology" and a "white theology."[3]

Philosophy seems relegated to discourse; it can only take part in stories about how science works, and other external and secondary issues. It has lost its grip on human reason, as much as it has lost touch with the fullness of the world we live in. Since the *Discourse,* philosophy has fallen into the bondage of scientific treatises, and no one seems able to tell whether or not there lies a truth behind the scientific fabric we have made of the world. This pessimistic view of the influence of Descartes's philosophy is most clearly expressed when Jaspers speaks of Descartes:

> In him one can see the origin and beginning of what will later be the enduring enemy of philosophizing, even in that place where one seeks his own truth. Descartes is a historical fate, in the sense that everyone who philosophizes has to decide about himself in the unavoidable appropriation of Descartes, through the manner in which he appropriates him.[4]

Contemporary philosophers have claimed in response to this point of view that a "post-Cartesian" or "non-Cartesian" philosophy must be created. Some think that the phenomenology of Husserl, Heidegger, and Merleau-Ponty has achieved this goal. Others try to find it in a narrative philosophy or in the Wittgensteinian conception of philosophy as (a) therapy.

In this way Descartes is either neglected or criticized for his limited view of science. But it may still be interesting to look at the *Discourse* in its own perspective, and analyze it in its own context.[5] For it may turn out that Descartes's view of the relation between science and philosophy was quite different from the outlook it has generated over the last 350 years.

In this essay such an analysis is undertaken. In the background stands an earlier analysis of the *Regulae.*[6] It will be argued that in the eyes of Descartes science and philosophy are in jeopardy, and need to be saved from criticism and judgments that are incorrectly grounded.

Descartes therefore seeks a new philosophy that gives a central place to the act of knowing, not only in science but also in metaphysics and morals. This act has above all a heuristic character in the search for a truth that is certain and indisputable.[7] In characterizing this search we may again follow the words of Jaspers:

> If certainty wishes to be truthful, then it is required that every truth should depend upon an origin which is substantial and which can be illuminated in the questioning process. And then the origin, which is not already true in its dimness, will be on its way to becoming true. Not in the movement of pure thought, but in the putting forward and the intimating of a thinking existence.[8]

In this process of "putting forward" (*Hervorbringen*), the *Discourse on Method* still has an impact on contemporary philosophy and its problems. And a journey to 1637 gives us the opportunity to reconsider our habits of thought, as the study of history ought to do (cf. AT VI, 6, ll. 19–25).

Method and Mind

Descartes wrote two works on method, the *Regulae ad Directionem Ingenii* (which was left unpublished and unfinished in 1628)[9] and of course the *Discours de la méthode* in 1637. The (sub)titles of the two works are related. The title "Discourse on Method" is followed by the phrase

> of rightly conducting one's reason and seeking the truth in the sciences [*pour bien conduire sa raison et chercher la vérité dans les sciences*]. (AT VI, 1; CSM I, 111)

The title of the *Regulae* contains similar language, as Marion shows in his French translation:

> Règles utiles et claires pour la direction de l'esprit en la recherche de la vérité [Useful and clear rules for the direction of the mind in the search for truth].[10]

Both titles combine two things within the search for truth—the method, or the methodological rules, and the mind, or reason. But they also display a slight but important difference. The *Regulae* conducts *the* mind, while the *Discourse* aims to conduct *his* reason. This difference seems indicative of the differences between the two works: the *Regulae* proceeds from rule to rule in a kind of dialectical process, while the *Discourse* follows a linear temporal scheme as in a story or tale. Philosophically speaking, the person who speaks in the *Regulae* seems to be an instructor, while the "I" of the *Discourse* is a storyteller, an individual placed in his own history.

The question how mind and method involve each other in the *Discourse* can be clarified by considering the *his* of "his reason" in the subtitle. Is reference made to the method (the French "*sa raison*" makes this possible), to Descartes, or to the reader of the story? The answer to this question is somewhat awkward: all three subjects are meant, albeit in different ways.

The first option finds its rationale in the French title "*Discours de la méthode.*" Grammatically, this phrase leaves more than one possibility for the genitive: it might be the case that the discourse is spoken *by* the method in order to conduct *his* (its) reason in the search for truth.

This interpretation, idealistic in the sense of the Hegelian Geist,[11] seems more than a little odd. Still, it cannot be dismissed too quickly. The storyteller not only wants to show a picture of his life; he also wants to convince the reader of the fruitfulness of the method in its own right. Consider this passage from Part II: "In short, the method which instructs us to follow the correct order, and to enumerate exactly all the relevant factors, contains everything that gives certainty to the rules of arithmetic" (AT VI, 21, ll. 13–17; CSM I, 121). At the end the storyteller says that he deserves to be praised not because of his discoveries, but only because he was convinced by reason (AT VI, 77, ll. 9–14). The persuasion is brought about by the method, which has even proved the existence of the storyteller's ego.[12]

But the second option also contains an element of truth. Even though he has assumed the anonymous disguise of a storyteller, Descartes says that he wants to show "what paths I have followed, and to represent my life . . . as if in a picture, so that everyone may judge it for himself."[13] He continues, "My present aim, then, is not to teach the method which everyone must follow in order to direct his reason correctly, but only to reveal how I have tried to direct my own" (AT VI, 4, ll. 1–3, 7–10; CSM I, 112). So Descartes clearly says that he wants to disguise himself as a storyteller in order to display his own reasoned conduct.

Still, this option too seems rather strange: what sense could there be in telling a story about how an anonymous person discovers a few scientific truths? Is there anything to be learned from it in epistemology or methodology? If there is, it is not from (auto)biographical coincidences, but only from the reasoning process which led to the discovery, as is well put at the beginning of the *Dioptrics* (AT VI, 81–93).

The third option also contains an element of truth. The opening lines of the *Discourse* already involve the reader in the search for truth: "Good sense is the best distributed thing in the world . . . for, as regards reason or sense, since it is the only thing that makes us men and distinguishes us from the beasts, I am inclined to believe that it exists whole and complete in each of us" (AT VI, 1, l. 17 and 2, ll. 26–29; CSM I, 111, 112). At several places Descartes states further that reasoning can be performed best only by someone who is in possession of his "*bon sens*" (e.g., AT VI, 12, l. 25–13, l. 1). These statements all invite the reader to direct his reason according to the method set forth.

What kind of common truth might lie behind these three possible options? The *Regulae* offers the clue to the puzzle. In Rule IV it is stated that the human mind contains something that might be called divine, in which the first seeds of useful thoughts are sown in such a way that they produce spontaneous fruits even while they are neglected and suffocated by controversial studies (AT X, 373, ll. 7–11). These fruits are present in the science of Antiquity, especially in mathematics. Descartes tries to develop these seeds methodically, and he uses mathematics only as an ornament of this development. His main goal, however, is a discipline that contains the first rudiments of human reason and can be extended to the truth in every subject matter (AT X, 374, ll. 7–11). Later, in Rule X, he admits, as he will in the *Discourse,* that from his youth he has gained long experience in using this method, and as in Rule IV (AT X, 374, ll. 11–13) he emphasizes its usefulness and power (AT X, 403, l. 24–404, l. 4). From Rule IV the method grows gradually, in Rules V–VII, with steps backward and forward, in order to direct the mind and to develop human reason in all the questions taken up in the remaining rules. This development of the mind goes hand in hand with that of the method in the discovery of the order of pure intellectual objects on which true science is based.

The Method in the *Regulae*

Nowadays the methodological precepts of the *Discourse* are commonly viewed as a revision and summary of the method of the *Regulae*. Like the *Discourse,* the *Regulae* begins with the claim that "*bon sens*" or the natural light of reason (*lumen naturale*) is present in everybody. But in this work it remains implicit, and the emphasis is immediately laid on the need to direct the mind in order to form solid and true judgments on everything that occurs. In the *Discourse* too it is said that the principal goal of the method is to apply the power of judgment correctly (AT VI, 2, ll. 12–14). But this statement is involved in a different set of problems, focusing on these questions: How can there be a problem about how to form correct judgments when everybody has the same power to do so? What goes wrong in the diaspora of meanings and theories? In the *Regulae* these questions are given short shrift. In Rule II Descartes simply says that whenever two people have a dispute, neither has the complete truth, because in that case he would simply convince the other one in the light of natural reason. In Rule I the chief mistake behind the formation of different theories is identified as the habit of translating one way of dealing with problems into other totally different kinds of problems. Making this mistake, men tend by habit to treat science as they do the arts. Arts, like playing the zither or agriculture, require specialized training; likewise, men tend to think, branches of science also need special attitudes of the mind or special skills. This, says Descartes, is certainly wrong. All sciences together are identical with human wisdom, which always remains the same, regardless of the subject matter to which it is applied. There is no need to confine the mind within any limits, for finding one truth may help in finding another in a totally different field. In this perspective the general purpose of the *Regulae* is to augment the natural light of reason so that all the sciences in their connections can be seen. This purpose makes it necessary to begin by occupying the mind only with those objects of which certain or indubitable knowledge can be acquired (Rule II). Starting with these objects (later characterized as the famous "simple natures"), science is to be generated by intuition and deduction (Rule III). Having already written Rules I, II, and III, what does Descartes mean by "method" when in Rule IV he says that a method is necessary to investigate the truth of things?

> By "a method" I mean reliable rules which are easy to apply, and such that if one follows them exactly, one will never take what is false to be true or fruitlessly expend one's mental efforts, but will gradually and constantly increase one's knowledge till one arrives at a true understanding of everything within one's capacity. (AT X, 371, l. 25–372, l. 4; CSM I, 16)

Are the rules mentioned in this passage only a favored subset, perhaps Rules V, VI, and VII, of those given in the *Regulae?* If they are, the question then is whether or not the remaining rules in the *Regulae* have epistemological status. If they did, they would seem to be both redundant, which is contrary to the definition of the method (*et nullo mentis conatu inutiliter consumpto* (AT X, 372, l. 2), and superfluous, because unlearned people with sharp minds seem to have been led by the method in a natural way (*vel solius naturae ductu* (AT X, 373, ll. 4–7).

The conclusion must be that the rules of the method are identical with those of the *Regulae*. During the development of the rules for the direction of the mind, the necessity of a method is discovered and understood. This reflects one aspect of the heuristic nature of methodological thought at the time, which is present as well in Ramus's pedagogical method, Francis Bacon's *ars inveniendi,* and even Lull's *ars magna.*[14]

The Cartesian method distinguishes itself from these forerunners by its doubly heuristic dimension. First, the method demands continuous exercise in problem-solving. As in the technical arts, one proceeds in science through a process of learning by doing (cf. Rules VI, IX, and X). According to Rule I this exercise brings about growth of the mental capacity for science.

Second, the method itself develops in a heuristic way. Going from rule to rule, Descartes frequently summarizes and recapitulates the results of what has gone before. The supposed rewritings of some parts (e.g., Rules IV, VIII, and XII) may be attributed to a heuristic development of the method itself. All problems are open at every stage of the thinking process until they finally appear in the right order, when they can be intuited and are accessible to deduction.

When both dimensions are taken together it becomes clear that the knowing mind, the method, and the attainment of scientific knowledge are bound together in one intellectual process.

The doubly heuristic success of the method requires intellectual steps to overcome prejudice. These steps are taken methodically in Rules I–III. In these rules the knowing process is freed to act in the light of reason. That light can only be recognized step by step, rule by rule. In other words, the knowing capacity of man grows in the act of knowing solid and indubitable objects. The rules themselves are the fruit of a knowing mind which enriches itself in this way. Method and the knowing activity that is directed to certain knowledge become indissolubly connected. The opening lines of Rule IV explicitly testify to this connection:

> But it is far better never to contemplate investigating the truth about any matter than to do so without a method. For it is quite certain that such haphazard studies and obscure reflections blur the natural light and blind our intelligence. (AT X, 371, ll. 14–17; CSM I, 16)

According to Rule I, all the sciences will fuse together in that natural light of reason and will remain the same human wisdom. Descartes compares this human wisdom with the light of the sun. Sunlight does not alter even when it illuminates a variety of different things. In just the same way, the act of the thinking intellect can illuminate all kinds of things, in nature and also in morals, without any alteration. The most obscure and complicated philosophical matters will therefore be revealed in the light of reason when this light is gradually developed according to the rules of the method. The knowing activity remains the same even in those questions that deal with the relation between the knowing mind and its object (Rules VIII, XII). Then it will reveal what kind of knowledge the mind is ultimately capable of.

The *Discourse on Method* presents the same process (see, e.g., AT VI, 66, l. 26–67, l. 27). The tale obscures the purity of the method, even as it better explains the obstructions that blind reason in the search for truth. But after arguing that the Method teaches the way to follow the true order, the storyteller reflects:

> But what pleased me most about this method was that by following it I was sure in every case to use my reason, if not perfectly, at least as well as was in my power. Moreover, as I practised the method I felt my mind gradually become accustomed to conceiving its objects more clearly and distinctly; and since I did not restrict the method to any particular subject-matter, I hoped to apply it as usefully to the problems of the other sciences as I had to those of algebra. (AT VI, 21, ll. 18–21; CSM I, 121)

This passage explicitly brings out the heuristic character of the methodical reasoning that has been alluded to earlier. But it may also be read as a comment on the *Regulae.*

The available rules, in which there exists no distinction between the extension of the method and the capacity of the mind, are confined to the development of true discourses in which only algebraic operations occur (cf. Rules XVII and XVIII, and the title of Rule XIX). The rest of the work is lacking. The production of true discourses is an extension of the knowing activity which rests on seeds of truth and of useful thoughts, innate to the mind (Rule IV: AT X, 373, ll. 8–11 and 376, ll. 12–20; and Rule XIV).

Can this activity be extended outside the field of mathematics? This question is not answered by the *Regulae,* whose second half is missing. Rules VIII and XII testify that Descartes is already engaged in such an extension; experiments in optics, magnetism, and perhaps medicine give him ample evidence of the success of his method in those fields. But a true scientific account of these experiments has probably not been elaborated. Such an account cannot rest on mathematics alone, as is made clear in the discussion of Kepler's *linea anaclastica* in Rule VIII. Either philosophy or experience is also needed (cf. AT X, 394). A report by Beeckman of a discussion with Descartes in 1628 suggests that Descartes was planning to complete his method by giving that true scientific account, in which philosophy and experience also take part:

> He told me that he has no more wishes concerning arithmetic and geometry. During the last nine years he has made as much progress in them as is possible for the human mind. He gave me examples of this which were not obscure. Immediately after his return to Paris he will either send me his Algebra, which he calls perfect, and through which one can obtain a perfect science of geometry, as far as any human knowledge can go, or he will return to edit and polish it himself in order to give us the opportunity to complete jointly what is left in science.[15]

After a short return to Paris, Descartes set out, probably with this plan in mind, for Friesland, where the famous scholar of optics Adriaen Metius was teaching at the University of Franeker. But during the following winter Descartes suddenly changed his plans. In all probability he left the project of the *Regulae* just because the method persuaded him (because he found out methodically) that the transition from mathematics to science and then to metaphysics required another order along which to think.

From *Regulae* to *Discourse*

The *Regulae* is intended as a stable treatise in which the method and the act of knowing—consisting of intuition and deduction—are worked out simultaneously with the possible objects of knowledge. As such it instructs the reader to search carefully for truth among all the types of questions that lie within the scope of the method. What made Descartes leave this project and instead write a *Discourse* in which the method is only explained in four precepts? Does the disguise of a storyteller not make it impossible to explain the heuristic character of the method according to which the capacity for reasoning grows with every step taken? These questions are difficult to answer.

The main difference between the *Regulae* and the *Discourse* lies in the fact that intellectual intuition is completely missing in the latter. Intuition, however, plays a crucial role in the *Regulae*. It is the only pure capacity of the intellect by which a simple indubitable concept can be gained. Only on the basis of intuition, for example, can mathematics count as certain knowledge or science (cf. AT X, 368, ll. 13–21; 365, ll. 14–18; and 410–424).

Furthermore, intuition forms the basis for all discursive reasoning (cf. AT X, 369, ll. 11–17). It must therefore be considered the fundamental intellectual act. Descartes defines intuition as

> the conception of a clear and attentive mind, which is so easy and distinct that there can be no room for doubt about what we are understanding. Alternatively, and this comes to the same thing, intuition is the indubitable conception of a clear and attentive mind which proceeds solely from the light of reason. (AT X, 368, ll. 13–19; CSM I, 14).

Nobody can make a mistake in this activity of forming concepts. Descartes gives these examples: to exist, to think, the bounding of a triangle by just three lines, and the single surface of the globe. These examples show a remarkable order. While the definition of intuition explicitly specifies the exclusion of any doubt, the first example of that which is intuited is: to exist. The methodological doubt of the metaphysics can already be recognized here; thought and examples from mathematics are made to follow.

Descartes was conscious of his unusual use of the word "intuition." He apologized for possible confusion and explained that he used only the Latin meaning of the verb "*intueri*" ("to look into"). In this use the metaphor of sunlight is implicitly recognizable. Intuition does not simply mean to know something a priori, or to see what is most real and eternal. One has to look into a subject matter in order to conceive, to become conscious by a clear and distinct concept. Thus conception means the discovery of something that is simple and can be clearly understood, as in the case of a globe. These simple things, well ordered, together make up a complex situation. The reality of a resulting concept depends on the clarity and distinctness with which it is intuited. Just as in technology, the difference between fantasy and discovery is just that the latter works or is connected with other concepts. A triangle, for instance, implies line, point, three, angle, and so on, which are parts of mathematics. A vacuum, by contrast, implies that nothingness is part of the existence of things, and must be rejected as a fantasy that cannot be connected with other concepts.

In the *Regulae* the simple things are called "simple natures," but reference can also be made to the "innate ideas" which are crucial in the *Meditations*. As in the case of the simple natures, innate ideas also play a prominent primary role in the knowing activity. When Hobbes questions the concept of innate ideas, he asks Descartes if souls even think with these ideas when they are sleeping dreamlessly. Descartes answers that when he speaks of an idea as innate he does not mean that it is always to be observed. Nothing is innate in that way. What is really meant is that everyone has the faculty to produce such ideas in his mind (AT VII, 189, ll. 1–4; AT IX, 147). Intuition likewise producees in the natural light of reason conceptions about which there can be no doubt.

Apart from intuition, Descartes recognizes in the *Regulae* two other intellectual functions, deduction and enumeration.

Deduction is first of all characterized by a movement of the intellect. When a chain of reasons is too long to intuit at once, deduction is the movement from one link to another. If the movement has been completed without missing a link, for example by repetition, and the chain can be looked over in one view, then deduction coalesces again into an intuition (cf. AT X, 387, ll. 3–8; 370, ll. 9–16). Schouls has nicely called it an "intuition on the move."[16] Indirect deduction appears in more complex questions when not everything is known. These questions sometimes arise out of a definable problem, as in a series of numbers in which some are lacking, or a geometrical construction. In such cases enumeration and analysis help, and a true discursus emerges when the unknown elements can be defined by known elements. The order in which the true discursus proceeds in unraveling the problem is again a matter of intuition (cf. Rules XVII and XVIII).

Other questions, like those belonging to physics, lack even such a supposed order that might be analyzed. Descartes places these questions in the (missing) third part of the *Regulae*. But he already mentions that in these cases only deduction, assisted by enumeration, can make it possible to compose things (e.g., hypotheses, concepts) in which some truth may be found (e.g., the metaphors of the *Dioptrics*). He also warns that many mistakes are made in this domain (e.g., the vacuum: cf. AT X, 424, ll. 19–24).

Descartes alludes to this point in the opening rule of the second part, Rule XIII, when he distinguishes perfect from imperfect questions. He promises that it will be shown how every imperfect question can be reduced to a perfect one which is accessible to intuition (AT X, 431, ll. 15–27). Thus in science everything can be reduced to the "true discourse" of Rule XVII, that is, the physico-mathematics.[17]

The development of the method in the *Regulae* and consequently the teaching of it are highly dependent on the intuition of simple natures. The omission of intuition in the *Discourse* can therefore be taken as the main explanation for Descartes's statement that he only talks about the method in that work without teaching it. He writes to Mersenne in 1637:

> However, I have not been able to understand your objection to the title; because I have not put *Treatise on Method* but *Discourse on Method,* which means *Preface or Notice on method,* to show that I do not want to teach the method but only to describe it. As can be seen from what I say, it is a practise rather than a theory. I call the following treatises *Essays in this Method,* because I claim that what they contain could never have been

> discovered without it so that they show how much it is worth. (AT I, 349, ll. 14–25; CSMK, 53)

Perhaps Mersenne was satisfied by this answer because he was then ignorant of the existence of the *Regulae*. But from the viewpoint of the *Regulae* the answer is not completely satisfying. Only a few weeks earlier Descartes had suggested another title:

> The Plan of a Universal Science to raise our Nature to its Highest Degree of Perfection, with the Dioptrics, the Meteorology and the Geometry; in which the most Curious Topics which the Author has been able to choose in order to give Proof of his Universal Science are Explained in such a Manner that even those who have Never Studied them can Understand them. (AT I, 339, ll. 18–25; CSMK, 51)

This title, in which universal science and the perfection of the mind are combined, strongly reflects the *Regulae*. But it seems incongruent with the contents of the *Discourse*. What happened in those few weeks? The question is a rhetorical one. All we know is that the definitive title surprised Huygens and Mersenne; both friends were at first unhappy with it.

Descartes's choice of a title seems logical, considered from another perspective. The Latin concepts of *intuitus* and *discursus* display a difference that in many respects resembles the difference between the *Regulae* and the *Discourse*. *Intuitus* is the pure intellectual activity in which true concepts are known. It is for example the fundamental epistemological act in the Platonic and Neoplatonic tradition. *Discursus* is the successive movement from one concept into another. It has the more rhetorical or dialectical function of combining words into arguments. The definitive title "Discourse" seems therefore the realistic consequence of the presentation of the method without the epistemological act.[18]

The presentation of the method by enumerating specimens of methodic reasoning, with biographical, epistemological, moral, metaphysical, physical and medical significance, but without an epistemological exposition of the act of knowing as in the *Regulae,* explains moreover why the method has to be conveyed in precepts: there is no longer an explicit unity between the growth of science and the growth of the reasoning capacity in the light of reason. The Instructor of the *Regulae* becomes a Preceptor in the *Discourse*.

When intuition disappears, the Neoplatonic attitude, according to which the intellect intuits—becomes insight into—the Good, and by doing so becomes wise and truthful, disappears as well.

In the *Regulae* the act of intuition which clears the ground for the fusion of all the sciences in the one human wisdom is not merely an act of discovery but also finally an act of objectifying self-knowledge, in the tradition that stretches from Plotinus and Augustine to the Oratory. This attitude disappears in the *Discourse* behind the mask or disguise of the storyteller. It is replaced by a literary style of writing in the skeptical tradition of Montaigne. For Montaigne's *Essays* form a "*moyen d'instruire*" by telling a story.[19]

But this influence in the *Discourse* raises questions as to the scientific character of the method. Montaigne wrote his *Essays* with a skeptical attitude that caused a real *crise pyrrhonienne* in France during the 1620s and 1630s.[20] The result of this crisis was a denial of scientific truth, along with the suspicion that atheism constituted the basis of the scientific attitude. Descartes strongly opposed these developments, and his "*projet d'une science universelle*" is also designed to reconcile science and wisdom, which had fallen apart in the work of such philosophers as Montaigne and Charron.

But now do not the literary form of the storyteller and the formulation of the method in precepts imply the impossibility of this reconciliation? The conclusion seems unavoidable that in the *Discourse* Descartes drops not only the concept of intuition but also one of his deepest philosophical ambitions, that of uniting science and wisdom.

Such a conclusion would obviously be mistaken. Although Descartes had a low opinion of skeptics like La Mothe le Vayer, he did not reject all the aspects of Montaigne's and Charron's philosophy. Like Mersenne—an even more outspoken opponent of skepticism who nonetheless maintained a life-long friendship with Gassendi—Descartes too remained friends with a moderate skeptic like Ogier. The latter defended Charron's *La Sagesse* against the Jesuit attack of Garesse in 1623.[21] He also signed the apology for Gucz de Balzac's letters in 1627, which Descartes in his turn eloquently praised in 1628.[22]

Balzac, who during that period was denied a high position at the court by Richelieu, wrote a series of discourses at the same time, which he dedicated to Descartes. The first one begins with a statement which Descartes rephrased in his "provisional morals" (cf. AT VI, 23, ll. 1–3): ". . . in the corruption of this Age, in which almost everyone revolts against faith, I do not want to believe anything to be more true than what I have learned from my mother and my wet nurse."[23] Neither Descartes nor Balzac were skeptics at the time, but this fact did not prevent them from using phrases which call to mind Montaigne and his fideism.[24]

In his third discourse Balzac caricatures the Stoic Zeno, and in the accompanying letter to Descartes teases him with it (cf. AT I, 570, ll. 7–14).[25] In the same letter Balzac reminds Descartes of his promise to write an "*Histoire de Votre Esprit*" (AT I, 570, l. 22–571, l. 3).

According to Gilson this reminder may refer to the *Discourse*.[26] But his suggestion that there is no relation between this "*Histoire*" and the *Regulae* is somewhat awkward. The *Regulae* have a Stoic tendency, like the *Studium Bonae Mentis,* and unlike the *Discourse.* But Descartes apparently abandoned the project of the *Studium* in 1625, and in 1627–1628 was working on the *Regulae* and the exposition of the method, as he promised at the meeting in the presence of Cardinal Bérulle. One can only suggest that Descartes was playing with the idea of writing such a history along with the *Regulae* (see Rule X). This intention was realized in the *Discourse;* and in 1637 Descartes sent Balzac a copy of the work to fulfill his promise (cf. AT I, 380–382).

The latter suggestion is an important one. If as early as 1628 Descartes had hit on the idea of writing a life story as a way of presenting his method and his conception of science, then the disguise of the storyteller is not wholly dependent either on the metaphysical meditations which he started in 1629 after his return to Holland[27]; or on the verdict on Galileo. The idea of defeating skepticism with its own weapons may also have been cherished for a longer time, perhaps even in 1627, at the time of the meeting in the presence of Cardinal Bérulle. The most powerful weapon in this struggle is the natural light of reason, stripped of all false intellectual prejudices. In the *Regulae* it is this metaphorical light in which intuition and deduction flourish.

The *Discourse* is even more subtle in its agonistic strategy: the disguise of the storyteller gives Descartes the opportunity to assume the moral and ethical position of an apparently genuine skeptic. This position enables him to deal with subjects that lie outside the scope of the *Regulae,* such as metaphysics, morals, and physics. But it also gives a new dimension to the knowledge that is obtained. While the intuition of the *Regulae* enables the pure intellect to grow with the searching activity developed by the method, the natural reason or "*bon sens*" of the *Discourse* makes it possible to take the whole person into account. The *Discourse* becomes "*consubstantiel à son auteur,*" to borrow Montaigne's famous phrase (*Essays* II, 18). The abstract or Platonic self-knowledge that is gained by the pure intellect is replaced by a self-knowledge that is aware of the full scope of the reasoning activity, extending into morals, physics, and metaphysics. The intuitive or intellectual conception of existence and thinking is then transformed into an actual experience which forms the basis for metaphysics and physics. In this sense the preliminary title of the *Discourse,* as a project of a universal science in which our own nature is brought to its highest perfection, is still the more correct one. Descartes, however, was fully aware of the consequences of this project. Only after publishing his metaphysics and his physics in the 1644 *Principles of Philosophy* does he dare to come back to this project in the 1647 preface of the *Principles.* Again a preface, like the *Discourse* (cf. CSMK, 53), but now written in the consciousness that his own method is completed. At the stage of the *Discourse* lacunae still remain, within the moral and political consequences of the metaphysics and the physics which he is eager to publish.

Metaphysics and Physics

The thesis that the *Discourse* is "consubstantial with the life of its author" seems to be contradicted by its anonymous publication: the author has a life only in his story (cf. AT I, 381, ll. 11–13).

Furthermore, it is not altogether clear whether or not the replacement of intuition by a storyteller alters the Cartesian doctrine of method. In order to see that there is no alteration and that the idea of an anonymous presentation has a special meaning, it is necessary to examine carefully the development of physics and metaphysics.

As I have mentioned, in 1628 Descartes returns to Holland with the purpose of solving all the scientific problems that lie outside the scope of mathematics. After his visit to Beeckman—who turns down the offer to cooperate—

Descartes perhaps returns to Paris. In the spring of 1629 he surprisingly chooses his domicile in Friesland at the University of Franeker. There, as previously mentioned, Adriaen Metius, a famous professor of optics, is lecturing. Descartes tries to persuade the craftsman Ferrier to join him; he is obviously involved with his dioptrics.

But in July 1629 Descartes writes a letter to Gibieuf. He tells the reverend father how involved he is in writing a small treatise, and reminds him of an earlier promise to correct it. A comment to Mersenne in 1637 makes clear that this treatise contains at least a part of the *Meditations* (AT I, 350, l. 19 – 351, l. 2; cf. 182, ll. 16–22). The letter, however, does not mention the subject matter, and it might therefore be argued that Gibieuf was already familiar with it. ("I would not have mentioned that it was done, if I were not afraid that time would let you forget your promise to me to correct it and to lay the last hand on it": AT I, 17; see also AT III, 237, ll. 2–7.)

Three months later Descartes writes to Mersenne about meteorological phenomena; he intends to write a little treatise on the subject. The language will be Latin and the work will be a specimen of his philosophy. He asks Mersenne to keep this information confidential ". . . because I have decided to set it out publicly, as a specimen of my Philosophy, and to remain hidden behind the scenery in order to listen to what people say about it" (AT I, 23, ll. 23–26).

He also mentions his philosophy's relation to medicine. In the same letter he speaks of a physician's opinion, adding ". . . and by now I have taken sides concerning the foundations of Philosophy" (AT I, 25, ll. 10–11).

Only a month later he changes his opinion concerning the writing of treatises, and claims to have found a way to set out all his thoughts without being contradicted by others (AT I, 70, ll. 12–16). Then, in December 1629, he alludes to a treatise he will publish—anonymously, because it is in conflict with the theology of Aristotle (AT I, 85, ll. 7–22). This treatise will no doubt contain his physics, but dioptrics will also find a place in it (cf. AT I, 120, ll. 5–9).

In short, during the period 1628–29 Descartes is occupied with all the subjects of the *Discourse,* with the exception of mathematics (cf. AT I, 139, ll. 5–12). Those subjects are intrinsically connected, so that explaining one implies explaining all. In November 1630 he identifies the project as *Le Monde.* Within a year he has sorted out his way to deal with physics, metaphysics, and medicine. The metaphysical thinking of 1629 has given him an enormous push forward. In April 1630 he gives Mersenne his reason for abandoning several other treatises he had started earlier in Paris:

> While I was working on them I acquired a little more knowledge than I had when I began them, and when I tried to take account of this I was forced to start a new project rather larger than the first. (AT I, 137, l. 29 – 138, l. 4; CSMK, 21)

He compares this situation with a change of architectural plans, a metaphor which has a central position in the *Discourse.* It reflects the methodic connection felt among all the parts of his philosophy, as had been laid down in the *Regulae*. The plans now include all the things which he promised in that treatise, but the way in which the method proceeds has altered. The change concerns the order in which all the subjects considered are to be conceived, but not the method in principle. The transition from mathematics to science and metaphysics still illustrates the methodological connection which is explained in the *Regulae*. No wonder that after the condemnation of Galileo a few years later he wants to burn all his papers. The movement of the earth is such an essential part of his physics and philosophy that he confesses, "if that is false, the whole foundation of my Philosophy is also a mistake" (AT I, 271, ll. 10–11). And although he makes a sharp distinction between faith and philosophy, he does not want the Church to disapprove of a single word (AT I, 271, ll. 14–18)—not because of a kind of submission of science to the Church, but because the certainty of the whole of his philosophy is jeopardized by the condemnation. For this reason alone he refuses to publish his physics (cf. AT VI, 8, ll. 18–29 and 60, ll. 4–25). The jeopardy results from Rule II of the *Regulae*, in which it is said that philosophy must speak for itself without allowing any room for debate, when it is a true philosophy. And so the *Discourse* emerges from a conscious deliberation: methodically it must speak for itself, but at the same time it must convince everybody that the verdict of the Church was philosophically mistaken. The method persuades everybody of this mistake in its own way by using the light of reason. At the end of the *Discourse* Descartes testifies once more to the resulting heuristic character of the science he intends to establish: "In short, if there was ever a task which could not be accomplished so well by someone other than the person who began it, it is the one on which I am working" (AT VI, 72, ll. 16–19; CSM I, 148).

Given full possession of the method, an adequate directing of the mind toward solid and true objects can provide the guarantee that the project can be finished. The *Discourse* therefore has a rhetorical function: it must persuade everybody that the Cartesian method is the only one in which the mind can be perfected. Only then can the true science of all things be attained.

The anonymous character of the storyteller is part of this persuasive activity: only in this way do the arguments speak for themselves independently of the man who developed them (cf. AT VI, 3, ll. 3–24 and 5, ll. 8–18). Precisely because everything in metaphysics, morals, and medicine is at stake, it is necessary to rule out every kind of interest in Descartes as a person. The storyteller will thus have to prove anonymously, as if he were method itself, what was stated at the beginning:

> . . . the power of judging well and of distinguishing the true from the false—which is what we properly call 'good sense' or 'reason'—is naturally equal in all men, and consequently . . . the diversity of our opinions does not arise because some of us are more reasonable than others but solely because we direct our thoughts along different paths and do not attend to the same things. (AT VI, 2, ll. 5–12; CSM I, 111)

In this way the *Discourse* pursues a method in science that is consubstantial with the elaboration of human nature.

Conclusion

The *Discourse* seeks to persuade people in possession of the natural light of reason of the following:

(1) There can be a science that is true and certain.
(2) This science must be acquired by using a heuristic method which proceeds like the method of analysis in mathematics: one learns the necessary insights through step by step exercise.
(3) The method does not stand on its own: through exercise the mind itself develops toward a perfect capacity even for metaphysical knowledge.
(4) In the process of development self-consiousness in moral issues will be reached on the basis of true metaphysics.
(5) The *Discourse* must persuade everybody, because if anything is wrong, the whole architecture collapses.

From these five points the importance of the *Discourse* for actual philosophizing might be inferred. First of all, Descartes places philosophy and metaphysics on a par with science when he develops his method along with his mental capacity. Philosophy's task is not only to control or to criticize science from an external position; nor does philosophy have the exclusive right to examine certain questions which demand a specific attitude. Philosophical, metaphysical, and scientific questions are interconnected in the search for truth. But that interconnection does not imply that philosophy loses its own way of dealing with questions. Precisely at the point where it must be decided whether or not pure scientific reasoning contains any real truth, the metaphysical question concerning the relation between simple, clear concepts and reality needs an answer. In the end, all scientific reasoning therefore becomes dependent on the apprehension of the thinking mind in the *cogito, ergo sum.* That dependence shows that Descartes, at the beginning of an era in which science is to assume large proportions, was aware of the fact that science is not merely a construction of the world "out there," but that it also develops and determines the thinking intellect itself. One must necessarily concede certain and true scientific knowledge, but only in philosophy and metaphysics can one become conscious of the consequences of that necessity.

The most intriguing of these consequences is already discussed in the *Regulae*. It concerns the limits of science and those of the mental capacities. Although it is according to Descartes no longer necessary to limit the mind to specific attitudes for any field of science and philosophy, this does not mean that mental activity—or, consequently, certain scientific knowledge—is unbounded. The faculty of knowing is finite, and this finitude is to be one of the main themes of the *Meditations*. There, as the apprehension of thinking activity is drawn out, the essential finitude of the mind becomes the foundation for recognizing or touching the infinity of God. Just as the human mind is not able to conceive God, to grasp a concept of the infinite, so too the mind is unable to conceive everything clearly and distinctly at first sight. In other words, the mind is capable of mistakes, and not every question can be perfectly understood. Although science may grow indefinitely, it still will be necessary to articulate that knowledge within the scope of human existence where practical, philosophical, political, and religious matters and purposes are in question. The mask of the anonymous storyteller is a manifestation of Descartes's belief that science will only yield limited results in those matters, but on the other hand that these results are valid, for they result from the natural light of reason. The combination of a scientific attitude with a literary, narrative style of expounding philosophy is therefore perhaps the most interesting problem for actual philosophizing that is raised by the *Discourse on Method.*[28]

Notes

1. The French version was nevertheless not very popular; it took almost twenty years before it was reprinted. The work's popularity derives mostly from the Latin version, especially in Holland and Germany.

2. J. Mittelstrass, *Neuzeit und Aufklärung* (Berlin, 1970), 388–396.

3. J.-L. Marion, *Sur l'ontologie grise de Descartes,* 2d ed. (Paris, 1981), 185–191, and *Sur la théologie blanche de Descartes* (Paris, 1981).

4. K. Jaspers, *Descartes und die Philosophie* (Berlin, 1956), 102.

5. Buchdahl has given a strong argument for such an analysis in *Metaphysics and the Philosophy of Science* (Oxford, 1969), 2.

6. See E. van Leeuwen, *Descartes' Regulae. De eenheid van heuristische wetenschap en zelfbewustzijn* (Amsterdam, 1986).

7. Cf. *Regulae ad Directionem Ingenii,* Rules II and III: AT X, 362–370.

8. Jaspers, *Descartes und die Philosophie,* 80–81.

9. Cf. J.-P. Weber, *La Constitution du texte des Regulae* (Paris, 1964).

10. R. Descartes, *Règles utiles et claires pour la direction de l'esprit en la recherche de la vérité,* trans. J.-L. Marion (mathematical notes by P. Costabel) (Haag, 1977).

11. Hegel was apparently struck by the interpretation of the *cogito* as an Anschauung instead of a syllogism; see *Enzyklopädie der philosophischen Wissenschaften,* 1830 (Hamburg, 1969), 91. Cf. J.-L. Marion: "Il ne s'agit pas la seulement ni d'abord d'un discours tenu *sur* la méthode, mais bien d'un discours tenu *par* la méthode sur ce qui des lors apparait comme un domaine sujet à son empire." ("La Situation métaphysique du *Discours de la Méthode,*" in *Le Discours et sa Méthode,* ed. N. Grimaldi and J.-L. Marion (Paris, 1987), 366.

12. The ego of "*je pense, donc je suis*" does not necessarily contain a personal reference to Descartes: the *Discourse* was deliberately published anonymously. Cf. G. Rodis-Lewis, *Descartes* (Paris, 1984), 205.

13. The meaning of the Greek "*methodos*" is "the way, the route that is to be taken."

14. The Greek verb "*heuriskein*" means something like "to find out consciously the thing to be sought." For a fuller discussion see E. van Leeuwen, *Descartes' Regulae,* chs. 4 and 7.

15. I. Beeckman, *Journal* (Haag, 1953) III, 94–95.

16. P. A. Schouls, *The Imposition of Method* (Oxford, 1980), 36.

17. The *Discourse on Method* is certainly not an example of the discursus of Rule XVII, but it does have a preparatory function which is comparable with the process of enumeration. Summing up all the items that are possibly involved makes it possible for a complete, sufficient, and/or orderly enumeration of all the aspects of the Method to emerge. The resulting order of enumeration is a matter of disposition, which may even be altogether arbitrary (cf. AT X, 391, ll. 13–14).

Rules VII and X show ways of doing this, and the text of Rule X shows some resemblance to the plan of the *Discourse on Method.* Rule X calls upon the reader to exercise the method, and the intellect, by re-searching previously made discoveries and artifacts that explain or presuppose an order. Descartes provides an example by recounting his own experience with the method, and continues by pointing to the work of craftsmen—weavers—and to number-play. All these activities presuppose a kind of order that may even be fictitiously imagined, but through which one can penetrate, almost playfully, into the intimate truth of things (AT X, 405, ll. 13–16). This playful penetration is totally absent in the dialectics of the school, which must therefore be rejected.

All the elements of Rule X are also present in the *Discourse on Method.* (In the latter Descartes also puts forward his own discoveries and artifacts.) Moreover, intuition is not mentioned in Rule X. According to Rule XI (cf. AT X, 408, ll. 11–16), Rule X is exclusively concerned with enumeration aimed at preparing all the possible orders of the elements to be disposed. After that preparation, the resulting order will coalesce into an object of intuition—the only human intellectual "instinct" (cf. AT II, 599, l. 8).

The *Discourse,* though not a true discursus in the sense of Rule XVII, can therefore still be seen as preparation for an intuition of the method, ensuring sufficient study of all relevant subject matters.

18. Rule XIII states that problems (*quaestiones*) only arise when intuitive understanding is not possible. Then judgment, which might be true or false, arises—and therefore, we might infer, discourse (cf. AT X, 432, ll. 11–22 and AT VI, 2, l. 5).

19. Brunschvicg has made a clear case for the influence of Montaigne on Descartes and Pascal; see *Descartes et Pascal, lecteurs de Montaigne* (Neuchâtel, 1945).

20. See R. A. Popkin, *The History of Skepticism from Erasmus to Spinoza,* (London, 1979), chs. 3, 4, 9; and E. M. Curley, *Descartes Against the Skeptics* (Cambridge, MA, 1978).

21. Cf. Popkin, *History of Skepticism,* 114.

22. Cf. AT I, 7–11.

23. L. Guez de Balzac, *Oeuvres* (Paris, 1665) II, 308.

24. Cf. Popkin, *History of Skepticism,* 120.

25. Balzac, the man of letters, probably thought of Descartes as the new Zeno, busy with an irrefutable and certain science.

26. Cf. E. Gilson, *Etudes sur le rôle de la pensée médiévale dans la formation du système cartésien* (Paris, 1930), 279. Gilson follows the suggestion of Cohen; see G. Cohen, *Ecrivains français en Hollande dans la première moitié du XVIIe siècle* (Paris, 1920), 416–418. See also G. Gadoffre, "La Chronologie du six parties," in *Le Discours et sa Méthode,* ed. Grimaldi and Marion.

27. Here the famous phrase of 1619 must be recalled: "Ut comoedi, moniti ne in fronte appareat pudor, personam induunt: sic ego, hoc mundi theatrum conscensurus, in quo hactenus spectator exstiti, larvatus prodeo" (AT X, 213). Furthermore, Burman

writes up his conversation with Descartes about the *Discourse* not in the usual dialectical way, but as real statements of Descartes in which the meaning of the author is explained (AT V, 177–178). So even in 1648, in a private conversation, Descartes seems to stick to his disguise. For a fuller discussion of the place of morals in the *Discourse,* see E. M. Curley, "Coherence ou incoherence du *Discours*?" in *Le Discours et sa Méthode,* ed. Grimaldi and Marion.

28. I want to thank Johan van der Hoeven who stimulated me in writing this paper and Stephen Voss who in his friendly manner kindled me with enthusiasm in preparing, correcting, and editing it.

16
From Metaphysics to Physics

Geneviève Rodis-Lewis

TRANSLATED BY FREDERICK P. VAN DE PITTE

The conclusion to Part IV of the *Discourse on Method* draws a contrast between the moral assurance that we possess a body and that a world exists, and the metaphysical certainty present only in clear and distinct ideas. At the end of the *Principles of Philosophy,* moral and metaphysical certainty take on a methodological function. The probability that an explanation is true grows with the number of properties deduced from first causes, even if these were merely suppositions to begin with. Metaphysical certainty grounds the rule of evidence in God, who is "the source of all truth," and then extends from mathematics to everything so demonstrated in physics, and the knowledge that material things exist.[1] Their existence has been proved at the beginning of Part II of the *Principles,* as it was in the Sixth Meditation, but moral assurance was sufficient for elaborating a scientific explanation of the universe.

What were "the foundations of physics"[2] that were provided by the commencement of metaphysics interrupted in 1629? How is Descartes led to take up "several metaphysical questions" when he composes *The World*—and what are they? When he writes on 15 April 1630, he is the process of discovering them, and he makes explicit only God's free creation of eternal truths. That principle's application to physics has been the object of several studies,[3] both with respect to its justification of a priori deduction and with respect to the complementarity between hypotheses and experiences. We shall simply provide clarifications of the continuity of this theme from the *Discourse on Method* to the *Principles,* in which the progress of moral certainty aims at enlarging the domain of laws established with metaphysical certainty. We shall examine in particular the stages of science's subordination to God, and some of its consequences: What are the meaning and limits of the "fable" of *The World?* What is the difference between hypotheses, which move toward a conjunction with the real, and the "comparisons" employed in the Essays, which are not based on "principles"? Is the modern notion of a model ruled out, and with what legitimacy? Science, liberated from all reference to divine exemplarism, is indeed the work of man. But in the statement of its laws, it cannot "dispense with God."[4]

The principal foundation gained in 1629 is the validation of our reason, when it sticks to what is clear and distinct, as in mathematics: the young Descartes was struck by "the certainty and evidence of its reasonings" (*Discourse* I: AT VI, 7). But the ideal of a "perfect science"[5] remained for the Scholastics an abstraction, derived from the physics of qualitative elements and substantial forms. As early as 1619 Descartes dares to hope that he can clarify the mysteries of nature with the laws of "mathesis."[6] He then elaborates a method in which the "certain and indubitable [*indubitata*] knowledge" (*Rules,* Rule 2: AT X, 362) of mathematics is opposed to probable opinions suspected of falsity. (The Latin "*probable*" suggests approval; in French he uses "*vraisemblable*" instead [*Discourse* I: AT VI, 8].) In 1637 the simplest reasonings of the geometers were placed in doubt (*Discourse* IV: AT VI, 32); the statement of the first precept of the method (*Discourse* II: AT VI, 18) introduces this action of the mind, which subjects ideas and the sensible to the hyperbolic rejection, as "absolutely false," of everything that can be shaken by "the least doubt," even by a simple imagination or fiction (*Discourse* IV: AT VI, 31). Descartes had not made all of his arguments explicit at the time, for fear of restricting the weakest minds.[7] The *cogito,* resistant to the reiteration of doubt, makes it possible for the precept of evidence to be stated as a "general rule" (AT VI, 33), a rule which the existence of God renders "assured" with "metaphysical certainty" (AT VI, 38). This subordination is renewed when Descartes passes to the "order of questions concerning physics" (title of Part V): he assumes "no other principle" than those which have demonstrated "the existence of God and the soul,"[8] accepting "nothing as true which does not seem to me to be more clear and more certain than the demonstrations of geometers had previously seemed."[9] But this divine guarantee in no way extends to the sensible.[10] The hypothesis of a generalized dream renders even belief in the world possibly illusory. The existence of God rules out universal error, and we can then be content with the "moral assurance" that bodies exist. For this is something that no one of good sense has ever doubted, the Synopsis of the *Meditations* goes on to say. And the proof added in the Sixth Meditation aims less at establishing it than at confirming that "the knowledge of God and our soul" is more certain than it is (AT IX, 12)—something which the *Discourse* had already stated (AT VI, 37). Descartes's purpose always remains "to withdraw the mind from the senses."[11] Their appearances (color, the size of the sun, and its movement) "can also deceive us very often without our being asleep," even though a geometer can invent a true demonstration in his dreams (cf. *Principles* I, a. 30): "whether we are awake or asleep, we must never permit ourselves to be persuaded except by the evidence of our reason, and never by our imagination or our senses" (AT VI, 39).

At the same time, our clear and distinct ideas impose themselves "in us" as "real things which come from God" (AT VI, 38). Descartes knows how to make good use of feigned ideas. He does not begin with a classification of the various kinds of ideas, as he does later in the Third Meditation: At the end of that Meditation, for the idea of God, and at the beginning of the Fifth, for geometrical essences, he discovers their innateness in parallel fashion by contrasting their internal necessity with fiction or with the fragile limitations of ideas perhaps received from without.[12] After the first demonstrations of the perfect God, on the basis of my imperfection and dependence, as in the Fifth Meditation, Descartes applies himself first to "the object of geometers," which he conceives (reflecting its evidence) "as a continuous body, or an indefinitely extended space" with the three dimensions of Euclidean space, "divisible into different parts which may have various shapes and sizes, and be moved and transposed in every way" (AT VI, 36). Because we have the moral assurance that there is a world, it matters little that these essences are only possible (for only the existence of God imposes itself as necessary). But has Descartes in this manner identified geometrical extension and matter? Here, perhaps, we have the major inadequacy of this second metaphysical foundation of physics, born of the initial meditations of 1629. In order better to destroy scholastic sensualism (AT VI, 37) Descartes maintained that the discovery of my thought, as having "no need of any place" and depending on "no material thing" (AT VI, 33), defined it as a "substance" separate from the always doubtful body; and that this helped us to think of God as pure spirit.[13]

Interested in the observation of an exceptional phenomenon, parhelia, Descartes uses this simple geometrical model to integrate it into the "orderly" explanation of "all meteorological phenomena" (to Mersenne, 8 October 1629: AT I, 23) and before long of "all of physics" (13 November: AT I, 70). In order to escape the traditional closed world, which God held in his hand "like a ball," and which the young man had perhaps aspired to possess in rivalry with God,[14] he invents the "fable" of a "new world," whose nonpolemical and methodological functions we must clarify. But if it is located in the "imaginary spaces" of the Scholastics, how can he succeed in distinguishing this abstraction from a matter which is really divided and in movement? It is in finding a way to do this that he is led to return to God and to take up "several metaphysical questions."

The difficulties and discoveries of this first stage may have pointed Descartes in the direction of a more rigorous "order of reasons" when, after 1637, he set about clarifying the excessively brisk and incomplete metaphysics. Before explicating the "question" taken up during the composition of *The World,* let us recall the contributions of the last stage: the Second Meditation deepens our distinct *knowledge* of thought and extension (to which the analysis of the piece of wax tends to reduce matter). After the proofs of God, the Sixth Meditation intervenes in the demonstration of the existence of bodies to demonstrate the real distinction between two types of substance.[15] Incorporating complementary considerations and a division of the material into brief articles for pedagogical reasons, which ultimately renders the sequence of reflections more difficult to follow, the *Principles* follows the same overall order.[16] This work, developing the rooting of physics in metaphysics, establishes, like the Second Meditation, the distinct knowledge of two essences

(*Principles* I, a. 8, "substance" being added in the French translation); then, as in the *Discourse,* contrasts God as pure spirit with "extension," which "constitutes the nature of bodies," and involves the imperfection of divisibility (a. 23). After mentioning the common notions referred to body (a. 48: size, three-dimensional extension, shape, movement, position, and divisibility), Descartes says that the principal attribute constituting the essence of substance is, for body, extension (aa. 52–54). Finally, article 60 lays down the *real* distinction between thinking substances and "extended or corporeal substance, although we do not yet know with certainty whether such a thing is present in the world." And article 1 of Part II, which accords its existence metaphysical certainty, after having recalled that we are "sufficiently persuaded" of it, explicates better than the *Meditations* the opposition between the two natures, which would make God a deceiver if either he or another mind "were presenting immediately to our soul . . . the idea of this extended matter." The end of the *Principles,* at article 206, recapitulates these metaphysical foundations—"God being . . . the source of all truth,"[17] and articles 22–24 of Part I having completed the *Meditations* account of the divine attributes and subordinated the deductive method in physics to "the author of everything which *is* or *can* be,"[18] which authorizes the progression of hypotheses toward the real.

Part IV of the *Discourse,* which corresponds to the beginning of the uncompleted metaphysics, is content with moral assurance concerning bodies. In pursuing "the whole chain of other truths," after he recalls the "principle" of evidence which governs all deductions, Descartes sets forth the correlation between "certain laws which God has *established* in nature, and of which he has imprinted such notions in our souls" that we discover them, with no doubt, "in everything which is or *occurs* in the world" (AT VI, 41)—the idea of a genesis being suggested here. The evocative element of the treatise follows: Descartes would very much like to get the public to desire its publication, if the difficulties which had made him postpone it were removed. He compares it to a "picture" (*un tableau*) which, starting with light, would pass from stars and all bodies to "man" who "is their spectator."[19] Interested to see how such a novel metaphysics as his would be received, Descartes had taken care to publish his physics while hiding behind the picture in order to overhear what was said about it.[20] Without employing the word "fable" here, Descartes says that he has resolved "to leave this whole world" to the "disputes" of the "learned," and to speak freely "of what would happen in a new one, if God were now to create somewhere, in imaginary spaces, enough matter to compose it" (AT VI, 42). This is the first use of the term "create" in the *Discourse;*[21] it refers to chapter 6 of *The World,* where "the invention of a fable" (heralded at the end of chapter 5; AT XI, 31) presents God as creator, also for the first time. Chapters 6 and 7, within the freedom provided by fiction, refer to the new "metaphysical questions" which Descartes is led to take up again, right up to the one made explicit in the letter of 15 April 1630, which he includes ("within fifteen days": AT I, 146) in the conclusion of chapter 7 on the evident "eternal truths" of mathematics: "God himself has taught us that he has disposed all things in number, weight, and measure" (Wisdom 11: 20): "the knowledge of these truths is so natural to our souls" (innateness, as always) that we distinctly conceive them as valid for all worlds, if God "had created several" of them (AT XI, 47), a phrase repeated almost verbatim in the *Discourse* (AT VI, 43, l. 10).

Before this recourse to God as creator both of the matter which excludes empty space (AT XI, 32) and of its laws (AT XI, 47), Descartes had begun by presenting sensible qualities as a language, in order to reject all resemblance to appearances. The investigator must work out its code, a notion which appeared in the *Rules for the Direction of the Mind,*[22] and recurred at the end of the *Principles* (a. 205) with details about the decoding process. Color and pain are the product of movement; like the strap which exerts discomforting pressure on the soldier, flame exerts pressure on our eyes, and if we approach it we experience a tickling sensation and then pain.[23] Descartes has set out from immediately accessible experience (and not from the stars), with concrete examples; and in order to explain these changes he must assume parts which move (ch. 2: AT XI, 7) with a "very quick and very forceful motion" (AT XI, 8). "I consider that there is an infinity of different motions in the world which endure permanently," declares the opening passage of chapter 3; and in the sequel empty space is denied, with the support of "some . . . experiments" (AT XI, 17–18 and 20–21). In this way the scientist has "recognized through different experiments that all the motions which occur in the world are in a way circular" (AT XI, 19). Chapter 5 denies the qualities that were paired off to give rise to the four "elements" of the "philosophers" (AT XI, 23–24 and 25–26). Instead, he proposes three elements: fire, which is very subtle and, with its minute and swiftly darting particles, capable of penetrating every crevice; air, which is composed of spheres juxtaposed like grains of sand; and earth, which has coarser and less mobile parts.

Then suddenly, in chapter 6, there begins the "fable" of a new world coming to be "in imaginary spaces," with the supposition that God, very distant from "all the creatures" he "made five or six thousand years ago, . . . creates anew . . . so much matter . . . that . . . no place can be perceived that is empty" (AT XI, 32). Why this sudden recourse or return to God at the heart of the "fable"? The primary aim acknowledged by Descartes is to avoid "disputes" with "the learned," by leaving "all of this world" to them—and since they surrender to him these indefinite "imaginary spaces" with which they surround it, he will suppose that God creates there "enough matter to compose [the new world]" by agitating "in various ways, and without order, the different parts of this matter" (*Discourse* V: AT VI, 42).

When he was beginning to write *The World,* Descartes asked Mersenne "whether there is anything definite in religion concerning the extension of created things, namely, whether it is finite or rather infinite, and whether in all those regions that are called imaginary spaces there are true created bodies" (18 December 1639: AT I, 86). The letter to Chanut of 6 June 1647 will recall that "the Cardinal of Cusa" thought "the world infinite" without being rebuked by the Church (AT V, 51). In 1629 Descartes had "no desire to deal with this question," but found himself "constrained to prove it" (AT I, 86). The possibility of confusing the infinite world with God had cost Giordano Bruno his life. But as early as chapter 3 of *The World,* Descartes spoke of "the origin and the source of all . . . motions" (AT XI, 12). He never admitted the necessary eternity of matter, as did Spinoza, whom Leibniz reproaches for rejecting an initial complete formation of the universe.[24] The letter to Chanut develops the difference between divine infinity, which alone is perfect, and the indefinite, the absence of limits (AT V, 51–52). Now, while the term "indefinite" is rare[25] (and often replaced by the expression "ad infinitum"), as early as the composition of *The World* it is applied to the divisibility of particles (ch. 3: AT XI, 12) and to the extension of matter (ch. 6: AT XI, 32). It is therefore no longer a question of juxtaposing another world, "*déréalisé,*"[26] in imaginary spaces, with the real world considered as finite. By substituting this indefinite universe within the Genesis narrative, Descartes avoids the temptation of a certain concordance[27] with the stages of scientific differentiation. The sacred history was "written for man," and seems to make of him "the end of creation," which increases our love for God (see to Chanut, 6 June 1647: AT V, 53–54; *Principles* III, a. 3, on this "pious thought"). That does not rule out the existence of "an infinity of other creatures" (to Chanut: AT V, 55) in worlds inaccessible to us but subject to the same "laws of nature"; for they have "no other principle than . . . the infinite perfections of God" (*Discourse* V: AT VI, 43) and are valid for every intellect. Descartes often insisted on the benefit of "this vast idea of the extension of the universe," which (expressly this time) rules out "imaginary spaces" as well as anthropocentrism: it is the third metaphysical foundation of morals (to Elisabeth, 15 September 1645: AT IV, 292; and to Chanut, 1 February 1647: AT IV, 609). Indirectly it also destroys geocentrism. Descartes derives a lesson for his own philosophy from the biblical narrative: creation was not conceived on the basis of a prior model; God always acts as a perfect Being, and because he has determined to make the things in the world, as Genesis says "they are all good."[28] And faith, always respected and distinguished from science, leads him to *believe* that Adam and Eve were created in a perfect and complete state of humanity (*Principles* III, a. 45).

But above all the new genesis has an explanatory function, and if there is a breach in the exposition of *The World* between the initial formation of the world from chaos[29] and the description of a "man" as a machine which is already complex (and functioning independently of its union with a soul), this is only because Descartes is unable to carry out enough experiments to enable him to describe its formation. "The multitude and order of the nerves, veins, bones and other parts of an animal does not show that nature is insufficient to form them, provided we suppose that this nature always acts according to the exact laws of mechanics, and that it is God who has imposed these laws on it."[30] With respect to inert as well as living bodies, Descartes permits mechanism alone to act in nature, but always "following the . . . laws established by God" (*Discourse* V: AT VI, 42). "God has established these laws so marvelously" that even beginning with "the most confused and the most complicated chaos . . . the parts of this chaos disentangle themselves, and dispose themselves in such good order that they have the form of a very perfect world" (*The World,* ch. 6: AT XI, 34–35). It matters little whether we suppose at the beginning a division into equal parts—a hypothesis less shocking to the minds of the young, for whom the *Principles* were intended (III, a. 46). The point is always to combine a real division of matter which excludes any vacuum with the movement that determines the different configurations progressively separating out the three elements. Part I of the *Principles* develops the metaphysical foundations, including the attributes of God in articles 22–24. Chapter 7 of *The World* ends with the correlation between the "eternal Truths" of mathematics and their innateness in our souls (AT XI, 47), after having stated at the beginning that "nature alone" could sort out "the chaos, following the laws that God has imposed on it" (AT XI, 36). Two planes can always be distinguished: "the laws of nature" which govern its "changes," and the immutability of God who "continues to maintain it in the same way in which he created it" (AT XI, 37). Descartes does not speak of a first movement (the fillip) and its temporal continuation. Through an immutable constancy, creation imposes an indefinite movement in a straight line. And thus there commences a differentiation which the impossibility of the smallest vacuum requires to proceed by vortices. Leibniz reproached Descartes for the vicious circle involved in the relativity between shapes (which are the effects of motion) and motions (which have no internal force, and refer to the position of shapes).[31] The *Principles* accentuates this relativistic presentation, perhaps in order to set up the language of Part III, which denies the motion of the earth without condemning Copernicus (aa. 17–19, 33, 38–39); and by insisting on "hypotheses" as such, the author forestalls any condemnation. But the immutability of God always grounds the initial division of matter and the conservation of the same quantity of motion (II, aa. 36–37).

The World discloses little by little these "metaphysical considerations" in which Descartes does not become involved: God is immutable (ch. 7: AT XI, 38). "For what more firm and solid foundation could one find on which to establish a truth . . . than to take the very solidity and immutability which are in God?" (AT XI, 43) "God alone is the author of all the motions in the world, insofar as they exist and insofar as they are straight; but . . . it is the different dispositions of matter which render them irregular and curved" (AT XI, 46).[32]

Now this combination of the effective and constant action of God with the passivity of moved and thus divided bodies introduces, through the model of the sling (AT XI, 45–46), a genuine centrifugal force, which seems to go beyond strict mechanism, but which also avoids the pure interchangeable relativity of motions and shapes, which would hold in an imaginary or abstract space when a geometer effects an ideal displacement. Eddies in rivers also display a dissociation between the lighter elements and the condensation of heavier ones: this image is developed in Part III of the *Principles.*[33] In Part V of the *Discourse,* the model of fermentation with its resulting heat is invoked in order to provide an account of cardiac expansion and the circulation of the blood.[34] In the absence of a scientific chemistry, and because the particles may be extremely small, the model implies elements which still escape observation. (Descartes uses "flea glasses [*lunettes à puces*]": *Dioptrics,* Discourse 7: AT VI, 155, the microscope not being perfected until the second half of the century.) He rejects any recourse to the occult, which Harvey's pulsific faculty seemed to him to be.

Thus complex phenomena are referred to combinations of variable structures and movements—shocks, undulations, and dissociations of elements progressively reduced to a dust much finer than what Morin had seen flitting in a ray of sunlight (12 August 1638: AT II, 304), above all crowding together "like a continuous liquid filling all the spaces which the coarsest bodies cannot occupy" (to Morin, 12 September 1638: AT II, 373). The same letter defends the comparisons employed in the Essays: unlike the Scholastics, who mixed together the spiritual and the corporeal, with qualities and forms, Descartes "compares only motions to other motions, or shapes to other shapes, etc.; that is, things which cannot be perceived by the senses because they are too small are compared to others which can be perceived" (AT II, 368). The comparisons of the Essays, and of the *Treatise on Man* (in which man is considered to be fully formed as a machine), are more an incentive to be content with mechanism than a model that can be directly transposed with its correlate. In biology, clocks or hydraulic machinery, organs or inflated sails, related by a difference of scale to physiological processes whose details escape us, are nice images, not precise explanations of each phenomenon. The comparisons of the *Meteorology* illustrate the effects of condensation or rarefaction resulting from simple motions.[35] The ones that open the *Dioptrics*[36] each accentuate an aspect of light, and are complete without being taken literally; it matters little that he who immediately receives a spatial modification by contact through a stick is blind.[37] The little spheres which "tend to fall in a straight line" (*Dioptrics* 1: AT VI, 87) in all directions are not crushed like grapes; in his response to objections sent to him Descartes insists on the difference between motion and simple pressure, in which the *tendency* to motion must be combined with the laws of equilibrium.[38] And the rebound of a ball can be totally deadened or absorbed—in the same way that the reflection of a ray of light (from bodies that we call white) can be absorbed when the light encounters what we perceive as black—or it can be directed along a different angle, as though losing velocity in passing through a cloth (a suggestion about refraction: Discourses 1 and 2: AT VI, 91–101); but in order to calculate such a thing, it is necessary "to appeal to experience" (2: AT VI, 102–105). Moreover, by "slanting" their rackets, tennis players are able to "graze" the ball, "a change which makes us see colors" (1: AT VI, 91–92, and *Meteorology* 8, on their "spinning": AT VI, 335).

Thus it is necessary to bring together "the three comparisons" in order to have all the "particulars" concerning what transmits a ray of light and causes us to see colors (AT VI, 104). These "comparisons . . . assist in . . . conceiving" light without "telling us truly what its nature is" (*Dioptrics* 1: AT VI, 83). Each of them has a precise function, whose concrete point of departure must remain outside of science.

Descartes also increases the number of images in order to hold the reader's attention, and to persuade him or her that the liveliness of qualitative appearances resolves itself into combinations of shapes and motions, even when they remain imperceptible. Fish swim very quickly without causing a ripple on the surface of the pond, if they are at the bottom (*The World,* ch. 4: AT XI, 19–20). Eels often slip into the *Meteorology,* like subtle matter into every crevice. In Discourse 3 salt, which is pointed and piquant to the tongue, is compared both to a diamond and to a "very pleasant odor of violets" (AT VI, 250, 258, 262); but when distilled, its parts become flat and cutting, like the leaves of an iris or a gladiolus (AT VI, 264). A letter discusses the passage of wind through wool, and invents ideal experiments with a tube or an inverted glass under which cooled air contracts: in giving this description Descartes writes "in haste" (to Reneri?, 2 June 1631: AT I, 205–208). The "particular truths" of the Essays are presented without the "general causes on which they depend," but their convergence with experiences should prompt us to judge that the scientist could not have "discovered them" without knowing these first causes (to Morin, 13 July 1638: AT II, 201).

"Since things could have been ordained by God in an infinity of different ways, it is by experience alone (*and not by the power of reasoning,* adds the translation) that we can know which of all these ways he has chosen" (*Principles* III, a. 46; cf. *Discourse* VI: AT VI, 64–65). Deduction was grounded in the *Principles* on the attributes of God, along with the creation and immutability of the laws of motion. Descartes accords them "metaphysical certainty," and extends it to "*the principal and most general*" things that have been demonstrated in physics "*by the principles of mathematics or by others at least as evident and certain*" (*Principles* IV, a. 206; emphasized passages added in the French translation). The Latin text already mentions the "stars" that are called "fixed," including the sun among them (III, aa. 13, 21, 23–24, 29, etc.—the earth's wandering indicating that it is a *planētos*—"a wandering star": a. 14). In spite of his precautions with language and his insistence on the relativity of astronomical hypotheses, Descartes has quite abandoned geocentrism, and admits the possibility of several worlds around each star (changing place—slowly for us—in relation to each other), in an indefinite universe. Science will take "several centuries" to explore it, since "particular experiments" must be directed by "very intelligent men" (*Principles,* Preface: AT IX-2, 20). Just as in our actions we progress from the best judgment possible toward the ideal of a perfect judgment,[39] the multiplication of experiments will reduce little by little the role of what is called moral certainty (a. 205), by confirming initial hypotheses. When this completely mechanical philosophy was found to be dull-witted or common (*crassa:* Froidmont, 13 September 1637: AT I, 406), Descartes clarifies the limits of our observation, first guided by "ratio," which is always mathematical and evident. Just as the dust in the ray of sunlight obscures the continuity of fine matter, so the tiny particles that are hardly visible in stones, trees, or meats must be divided still further in order that what is no longer perceived by our senses "*propter nimiam exiguitatem*" because its fineness is too extreme, might be considered "*ad exemplum et similitudinem*" after the model of and the resemblance to what we see.[40] Because Descartes was conscious of the limits of our observation, he projects into the chemical model of boiling or fermentation completely mechanical effects, in order to rule out any "vegetative or sensitive soul," which no one would suppose present in wet stacked hay (*Discourse* V: AT VI, 46).

In the same way, after observing eddies in water, playing with a sling, and rotating a vessel filled with shot and wood chips,[41] he describes what has since been called centrifugal force—without, however, integrating a true force into matter. This motive force (*vis movens*) is that of God himself (*ipsius Dei*), "who preserves as much motion in matter as he had imposed [*posuit*] on it at the first moment of creation" (to More, August 1649: AT V, 403–404). And he denounces the anthropomorphism of More, who projects into bodies (even at rest, when he speaks of resistance) the power our soul has to move our body.[42] But the creative and continuous act of God remains transcendent; it is not immanent in nature like the world soul of the Platonists.[43] Descartes thus thought that he had established forever the "principles" from which "all truths" would be deduced (*Principles,* Preface: AT IX-2, 20).

Principles or "first causes" are the point of departure for all deduction. After Descartes has made much use of the architectural image of "foundation,"[44] the 1647 Preface accentuates continuity of development by comparing all of philosophy with a tree (AT IX-2, 14–15; ever since the onset of systematic doubt, Descartes spoke of "uprooting" "wrong opinions" or "errors": *Discourse* II and III: AT VI, 22 and 28). Its metaphysical roots include "the principles of knowledge," along with "the explanation of the attributes of God," from which flow the creation of the universe, the constancy of its laws, and their enactment, as well as "all the clear and simple notions which are in us," permitting deductions on the model of mathematical reasoning. Between God and the criterion of evidence, the philosopher mentions "the immateriality of our souls": this element will intervene in morality at the top of the tree, and before that it will exclude from physics, by the distinction of two types of substance, every "form" (the soul alone can be the form of the body) and everything the Scholastics had inappropriately projected from the psychic onto the physical.[45] Physics, then, constitutes "the trunk," which takes in the properties and functions of all bodies, both inert and living. It nourishes the many branches above: all the "useful" applications that Descartes disdained in his youth[46] and then exalted at the end of the *Discourse* (VI: AT VI, 61–62). Ten years later, medicine, one of the three principal branches, with mechanics, is disconnected from morals, so much progress is still to be made. This higher morals will also progress, in proportion to the certainty due to continual confirmation of its principles by their agreement with experiences (*Principles* IV; a. 205).

But what happens if the trunk dies? Descartes would never have thought that certain of his scientific hypotheses would last by being grafted onto principles other than his. Christian Huygens[47] and Newton deepened our understanding of centrifugal force within a totally different context. Roemer applied the principle of observing eclipses of a satellite to measure the velocity of light; Descartes had chosen the moon, which is too close—the blind man's stick was too short. And he linked the truth of his whole system to the instantaneous transmission of light.[48] At the end of the century Malebranche discovered the explanation of colors in terms of frequency of vibration, by abandoning the hardness and immobility of tiny spheres with a tendency to spin. And he contemplated directly in God the truths of intelligible extension, distinguished from matter.[49] In the hands of Einstein[50] does matter once again become the explanation of physical phenomena simply by its extended structure? But for Descartes, a created mind cannot conceive any geometry other than Euclid's. The reduction of the physical object to a three-dimensional, homogeneous, and undifferentiated space produces all the impasses of strict mechanism. By the constant subordination of its laws to God, Descartes wanted to make the sap rise in this tree. Will it rise far enough, through the metaphysical discovery of freedom in man, to bring to maturity its fruit—generosity?[51]

Notes

1. *Principles of Philosophy* IV, a. 206. If they do not call for further detail, we give references in parentheses in the text. We emphasize in a special way the additions of the French translation, which are important in articles 204–206, and are found in italics in volume IX-2 of the Adam-Tannery edition.

2. To Mersenne, 15 April 1630: AT I, 144: the expression refers to reflections during the first nine months spent in the Netherlands, before August–September 1629, when he interrupts his composition. Then, when writing his physics, he will "encounter several metaphysical questions" (AT I, 145).

3. F. Alquié, *La découverte métaphysique de l'homme chez Descartes* (Paris, 1950), sees, following E. Bréhier (in three articles of 1937, in *La philosophie et son passé* [Paris, 1937]), the emancipation of physics and the perfection of mechanism (Alquié, *Découverte,* 92–94, 114). Both affirm that Descartes does not return to the doctrine of eternal truths in his finished works. In *L'Oeuvre de Descartes,* 2 vols. (Paris, 1971), we show the echo of this doctrine in chapter 7 of *The World,* in the *Discourse on Method* (Parts V and VI), and in *Principles* I, aa. 22–24. On the letter of 15 April 1630 and its connection with the physics of the creation of truths, E. Garin, *Vita e opere di Cartesio* (Bari, 1984), 87–90, indicates in conclusion what we are developing here: "Si preoccupi dei fondamenti metafisici della sua fisica o . . . di non collocare la struttura su un piano di assolutteza autonoma." In 1949, M. Noda published an article in Japanese in *Le Sens* on "Physique et métaphysique chez Descartes" (excerpts trans. by M. Kobayashi appear in our *Descartes, textes et débats* [Paris, 1984], 385–386). His doctoral thesis deals with "l'articulation de la physique et de la métaphysique chez Descartes." In June 1987, Kobayashi presented to the Centre National de Recherche Scientifique (CNRS) "La position de la philosophie naturelle du *Discours* dans les oeuvres de Descartes," published in *Problématique et réception du Discours et des Essais,* ed. Henry Méchoulan (Paris, 1988). He examines the double relation between hypotheses and indicative and discriminative experiments in the texts of *Discourse* V and VI. This point is also treated by W. Röd, "L'explication rationelle entre méthode et métaphysique," in *Le Discours et sa méthode,* ed. N. Grimaldi and J.-L. Marion (Paris, 1987), 91–94, 111–117, proceed-

ings of the Sorbonne colloquium of January 1987. On "Science et hypothèses chez Descartes," see M. Martinet, *Archives internationales d'histoire des sciences* (1974), 319–339, also in our collection of articles in French, *La Science chez Descartes* (New York: Garland, 1987). The fifth part of our *Descartes, textes et débats,* 381–522, develops and comments on texts concerning deduction, moral and metaphysical certainty, "fable," hypotheses, suppositions and images—without, however, distinguishing in the way done here certain "models" which involve an explanation by the laws of nature as they are established by God. In *Un autre Descartes* (Paris, 1980), P.-A. Cahné unites literary and critical points of view (see p. 81, "on the creative and non-illustrative force" of the image, and the "logical trickery" reducing analogy to the equality of an equation).

4. Pascal's phrase, according to his niece (*Pensées,* Brunschvicg ed., no. 77): after the initial "fillip," Descartes "has nothing more to do with God." This materialist tendency was evident in several of the presentations in the "Tavola rotonda" at Lecce (23 October 1987), where G. Giorello concluded that he "dispenses with God," and the materialist tendency was affirmed by Paolo Rossi and L. Geymonat. Their contributions are recorded in *Descartes: Il Discorso sul Metodo e i saggi di questo metodo, Atti del convegno di Lecce, Instituto dell'Enciclopedia Italiana,* 2 vols. (Rome, 1990). See also the presentations by A. Gabbey, "Explanatory Structures and Models in Descartes's Physics," and Archangelo Rossi, "Forze e moti circolari nella fisica di Descartes dalle *Météores* ai *Principia,*" I, 341–346. Many of these works refer to hypotheses and models, suggesting this complementary reflection to us. In a paper given at Edinburgh in 1977 on "Physique et métaphysique chez Descartes," P. Costabel emphasizes that the new metaphysics comes before physics, and no longer after it, so that it may justify physics without interfering "with the science of natural phenomena" (in *Démarches originales de Descartes savant* [Paris, 1982], 188). He reminds us (p. 182) of G. Bachelard's criticisms of "the metaphysics of the sponge," which mixes the concrete image (an aid to our conceiving the phenomenon) with the exclusion of the void by the essence of extended matter (which is metaphysics).

5. Scholastic texts are cited by E. Gilson, *Discours de la Méthode, texte et commentaire* (Paris, 1962) (on AT VI, 7, ll. 24–25); Gilson, *Index scolastico-cartésien* (Paris, 1979), entries on "Science"; and J. Sirven, *Les années d'apprentissage de Descartes* (Paris, 1928; reprint, New York: Garland, 1986), 185–186. We comment on a text by Clavius in our paper "Descartes et les mathématiques au collège: Sur un lecture possible de J.-P. Camus," *Discours et sa méthode,* 190 and 194–195; and Michelle Beyssade translates important extracts from it in an appendix to this paper, pp. 207–212.

6. Epitaph on Descartes composed by Chanut (quoted by Charles Adam, *Vie et oeuvres de Descartes.* AT XII, 590). We translate "Matheseos" by "of Mathematics" (*L'Oeuvre de Descartes,* 47: "*de la Mathématique*"); for in the spring of 1619, Descartes seeks to unify the sciences of the continuous and the discontinuous. The wonderful discovery of November, giving rise to the enthusiasm which preceded the dreams, spurs on "mathesis universalis." Chanut classes it as "Adolescens"; and, at the end of Part II of the *Discourse,* Descartes does not consider himself (at 23 years of age) sufficiently mature to establish the "principles" of "philosophy," whence the nine years of waiting and exercise in the method (*Discourse* III: AT VI, 28–30).

7. We develop this point in "Du doute vécu au doute suprême: ses limites dans de *Discours,*" presented at the 29 September 1987 conference on Descartes at Barcelona-Sitges, and published in Carlos Martin Vide, ed., *Simposio: 350 años del Discurso del Método de Descartes. Actas del III congreso de lenguajes naturales y lenguajes formales* (Barcelona, 1988), III-2, 865–885. See the letter to Mersenne, spring 1637: AT I, 350.

8. *Discourse* V: AT VI, 41. Descartes always follows this order of ontological

priority (and not of discovery) when he speaks of the content of the beginnings of metaphysics (to Mersenne, 15 April and 25 November 1630: AT I, 144 and 182: the "existence of God, and that of our souls when they are separated from our bodies, from which their immortality follows"). See the titles of the *Meditations* (as early as 1641, the Synopsis makes clear that immortality is not demonstrated, but follows from the real distinction between soul and body: AT VII, 13–14; AT IX, 10).

9. *Discourse* V: AT VI, 41. This confirms that they are placed in doubt and that they are subordinated to God. From the time when Descartes first speaks of his metaphysics, he claims to have demonstrated its truths "in a manner which is *more* evident than the demonstrations of geometry" (15 April 1630: AT I, 144).

10. Contrary to the conclusions of J.-M. Beyssade on the rehabilitation of "sensible certainties," guaranteeing "the infallible superiority of waking over dreaming," in "Certitude et fondement. L'évidence de la raison et la véracité divine dans la métaphysique du *Discours de la Méthode,*" *Le Discours et sa méthode,* 343, 347 and 348.

11. This formulation is repeated in Latin in the letters of 1637 (AT I, 351, 353) and 1638 (AT I, 560), as well as in the Synopsis of the *Meditations* (AT VII, 12; AT IX, 9).

12. We show this probable implications in the first manuscript in "On the Complementarity of Meditations III and V: From the 'General Rule' of Evidence to 'Certain Science'," in *Essays on Descartes' Meditations,* ed. A. Rorty (Berkeley, 1986). The developments of the Third Meditation, classifying three sorts of ideas (without permitting this to go further at that time) and then distinguishing their formal and objective reality, would come later. See "Hypothèses sur l'élaboration progressive des *Méditations* de Descartes," *Archives de philosophie* (1987), 109–123.

13. To Mersenne, spring 1637: AT I, 349–350: This insufficiently explained distinction renders the demonstration of God "difficult to understand." We develop the point in "L'état de la métaphysique cartésienne en 1637," in *Descartes: Il Discorso sul Metodo* I, 105–118.

14. The letter to Chanut of 1 February 1647, after having mentioned the "very great error of wanting to be gods," rejects the finite world, enclosed "in a sphere" (AT IV, 608 and 609). For the relationship between the "melon" of the first dream of 1619 and the insignia of power over the world, see *L'Oeuvre de Descartes,* 52–53, and notes on 452–453. We go more deeply into the temptation and the nightmare in "L'alto e il basso e i sogni di Descartes," *Rivista di Filosofia* (1989), 189–214.

15. Gilson having considered this order to be a "paradox" (*Etudes sur le rôle de la philosophie médiévale dans la formation du système cartésien* [Paris, 1951], 300), M. Gueroult justifies it (*Descartes selon l'ordre des raisons* [Paris, 1953], II, 173–174), without making explicit the double role of the distinction. More neatly stated in the *Principles* (II, a. 1), it appears in the Sixth Meditation as the opposition of "intellectual substance" to a "corporeal or extended substance" (AT IX, 62–63).

16. J.-M. Beyssade nicely analyzes "L'ordre dans les *Principia,*" in *Etudes philosophiques* (1976), 387–403, included in our collection of articles in French: *Méthode et métaphysique chez Descartes* (New York: Garland, 1987).

17. *Fons veritatis* is found in St. Augustine (*Confessions* XII, 30, 41), without God's *creation* of truth; and at the end of the First Meditation, in the (hypothetical) opposition of the true God to the fiction of an evil spirit (AT IX, 17).

18. In *Descartes, textes et débats* (p. 383), we emphasize how this specification of method in physics anticipates the order of reasons. In 1987, T. Nishimura defended a *these de 3e cycle* on "La création radicalement universelle dans la théorie de la science chez Descartes," justifying this composition of the *Principles.* (We observe that a. 28,

which rejects the examination of the "purposes" of God in "creating the world," continues as follows: "he is the author of all things," which allows "the faculty of reasoning which he has placed in us" to find how these things "could have been produced": hypothesis goes in advance of reality.) M. Kobayashi ("La position . . .") emphasizes the *Discourse on Method*'s concern with "everything that is or can be in the world, without considering anything . . . but God alone who created it" (*Discourse* VI: AT VI, 64).

19. *Discourse* V: AT VI, 41–42. This already suggests the relation of appearances to our vision. Above all, the study *Treatise on Man,* which begins with chapter 18, must have been a part of *The World,* which was interrupted at chapter 15. As early as 18 December 1629, Descartes wanted "to begin the study of anatomy" (to Mersenne: AT I, 102).

20. To Mersenne, 8 October 1629: AT I, 23. At this time he was anticipating the publication of the *Meteorology* "as a sample" of his "Philosophy," and by 13 November he wanted "to explain all the phenomena of nature, that is, all of physics" (AT I, 70).

21. P.-A. Cahné's *Index du "Discours de la méthode" de René Descartes* (Rome, 1977) lists six instances of "*créer*" in Part V (and one of "*création*"), as well as one instance in Part VI.

22. This point is developed in J.-L. Marion, *Sur la théologie blanche de Descartes* (Paris, 1981). Chapter 12 deals with the *Rules* (see also his translation and notes to it), as well as the progress in the *Dioptrics,* where Descartes attempts to use shapes to bring about "an understanding of the nature of things" (p. 248).

23. Chapter 2: AT XI, 9–10: tickling is the gentle pleasure felt by the sleeping infant when its lips are brushed with a feather; there is no resemblance between the mechanical cause and the qualitative effect.

24. P. Rossi recalled this at Lecce (see n. 4); by contrast, Boyle and Newton distinguish a first phase in the final constitution of the world, before it is submitted to the laws of mechanism.

25. In the *Conversation with Burman* (AT V, 167, on *Principles* I, a. 26), Descartes claims to have been the first to distinguish between "infinite" and "indefinite." The *Discourse* presents (once) "continuous body" as "indefinitely extended space" (IV: AT VI, 36). The adverb "indefinite" (without "*infinitum*") appears twice in the *Meditations* (AT VII, 51; translated by "*sans cesse*" and "*indéfiniment*" in the French: AT IX, 41). Other details (following the Japanese indexing) will be found in n. 28 of our contribution at Lecce (see n. 4 and n. 13)

26. In employing this term (*Découverte,* 94, 105, 114, etc.), F. Alquié has in mind the theory of a "technical science" (p. 104) oriented toward "conventionalism" (p. 114). The *Discourse* issues a call for increased "experiments" (Part VI), under the direction of the philosopher who interprets them; and the fable rejoins the "true world" (*The World,* chs. 6 and 9: AT XI, 35 and 63; it is similar to ours, ch. 15: 104; similarly for the "true earth" and the "true moon," chs. 10 and 12: 72, 80, and 83).

27. He had begun to learn Hebrew in order to read Chapter One of Genesis, which he thought closer to his system than traditional interpretations (fragment of a letter, added to the end of AT IV, at p. 698; dated 14 October 1630 in the De Waard edition of the Mersenne correspondence: see AT [revised edition] IV, 816). This hope recurs in 1641 (to Mersenne, 28 January: AT III, 296). But he later tells Mlle. de Schurman that he has found nothing clear and distinct there (AT IV, 700–701); and in the *Conversation with Burman* (AT V, 169, on *Principles* III, a. 45) says that the text is metaphoric, confusing sky and air. The Cartesian Cordemoy published a letter in 1668 to the Jesuit Cossart, maintaining the agreement between the first pages of the Bible

and what Descartes had written (*Oeuvres philosophiques,* ed. Clair-Girbal [1968], 258ff.): light appeared before the sun and vegetation appeared with no need for souls; he discusses the Hebrew term giving "living souls" (*Vulgate*) to animals, which he says signifies "living individuals" quite distinct from the mind (*mens*) breathed into man (pp. 268–269).

28. Chapter One of Genesis repeats six times "God saw that it was good," after the principal stages of creation, and summarizes in verse 31 "God saw all that he had made, that it was very good." Descartes cites this text in sec. 8 of the Sixth Responses (AT VII, 435–436), where the matter is raised by his spontaneous affirmation of the free creation of the essences of things, and of the mathematical truths that can be known about them (AT VII, 380). Previously, he had independently reinforced the foundation by extending the liberty of indifference in God to the creation of the true *and the good* (Sixth Responses, sec. 6: AT VII, 431–432). This is the principal text on the subject published by Descartes, in the same period as the *Meditations,* which had put off the study of the attributes of God (end of the Third Meditation and beginning of the Fifth Meditation).

29. On 23 December 1630, Descartes spoke with enthusiasm to Mersenne about it, clarifying his intentions and the significance of the project: "I am currently trying to disentangle chaos in order to let light shine forth from it, and this is one of the most profound and one of the most difficult matters that I could ever undertake; for nearly all of physics is included in it. I have to consider a thousand different things all together, in order to find a device by means of which I can speak the truth, without shocking anyone's imagination or offending against commonly held opinions" (AT I, 194).

30. To Mersenne, 20 February 1639: AT II, 525: he "believes in particular that he can explain its formation by natural causes," just as he had done in the *Meteorology* for the formation "of a grain of salt, or a little crystal of snow." If he could take up again his work on *The World* (that is, the part published separately under the title *Treatise on Man*), he would study in the animal "the causes of its formation and its birth." He attempts this in 1648 for "the animal in general" and not "man in particular" (to Elisabeth, 31 January: AT V, 112). We explain the parallel between the natural differentiation of elements and the genesis of organisms following the laws of nature, instituted by God, in "Limites du modèle mécanique dans la 'disposition' de l'organisme," in our collection *L'anthropologie cartésienne* (Paris, 1990).

31. *De ipsa natura* 13: the Schrecker translation is given in *Descartes, textes et débats,* 424–425.

32. The "theologians," Descartes adds, say that God is the author of all our actions insofar as they are right; we divert them (AT XI, 46–47). In Malebranche this becomes the infinite movement which the will receives from God.

33. *Principles* III, a. 30, on water whirling and carrying straws along. The planets are enclosed within subtle matter turning around "as well as a vortex having the sun at its center." In a. 55, this "impulse" (*vis*) "thrusts the globules of light away from the center": "*recedere conantur*"; in the revised edition, AT VIII-l, 351, cf. the similarity with the thought of Pascal (Brunschvicg ed., no. 368) on "light" spoken of as "*conatus recedendi*": "all this is crude like a blow from a stone" (with a sling). The meeting of two curvilinear currents also enables us to understand the passage of comets from one firmament to the other (*The World,* ch. 9: AT XI, 58–61).

34. In *The World* (ch. 4) Descartes maintains that "the heat of our heart is greatest, but we do not feel it because it is the normal state of things" (AT XI, 21). This scholastic belief is accepted as experiential.

35. On their discussion in the correspondence of 1637–38, and on the literal quotations from Father Fournier in his *Hydrographie* (1643), see our "L'accueil fait aux *Météores*" (in *Problématique et réception . . .*). On the limits of the image of eels in ch. 1, see the letter to ***, March 1638: AT II, 43.

36. G. Leisegang employs the term *Denkmodell* in his edition of *Descartes Dioptrik* (1954). In *L'Oeuvre de Descartes* (p. 506, n. 78) we also refer to E. Cassirer, C. F. von Weizsäcker, and H. Herz. In "Méthode cartésienne et modèle mathématique," *Modèles et interprétation* (Lille-III, Centre de recherche sur l'analyse et la théorie des savoirs, 1978), R. Lefèvre focuses on the mathematical model (as a purely rational analogy) and distinguishes it from "physical models drawn from the imagination" (p. 91: these are "utilitarian models, instruments of method"; but he does not stipulate their limits). We distinguish them here from "simple comparisons." (We dealt with these in turn in *L'Oeuvre de Descartes,* 182–185 and corresponding notes, 506–507; *Descartes, textes et débats,* 434–436, 442–456, and 478–488, with quotations from the *Treatise on Man* and commentary by P.-A. Cahné.)

37. The paradox is emphasized by M. Serres ("L'évidence, la vision, et le tact," *Etudes philosophiques,* 1968, 193), and licensed by A. Glucksmann (*Descartes, c'est la France,* ch. 4, sec. 2, "L'aveugle-roi," 212–221).

38. To Ciermans, 23 March 1638: AT II, 72 and 78: "*inclinationem sive propensionem ad motum.*"

39. From *Discourse* III (AT VI, 28) to the *Passions of the Soul* (a. 148), Descartes is content "with judging the best that one can, in order also to do his best," after having stated the ideal of the highest morality (*Principles,* Preface: AT IX-2, 14: "the highest degree of wisdom," it presupposes "a complete knowledge of the other sciences"): "It is sufficient to judge well in order to do well" (*Discourse* III: AT VI, 28). On the parallel with the two forms of certainty at the end of the *Principles,* cf. G. Canziani, *Filosofia e scienza nella morale di Descartes* (Florence, 1980), extracts of which are translated in *Descartes, texts et débats,* 406–409.

40. To Plempius for Fromondus, 3 October 1637; Latin, I, 421. In the letter to Plempius, 15 February 1638, Descartes describes a vivisection as a crucial experiment (without employing this term from Bacon's *Novum organum* IV, 67, though he mentions "Verulam" several times); the experiment is directed against Galen, who regarded arteries as bellows (AT I, 526–527; see the translation by Liard, and commentaries, in *Descartes, textes et débats,* 172 and 490).

41. An experiment described to Mersenne, 16 October 1639: AT II, 593–594: thus "the subtle matter which turns around the earth drives heavy bodies toward the center."

42. August 1649: AT V, 404: "*mentis nostrae . . . cui* [*Deus*] *vim dederit corpus movendi.*" This "force which the soul has to move the body" is a primitive notion which characterizes their union (to Elisabeth, 21 May 1643: AT III, 665). It is made progressively more precise, beginning with the Sixth Meditation.

43. In all of this correspondence with More, Descartes distinguishes the omnipresence of God from true extension, which is imaginable and divisible (5 February 1649: AT V, 270). For More, any spirit acting on matter is in some fashion present to it (5 March: AT V, 314–315). Concerning the impulse and the resistance attributed to two men attempting to launch a boat grounded in shallow water, one standing on the shore, the other in the boat, see the letter of 15 April 1649: AT V, 345–346.

44. On the employment of this term in the early works, see the references to AT X, 134, 179, 194, 216, 220, by J.-L. Marion, "Les trois songes ou l'éveil du philosophie," in *La Passion de la raison: Hommage à Ferdinand Alquié,* ed. J. Deprun and J.-L. Marion (Paris, 1983), 60. The two Latin quotations given by Baillet say, for

10 November 1619, "*mirabilis scientiae fundamenta*" (the enthusiasm preceding the dreams); and for 11 November 1620, "*fundamentum inventi mirabilis*" (AT X, 179). "One calls 'foundation' " that on which "one builds all the rest" (to Mersenne, 18 December 1629: AT I, 87). Descartes's reference to his studies at La Flèche contrasts the insignificance (techniques) of what has been "built" on the "very firm and very solid foundations" of mathematics with the superb palaces of classical morality, "which were built only on sand and mud" (*Discourse* I: AT VI, 7–8). The *Discourse* announces "the foundations of metaphysics" (AT VI, 1), after having rejected "shifting earth and sand in order to find rock and clay" (III: AT VI, 29): the *cogito* is the first stable bed, resting on the divine rock. The term is frequently employed both in major texts and in the correspondence; Descartes will repeat for the *Meditations* what he had said in 1630 (AT I, 144) for the first metaphysical reflections: that they "contain all the foundations of my physics" (to Mersenne, 28 January 1641: AT III, 298). Galileo had indeed examined "physical matters by means of mathematical principles," but "he built without foundation" (to Mersenne, 11 October 1638: AT II, 380), etc.

45. Sixth Responses, sec. 10, on the conception of weight, and of all the real qualities and substantial forms, on the basis of lived experience of the soul acting on the body (AT VII, 441–443; AT IX, 240–241).

46. Concerning the disdain for techniques, current at that time, and the reversal in Part VI of the *Discourse,* when the new physics has replaced the "speculative philosophy" of the "schools" (AT VI, 61–62), see "Descartes et les mathématiques au collège . . . ," in *Le Discours et sa méthode,* 191–194.

47. T. Gregory quotes Baillet's remarks on the life of Descartes in which Christian Huygens specifically reproaches Descartes for wanting "to make people believe that he had found the truth . . . by establishing himself . . . and glorifying himself in the privacy of the beautiful network of his expositions." *Scetticismo ed empirismo. Studio su Gassendi* (Bari, 1961), 78–79.

48. To Beeckman, 22 August 1634: AT I, 307–308; and 312 on the eclipse of the moon precisely when it is on a straight line with the sun and the earth: there is not even a half-minute of time lag; cf. to Mersenne, 11 October 1638: AT II, 384. In the article "Light" in his *Encyclopedia,* d'Alembert emphasizes that if he "was in error concerning the motion of light," Descartes "had imagined the means for determining the time light takes to traverse a certain space." Unfortunately, "the moon was too close". . . .

49. G. Rodis-Lewis, "Les limites initiales du cartésianisme de Malebranche," in *La Passion de la raison,* 231ff., esp. 239–247. Concerning the explanation of colors, see Malebranche, *Recherche de la vérité,* Eclaircissment XVI, with commentary by P. Costabel, in *Oeuvres complètes* III, 383–418.

50. The relationship is discussed by F. Le Lionnais, "Descartes et Einstein," *Revue d'histoire des sciences* (1952), 139–150; reprinted in our edition *La Science chez Descartes.*

51. "Le dernier fruit de la métaphysique cartésienne: la générosité," *Etudes philosophiques* (1987), 43–54.

17

Reason, Nature, and God in Descartes

Gary Hatfield

Descartes was a scientist before he was a metaphysician. The Descartes we know today, the Descartes of the evil demon and the *cogito,* was the later, metaphysical Descartes, who used his philosophy to ground his physics. The earlier Descartes studied mathematics, music, optics, and mechanics, and he was rumored to possess a special method that would guide the way to certain knowledge in any field. But he was not a metaphysician, and he gave no indication of having envisioned a general physics. He did not have the deep foundational aspirations of the Descartes we know.

The transition from the early to the mature Descartes—his "metaphysical turn"—is of great interest. Some of its distinguishing features are well known: the mature Descartes, by contrast with the early Descartes, employed skeptical arguments, presented metaphysical arguments for the existence of God and the real distinction between mind and body, and claimed to have discovered the metaphysical foundations of physics. He also proposed the remarkable doctrine that the eternal truths are God's free creations. French interpreters, especially, have contended that this last fact provides a key to understanding Descartes's metaphysical turn.[1] As we shall see, it is a key best understood in the context of Descartes's attempt to secure foundations for his physics through a reformulated theory of the human intellect and its objects.

Descartes's metaphysical turn shows itself in the contrast between his early *Rules for the Direction of the Mind* (abandoned in 1628–29) and his mature metaphysical works, the *Meditations* and the *Principles of Philosophy.* The *Rules* is a general methodological treatise that gives instructions for guiding the mind to certain and evident knowledge. Unlike Descartes's later works, it claims no greater certainty for the products of this method than that found in ordinary arithmetic and geometry; the veracity of human cognition is never questioned, and there is no hint of skepticism.[2] The work of the mature Descartes differs in two respects. First, he now envisions a comprehensive, unified physics of the entire universe, in which all explanations of natural phenomena are reduced to a few principles governing matter in motion; this unification of explanatory principles does not appear in the *Rules,* which merely claims methodological generality.[3] Second, this general physics is provided with a deep metaphysical foundation established through a radical process of doubt, in which even the truths of mathematics are called into question. Within the hierarchical structure of knowledge built upon this new foundation, the existence of God and the spiritual nature of the human mind are known as well as, or better than, the simplest of mathematical propositions, such as that two and three make five (AT VII, 4, 157).

It has become a commonplace of Cartesian scholarship that Descartes's metaphysics was wholly or largely in the service of his new physics—and indeed Descartes himself suggested this connection in two oft-cited letters to Mersenne (AT III, 233, 297–298). But some commentators have questioned whether the new physics actually required deep foundations. Within physics itself, they argue, Descartes demanded no greater certainty than that of mathematics, and with respect to his various particular mechanistic hypotheses, he was willing to accept an even weaker standard of certainty.[4] Why, then, should Descartes have changed his strategy after the *Rules,* instead of simply extending the methodology of that work to the case of a general physics? Why did he need to adopt the radical skepticism of his mature works?

There have been three answers to this question. (1) Among intellectual historians, the typical answer has been that in 1628 or 1629, not long after abandoning the *Rules,* Descartes found himself in the grip of a skeptical crisis—a *crise pyrrhonienne*—which called all knowledge into question, including rational knowledge of God.[5] Descartes met the crisis by developing the *cogito* and the proof of a veracious God, and he chose to share these remedies with his contemporaries in the *Discourse on Method* and the *Meditations.* According to this interpretation, the doubt functioned in these works to defeat a very real skepticism by presenting and defeating its strongest arguments.[6] (2) The second answer emphasizes the methodological character of the doubt, and does not require that Descartes took the doubt seriously on its own terms. According to this interpretation, the radical doubt was used as a device, as a kind of touchstone, for separating the absolutely certain from the even minimally uncertain; the doubt was simply the flip side of the quest for absolutely unshakable knowledge, and the invocation of a deceiving God in the *Meditations* was simply a way of taking this methodological doubt to its extreme.[7] (3) The third answer also does not take the doubt literally, but for a different reason: both the doubt and its solution are regarded as products of dissimulation. According to this interpretation, the appeal to God in overcoming the doubt was camouflage for an inherently materialistic physics; the doubt and its resolution were elements in a carefully prepared Straussian ruse perpetrated to deflect the gaze of the Inquisition from, and to enlist the considerable authority of the Church in support of, Descartes's genuine intellectual product, his new physics.[8] Hence, his extended discussion of God and the soul and his use of hyperbolical doubt were elements of rhetorical strategy, not of philosophical argumentation.

Although I think that all three of these positions are correct inasmuch as they make the relation between God and the doubt paramount for understanding the deep foundationalism of the mature Descartes, I reject each of the proposed conceptions of that relationship. As I see it, the dissimulation hypothesis is correct in stressing that Descartes's overriding concern was his new physics, but it errs with respect to the role of God in Descartes's philosophy. The standard methodological reading of the doubt is on the right track, but it strays from the path in treating certainty as the chief, or perhaps the only, methodological aim. And although Descartes no doubt was pleased that his *Meditations* contained an answer to skepticism, answering the skeptics was the least of his concerns.

In my view, there are two levels at which to read the hyperbolic doubt and the metaphysical turn. The first grants a methodological role to the doubt, but one that goes beyond the mere quest for certainty, to a reform of the mind's cognitive practices. Descartes believed that the Aristotelian conception of the intellect and its objects was incorrect, and he used the doubt as a device to acquaint the reader of the *Meditations* with the proper function and objects of the intellectual faculty. The second, and deeper, level at which to read the metaphysical turn focuses on the relations among reason, nature, and God in Descartes. Specifically, it finds the root of the metaphysical turn in Descartes's reconception of the metaphysics of the relation between God and the essences of created things as expressed in his doctrine that the eternal truths are God's free creations. This doctrine allowed Descartes to affirm that essences of created things are completely comprehensible to human beings—and thereby to clear the way for the metaphysical foundations of his physics—while avoiding the obstacles to such conceivability implicit in scholastic metaphysical theology. At the same time, the new conception of the relations among God, essences, and the mind yielded an explanation of how the intellectual faculty can gain access to the objects of knowledge in the manner newly discovered through the practice of radical doubt.

The interpretation offered here seeks to make sense of Descartes's texts and the pattern of their development by placing them in a context sufficiently broad to include the fact that when Descartes wrote, innovation in metaphysics and natural philosophy could draw the scrutiny of Church authorities who wielded considerable power. But it should not be concluded that this interpretation will, therefore, explain Descartes's intellectual development in nonintellectual terms. In fact, I shall be attributing to Descartes an intellectual strategy that, I claim, allowed him to attack the intellectual basis for one aspect of what he considered to be the overly close relation between theology and metaphysics. Others who have dealt with the relation between philosophy and theology in Descartes have tended to focus on the sincerity of his religious convictions. Those who accuse him of dissimulation write as if he mendaciously brought religion and theology into his philosophy, while his defenders typically respond with evidence that he was sincere in attempting to prove both the existence of God and the distinction between the soul and the body.[9] I shall not question his sincerity; instead, I will attempt to show that Descartes responded to his context with an intellectual strategy that included his metaphysical turn, a strategy which, if successful, would allow him to pursue an innovative metaphysics and natural philosophy while giving metaphysics and theology each its due.

Intellectual Intuition of God and the Soul: Preparing the Intellect to Know Matter

The earliest known document in which Descartes refers to deep metaphysical foundations for physics is the letter to Mersenne of 15 April 1630, in which he also announces that the eternal truths are God's free creations. Just prior to that celebrated announcement Descartes writes that his attempts to know God and the soul by natural human reason had enabled him "to discover the foundations of Physics." Intensive study of God and the soul, he revealed, had already yielded considerable dividends. For, he continued, "I think that I have found how to demonstrate the truths of metaphysics in a manner that is more evident than the demonstrations of Geometry" (AT I, 144; CSMK, 22). According to Descartes, his studies of immaterial beings had opened a path to metaphysics and physics alike.

Descartes's suggestion that contemplation of God and the soul led him to the foundations of physics is intriguing. The claim is not entirely surprising, for in the *Meditations* consideration of God and the soul dissolves the radical doubt, through the *cogito* and the divine guarantee of intellectual perception, and hence prepares the way for positive claims to knowledge. But I wish to suggest an even tighter interconnection among radical doubt, contemplation of God and the soul, and the discovery of the foundations of physics than that effected by the use of the doubt to vindicate clear and distinct perception. This connection arises with a use for the doubt that differs from the methodological and antiskeptical uses described previously. As Descartes explains to Hobbes, he employed the arguments for doubting in the *Meditations* not only to achieve certainty and to defeat the skeptic, but also "to prepare my readers' minds to consider things which are related to the intellect, and help them to distinguish these things from corporeal things," and he adds that "such arguments seem to be wholly necessary for this purpose" (AT VII, 171–172). Elsewhere he describes this function of the doubt as "the withdrawal of the mind from the senses" in preparation for contemplating objects of the intellect.[10] In asking readers to withdraw their minds from the senses Descartes was not merely preparing them to make judgments about sensory things without following the "prejudices of the senses," nor was he simply helping them to consider immaterial beings, such as God and the soul, that do not fall under the senses. Although he surely had both of these aims, he was, I contend, primarily interested in having readers discover the proper use of the intellect itself as an epistemic faculty. This aim differs from simply weakening the grip of the senses on the intellect, for it will lead to the revelation that, contrary to Aristotelian doctrine, there is thought without a phantasm, there are objects of the intellect that can be known without considering images from the senses or in the imagination. God and the soul constitute two such objects. They are the objects first known in the order of the *Meditations,* but they are not the only things to be considered by pure intellect. Descartes contends that geometrical objects, too, can be understood independently of the imagination (AT VII, 72–73), and he uses this purely intellectual knowledge of extension or pure quantity to ground his claim that extension is the essence of matter (AT VII, 63; AT VIII-1, 41–42).

The purported discovery of a pure intellect sufficient in itself for the intuition of God, the soul, and the essence of matter marks the transition from the early to the mature Descartes.[11] The *Rules* predates Descartes's mature theory of the intellect, for in that work he considered the imagination to be essential to mathematical knowledge.[12] Nor is the mature theory presented outright in the *Discourse.* In the latter work the doubt figures merely as the counterpart to certainty. The doubt of Part I is a conventional skeptical doubt, deriving from disagreement among the learned over the propositions of a given subject matter; only mathematics exhibits the sort of agreement that does not induce doubt (AT VI, 7). These first doubts lead to the project of cognitive renewal in Part II, which is described in the familiar Cartesian metaphor of razing all that is uncertain and seeking a new method with which to construct a new edifice (AT VI, 11–14). There follow the four steps of the method and a description of a general science of proportion (AT VI, 18–20)—both reflecting the *Rules*—succeeded by announcement of the project to discover the principles of philosophy (AT VI, 22). In these passages doubt is used as a counterpart to the search for certainty, but the deep doubt of the *Meditations* does not appear. An approximation of the latter doubt is introduced in Part IV, in a quick survey of the arguments and conclusions that appear later in the *Meditations* (AT VI, 31–32); but the radical hyperbolical doubt of the evil deceiver is never broached in the *Discourse.* Interestingly, the metaphysical doctrine that extension is the essence of matter is not expressly stated either. Although the equation of matter with extension is indicated in the précis of *The World* contained in Part V (AT VI, 42–43), it is given the same hypothetical status there that it had received in the earlier, suppressed work (AT XI, 31–33) and as it would receive in the *Meteorology* (AT VI, 233).

The absence from the *Discourse* of both the radical doubt and the foundational metaphysics are, I believe, explained in a letter from Descartes to Mersenne. Descartes is responding to Mersenne's charge that in the *Discourse* he has not sufficiently explained the origin of his knowledge of God and the soul. He explains that the light treatment given to skepticism in that work precluded an adequate explanation of such knowledge:

> I could not deal any better with this topic without explaining in detail the falsehood or uncertainty to be found in all the judgments that depend on the senses or the imagination, in order to show in the sequel which judgments depend only on the pure understanding, and what evidence and certainty they possess. I left this out on purpose. . . . But about eight years ago I wrote in Latin an introduction into metaphysics, where all of this is deduced

> at sufficient length, and if this book [the *Discourse*] is translated into Latin, as has been suggested, I could have it included. However, I am convinced that those who study my arguments for the existence of God will find them the more demonstrative the more carefully they seek their faults. I claim that these arguments are clearer in themselves than any of the demonstrations of the Geometers; in my view they are obscure only to those who cannot withdraw their mind from the senses, as I wrote on p. 38.[13]

The Latin work that he envisions publishing is surely the *Meditations*. Thus, the suggestion of hyperbolical doubt, the use of doubt to withdraw the mind from the senses, and the deep foundationalism (in the form of the greater evidence of metaphysics over mathematics) all come together in the announcement of the *Meditations* as a work that will supply the arguments missing from the *Discourse*. But, as Descartes would soon reveal to Mersenne (AT III, 233, 297–298; CSMK, 157, 173), the *Meditations* was not solely, or perhaps even primarily, a work intended to prove the existence of God, for it contained the foundations of his physics, foundations that were promised but not revealed in the *Discourse* and *Essays*.

Let us take seriously for a moment the idea that the primary methodological function of radical doubt in the *Meditations* was intended to be the discovery of the pure intellect as an instrument of cognition, rather than the attainment of mere certainty. This understanding of the aim of the doubt explains how Descartes could hold that the *Meditations* would simultaneously reveal the foundations of his physics and "destroy the principles of Aristotle" (AT III, 297–298; CSMK, 173). First, Descartes claims to reveal to the reader that she has a maximally clear and distinct intellectual intuition of God and a direct apprehension of her own mind. If true, this claim entails that the scholastic Aristotelian theory of cognition is in error, for according to that theory (1) "intelligible species" (immaterial entities that represent intelligible things) are required for the act of understanding, (2) intelligible species can be produced naturally in the human mind only in conjunction with a "phantasm," or material image, in the imagination, but (3) there are no phantasms of immaterial begins such as God and the soul, which means that (4) an embodied intellect "cannot naturally possess clear and distinct cognition of immaterial substance," including God and the human soul.[14] Thus, by uncovering an "utterly clear and distinct" idea of God (AT VII, 46), and an idea of his own mind (VII, 43),[15] Descartes would provide immediate experiential evidence that contradicts (4) and undermines (2), given that (3) was common ground (VII, 181, 183).

Second, beyond providing this potentially devastating counterexemplification to the Aristotelian theory of cognition, Descartes directs the reader toward her innate idea of extension as the object of geometry, an idea that, he maintains, exhibits the essential attribute of matter (AT VII, 63, 71). But if it can be established that intellectual intuition of the sort that revealed God and the soul also makes evident that the essence of matter is extension, Descartes would have a basis for excluding sensory qualities such as color or heat—the "real qualities" of Aristotelian physics—from the ontology of matter. It would be difficult to establish the ontological priority of shape (a mode of extension) over color (an apparent property of sensible things) by reflection on sensory ideas alone; in vision shape and color always co-occur, and phenomenal color seems no less "clear" than does phenomenal shape.[16] However, if Descartes could provide grounds for rejecting the Aristotelian claim that knowledge of essences must be abstracted from sense experience, grounds he offers in his (alleged) discovery of purely intellectual knowledge, he would, given his doctrine that extension is an object of pure intellect, be able to provide justification for the claim that shape has primacy over color—for color is not an object of pure intellect at all.[17] On this reading the feature of the doubt that was missing from the earlier works, its use to "withdraw the mind from the senses," is the very feature that allows the *Meditations* to provide deep foundations for physics.

This reading may explain the curious juxtaposition of "the essence of material things" and "the existence of God" in the Fifth Meditation. The seemingly offhand transition from triangles to God (AT VII, 65) would be explained if Descartes intended to show thereby that the idea of a triangle, or of any mode of extension, is not an adventitious but an innate idea, with the same stubborn presence to reason that he accorded the idea of God. The juxtaposition of God and extension in the Fifth Meditation serves to demonstrate that both can be known through pure intellect. If we now recall Descartes's indication that it was by considering knowledge of God and the soul that he came to the foundations of his physics, we may be tempted to see the role of the *cogito* and the contemplation of the idea of God in the *Meditations* as preparatory to the discovery that extension is the essence of matter.

If this reading is correct there may be an element of dissimulation in the *Meditations,* but it is one that has been well remarked. When Descartes confided to Mersenne that the *Meditations* contained the foundations of his physics, he asked his friend not to reveal this fact, "for that might make it harder for the supporters of Aristotle to approve them."[18] Here is direct evidence for Cartesian dissimulation,[19] for in the prefaces to the work itself he told his readers, as well as the theologians of the Sorbonne, that his purpose was to prove the existence of God and the distinction of the soul from the body (AT VII, 2–3, 7, 9), but he hid from them the fact that the work was intended to provide foundations for his physics. Is it such a large step, then, to suppose that the investigation of the soul and God has as a primary purpose the preparation of the mind to perceive pure quantity, the essence of matter?

The conclusion that Descartes was more interested in using the light of nature for the pursuit of physics than for securing the rational foundations of faith need not cast suspicion on the sincerity of his religious convictions. As he wrote to an unknown correspondent regarding matters of faith, "No one who really has the Catholic faith can doubt or be surprised that it is most evident that what God has revealed is to be believed and that the light of grace is to be preferred to the light of nature."[20] We can, in other words, take Descartes literally when he writes to the theologians at the Sorbonne that as members of the faithful, "we must believe in the existence of God because it is a doctrine of the Holy Scripture, and conversely, that we must believe Holy Scripture because it comes from God" (AT VII, 2). If he goes on to invoke the standard motivation for rational proofs of God's existence—the need to address the unbeliever[21]—we need not see this as a manifestation of Descartes's evangelical zeal, because we know that the converts he wished to attract through the *Meditations* were converts to his philosophy, not to his faith. As a religious man, he gave the light of grace primacy over the light of nature. But as a natural philosopher, he claimed to have discovered the foundations of his physics through the contemplation of God and the soul, and he enjoined others to meditate with him in the pursuit of metaphysical knowledge (AT VII, 9).

Descartes and Theology

Consider the challenges facing Descartes. He wished to replace the old natural philosophy, which he found wanting, with a mechanistically conceived physics. His path was uphill and fraught with peril. Uphill, because the Aristotelian natural philosophy, with its appeal to substantial forms and real qualities, was deeply embedded in a widely accepted metaphysics of substance and a sense-based conception of the intellect. Perilous, because this metaphysics and epistemology were themselves closely connected with both natural theology and matters of faith, and apparent or actual disagreement with orthodox positions could be dangerous.[22]

Let us focus for a moment on the threat to natural philosophy from those who wielded, or who could influence, religious authority. Descartes's sensitivity to this threat is apparent from his reaction to Galileo's condemnation. Not only did he suppress his *World* upon hearing the outcome of Galileo's trial, he also contemplated burning all his papers (AT I, 270–271). Further, when he did publish his complete physics in the *Principles of Philosophy,* he disguised his affirmation of the Copernican system through the verbal ploy of arguing that the earth is at rest with respect to the surrounding ether, even while it is carried around the sun yearly by that same ether (III, aa. 19–29). Moreover, he was careful to affirm the doctrine that the universe was created fully formed, while at the same time restating his "hypothetical" account from *The World,* according to which the universe develops out of chaos in accordance with the laws of nature alone, without providential intervention (III, aa. 45–47). Finally, he explicitly placed divine authority above human reason (I, a. 76) and submitted all of his "opinions" to the authority of the Church (IV, a. 207).

Facts such as these led Charles Adam to propose that upon hearing of the Galileo affair, Descartes expanded his metaphysics—and especially his discussions of the soul and God—because he needed a "flag" to cover the "merchandise," that is, to cover his work in natural philosophy.[23] Yet even though Descartes reacted intensely to Galileo's condemnation, it would be an error to assume that his concern to be at peace with the Church stemmed solely from worry over that event. From as early as 1629 Descartes had complained about the intrusive intermixture of Aristotelian philosophy with theology, and over the next few years (prior to 1633) he showed interest in squaring his own teachings with official Church doctrine (AT I, 85–86, 150, 153, 179). So the Galileo affair could not have been the instigator of Descartes's concern with the relation between philosophy and orthodox doctrine. Even more importantly, it would be misleading to assimilate Descartes's concerns to the standard complaint, familiar from Galileo's letter to Christina,[24] that religious teaching (based on Biblical passages) was being imposed on natural philosophy when no article of faith was at stake. Although Descartes disapproved of such impositions, his own concern with the relation between theology and philosophy was focused elsewhere. With respect to what he termed "theology proper," he focused on cases in which philosophical teachings had become conjoined with theological interpretations of the objects of faith; with respect to natural theology or the metaphysics of God, he focused on the relations among God, essences, and human knowledge.

Within scholastic theology an intricate relation existed between natural reason and the objects of faith. In the tradition of theological science stemming from Thomas Aquinas, "theology proper," which was part of the sacred teaching of the church (*sacra doctrina*), receives its first principles from revelation rather than from natural reason.[25] Nonetheless, Aquinas allowed that natural reason could make at least four types of contribution to theology. First, natural reason could, independently of revelation, prove what were known as the "preambles of faith"; these preambles were the province of what Aquinas called "the theology which is part of philosophy" (later known as "natural theology").[26] Natural reason could be used, second, to defend the articles of the faith from attack by outsiders, for example, by reasoning from a shared revelation, as could Christians with Jews; third, to systematize sacred doctrine by deriving lesser known articles of faith from those better known; and, fourth, to make more comprehensible the objects of faith, as in explications of the trinity through analogies, or explanations of what happens to the substance and accidents of the bread and wine when (as faith revealed) the latter undergo transubstantiation. In this fourth case, the objective is not to prove by natural reason that the object of faith—for instance, the body and blood of Christ under the appearance of bread and wine—exists or has certain properties, but rather, given that it does exist with certain properties, to "make comprehensible to the human mind" or to "elaborate the contents" of the corresponding article of faith.[27] As a result of this last function of reason in theology proper, many features of Aristotelian philosophy became bound up with an orthodox understanding of the objects of faith. Indeed, the Council of Trent effectively made Aquinas's Aristotelian explanation of transubstantiation, which involved the alteration of one substance into another while the accidents of the first are preserved, an article of faith.[28]

Descartes objected especially to the use of Aristotelian philosophy to explicate the objects of faith. He, along with others of his acquaintance, including Pierre de Bérulle, Charles de Condren, and Guez de Balzac, envisioned a firm division between philosophy and theology, so that sacred doctrine would not be encumbered by philosophical explanation.[29] In his correspondence from 1630 onward Descartes enforced a strict division between questions that belong to theology proper and those that pertain to metaphysics; he treated any question resolvable by the natural light, including those about God, as properly metaphysical, leaving theology to address the mysteries of the faith.[30] He codified this strict division in his *Comments on a Certain Broadsheet,* which urges that in considering the relationship between reason and revelation three types of questions must be kept distinct:

> First, some things are believed through faith alone—such as the mystery of the Incarnation, the Trinity, and the like. Secondly, other questions, while having to do with faith, can also be investigated by natural reason: among the latter, orthodox theologians usually count the questions of the existence of God, and the distinction between the human soul and the body. Thirdly, there are questions which have nothing whatever to do with faith, and which are the concern solely of human reasoning, such as the problem of squaring the circle, or of making gold by the techniques of alchemy, and the like.[31]

His objections to scholastic theology focused on the importation of philosophical explanations into questions of the first sort. As he complained in a letter to Mersenne in 1629, theology had become "so bound to Aristotle that it is almost impossible to expound any other Philosophy, without it seeming at the outset to be contrary to faith" (AT I, 85–86). If we can trust Burman's record, nearly twenty years later Descartes bitterly attacked "Scholastic Theology," asserting that it "should above all else be stamped out," contending that "the simpler we keep it, the better Theology we shall have," and noting that, since "rustics" have as much chance to get to heaven as anyone else, "it is much more satisfactory to have a Theology as simple as theirs than one which is plagued with countless controversies" (AT V, 176; CB, 46–47). He did not go so far as to contend that theologians should refrain from using the light of reason in theology, but he assigned to reason the limited role of showing that things believed through faith are consistent with the "natural light" (ibid.; also, AT VIII-2, 353); presumably, this would not involve "explaining" or "elaborating" articles of faith, for, Descartes observed, "Theology must not be subjected to our human reasoning, which we use for Mathematics and for other truths, since it is something we cannot fully grasp" (AT V, 176; CB, 46). It is in the spirit of showing the consistency of his philosophy with transubstantiation that we should, I believe, read Descartes's discussions of the Eucharist.[32]

Descartes intended to show, by explicitly distinguishing metaphysics from theology proper, that one could deny Aristotelian philosophy without contradicting articles of faith. But he was also interested in another relationship between Aristotelian philosophy and theology, one pertaining to natural theology—or so I will argue.

Knowledge of God and Knowledge of Created Essences

Descartes positioned himself in direct opposition to the central teachings of Aquinas and his followers on how God is known. Within scholastic Aristotelian metaphysics in the Thomistic tradition, knowledge of God was deeply connected with knowledge of nature. God is known through nature as its prime mover and first, necessary, and highest cause. Further, God's purposes are revealed in the creation inasmuch as he is the designer of the universe; Aquinas and others used the notion of God as designer in the argument from governance (a version of what was later known as the argument from design). Descartes described a different route to knowledge of God, an inward path that avoided appeal to visible (corporeal) things. His proofs appealed, in one way or another, to the idea of God he claimed to uncover through pure intellection. He denied that human reason is privy to God's designs, banishing appeal to God's final causes from his natural philosophy.[33] In so doing he forsook use of the argument from governance as a proof of God's existence. (He of course offered his own version of a "cosmological" argument in the Third Meditation proof based on the idea of God.)

I think that Descartes also positioned himself in opposition to a less explicit connection between knowledge of nature and knowledge of God in scholastic metaphysics, one that rested on Aquinas's and Suarez's understanding of the implications about God contained in claims to know natural essences by natural means. From an Aristotelian perspective, "scientific" (systematic and necessary) knowledge of nature requires knowledge of essences, which means (in the first instance) knowledge of the necessary connections among the properties proper to individuals *qua* instances of a species of substance.[34] Thus, to know the essence of human beings is to know that human beings are animals; but, since animals necessarily are sentient, it follows that human beings necessarily are sentient. Aristotelian philosophers, including Suarez (citing Aquinas), explained these necessary connections by appeal to "real essences";[35] such essences ground the necessary connections in question by delimiting what properties a human or other kind must have. But what determines the domain of real essences? Suarez (as Aquinas) appealed to God's creative power in explicating the metaphysics of real essences, maintaining that the necessary connections between the properties of a real essence are at once dependent on God but independent of God's will.[36] Such connections are founded in the potentiality of real essences in God's creative power; hence, *humanity* is a real essence because a human being can be created, and *chimera* is not because one cannot.[37] In this way, these authors could explain how the truths about such essences can be necessary and eternal (being grounded in an eternal being). But this explanation implied that to claim to understand the necessary connections contained in such essences, such as the connection between humanity and sentience, is to claim to understand the limits of God's creative power.

Descartes's remarkable (and novel) theory that the eternal truths depend in an unlimited way on God's power can be seen as a response to these doctrines. In his famous letter to Mersenne of 15 April 1630, Descartes proclaimed "the mathematical truths which you call eternal have been established by God and depend entirely on him no less than do the rest of his creatures" (AT I, 145; CSMK, 23); he subsequently affirmed that God "is no less the author of creatures' essence than he is of their existence" (to Mersenne, 27 May 1630: AT I, 152; CSMK, 25).[38] I shall argue that this doctrine allowed Descartes to sever the relation between knowledge of essences and knowledge of God found in Aquinas and Suarez, and thereby to avoid what he took to be the unacceptable consequences of their doctrine for one who affirmed, as did he, that human beings fully grasp the essences of created things.[39] Further, I will suggest that this doctrine facilitated his reformed conception of the intellect and its objects by rendering acceptable his posited a priori access to such essences. If these suggestions are correct, then in one fell swoop Descartes could make progress on both of the challenges described at the outset of the previous section.

In order to understand how the doctrine that the eternal truths are created could serve as a counter to the scholastic Aristotelian conception of a strong connection between knowledge of God and knowledge of nature, it will be necessary to delve more deeply into scholastic doctrine, especially as presented by Suarez and interpreted by later authors.[40] The doctrine is complex and verbal pitfalls abound. For instance, Suarez affirmed that there are no real essences independent of existence; in fact, he denied that essence and existence are ontologically distinct. In this sense, he affirmed the creation of essences along with the creation of things, a verbal formulation that might be confused with the creation of the eternal truths. But Suarez did not think that the eternal truths are created, nor even that they depend on the actual existence of things; for he also maintained that there would be necessary (and eternal) truths (and hence "scientific knowledge") pertaining to essences, or to essential connections between essence and predicate, even if God chose not to create. For this reason, in seeking to understand Suarez on the eternal truths it will be useful to examine the status of the essences of creatures prior to (or rather, independently of) creation.[41]

Suarez reviewed four positions on eternal truths pertaining to essential connections, such as that "man is an animal," and he affirmed the fourth (DM XXXI.12.38–47; see also 2.1–5). (The knowledge in question is, in the first instance, divine knowledge, as is clear from the fact that it pertains to essences prior to, or even in the absence of, God's creative act.[42]) First, there is the position that such assertions are true only when human animals exist, a position that Suarez rejected out of hand; for although he thought that God is creator of essences and that the essence of (say) human beings exists only when human beings exist, he nonetheless held that a science of essences is possible and that this science can exist whether or not the essences in question (and the things that realize them) exist in actuality.[43] Truths about essences are eternal, whether things possessing those essences exist or not. In this manner, Suarez himself cast the question of whether there are eternal truths about essential connections as a question about such truths prior to creation.

According to the second position, essential truths are known from eternity in the divine intellect. Although Suarez agreed that essential truths are known by God from eternity, he did not hold this knowledge sufficient by itself to explain the eternal truths about essential connections. According to him, knowledge of everything, including contingent truths and truths about merely fictive beings, is in the divine intellect from eternity.[44] Given the extensive contents of the divine intellect, the problem becomes that of distinguishing knowledge of contingent truths (or of fictive beings) from knowledge of real essences or essential connections. Mere appeal to God's foreknowledge does not suffice, for this knowledge covers both contingent and necessary truths; furthermore, Suarez asserts, those propositions "wherein essential predicates are affirmed of subjects" would be known by God to be true "even if God had ordained that nothing would come to be in time." According to Suarez, there would be truths known by God about essential connections even had God chosen not to create anything at all and therefore had no foreknowledge of what would be created. Indeed, he maintains, these truths are true independently of God's intellect; they have eternal truth "not only as they are in the divine intellect but also in themselves and prescinding from it."[45]

These considerations lead to the third position, which addresses the problem of a science of essential truths by setting up these truths as necessary and eternal, seemingly independent of God. Surprisingly, this position, which Suarez labeled "the common opinion," is consistent with his favored doctrine that actually existing essences are created. For according to this third position, "the essences of creatable things are not eternal, absolutely speaking . . . but the connections of the essential predicates with the essences themselves are eternal"; each essential connection "of itself is necessary and eternal." Thus, even though the actual existence of essential connections in creatures is not eternal, the truths about such connections are; hence, a science of essential truths is possible (DM XXXI.12.41; W, 201). Yet Suarez rejects this position as well, precisely because it offers no explanation for the "eternal truth" of essential connections.

> If that connection of such a predicate with a subject is eternal, I ask what it is outside God? For, it is either something or nothing. If someting, how is it eternal without an efficient cause? If nothing, it is indeed not surprising that it does not have an efficient cause; but it is surprising that it could be eternal or that there would be a real connection, if it is nothing. (DM XXXI.12.42; W, 201–202)

He goes on to affirm that "not only do essences come to be but also the essential connections as well" (ibid.; W, 202).

It may seem as if we have now come full circle, back to the creation of essences and of (so-called) eternal truths, even as regards necessary connections. Yet Suarez does not draw this conclusion. Instead, he provides a closer analysis of the ways in which there might be eternal truths about as yet uncreated (and perhaps never to be created) essences. He frames his explanation as an analysis of the copula, though in fact the solution depends on his doctrine of real essences. He starts by distinguishing two senses of the copula "is." In the first sense, it indicates "a connection, actual and real, of the terms existing in the thing itself," in which case the proposition "a man is an animal" is true only when there are actual humans. In the second sense, the copula "only indicates that the predicate is of the nature of the subject, whether the terms exist or not" (DM XXXI.12.44; W, 203). The latter sense is the one needed to explain the possibility of a science of finite essences independent of creation. In explaining this second sense of the copula, Suarez compares propositions about essences with hypothetical conditionals: "just as this conditional proposition is eternal: 'If it is man, it is animal', . . . so, too, this is eternal: 'man is an animal'." In each case, there can be an eternal truth without the actual existence of human beings or of the essence *humanity* (DM XXXI.12.45; W, 204). But now Suarez introduces a final distinction, between two sorts of eternal and necessary truths involving the copula (and corresponding hypothetical conditionals); this distinction brings us to his actual explanation of the possibility of a science of essences independent of creation.

First, there are necessary and eternal propositions involving the copula which, "if we take our stand formally and precisely on their truth," do not depend either on the actual existence of things or on a cause capable of creating things. Suarez gives as examples conditional truths about both impossible and possible things: "If a stone is an animal, it is able to sense," "If man is an animal, he is able to sense," and concludes that just as these can be true without the existence of human beings or animals or causes able to produce them, so, more generally, the truth of " 'Every animal is able to sense' does not of itself depend on a cause which can effect an animal." In a startling continuation that has led many commentators to conclude that Suarez was willing to assert the truth of such propositions even if God did not exist, he adds that "if, by way of the impossible, there were no such cause, that enunciation would still be true, just as this is true: 'A chimera is a chimera,' or the like."[46] But these truths are unable to provide the desired explanation of real essences, as Suarez himself makes clear in introducing the second sort of eternal and necessary truth, that which is grounded in God's creative power:

> Yet, on this point, we should assign a difference between necessary connections, conceived and enunciated between possible things or real essences, and between imaginary things or beings of reason, that in the former the connection is so necessary in terms of an intrinsic relationship of terms abstracting from actual existence, that it is still possible in relation to actual existence. This whole can be indicated by the copula "is," even as it abstracts from time, so that when it is said: "Man is a rational animal," it is indicated that man has a real essence so definable, or (which is the same thing) that man is a being, which is not a fiction but real, at least possible. In this respect, the truth of such enunciations depends on a cause able to effect the existence of the terms. (DM XXXI.12.45; W, 205)[47]

Essential connections pertaining to uncreated but nonetheless "real" essences are true because such essences really could come into existence; by contrast with predications pertaining to fictive beings, essential connections are based on a connection of properties in an essence that exists "in its cause." In order to explain the necessity of these connections, it is not enough to appeal simply to the copula "is" or to compare certain predications with hypothetical conditionals; rather, the necessity of essential connections is grounded in the notion of *real essence.* As Suarez explained earlier in Disputation XXXI, such essences exist prior to creation "in the potency of God" (2.2; W, 58). Indeed, in Disputation II he defined a real essence as one "that can really be produced by God."[48] Thus, a proposition asserting an essential connection can be eternally true irrespective of the actual existence of the essence because it pertains to the essence as it exists "in its cause," that is, in God's creative power.[49]

There can be eternal truths about nonexisting finite essences, truths that depend on God but are not subject to his will, because God understands his own creative power and so understands which beings (and therefore which essences) are creatable and which beings are merely fictive (and cannot be made real). Essential propositions have eternal and necessary truth, not because the essences are independent of God, and not simply because of divine foreknowledge (say) that human beings will come into existence, and not simply because essences are "beings" of God's reason, but because God's knowledge of such essences arises from a necessity pertaining to human beings considered "in their cause." In this way, the doctrines that all truth depends on God and that God is the creator of essences can be maintained, without subjecting the essences to God's will, and therefore without undermining the possibility of a science of essences.

Mersenne, in his attack on Aristotelian natural philosophy in the years prior to and after 1630, affirmed that in the Aristotelian ontology and theory of cognition scientific knowledge of essences is equivalent to knowing the extent of God's creative power. Mersenne himself accepted that "the possibilities of things" and "the eternal and immutable truths" flow from God's being,[50] but argued that physical knowledge of the kind sought in Aristotelian natural philosophy is unattainable, because the human mind ultimately is unable to penetrate to the essence of a thing; to do so would be "necessarily to know it perfectly as God knows it."[51] In the face of this problem, he retreated to a kind of probabilism in physical science, which effectively denied the Aristotelian conception of physics. At the same time, he elevated the mixed sciences, such as astronomy, optics, music, and mechanics, all of which depend on mathematics; he contended that certainty is possible in mathematics, and that here the human mind can aspire to knowledge equivalent to God's.[52] These two positions need not be seen as contradictory. According to scholastic doctrine, mathematics pertains to the accidental in physical things, and therefore we can know it without knowing the true essences, which depend on God himself.

Given this situation, in which a consistent refusal audaciously to regard the human intellect as sufficient for comprehending divine power would naturally lead to skepticism with respect to a science of essences, we are in a position to appreciate Descartes's insight with respect to essences and eternal truths. First, in his well-known identification of the essence of matter with extension, he attributed to matter an essence that was the accepted paradigm of intelligibility; given this identification, there could be no doubt that the human intellect can grasp matter's essence. But, second, in adopting the doctrine of the creation of the eternal truths, including the eternal truths of mathematics, he could avoid the kind of audacity with respect to knowledge of natural essences that Mersenne found objectionable.[53]

Descartes's strategy comes into relief through consideration of what, precisely, was new in his account of the eternal truths. Suarez and Mersenne believed in the creation of essences and maintained that the truth with respect to both actual and merely possible essences depends on God. Descartes agreed on both points. Still, his doctrine marked a fundamental departure from Suarez and Mersenne.[54] According to the latter thinkers, the eternal truths are not subject to God's will; they are grounded in his creative power, and hence are realized in his understanding of himself. Moreover, these authors allowed that it is within the ambit of human reason to posit an intelligible connection between God and the eternal truths (though Mersenne doubted that we could grasp the connection). It was the intelligibility of this connection that Descartes denied in saying that the eternal truths are subject to the will of God, or that there is no distinction among God's understanding, willing, and creating (to Mersenne, 27 May 1630: AT I, 153; CSMK, 25–26).

But, further, Descartes's position allowed him to reject the scholastic Aristotelian theory of knowledge without adopting a Neoplatonic atlernative. Neoplatonists held that the essences of created things are an emanation from God. There were two ways of conceiving human knowledge of such essences, both of which ensured that the essences perceived by humans would serve for knowledge of the actual essences of things. According to the first conception, the human mind perceives the forms or archetypes of things in the divine mind;[55] it has direct epistemic access to the "originals" of the things in the world. Aquinas criticized this position for granting human beings a direct vision of God, and Suarez rejected it on similar grounds.[56] According to the second conception, the human mind possesses ectypal copies of the archetypal ideas in the mind of God.[57] Humans can know the essences of things without direct insight into the mind of God, but this position nonetheless implies that human knowledge of essences parallels divine knowledge, a position which, I have argued, Descartes was at pains to avoid.

Descartes's position allowed him to avoid both versions of Neoplatonism while nonetheless maintaining that the essences grasped by the human intellect serve for knowledge of the actual essences of things. According to the doctrine of the creation of the eternal truths, the created world and the knowing mind come as a package: matter is created with the essence *extension,* and human minds are created with an innate idea of—or an innate basis for the intuitive apprehension of—pure extension. There is a "pre-established harmony" between the ideas of the intellect and the essences of things.[58]

However, the implication of Descartes's doctrine is that this harmony should be conceived as mediated by God's will, rather than either by his intellect or by an intelligible connection between his power and his ideas. Descartes could adopt an innatist conception of the cognition of essences, without being forced to claim that the innate ideas he attributed to the human mind were reflections of the essential structure of God's intellect. In this way, the doctrine of the creation of the eternal truths could support Descartes's reformed conception of the pure intellect as a faculty capable of intuiting the essences of things.

Knowledge of God by the Natural Light

In the previous sections I have argued that we can make sense of Descartes's doctrine of the creation of the eternal truths by seeing it as part of a strategy to divest claims to knowledge of natural essences from the implication that such claims presuppose knowledge of God's creative power. Assuming that this interpretation is correct, it raises the question of how Descartes could claim to derive some of his most fundamental claims—such as that God is not a deceiver—from knowledge of God attained through the natural light. The problem of how the natural light can be used to prove the existence of God if its own veracity must first be guaranteed by God has long been raised in objection to the proofs for the existence of God in the Third and Fifth Meditations (see, e.g., AT VII, 214). The use of the natural light to prove the existence of God seems even more problematic if the natural light and the eternal truths it contemplates are themselves viewed as creations of God; for if the eternal truths are alleged to be creations of God, how could they provide an independent argument for God's existence? Moreover, if the separation of natural theology and natural philosophy was an intended implication of the doctrine of the creation of the eternal truths, it appears that Descartes directly contradicted this implication as early as *The World,* for there (AT XI, 37–38) and in the *Principles* (II, aa. 36–37, 39) he claimed to derive specific knowledge of the physical world from his knowledge of God, when he claimed that his three laws of motion follow from God's immutability. Both the proofs of God's existence and the derivation of the laws of motion seem counter to the idea that the relation between God and creation is unintelligible.

There appears to be a deep tension in Descartes's thought at this juncture. On the interpretation offered thus far, the creation of the eternal truths is a fundamental tenet of Descartes's mature metaphysics. But the proofs of the existence of God and the appeal to divine immutability are no less fundamental. However, the tension may not be as direct as it appears at first glance, for the truths about God used to prove his existence and to secure the laws of motion most likely are not created truths. Surely it is not a created truth that God exists, or that he is immutable—as Descartes seems to have recognized.[59] Perhaps, then, he avoided aggravating the charge of circularity by maintaining that there are uncreated truths about God that human reason can grasp—

truths pertaining to his immutability, his status as necessary being and cause of himself, and his perfection (which precludes deception). If so, it would seem that in the end Descartes did, after all, subject God to the tribunal of the natural light, inasmuch as the natural light grasps these truths.

This latter thought should give us pause, because taken in one way it yields incoherence. If the natural light is itself created by God, if he is responsible for its very consitution, then it is deeply problematic to say that he is subject to it. That would be like saying that the human mind, in its attempt to chart the conceptual space of both the mundane and the divine, could discover independent principles of God's being despite the fact that it was God who provided the mind with its charts and instruments. If the natural light is a created light, then whether or not there are uncreated eternal truths, the mind can be privy to those truths only through the natural gift of God (a gift dispensed to one and all, and one that is distinct from the gift of grace). God is subject to the natural light only to the extent that he chooses to be, which is to say that it is by his choice that we understand him in any way at all.

Interestingly, we find Descartes affirming a position very much along these lines in Part I of the *Principles,* in articles 22 and 28. He has already gone through the doubt and found his final reprieve in various proofs for the existence of God. Having recognized that God exists and that our existence depends on him, he begins to reflect on the attributes of God. In article 22 he describes God as, among other things, "the source of all goodness and truth," a phrase in which some have detected the doctrine of the creation of eternal truths.[60] I agree that the doctrine is to be detected here. However, the turn of phrase most revealing for present purposes comes six articles further on, where Descartes considers how knowledge of God could lead to knowledge of nature, as knowledge of an effect through its cause. Having inveighed against the arrogance of those who would claim to share in God's plans, he goes on to specify the way in which we can know nature through God:

> We should, instead, consider him as the efficient cause of all things; and starting from the divine attributes which by God's will we have some knowledge of, we shall see, with the aid of our God-given natural light, what conclusions should be drawn concerning those effects which are apparent to our senses. (*Principles* I, a. 28)

Knowledge of God's attributes is here attributed to human reason, but only as a result of divine will. It is by God's will that we can know his attributes, such as immutability. The knowledge revealed to us by the divine will in this instance is not a gift of revelation, known through the light of grace; it is known by the light of nature. But the light of nature itself, and its ability to afford knowledge of God, is a gift from God.

In the last passage Descartes was perhaps anticipating the derivation of the laws of motion from God's immutability. There seems no reason to believe that Descartes's position would be different regarding other things we allegedly know about God, including that he is infinite, perfect, cause of himself, and so on. These attributes of God are themselves known only through the idea of himself that God has implanted in our soul, like "the mark of a craftsman stamped on his work" (AT VII, 51). Thus, human reason has no independent purchase on the attributes of God or on the conditions for his existence. But that is just what we would expect if it did not have access to any logical or essential truths except as provided by God. Which is not to say that there is no truth that is not subject to God's will, but rather that such uncreated truths as there may be are not comprehensible by us (AT I, 145; CSMK, 23; and AT VII, 152). The best that can be said is that, by God's will, we know some of the uncreated eternal truths that pertain to God, without comprehending them.[61] But the suspicion that there is uncreated truth of this sort is of no metaphysical or epistemological import for us, for we have no access to such truths independent of the natural light that has been bestowed upon us by God, and this light reveals the conditions of his existence only to the extent that he wills it so.

This reading frees Descartes of the alleged tension between knowledge dependent on God and knowledge of God. Such freedom may seem like cold comfort, for it may appear that the alleviation of this tension has been purchased at the price of strengthening the case for circularity. God is known through a natural light which itself is a gift from God. Of course, the question of whether this makes the circle worse depends on what one takes the problem of the circle to be, and on what one thinks Descartes needs from the divine guarantee. If reason must be vindicated unconditionally, without the use of reason, then Descartes's project is already hopeless. If Descartes needs to prove God's veracity by grasping the truth about God independently of the God-given natural light, hopelessness is added to hopelessness. Fortunately for Descartes, there are other construals of what he needs from the divine guarantee, construals in which the scope of the doubt is limited, thereby placing less demand on the guarantee.[62] For if the contemplation of God in the Third Meditation needs only to show that the deceiving-God hypothesis is ill-formed and so ultimately is unable to provide a "powerful and well thought-out" reason for doubting (AT VII, 21), then there may be hope after all.

We have examined two aspects of Descartes's metaphysical turn. The first was the reform of the intellect. Methodologically, this amounted to teaching the reader of the *Meditations* to seek the basic truths of metaphysics in the clear and distinct perceptions of the pure intellect, independent of the senses and imagination. The second was the creation of the eternal truths. This doctrine provided a metaphysical apology for the reform of the intellect; specifically, it explained the ability of the human intellect to perceive the essences of things by appeal to the alleged fact that both the mind and the essences were mere creatures of God, placed in harmony with one another.

I have further argued that Descartes separated metaphysics from natural theology by making the eternal truths more radically dependent on God than had others before him. In a deft bit of metaphysics, he explained how we can have knowledge of the essences of natural things without insight into the divine mind. Metaphysics and physics were to proceed without claiming any special knowledge of God's purposes and without presupposing comprehension of God's creative power. Descartes effectively widened the range of the natural light with respect to the world but narrowed it with respect to God. He joined this reconception of the natural light with an insistence that the traditional distinction between the light of nature and the light of grace should mark the divide between philosophy and theology proper; the light of nature is to be directed only on things known naturally (including a "natural"—innate—idea of God, and an idea of the soul), and is not to be mixed with the light of grace in philosophical "explanations" of things believed through faith. Descartes emphasized that revelation, not reason, is the true basis of theology proper, and that in matters of religion the light of grace is superior to the light of nature. If Kant would later deny reason to make room for faith, in an earlier day Descartes could recall the primacy of faith to make room for reason.

Notes

I am grateful to Rose Ann Christian for comments on various drafts, and to James Ross for discussions on Aquinas and Suarez, though I would not imply that he agrees with the positions I adopt. An earlier version of this paper was published under the same title in *Science in Context* (Cambridge: Cambridge University Press, 1989), 3: 175–201. Revised version reprinted with permission.

In addition to the forms listed in the Abbreviations (p. ix) and used throughout this book, I use these abbreviations in this essay:

CB René Descartes, *Descartes' Conversation with Burman,* trans. John Cottingham (Oxford: Oxford University Press, 1976).

DM Francisco Suarez, *Disputationes metaphysicae;* cited by disputation, section, and article. I use the Vives edition, the Paris edition of 1605, and the Wells translation.

ST Thomas Aquinas, *Summa theologiae* (Cambridge: Blackfriars, 1964–81); cited by part, question, and article.

Vives Francisco Suarez, *Opera omnia,* 26 vols. (Paris: Vives, 1856–77).

W Francisco Suarez, *On the Essence of Finite Beings as Such, on the Existence of that Essence and their Distinction,* DM XXXI, trans. Norman J. Wells (Milwaukee: Marquette University Press, 1983).

1. Emile Boutroux, *Vérités éternelles chez Descartes,* trans. M. Canguilhem (Paris, 1927; reprint, Paris: Vrin, 1985); Emile Bréhier, "The Creation of the Eternal Truths in Descartes's System," in *Descartes: A Collection of Critical Essays,* ed. Willis Doney (Notre Dame: University of Notre Dame Press, 1968), 192–208; Etienne Gilson, *La liberté chez Descartes et la théologie* (Paris, 1913; reprint, Paris: Vrin, 1982), pt. 1, ch. 2; and J.-L. Marion, *Sur la théologie blanche de Descartes* (Paris: Presses Universitaires de France, 1981), bk. 1. I have learned especially from the latter three authors, although my interpretation differs significantly from each of theirs.

2. I examine the relations among the *Rules, Discourse on Method,* and *Meditations* in my "Science, Certainty, and Descartes," in *PSA 1988,* ed. Arthur Fine and Jarrett Leplin, 2 vols. (East Lansing, MI: Philosophy of Science Association, 1989) II,

249–262, secs. 1–2, and date the metaphysical turn from 1629. Etienne Gilson, *Études sur le rôle de la pensée médiévale dans la formation du système cartésien* (Paris: Vrin, 1930), pt. 2, ch. 1, dates it from that year; but whereas he sees Descartes's scientific program as having been essentially set prior to this turn, I maintain that the turn itself helped to engender his unified physics. Edwin M. Curley, *Descartes Against the Skeptics* (Cambridge, MA: Harvard University Press, 1978), ch. 2, effectively contrasts the project of the *Rules* with the deep foundationalism of the later works.

3. In Rule 14, Descartes affirms that "the weight of a body is something real" (AT X, 448); in his later work, the denial that weight is a real property serves as a prime instance of his reduction of all natural properties to matter in motion (e.g., *Principles of Philosophy* IV, a. 20: AT VIII-1, 212). In his discussion of an optical problem, Descartes's regressive method leads to an unspecified "natural power in general" but he gives no hint that it must reduce to matter in motion (AT X, 395).

4. Hiram Caton, *The Origin of Subjectivity: An Essay on Descartes* (New Haven: Yale University Press, 1973), 66–73. Desmond Clarke, *Descartes' Philosophy of Science* (Manchester: Manchester University Press, 1982), ch. 6, observes that Descartes did not demand hyperbolic certainty of scientific hypotheses and he downplays the role of metaphysics in Descartes's mature work (ibid., chs. 1, 4). Gerd Buchdahl, *Metaphysics and the Philosophy of Science. The Classical Origins: Descartes To Kant* (Cambridge, MA: MIT Press, 1969), ch. 3, recognizes Descartes's lowered standard of certainty in physical science without downplaying the foundational role of metaphysics; see also my "First Philosophy and Natural Philosophy in Descartes," in *Philosophy, Its History and Historiography,* ed. A. J. Holland (Dordrecht: Reidel, 1985), 149–164, and "Science, Certainty, and Descartes," secs. 4–5.

5. Richard H. Popkin, *The History of Scepticism from Erasmus to Spinoza* (Berkeley: University of California Press, 1979), ch. 9.

6. Henri Gouhier, "Doute méthodique ou négation méthodique?," *Études philosophiques* 9 (1954): 135–162, sec. 4.

7. Martial Gueroult, *Descartes' Philosophy Interpreted According to the Order of Reasons,* trans. Roger Ariew, 2 vols. (Minneapolis: University of Minnesota Press, 1984–85), ch. 2; Margaret Wilson, *Descartes* (London: Routledge & Kegan Paul, 1978), ch. 1, secs. 3, 9.

8. Caton, *Origin of Subjectivity,* chs. 1, 3; see also Kenneth Dorter, "Science and Religion in Descartes' *Meditations,*" *The Thomist* 37 (1973): 313–340. Louis Loeb, "Is There Radical Dissimulation in Descartes' *Meditations?,*" in *Essays on Descartes' Meditations,* ed. A. Rorty (Berkeley: University of California Press, 1986), 243–270, adopts a more moderate tone than Caton or Dorter in identifying in Descartes "a nontheological epistemological position compatible with the dissimulation hypothesis" (p. 245). According to Caton, *Origin of Subjectivity,* chs. 1, 4, not only did Descartes disingenuously profess a belief in God in order to promote his mechanistic physics, but through the patent circularity of his proof for God's existence and the resulting debilitation of his metaphysical argument for the substantiality of the soul, he sought to reveal the intellectual weakness of theism.

9. Wilson, *Descartes* (3, esp. n. 3), casts the question of whether Descartes's primary philosophical goal was to found his physics as a question about his religious sincerity (e.g., whether he was serious in proving the existence of God, or was an atheist). She rejects Caton's arguments and commends A. B. Gibson's view as "the correct perspective." Gibson, in his *Philosophy of Descartes* (New York: Russell, 1967), 50–62, does not see Descartes as choosing between science and religion, but suggests that he was attempting "to construct a system in which the religious and the

scientific consciousness of humanity both take their place in their own right in the totality of experience" (p. 50); nonetheless, he casts the problem in terms of Descartes's religious sincerity in the *Meditations.* Henri Gouhier, *La pensée religieuse de Descartes,* 2d ed. (Paris: Vrin, 1972), reviews scholarship which poses the question of whether Descartes was primarily a metaphysician or physicist as a choice between science and religion (pp. 18–24); I agree with Gouhier that the problem should not be posed thusly, but differ with his contention that Descartes was first and foremost a Christian apologist who developed his physics for apologetic reasons (pp. 167–170).

10. Descartes typically makes "withdrawal of the mind from the senses" prominent when describing the doubt of the *Meditations:* see the review of the past few days' meditations at the opening of the Fourth Meditation and the similar imagery of withdrawing from the senses at the opening of the Third Meditation; also, the discussions from the second and fifth sets of Objections and Replies (AT VII, 131, 350).

11. Reflection on the metaphysical foundations of the new physics may well have facilitated a transition in Descartes's thinking from *sciences* of nature and their methodology to a single, general science of nature: see my "Science, Certainty, and Descartes," secs. 1–2. Gilson, *Études sur le rôle,* 166–167, stresses the function of Descartes's metaphysical turn in the consolidation of the new physics, but he sees the new physics as having already been essentially completed in a piecewise fashion (pp. 146–149).

12. Descartes explained the usefulness of the imagination in mathematics by remarking that in using this faculty, one is actually considering a sample of extension in the corporeal imagination, that is, in the brain (Rule 12: AT X, 416–417); by contrast, he described the pure intellect as a potential source of error in considering extension (Rule 14: AT X, 440–446): "For although someone may convince himself that it is not self-contradictory for extension *per se* to exist all on its own even if everything extended in the universe were annihilated, he would not be employing a corporeal idea in conceiving this, but merely an incorrect judgment of the intellect alone." It is not clear that Descartes meant to preclude the possibility of purely intellectual knowledge of extension in the *Rules,* but he did hold that insofar as extension is known as pertaining to body, it is known through the imagination: there is no talk of grasping the essence of matter by pure intellect. By contrast, in the *Meditations* and later writings the imagination is a useful aid in geometry, but not an essential faculty: AT VII, 72–73; Descartes to Elisabeth, 28 June 1643: AT III, 691; CSMK, 227.

13. 27 February 1637: AT I, 350–351, translation modified from CSMK, 53. The phrase "withdraw the mind from the senses" is given in Latin in a letter otherwise in French. It obviously is not a direct quotation from p. 38 (AT VI, 37); the same Latin phrase does occur twice in the *Meditations:* AT VII, 9, 52.

14. The quoted phrases and the other points occur in Francisco Toledo, *Commentaria una cum quaestionibus in tres libros Aristotelis De anima* (Köln, 1594), III.7, q. 21 (fols. 164v, 165r), and q. 23, concl. 3: "Intellectus in corpore non potest habere naturaliter claram & distinctam cognitionem substantiae immaterialis" (fol. 168ra); also, concl. 4: "Substantiae immateriales a nobis confusem in hoc statu cognoscuntur" (fol. 168rb). Similar points are found in Eustache de Saint Paul, *Summa philosophiae quadripartita* (Köln, 1638; 1st ed., Paris, 1609), pt. 3, "Physica," III.4, disp. 2, qq. 4–5, 7, 10 (III, 287–289, 290–293, 298) and Antonio Rubio, *Commentarii in libros Aristotelis Stagyritae philosophorum principis, De anima* (Lyon, 1620), "Tractatus de natura et ratione atque officio intellectus agens," qq. 2–3, 5–6 (pp. 637–646, 680–684); also in the Jesuits of Coimbra College, *Commentarii in tres libros De anima Aristotelis* (Köln, n.d.; 1st ed., 1598), III.5, q. 3, a. 2, q. 5, a. 2 (pp. 383–384, 402–

403), III.8, q. 7, a. 2, q. 8, a. 2 (pp. 449, 453–455), though (4) is not drawn as clearly and firmly (pp. 402–403). Descartes remembered the scholastic authors just cited from the period when he read such literature, which, he says in 1640, ended twenty years previously: Descartes to Mersenne, 30 September 1640: AT III, 185; CSMK, 153–154. The four points occur also in Thomas Aquinas, *Summa theologiae* (Cambridge: Blackfriars, 1964–81) I.84.6–7, 87.1, 88.1–3 (henceforth abbreviated ST).

15. In the Third Meditation Descartes speaks of the "idea" of his own mind; at the end of the Second Meditation he purports to show that the mind is better known than body (AT VII, 33–34). Of course, one may question the truth of Descartes's premises grounded in allegedly immediate intuitions; notoriously, even his claim to have an idea of his own mind presents grave difficulties, on which see Wilson, *Descartes,* ch. 2, sec. 6.

16. Descartes admits as much with respect to color, etc., regarded as sensory ideas: "sensations . . . may be clearly perceived provided we take great care in our judgments concerning them to include no more than what is strictly contained in our perception—no more than that of which we have an inner awareness" (*Principles of Philosophy* I, a. 66: AT VIII-1, 32).

17. See my "The Senses and the Fleshless Eye," in *Essays on Descartes' Meditations,* ed. Rorty, 45–79, sec. 4.

18. Descartes to Mersenne, 18 March 1641: AT III, 297–298; CSMK, 173; he hoped for the approbation of the Sorbonne, AT III, 233; CSMK, 157.

19. Charles Adam, *Vie et oeuvres de Descartes* (Paris: Cerf, 1910), 304–305; Caton, *Origin of Subjectivity,* 17.

20. Descartes to Hyperaspistes, August, 1641: AT III, 426; CSMK, 191.

21. Dorter, "Science and Religion," 318–320, finds Straussian undertones in the "circular" appeal to God and Scripture, where he should hear the commonplace; on the position that Scriptural authority is sufficient for belief in the existence of God, as well as its detractors, and on the orthodox belief that rational proofs for the existence of God were needed to address the unbeliever, see Alan Kors, *Atheism and Learning in Early Modern France: 1650–1729,* 2 vols. (Princeton, NJ: Princeton University Press, 1990–), vol. 1, ch. 4. The Fifth Lateran Council had effectively made it an article of faith that there exists a rational proof for the existence of God using natural reason alone, not revelation (Kors, ibid., 1:115–116), and that Averroist doubts about personal immortality are in error and could be so proven philosophically (Eckart Kessler, "The Intellective Soul," in *Cambridge History of Renaissance Philosophy,* ed. Charles Schmitt (Cambridge: Cambridge University Press, 1988), ch. 15, on p. 495; Toledo noted this charge to philosophers, *Commentarii De anima,* fol. 6v). Descartes promised the theologians of the Sorbonne that he would deliver on both accounts (AT VII, 1, 3), though of course he did not explicitly state his proof for the immortality of the soul (VII, 13).

22. The fact that innovative authors could feel the threat of Church authority does not entail the old simplistic view that there has been a general warfare between science and religion—a view whose historiographic fortunes and intellectual limitations have been admirably reviewed in David C. Lindberg and Ronald L. Numbers, eds., *God and Nature: Historical Essays on the Encounter between Christianity and Science* (Berkeley: University of California Press, 1986), introduction.

23. Adam, *Vie et oeuvres,* 165–179, 304–307. Adam was careful to avoid treating Descartes's metaphysics as mere camouflage (pp. 306–307), although citations of his work by Caton, *Origin of Subjectivity,* 11, 71, 205, would suggest otherwise. Gouhier, *Pensée religieuse,* 23–24, reviews older French scholarship emphasizing the motivational priority of the physics.

24. Galileo Galilei, "Letter to the Grand Duchess Christina," in *The Galileo Affair: A Documentary History,* ed. Maurice A. Finocchiaro (Berkeley: University of California Press, 1989), 87–118; for discussion see William Shea, "Galileo and the Church," in *God and Nature,* ed. Lindberg and Numbers, 114–135.

25. M.-D. Chenu, *La théologie comme science au xiiie siècle,* 3d ed. (Paris: Vrin, 1969), provides a clear and informative discussion of thirteenth-century positions on whether theology is a science and, if it is, whence its principles derive and how reason may be used in it; he discusses Aquinas in ch. 4, sec. 3 and ch. 5. A concise treatment of "scientific" theology in Aquinas, his contemporaries and successors may be found in M.-J. Congar, "Théologie," sec. 6, in *Dictionnaire de théologie catholique,* ed. A. Vacant, E. Mangenot, et al., 15 vols. (Paris, 1903–50) XV-1, 374–410.

26. ST I.1.1, ad 2: "Sciences are diversified according to the diverse nature of their knowable objects. . . . Hence there is no reason why those things which are treated by the philosophical disciplines, so far as they can be known by the light of natural reason [*lumine naturalis rationis*], may not also be treated by another science so far as they are known by the light of divine revelation [*lumine divinae revelationis*]. Hence the theology [*theologia*] included in sacred doctrine [*sacra doctrina*] differs in genus from the theology [*theologia*] which is part of philosophy."

27. The quoted phrases are (respectively) from M.-J. Congar, "Théologie," col. 382, and Chenu, *Théologie comme science,* 77. On the fourth use see also Aquinas, ST I.1.5, ad 2. Congar lists the four uses given here; Chenu's list is more finely distinguished (pp. 77–78).

28. F. Jansen, "Eucharistiques (Accidents)," in *Dictionnaire de théologie catholique* V-2, 1368–1452, secs. 5.3–4 (cols. 1418–1422); see also L. Godefroy, "Euchariste d'après le concile de Trente," ibid. V-2, 1326–1356, in cols. 1347–1350. Godefroy observes that the council did not intend to join purely philosophical doctrines with Eucharistic dogma (ibid., cols. 1348–1349), but that it knew only one philosophy: "la philosophie scholastique" (col. 1348).

29. On Bérulle and Condren see Gouhier, "La crise de la théologie au temps de Descartes," *Revue de Théologie et de Philosophie* (ser. 3) IV, 19–54, as reprinted in his *Pensée religieuse,* 279–309, on pp. 296–297. Guez de Balzac, *Socrate chrestien,* in his *Oeuvres,* 2 vols. (Paris, 1665; reprint, Geneva: Slatkine, 1971) II, 201–280: "Nous entreprenons de discourir de sa [God's] Nature & de son Essence, de faire des Relations de sa Conduite & de ses Desseins, avec le jargon de la Philosophie d'Aristote. Pour ne rien dire de plus rude, nos pretentions sont trop hautes; nos entreprises sont trop disproportionées à nostre force" (p. 223); on philosophy and religion, p. 232, and on theology, p. 266. Balzac was an intimate friend of Descartes ca. 1628–31 (AT I, 5–13, 132, 196–204, 322, 569–572). Congar, "Théologie," describes several reactions against the use of natural reason in the elaboration of the objects of faith (cols. 392–398, 423–424, 426–430).

30. Descartes employed this usage in the letter to Mersenne from 15 April 1630: "As to your question in Theology, although it surpasses my mental capacity, it does not seem to lie outside my calling, for it does not at all concern that which depends on revelation, which is what I call Theology proper; it is instead metaphysical and ought to be examined by human reason" (AT I, 143–144; CSMK, 22); to Mersenne, 6 May 1630: "I do not want to meddle with Theology" (AT I, 150; CSMK, 25); to Mersenne, 27 May 1630: "As for. . . , it is a question of Theology: that is why you will absolutely permit me, if you please, to say nothing about it" (AT I, 153; CSMK, 26; also ibid., two paragraphs later); further, AT I, 366.

31. At VIII-2, 353: Descartes is criticizing his one-time disciple Henry Regius for

invoking Scripture in a question of the second sort (pertaining to the distinction between mind and body, AT VIII-2, 343) without showing that the same conclusion could be achieved through the natural light (AT VIII-2, 353). He also condemns the abuse of Scripture that results from presuming "to solve problems of the third sort on the basis of some mistaken interpretation of the Bible" and he equally contends that "it diminishes the authority of Scripture to undertake to demonstrate questions of the first kind by means of arguments derived solely from philosophy" (ibid.). His threefold division would have posed no problem for Aquinas: the first two parts of Descartes's division are implicit in Aquinas's discussion of the relation between things known by natural reason and those that depend on revelation: ST I.1.1. Aquinas does not explicitly describe questions of Descartes's third kind and he maintains the primacy of revealed knowledge over reason (I.1.6, ad 2); nonetheless, the same passages make clear that he granted a wide scope to natural knowledge, and he was willing to allow that it could make an independent contribution to theology proper (I.1.5, ad 2). Further, as Galileo argued, perhaps too cleverly, such a division is consistent with many passages in Augustine (Galileo, "Letter to the Grand Duchess").

32. From as early as 1630 Descartes was also concerned to show that the principles of his physics as expressed in the account of colors found in his *Dioptrics* could "explain how the whiteness of the bread remains in the holy Sacrament" (Descartes to Mersenne, 25 November 1630: AT I, 179; CSMK, 28); in a letter to Vatier (22 February 1638: AT I, 564; CSMK, 88), he favorably compared his account of transubstantiation with the usual one, claiming that in his philosophy transubstantiation is easily explained and noting that the Calvinists think it cannot be explained on the ordinary philosophy. In response to Arnauld's query, he attempted to show in the Fourth Replies that he could construct a metaphysical account of the Eucharist that did not violate Church teaching—or rather, what he portrayed as essential to Church teaching, for he maintained that "as far as I know, the Church has never maintained that the 'forms' of the bread and wine that remain in the sacrament of the Eucharist are real accidents" (At VII, 252), although in the second edition he added an explanation of how theologians could have concluded there was "no doubt" about the reality of the accidents (AT VII, 253). In the letter to Father Dinet he described this explanation as an example of how his philosophy was not "in conflict" with theology, and he promised to show that his views did not conflict with "theological certainties" where the "commonly accepted" philosophy did (AT VII, 581). By the way, in 1663 Descartes's works were placed on the *Index* as requiring correction primarily because his philosophy challenged the orthodox interpretation of the Eucharist (Gouhier, *Pensée religieuse*, 1; William Ashworth, "Catholicism and Early Modern Science," in *God and Nature,* ed. Lindberg and Numbers, 136–166, on p. 151).

33. Fourth Meditation: AT VII, 55; *Principles* I, a. 28; III, a. 2. Norman Kemp Smith, *New Studies in the Philosophy of Descartes* (London: Macmillan & Co., 1953), ch. 7, discusses Descartes's rejection of Aquinas's ways of proving God's existence (pp. 163–170, 174–177).

34. Eileen Serene, "Demonstrative Science," in *Cambridge History of Later Medieval Philosophy,* ed. Norman Kretzmann and Jan Pinborg (Cambridge: Cambridge University Press, 1982), 496–517, on pp. 504–506; Nicholas Jardine, "Epistemology of the Sciences," in *Cambridge History of Renaissance Philosophy,* 685–711, on pp. 686–693. Francisco Suarez, *Disputationes metaphysicae* (henceforth abbreviated DM) disp. XXXI, sec. 2, a. 10, mentions this aspect of "scientific" knowledge. I have used, and usually adopted, the translation of Disputation XXXI by Norman J. Wells, entitled *On the Essence of Finite Beings as Such, on the Existence of that Essence and their Distinc-*

tion (Milwaukee, Wisconsin: Marquette University Press, 1983) (henceforth abbreviated W).

35. DM II.4.6; Suarez cites Aquinas, *De Ente et Essentia,* ch. 2, trans. Robert P. Goodwin, "On Being and Essence," in *Selected Writings of St. Thomas Aquinas* (Indianapolis: Bobbs-Merrill, 1965). In the cited chapter Aquinas does not use the term "real essence," but he affirms that "essence is that according to which a thing is said to be" (p. 38), and the discussion suggests that essences determine essential predications.

36. Suarez, DM XXXI.12.40; W, 200: "those enunciations [pertaining to essential predications] are not true because they are known by God, but rather they are thus known because they are true; otherwise no reason could be given why God would necessarily know them to be true. For if their truth came forth from God Himself, that would take place by means of God's will; hence it would not come forth of necessity, but voluntarily." If the truths "came forth" or were created by God himself they would depend on his will because God is under no necessity to create but does so voluntarily; as we shall see, although in one sense the truths do "come to be" inasmuch as they are made actual by God, in another sense the truth of essential connections is not created by God but nonetheless depends on his existence, being grounded in his creative power. Aquinas allowed that prior to creation essences exist only in God's creative power and intellect (*On the Power of God,* trans. English Dominican Fathers, 3 vols. [London: Burns Oates & Washbourne, 1932], q. 3, a. 5, ad 2 (I, 110); he held that God knows the natures of things before creation inasmuch as he knows his own power (ST I.14.5 corpus, 14.9) and that he so knows them "in their own proper natures" (ST I.14.6 ad 1).

37. DM XXXI.2.6, 10; W, 61, 63. Suarez was willing to derive conclusions about limitations on God's absolute power from metaphysical arguments, as when he argued that it is beyond God's power, considered absolutely, to preserve a created essence without existence (DM XXXI.12.5, 7). In a sense the present argument does not restrict God's absolute power, for his omnipotence exhausts the domain of creatable being (DM XXX.17.10, 15).

38. I understand the doctrine of the creation of the eternal truths as did Gilson, *Liberté chez Descartes,* 50, and Boutroux, *Vérités éternelles,* pt. 1, sec. 5, according to whom Descartes held that logical, mathematical, and essential truths are necessary with respect to our knowledge (and to the actual operation of nature) but contingent with respect to God; to put the point in a vocabulary that Descartes tended not to use, it was within God's absolute power to create other logical, mathematical, and essential truths, but the created world is administered through God's ordinary power in accordance with the truths he did create (as Descartes did put it, even though the truths were freely created by God, because God is immutable they are "immutable and eternal," that is, he would not violate the truths he decreed; AT I, 145–146, AT VII, 380). Amos Funkenstein, *Theology and the Scientific Imagination* (Princeton, NJ: Princeton University Press, 1986), ch. 3, discusses the role of the distinction between absolute and ordinary divine power in the rise of the new science. As discussed by theologians and theological metaphysicians during the High Middle Ages, the distinction pertained especially to God's choice of a standard of justification for salvation and his ordinary application of that standard, together with his knowledge of future contingents and his causal role in predestination; most discussions of "voluntarism" occurred in this context; see Alister McGrath, *Iustitia Dei: A History of the Christian Doctrine of Justification,* 2 vols. (Cambridge: Cambridge University Press, 1986), vol. I,secs. 11–18 and McGrath, *Intellectual Origins of the European Reformation* (Oxford: Basil

Blackwell, 1987), 83–85. In an early letter, Descartes refused to answer a question pertaining to justification because it belonged to theology (AT I, 153; CSMK, 26).

39. I have benefited from Bréhier's remarks, in "Creation of Eternal Truths," on Descartes's need to explain how the human mind could have certain knowledge of essences and on the obstacle to this desideratum posed by Aquinas's and Suarez's understandings of the basis of eternal truths in God's understanding of himself (pp. 194–198); however, I differ with Bréhier on the "Neo-Platonism" of Aquinas and Suarez, on his attribution to Suarez of the position that the eternal truths are independent of God (p. 198), and on his linkage of Descartes's doctrines with the hyberbolic doubt (pp. 199–201).

40. Many scholars have concluded that Suarez was Descartes's intended "adversary" in his advocacy of the creation of the eternal truths: Gilson, *Liberté chez Descartes,* pt. 1, ch. 2; T. J. Cronin, "Eternal Truths in the Thought of Descartes and of His Adversary," *Journal of the History Of Ideas* 21 (1960): 553–559; Marion, *Sur la théologie blanche,* 43–63, 135–139; and E. M. Curley, "Descartes on the Creation of the Eternal Truths," *Philosophical Review* 93 (1984): 569–597. I think that in fact Descartes was moving against a position held by Suarez, but not the one attributed to him by these authors, who maintain that Suarez granted the eternal truths their truth independent of God. Suarez attributes such a doctrine to other authors (including Henry of Ghent and Godfrey of Fontaines) but rejects it himself (DM XXXI.2.1–3); Descartes, in rejecting the view that the truths are independent of God (AT I, 149–150; CSMK, 24–25), could have been opposing the position described by Suarez or a version of it found in another author (identity unknown). Norman J. Wells contends that beyond Henry and Godfrey (as mentioned by Suarez), certain Thomists (including John Capreolus, Paul Soncinas, and Cajetan) held the dreaded doctrine ("Descartes and the Scholastics Briefly Revisited," *New Scholasticism* 2[1961]: 172–190).

41. Suarez lays out the problem along the lines sketched in this paragraph in DM XXXI.1–2; the question of the status of essences prior to creation is discussed especially in DM XXXI.2.1–2, 7–8, 10–11.

42. According to Aquinas (ST I.16.5), God's knowledge is the standard against which human knowledge is compared.

43. DM XXXI.12.39; criticism of the position continues in 40.

44. On fictive beings: DM XXXI.2.10; on contingent truths, 12.40.

45. DM XXXI.12.40; W, 200–201; another part of this passage is quoted in n. 36 of this essay. Many authors, arguing from these and similar passages, attribute to Suarez the doctrine that truths about essential connections are true independently of God: Gilson, *Liberté chez Descartes,* 43–49; Bréhier, "Creation of Eternal Truths," 195; Cronin, "Eternal Truths in Descartes," 557–559; Wells, "Descartes and the Scholastics," 188, n. 47 (but in the introduction to his translation of DM XXXI, Wells gives a more nuanced reading, 17–27): Marion, *Sur la théologie blanche,* 59–60; and Curley, "Descartes on the Creation," 585–587. I argue that Suarez holds these truths to be true independently of God's intellect, but not of God himself.

46. As the subsequent passage (to be quoted in this paragraph) makes clear, Suarez places much weight on his assimilation of this usage of the copula to statements about fictive or imaginary beings. As he states in DM XXXI.2.11, such truths suppose merely "the being of the truth in a proposition or in knowledge"; in this way, truths about fictive beings differ from truths about essences, for the latter truths do not depend just on the intellect but are grounded in the fact that the essences are "apt for existing" (W, 64), or exist "in their cause."

47. Authors who attribute to Suarez the doctrine that eternal truths about essences are true independently of God end their analyses of DM XXXI.12.45 just prior to this quotation: Gilson, *Liberté chez Descartes,* 47–48; Cronin, "Eternal Truths in Descartes," 558–559; Marion, *Sur la théologie blanche,* 62, n. 23; and Curley, "Descartes on the Creation," 586.

48. DM II.4.6; Paris I, 62a (Vives XXV, 89b, II.4.7):

> Quid autem sit essentiam esse realem, possumus aut per negationem, aut per affirmationem exponere. Priori modo dicimus essentiam realem esse, quae in sese nullam involvit repugnantiam, neque est mere conficta per intellectum. Posteriori autem modo explicari potest, vel a posteriori, per hoc, quod sit principium vel radix realium operationum, vel effectum, sive sit in genere causae efficientis, sive formalis, sive materialis; sic enim nulla est essentia realis, quae non possit habere aliquem effectum vel proprietatem realem. A priori vero potest explicari per causam extrinsecam (quamvis hoc non simpliciter de essentia, sed de essentia creata verum habeat), et sic dicimus essentiam esse realem, quae a Deo realiter produci potest, et consistitui in esse entis actualis.

I gloss the negative definition, by way of nonrepugnance, in the next note. Of the two positive explications, the a posteriori one, from effects, allows one to infer a real essence from actual operations or effects; the a priori one, from causes, explains real essences in relation to their extrinsic cause, God. It is the eternity of this cause that grounds the eternity of truths about essential connections, as Suarez explains in DM XXXI.2.2 and 10.

49. In the introduction to his translation of DM XXXI, Wells questions whether Suarez maintained this explanation consistently, and argues that Suarez was torn between two understandings of the status of real essences prior to creation, one of which depends on an "extrinsic denomination" forthcoming from divine omnipotence, and one of which does not. While allowing that Suarez "did not intend to go beyond divine omnipotence and a potential efficient cause" (p. 34, n. 67), Wells maintains that he nonetheless effectively appealed to a "nonrepugnance" of essences to being, or to the "real possibility" of such essences, independent of God (pp. 18, 19, 21, 23–25). To support the latter he cites passages in which Suarez assigns a "nonrepugnance to being produced" to creatable essences (e.g., DM XXXI.2.2; W, 59; and DM XXXI.6.13; W, 95), which often seem to support his position. That Suarez did not intend any other than the first explanation is clear from DM XXXI.2.3–5. Nonetheless, a full examination of Wells's meticulous argument would require a separate essay chapter by itself. But in support of my own reading I would emphasize passages in which Suarez speaks directly to the notion of nonrepugnance, and here I think he makes clear that what "alone bespeaks a nonrepugnance to being produced" is the possibility of being made real "by receiving true entity from its own cause" (DM XXXI.2.2; W, 58–59; Suarez is discussing the position of Capreolus, but then states his own elaboration [beginning on W, 58 sub], "In this sense . . ."; see also DM XXXI 2.10–11; W, 63–64, where he refers back to this explanation as his own, and 2.4, where he rejects the position he ascribes to Capreolus, which assigns "a real receptive and unproduced potency" to uncreated finite essences themselves [W, 60].

50. Marin Mersenne, *Questions theologiques, physiques, morales, et mathematiques* (Paris, 1634); reprinted in his *Questions inouyes,* ed. André Pessel (Paris: Fayard, 1985), epistre; he compares the sciences (and their eternal truths) with "rays of divinity" (ibid.).

51. Marin Mersenne, *La verité des sciences contre les sceptiques ou pyrrhoniens*

(Paris, 1625), 14–15, as cited in Peter Dear, *Mersenne and the Learning of the Schools* (Ithaca: Cornell University Press, 1988), 40.

52. Dear, *Mersenne and the Schools,* 53–54, 68–72; Mersenne, as cited in Marion, *Sur la théologie blanche,* 170–171; Mersenne, *Questions theologiques,* epistre.

53. As Bréhier, "Creation of Eternal Truths," 203, has observed, Pierre Poiret, *Cogitationum rationalium de deo, anima, et malo* (Amsterdam, 1677), later argued in favor of Descartes's doctrine and maintained that to suppose that the eternal truths flow from God's essence is to place him on the level of created minds that understand such truths (p. 123). Kemp Smith, *New Studies,* ch. 7, collects texts in which Descartes stresses the incomprehensibility of God and of his relation to the eternal truths.

54. I have benefited from discussions of the relations among Descartes, Suarez, and Mersenne in Marion, *Sur la théologie blanche,* 161–178, and Dear, *Mersenne and the Schools,* ch. 4, although my interpretation of those relations differs fundamentally from each of theirs. Marion has Suarez and Mersenne affirm the independence of eternal truths (p. 176), whereas Dear finds Suarez and Mersenne affirming the dependence of those truths on God in a manner that brings their position closer to Descartes's than he realized (pp. 58–60); I argue that Suarez and Mersenne did affirm the dependence of the eternal truths on God, but that their positions differed greatly from Descartes's.

55. Michael J. B. Allen, *Marsilio Ficino and the Phaedran Charioteer* (Berkeley: University of California Press, 1981), 120–125, 152–157.

56. Aquinas, ST I.84.5, I.12.11; Suarez, *De anima* IV.6.5–7 (Vives, III, 736b–737b).

57. Kessler, "Intellective Soul," 497–500, 523–526.

58. In fact, Aquinas and later Aristotelian Scholastics also posited a harmony between the agent intellect and created material things, not in the form of innate species, but inasmuch as the agent intellect possesses the power to "make all things" (ST I.79.3, sed contra), i.e., to produce, on the occasion of the reception of material phantasmata, intelligible species of any of the naturally occurring kinds (ST I.79.4 corpus; *On Truth,* q. 1, a. 4, ad 5; Suarez, *De anima* IV.2.12; Vives III, 719b); to this extent, the intellect contains "seeds" of all the intelligible species (*On Truth,* q. 11, a. 1, ad resp.). Descartes is able to posit such a harmony without affirming that the human mind is "a participated likeness of the uncreated light" (ST I.84.5, corpus).

59. From the letter to Mersenne, 6 May 1630: "the existence of God is the first and the most eternal of all possible truths and the one from which alone all others derive" (AT I, 150; CSMK, 24). But then this truth could not itself be created. See Norman J. Wells, "Descartes' Uncreated Eternal Truths," *New Scholasticism* 56 (1982): 185–199.

60. Geneviève Rodis-Lewis, *Idées et vérités éternelles chez Descartes et ses successeurs* (Paris: Vrin, 1985), 13; she also cites a relevant passage in a. 24. Although Descartes makes both the true and the good depend on God, recall that in an early letter to Mersenne he sidestepped the theological question of justification (see n. 38 in this essay).

61. See Wells, "Descartes' Uncreated Eternal Truths," 194–195.

62. Curley, *Descartes Against the Skeptics,* ch. 5.

18

Descartes and Experiment in the *Discourse* and *Essays*

Daniel Garber

It is generally recognized that knowledge for Descartes is the clear and distinct perception of propositions by the intellect; knowledge in the strictest sense is certain, indeed indubitable, and grounded in the purely rational apprehension of truth. But it is also generally recognized that Descartes was a serious experimenter, at least in his biology and his optics, and that in these areas, at least, he seemed to hold that knowledge requires an appeal to experience and experiment. Writing, for example, in Part VI of the *Discourse on Method,* Descartes laments the fact that he has neither the time nor the resources to perform all of the experiments (*expériences*) necessary to complete his system, and calls upon his readers to "communicate to me those that they have already made, and to help me in performing those which remain to be done" (AT VI, 65). (One can see in the *Discourse* a clear anticipation of an important later literary form, the grant application.)

To the twentieth-century philosopher this looks a bit puzzling: how can Descartes be *both* a rationalist, who sees knowledge as deriving from the intellect, and an experimentalist, who sees experiment and observation as essential to the enterprise of knowledge? This is the puzzle I would like to address in this essay. I shall argue that not only is there no contradiction here, but that the appeal to experience is an essential part of the method for constructing a deductive science. We shall begin with a brief account of Descartes's procedure for constructing his science, his method. While Descartes's method is discussed at great length in any number of books and papers, there is hardly a clear account of what it is in practice in any of the literature. Then, once we have a clear picture of what Descartes's method is, and the precise deductive structure of the body of knowledge that he is building, we can then turn directly to the question of experiment, and see how it fits into the program.

Method

I hold the view that Descartes, in an important sense, gave up his famous method sometime in the late 1630s or early 1640s, and so I do not want to identify the question of Descartes's scientific procedure with that of his method.[1] But to understand Descartes's procedure in science it will be helpful to begin with a brief account of the method as it is in itself and as it is in application, and work from there. In discussing the method, I shall concentrate on the account Descartes gives in the early *Rules for the Direction of the Mind,* which Descartes worked on intermittently from 1618 or so until 1628 or thereabouts; though never finished and never published, it is by far the most thorough account of method in the Cartesian corpus, far more intelligible than the brief and enigmatic account of the method Descartes gives in Part IV of the *Discourse.*

In order to understand the method, we must understand the goal of inquiry in the *Rules,* for the method of the *Rules* is precisely a method of attaining that goal. The goal of inquiry is the subject of the first two rules:

> The goal [*finis*] of studies ought to be the direction of one's native abilities [*ingenium*] toward having solid and true judgments about everything which comes before it. . . . We should concern ourselves only with those objects of which our native abilities seem capable of certain and indubitable cognition. (AT X, 359; AT X, 362)

By "certain and evident cognition" here, Descartes seems to mean knowledge grounded in what he calls intuition and deduction. In Rule III Descartes defines intuition:

> By intuition I understand not the fluctuating faith in the senses, nor the deceitful judgment of a poorly composed imagination, but a conception of a pure and attentive mind, so easy and distinct that concerning that which we understand no further doubt remains; or, what is the same, the undoubted conception of a pure and attentive mind, which arises from the light of reason alone. (AT X, 368)

Deduction is defined in terms of intuition; it is a chain of intuitions, the intuitive grasping of a connection between one proposition and another. (AT X, 369–370, 407) This, Descartes argues in the *Rules,* is the only way to knowledge (AT X, 366).

Method is what, in the *Rules,* is supposed to lead us to such knowledge. But what is this method? Descartes writes in Rule IV:

> By method I understand certain and easy rules which are such that whoever follows them exactly will never take that which is false to be true, and without consuming any mental effort uselessly . . . will arrive at the true knowledge [*vera cognitio*] of everything of which he is capable. (AT X, 371–372)

Descartes summarizes these "certain and easy rules" in Rule V:

> The whole of method consists in the order and disposition of those things toward which the mental insight [*mentis acies*] is to be directed so that we discover some truth. And this rule is observed exactly if we reduce involved and obscure propositions step by step to simpler ones, and thus from an intuition of the simplest we try to ascend by those same steps to a knowlege of all the rest. (AT X, 379)

Descartes's rule of method has two steps, a *reductive step,* in which "involved and obscure propositions" are reduced to simpler ones, and a *constructive step,* in which we proceed from simpler propositions back to the more complex.[2] But the rule makes little sense, nor does it connect very clearly with the account of knowledge and certainty in terms of intuition and deduction, unless we know what Descartes means here by the reduction to simples, and the construction of the complex from the simples.

The precise method Descartes has in mind is nicely illustrated by an example he gives of methodical investigation in Rule VIII (see Table 18.1). The problem Descartes poses for himself is that of finding the anaclastic line, that is, the shape of a surface "in which parallel rays are refracted in such a way that they all intersect in a single point after refraction" (AT X, 394). Now, Descartes notices—and this seems to be the first step in the reduction—that "the determination of this [anaclastic] line depends on the relation between the angle of incidence and the angle of refraction" (AT X, 394). But, Descartes notes, this question is still "composite and relative," that is, not sufficiently simple, and we must proceed further in the reduction. Rejecting an empirical investigation of the relation in question, Descartes suggests that we must next ask how the relation between the angles of incidence and refraction is caused by the difference between the two media, for example, air and glass, which in turn raises the question as to "how the ray penetrates the whole transparent thing, and the knowledge of this penetration presupposes that the nature of the illumination is also known" (AT X, 394–395). But, Descartes claims, in order to understand what illumination is we must know what a natural power (*potentia naturalis*) is. This is where the reductive step ends. At this point, Descartes seems to think that we can "clearly see through an intuition of the mind" what a natural power is (AT X, 395). Other passages suggest that this intuition is intimately connected with motion.[3] Once we have such an intuition, we can begin the constructive step, and follow, in order, through the questions raised until we have answered the original question, that of the shape of the anaclastic line. This would involve understanding the

Table 18.1 Anaclastic Line Example (*Rules for the Direction of the Mind,* Rule VIII)

Q1. What is the shape of a line (lens) that focuses parallel rays of light to the same point?

Q2. What is the relation between angle of incidence and angle of refraction (i.e., the law of refraction)?

Q3. How is refraction caused by light passing from one medium into another?

Q4. How does a ray of light penetrate a transparent body?

Q5. What is light?

Q6. What is a natural power?

Intuition: A natural power is. . . .

Construction: The construction consists in traversing the series of questions from Q5 to Q1, deducing the answer to each question from that of the preceding question.

nature of illumination from the nature of a natural power,[4] understanding the ways rays penetrate transparent bodies from the nature of illumination, and the relation between angle of incidence and angle of refraction from all that precedes. And finally, once we know how angle of incidence and angle of refraction are related, we can solve the problem of the anaclastic line.[5]

This example develops the programmatic statement of the method as given in Rule V in a fairly concrete way. If we take the anaclastic line example as our guide, then methodical investigation begins with a question, a question which, in turn, is reduced to questions whose answers are presupposed for the resolution of the original question posed (i.e., Q1 is reduced to Q2 if and only if we must answer Q2 before we can answer Q1). The reductive step of the method thus involves, as Descartes suggests in Rule VI, ordering things "insofar as some can be known from others, so that whenever some difficulty arises, we will immediately be able to perceive whether it will be helpful to examine some other [question], and what, and in what order" (AT X, 381). And so, in a sense, the reduction leads us to more basic and fundamental questions, from the anaclastic line, to the law of refraction, and back eventually to the nature of a natural power and to the motion of bodies. Ultimately, Descartes thinks, when we follow out this series of questions, from the one that first interests us, to the "simpler" and more basic questions on which it depends, we will eventually reach an intuition. When the reductive stage is taken to this point, then we can begin the constructive stage. Having intuited the answer to the last question in the reductive series, we can turn the procedure on its head, and begin answering the questions that we have successively raised, in an order the reverse of the order in which we have raised them. What this *should* involve is starting with the intuition that we have attained through the reductive step, and *deducing* down from there, until we have answered the question originally raised. Should everything work out as Descartes hopes it will, when we are finished it is evident that we will have certain knowledge as Descartes understands it in the earliest portions of the *Rules;* an answer arrived at in this way will constitute a conclusion deduced ultimately from an initial intuition.

Descartes's strategy here is extremely ingenious. The stated goal of the method is certain knowledge, a science deduced from intuitively known premises. What the method gives us is a *workable procedure* for *discovering* an appropriate intuition, one from which the answer to the question posed can be deduced, and it shows us the path that deduction must follow. This workable procedure is the reduction of a question to more and more basic questions, questions that we can identify as questions whose answers are presupposed for answering the question originally posed; this reduction both leads us to an intuition, Descartes thinks, and shows how we can go from that intuition back to the question originally posed.

This is the story as of 1628 or so, when Descartes abandoned the composition of the *Rules.* As noted earlier in this section, I think that Descartes's thinking about method changes in his later years. Put briefly, while Descartes always maintains the view that knowledge is to be grounded in intuition, in the immediate apprehension of truths, he changes his mind about which truths lie at the bottom, and about how it is that we are to find them. In the *Rules* he seems to take the view that our knowledge of the physical world is grounded in certain truths, immediately grasped, about the nature of bodies, natural powers, and so forth.[6] But in the later writings, the grounding is ultimately in metaphysics, our knowledge of ourselves and God, and in God's role as the guarantor of our clear and distinct perceptions; in the later writings, the intuitions he takes for granted in the *Rules* must be grounded in God our creator and in us, God's creation. And furthermore, in the latter writings, the reductive step of the method, a step that can lead us only as far as the unjustified intuitions, is abandoned in favor of a direct attack on the foundations.[7] Despite these changes, though, it will be helpful to begin attacking the question of experiment in Descartes by examining the role it plays in his method.

Method and Experiment

In the previous section of this paper I emphasized what might be called the deductive structure of Descartes's project, the view of a completed science as a deduction from initial intuitions. In calling the structure deductive I do not mean to say that it is deductive in precisely the modern sense, or that it is deductive in any precise sense at all. It must be remembered that when Descartes introduces the notion of deduction in the *Rules* it is in explicit contrast to the formal logic of the schools, indeed, in explicit contrast to any formal procedures at all. For Descartes, intuition and deduction are the immediate grasping of the truth of propositions and the inferential connections between propositions, and so there is no in principle reason why a deduction cannot be an ampliative inference in the modern sense of the term, as, for example, the *cogito* seems to be.[8] But despite Descartes's refusal to pin down the notion of a deduction in any formal way, a completed science is supposed to be deductive for him in a rather strict sense; derivative and more complex propositions are supposed to be deduced in his sense from propositions more basic and simpler, and grounded ultimately in intuition.

However, Descartes is clear, his natural philosophy is definitely *not* supposed to be a priori in the modern sense of the term, knowledge obtained without the help of experience. Although Descartes seems to want to proceed deductively, experience and experiment have a significant role to play in this business. It is, of course, well known by now that Descartes was a dedicated experimenter, observer, and dissector, and that the empirical investigation of nature is given significant attention in the *Rules,* the *Discourse,* and other writings where he discusses his natural philosophy. Of course, this raises an important problem: how is the appeal to experience consistent with the apparently deductive structure of Descartes's project? There is a considerable literature on this basic question, and answers range from denying (or better, ignoring) the interest in experiment, to denying that Descartes's science was ever intended to be deductive, to claiming that Descartes was simply inconsistent—

deductive in theory, and empirical in practice.[9] This is the problem I would like to address in this section. I shall try to show something that may sound a bit paradoxical, that for Descartes experiment functions as an important and, in fact, indispensable tool for discovery in his deductive science, and it is to experience that we must turn to help us sort our the details of the deductive hierarchy of knowledge.

A reasonable place to begin is with a passage from Part VI of the *Discourse,* where Descartes attempts to explain to the reader the use of experiment in his thought. The passage begins with a lengthy account of where experiment is *not* really necessary. Descartes reports that he began his investigations with "the first principles or first causes" of everything, which can be discovered from "certain seeds of truth which are naturally in our souls." From this Descartes derived "the first and most ordinary effects that one can deduce from these causes," the heavens, stars, the earth, water, air, fire, and so on. The passage then continues as follows:

> Then when I wanted to descend to those which were more particular, I was presented with so many different kinds of things that I did not think that it was possible for the human mind to distinguish the forms or kinds of bodies which are on the earth from an infinity of others that could have been there, if God had wanted to put them there, nor, consequently, to make them useful to us, unless one proceeded to the causes through their effects, and attended to many particular experiments. Afterward, reviewing in my mind all of the objects which have ever been presented to my senses, I venture to say that I have never noticed any thing that I could not easily enough explain by the principles that I have found. But I must also admit that the power of nature is so ample and so vast, and that these principles are so simple and so general, that I have found hardly any particular effect which from the first I did not know could be deduced in many ways, and [I admit] that my greatest difficulty is ordinarily to find in which of these ways it depends on these principles. (AT VI, 64–65)

Experiment seems not to be at issue in the early stages of investigation. Where experiment becomes important, Descartes indicates, is when we move from the very most general features of the world, and, as he puts it, descend to particulars. There, he says, the direct deduction from first principles must stop, and we must "proceed to the causes through their effects, and attend to many particular experiments." This has suggested to many, and not implausibly, that at this stage science must become a posteriori, arguing from effect to cause by a kind of hypothetico-deductive method of the kind practiced in the *Essays* and defended in the correspondence of 1637 and 1638.[10] While this may describe Descartes's views later, in certain pessimistic sections of the *Principles,* this is not, I think, what Descartes had in mind in the *Discourse.*[11] In the passage in question, Descartes seems clear that he is still interested in deduction, even after he has descended to particulars. The problem is that in any given case, there are many possible ways in which one can deduce from the general principles, "so simple and so general," to the particular effects we observe. Experiment is somehow supposed to help us find the *right* deductions, the ones that pertain to our world and to the phenomena that concern us. In this way, experiments seem not to *replace* deductions, but to *aid* us in making the *proper* deductions.[12]

The view is initially quite paradoxical. How can some deductions be right and others wrong? How can it be that experiment is essential for a deductive explanation of a phenomenon? And how could Descartes possibly have maintained a deductive structure in his science, if he admits that there are curcumstances in which we must "proceed to causes through their effects"? To see how this might work, let us turn to some examples.

As discussed previously, the anaclastic line problem from Rule VIII involves finding the shape of a surface that refracts all parallel rays into a single point. Descartes's solution to the problem requires us to follow a certain series of steps, first a reduction of the problem to a series of simpler ones, then a constructive step, where the reductive series is traversed backwards, resulting in a deductive solution to the problem, if all works well. Descartes never tells us here where we can or must appeal to experience; experience comes up only in a negative way, where Descartes asserts that we should not try to discover the relation between the angle of incidence and the angle of refraction through experiment, for that would violate Rule III, which tells us that only intuition and deduction are sources of real knowledge (AT X, 368). But there is at least one place in the reduction where an appeal to experience would seem to be helpful, if not altogether obligatory. In the very next step of the reduction, Descartes says that the investigator must notice that the relation between the angles of incidence and refraction itself depends on the changes in these angles due to the differences in the media through which the ray is passing (e.g., from air into glass, or water into air), and that these changes, in turn, depend on the way in which the ray penetrates the transparent body (AT X, 394). Descartes does not mention experiment or experience in this context. But it is difficult to imagine that this is a step that we can make on the basis of the "seeds of truth" alone. While it may not require sophisticated optical experiments, it seems that we at least require some minimal experience with light rays and lenses, or other actual instances of refraction, in order to see that light is typically bent by passing from one medium into another, and to come to the realization that in order to discover the law refraction obeys we must first understand how light passes through media of different sorts. In this way experience would seem to help us to see how we might proceed in our investigation by suggesting what further questions it might be useful for us to look into.

Experiment comes up at best only implicitly in the anaclastic line example. But it is quite a visible feature of another example Descartes gives of his method. The example I have in mind is the account Descartes gives of the rainbow in the Eighth Discourse of his *Meteorology.* This passage contains the *only* explicit mention of the method in all of the *Essays,* and it is singled out in a letter from 1638 as an exemplary use of the method in practice (See AT VI, 325; Ols 332 and Descartes to Vatier, 22 February 1638: AT I, 559; CSMK, 85). The example is a very complicated one, one of Descartes's best but most complex scientific arguments. I shall begin by summarizing the argument, and then try to show how the mass of experimental detail and complex argument sorts itself out into a methodical framework (see Fig. 18.1).[13]

The problem is to explain how it is that rainbows come about. The account begins with the *observation* that rainbows appear when and only when there are water droplets in the air. Descartes then turns to the study of large spherical flasks of water which, he claims, duplicate the effects seen in individual droplets of water that appear to cause the rainbow. Observations on the flask allow Descartes to measure the angles at which colors are observed, and allow him to determine that there are two regions of color whose red portions are about 42 and 52 degrees from the angle at which they are hit by the rays of the sun (see Fig. 18.1). These experiments also allow Descartes to determine that these two regions of color derive from two different combinations of reflection and refraction within the water flask; the brighter color region (which corresponds to what is now called the primary bow) at 42 degrees results from two refractions and one internal reflection, while the dimmer color region (the secondary bow) at 52 degrees results from two refractions and two internal reflections. (The two paths can be discerned within the flask represented in Fig. 18.1). These investigations lead Descartes to two further questions,

Figure 18.1

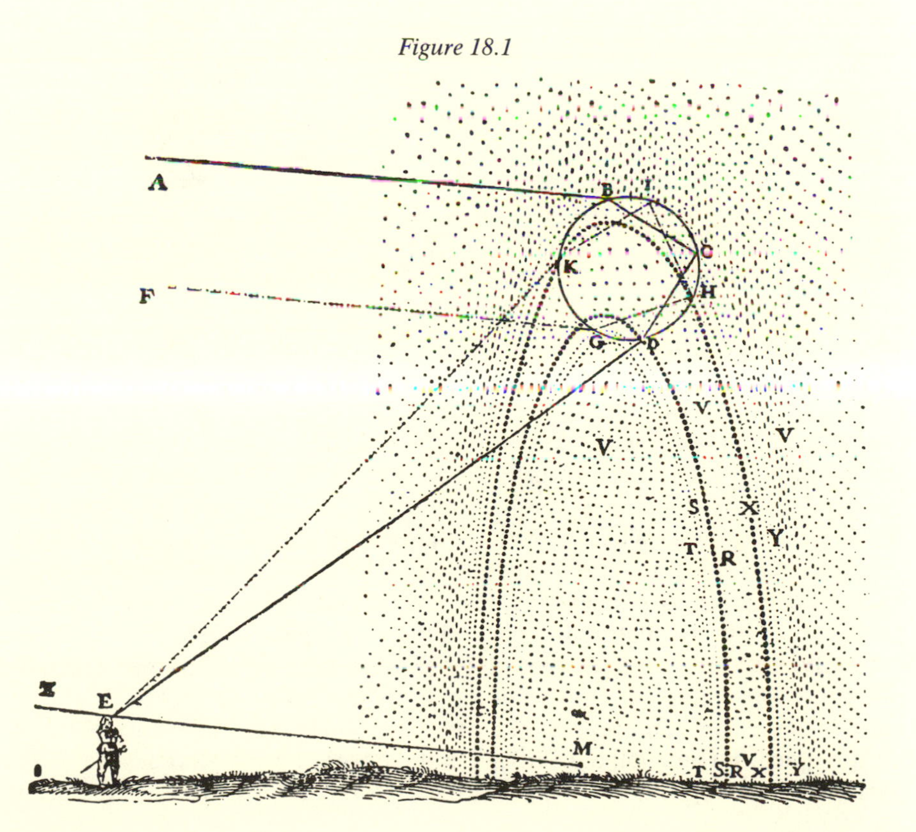

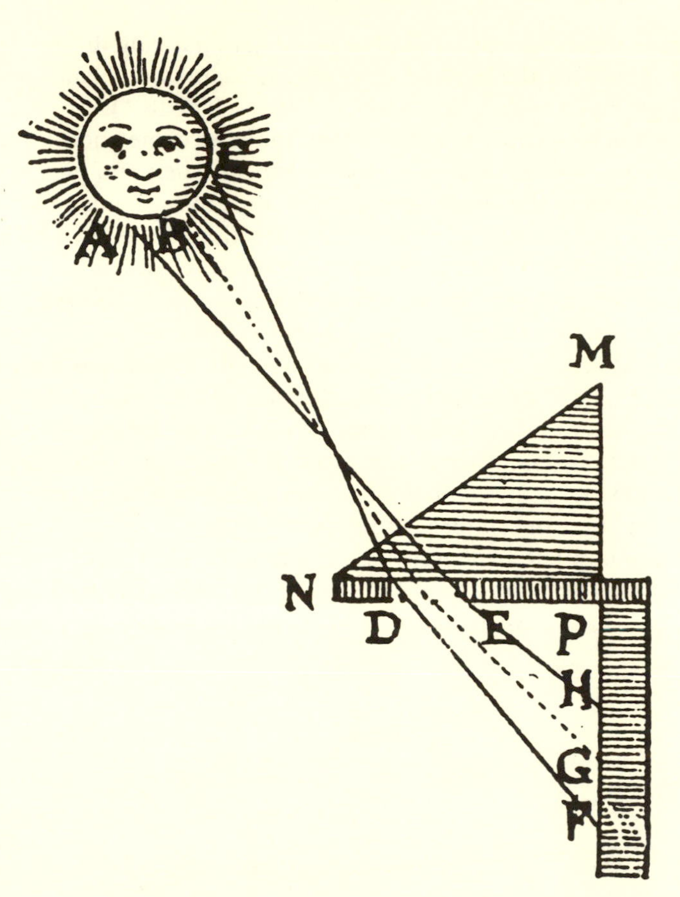

Figure 18.2

why there is color at all in these cases, and why it is that the colors appear at two specific angles. The first question, that of color, is explored experimentally, through a prism, in which, like the flask, colors are produced through the reflection and refraction of light (see Fig. 18.2). Observations made with the prism show that a curved surface, like that of the raindrop or the flask, is not needed to produce color; nor is a reflection necessary, Descartes discovers through experiment. What seems to be necessary, Descartes finds, is at least one refraction, and a restricted stream of light. But in order to understand how the refraction of a restricted beam of light can produce color, we must press deeper into the nature of light and the way it passes through a transparent body, the very questions that we were pressed back into in the anaclastic line case. The nature of light we know from the *Dioptrics:* "[The nature of light is] the action of movement of a certain very fine material whose particles must be pictured as small balls rolling in the pores of earthly bodies" (AT VI, 331; Ols 336).[14] And, Descartes argues, what happens when a restricted beam

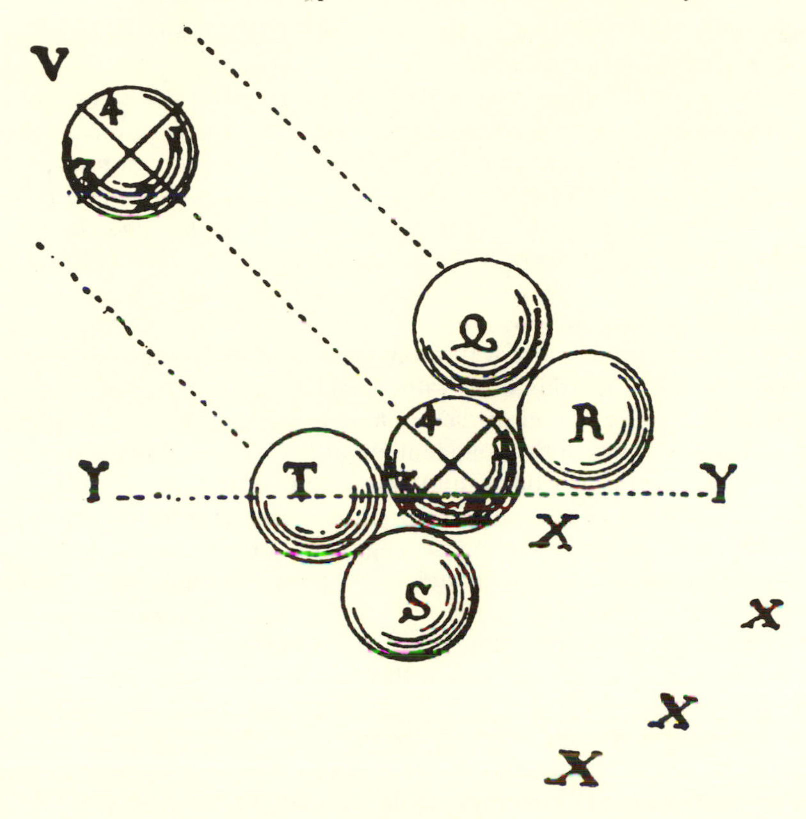

Figure 18.3

of light passes from one medium into another in refraction is that the balls are given differential tendencies to rotate, depending on where they are in the stream (see Figs. 18.2 and 18.3). Since, refraction aside, that is the only mechanical effect that passing from one medium into another has on the light, Descartes argues that color just *must* be caused by the differential tendency to rotation. Those balls with a greater tendency to rotate produce the color red in us, Descartes claims, while those that have a lesser tendency to rotate produce the color blue/violet in us. (Remember, of course, Descartes held that in the strictest sense, color is only in the mind, and not in bodies.) And so, from the nature of light and the way it passes through media, we have shown how colors are produced, Descartes thinks. But it still remains to show why the colors are produced in two discrete regions, at characteristic angles from that of sunlight. To solve that problem, Descartes turns back to the flask. Appealing to the law of refraction, which Descartes alludes to in the anaclastic line example, and derives (after a fashion) in the Second Discourse of the *Dioptrics,* he demonstrates that after two refractions and one reflection, the vast majority of a bundle of parallel rays hitting the flask, wherever they may hit, will emerge from the flask between 41 and 42 degrees with respect to the angle of the incident light, and after two refractions and two reflections, the majority will emerge at between 51 and 52 degrees (AT VI, 336ff.; Ols 339ff.)[15] From this it follows that at those two regions on the surface of the sphere, there will be two discrete streams of light that emerge from the flask, moving from one medium into another. And from the previous argument, this will result in two regions of color at the two angles earlier observed. And so, from the nature of light, the way it passes through media, and the law of refraction, it follows that the rays of sunlight hitting the flask will result in two regions of color at two characteristic angles. When we have a multitude of such drops, we have a rainbow.

It is by no means obvious how this somewhat confused mass of experiment and reasoning can be fitted into the rather rigid mold of Descartes's method. The schematic representation of the argument given in Table 18.2 indicates one plausible way in which the argument might fit. In the schematic representation of the argument, Q1 through Q5 represent the reduction, which leads us from the question originally posed, "what is the cause of the rainbow," back to the intuitions which are the starting point of the Cartesian deduction, intuitions about the nature of light and how it passes through media. But the important thing is, of course, the specific path that Descartes follows to go from the initial question to the intuition, for it is that path that will determine the path followed in the deduction. In this case Descartes proceeds by splitting the question into two questions, one about color and one about the two regions. Included in square brackets are the empirical results derived from experiment at the point in the argument in which Descartes appeals to them. The path followed after the intuition is relatively straightforward. Here we are dealing with the same steps followed in the reduction, only in the reverse order, as we pass from intuition to the final answer to the question originally posed. But unlike the reduction, experiment and its results seem to play no role in this part of the argument. The example is certainly much more complex than the anaclastic line example, but it seems to have much in common with it in structure.

Before turning back to my main theme, the use of experiment in these arguments, I would like to comment on the kind of deduction that is involved in this case. In the anaclastic line case, we had a definite question, the shape of a lens with such-and-such properties, and at the conclusion of the procedure we can expect a deductive answer to the question, a deduction from basic principles (ultimately, the nature of a natural power) that a lens with this-or-that shape will have such-and-such characteristics. But the situation here is a bit different. What we are seeking is the *cause* of the rainbow. The answer to this question is, in a sense, not deduced; rather, it is revealed in the deduction itself. The deduction shows us how we can go from the nature of light to the phenomenon of the rainbow; what is deduced, strictly speaking, is just the phenomenon itself, the patches of color in the sky. But the path followed in deducing the phenomenon shows us that the cause is the passing of light from one medium to another, the differential tendency to rotate this passage gives the particles of light, and the way that the law of refraction causes light rays to

Table 18.2 Descartes's Account of the Rainbow (*Meteorology,* Eighth Discourse)

Q1. What causes the rainbow (two regions of color)?

[Rainbows appear only in the presence of water droplets; size is irrelevant to the phenomena.]

Q2. What causes the two regions of color in any spherical ball?

Q2a. What causes the two regions?

[The two regions result from two combinations of reflection and refraction.]

Q3a. Why do the two combinations of reflection and refraction result in two *discrete* regions?

Q2b. What causes the color?

[Color is produced without a curved surface and without reflection; it requires a restricted stream of light, and a refraction.]

Q3b. How does *refraction* cause color under appropriate circumstances?

Q4. How does light pass through media?
Q5. What is light?
Intuition: The nature of light, and how it passes through media [Cf. Q5, Q4.].

D1a. Law of refraction

D2a. All parallel rays of light converge into two discrete streams after two refractions and one or two reflections, emerging from the drop (flask) in two discrete regions. [Cf. Q3a]

D1b. The only change in a restricted stream of light passing from one medium to another (refraction aside) is a differential tendency to rotation.

D2b. Color can only be the differential tendency to rotation produced in passing from one medium to another in refraction [Cf. Q3b].

D3. Parallel rays of light produce two discrete regions of color on a spherical ball of water [Cf. Q2].

D4. Sunlight (parallel rays of light) on a region of water droplets will produce two regions of color [Cf. Q1].

converge into two discrete streams at two characteristic angles. This a deduction, but a deduction of a very different sort than the one in the anaclastic line example. One can quite plausibly ask if Descartes can *really* be sure that he has given the true sequence of causes that produce the rainbow, as opposed to a possible sequence that produced the same appearances. Descartes himself will later come to see that as a problem.[16] But in the *Meteorology* it is not; he seems confident that the methodical procedure of investigation he is following assures him that he has captured the real causes.

To return to my main thread, a number of interesting things emerge from these two examples. First of all, it would appear that experiment functions strictly at the *reductive* stage of method, the stage in which we are trying to go from a question posed to the intuition from which the answer is to be derived; experiment seems not to be involved in the actual deduction. And in that initial stage of inquiry, it seems to function in two not altogether separable roles. First of all, it helps better define the phenomenon to be deduced or the problem to be solved. This is not at issue in the anaclastic line example, where the problem is set with sufficient precision. But it is an important function of experiment in the rainbow example, where Descartes appeals to experiment to fix what the rainbow is, that it consists of two separate bows, and that the two bows are always at such-and-such an angle with respect to the rays of the sun; in this way, experiment clarifies the question that is to be answered.[17] But just as importantly, experiment aids the reduction by suggesting how things depend on one another, and, in that way, suggesting at a given juncture what question we might turn to next. It is because we know from experiment that refraction depends on a light ray passing from one medium to another that we know that we must investigate light rays, media, and how light passes through a medium in order to determine the law of refraction. Similarly, it is because of experiments with the prism that we know that reflection is irrelevant to color, but refraction is not, and it is because we know that colors can arise from the refraction of light that we know that the nature of color is to be sought in an examination of what light is, and how it is altered by refraction. Once we understand Descartes's method and the roles that experiment does (and does not) play in it, it should come as no surprise that Descartes might suggest that "it would be very useful if some . . . person were to write the history of celestial phenomena in accordance with the Baconian method . . . without any arguments or hypotheses" (Descartes to Mersenne, 10 May 1632: AT I, 251; CSMK, 38) The sorts of tables that Bacon recommends to the investigator in Book II of his *Novum Organum* can tell us, for instance, that factor A (color, say) is always accompanied by factor B (refraction, say), but the factor C (say reflection) is present in some cases but absent in others. In an investigation of A, this could lead us to questions about B, and prevent us from raising irrelevant questions about C, as when in the rainbow example we learn that refraction is relevant to color, but reflection is not. Such tables of phenomena and their correlations with one another, independent of any theory, are precisely what Descartes needs to define problems and to determine the relations of dependence of one phenomenon on another necessary to perform the reductive step of the method.

In this way, it seems that *experiment is not a replacement for deduction, but part of the step preliminary to making a deduction.* Science remains deductive for Descartes; in the end our knowledge of the cause of the rainbow depends on our performing a deduction of the phenomena from an initial intuition. But experiment seems to play its role in preparing the deduction. Insofar as it helps perform the reductive part of the method, the sequence of steps that leads from a question to an intuition, it helps determine the deduction, the same steps followed in reverse order that leads from intuition to the answer to the question posed. The deductive chain that the Cartesian scientist seeks in reason, the chain that goes from more basic to less, is exemplified in the connections one finds in nature itself. Insofar as these latter connections are open to experimental determination, we can use experiment to sketch out the chain of connections in nature and find out what depends on what, *and thus we can use the connections we find in nature as a guide to the connections we seek in reason.* It may not be obvious to us at first just how we can go deductively from the nature of light to the rainbow, but poking about with water droplets, flasks, and prisms may suggest a path our deduction might follow.

This understanding of how experiment and observation may be useful in a deductive science of the sort that Descartes was attempting to construct allows us to make some sense of some of the more puzzling aspects of Descartes's remarks. On this understanding, we do *find* causes through their effects, in a sense; experiment is quite necessary in solving problems and helping us to discover the real causes of phenomena in our world. But in no sense are we replacing deductive with *a posteriori* reasoning. Though we must appeal to experiment, experiment only prepares the deduction that will establish the cause. Furthermore, we can now see how experiment can point the way to the "correct" deduction, and eliminate the "incorrect" deductions. There can be alternative derivations of a given phenomenon in the sense that the same *bare* effect may be produced by different chains of causes. For example, a distribution of colors in a pair of bows in the sky (a bare effect) may be produced by the reflection and refraction of light through raindrops (as it actually is in our world), or by a distribution of tiny colored balls suspended in the air, or by colors projected by a slide projector on a cloud of dust, or by any number of other perverse means. But experiment helps us find the correct deduction, that is, the correct chain of causes, by making the phenomenon more precise, and suggesting how it is that the phenomenon is actually produced in this world. In this way experiment can lead us to the correct derivation, correct in the sense that it represents the way the phenomena are caused in our part of the universe. Alternative deductions are not wrong, strictly speaking; one might be able to produce something that looks to us very much like a rainbow in any number of ways. But it's just that it is not the way things are done *here,* at least not the way it is done in nature.

So far I have talked about experiment in the context of Descartes's official method. But, as I pointed out at the very beginning of this essay, I think that Descartes later came to set his method aside. In his later writings, those that follow the *Discourse,* I would argue that Descartes abandoned the reductive stage of his method in favor of a direct attack on the tree of knowledge, starting from intuition (or, rather, first principles, first philosophy) and deducing on down from there. But I think that much of what I said about experiment in the method also holds good for the system-building orientation of later works like the *Principles of Philosophy.* Though in the later writings an explicit reductive step is not in evidence, Descartes must find some way of constituting his deductive chain, and here experiment will be useful for the same reason it is in the method. It is, I think, no accident that at the moment that Descartes was working on extending the system of the *Principles* from the inanimate world, derived by the laws of nature from an initial chaos, to the world of plants and animals, Descartes was also doing experiments on the formation of the fetus.[18] I am certain that Descartes thought that in sexual reproduction, the development of a living body from mechanical causes, he might find clues about how living bodies originally arose on this earth through mechanical causes, and that such clues would help him extend the deduction of terrestrial phenomena began in the *Principles* to living things.

Experiment and the Priority of Reason

In the previous section I tried to show how experiment plays a role in Descartes's scientific procedure, how experiment is needed in at least certain circumstances to aid in the deduction that leads us to genuine knowledge through deduction. But this raises an interesting question. Descartes is usually identified, and rightly so, as the philosopher of reason, the philosopher who rejected the dependence on the senses that characterizes the Aristotelian philosophy that he was eager to replace, in favor of dependence on clear and distinct perception, the immediate dictates of the light of reason. I have tried to show how Descartes's deductive science is not compromised by the way in which he appeals to experiment, how the particular conception Descartes has of the deductive structure of knowledge is fully consistent with the use of reason as an auxiliary to the reductive step of his method. But a deeper question still remains, how *any* use of experiment *at all* is consistent with his strictures against the appeal to experience.

Descartes certainly does oppose naive dependence on the senses in passages too numerous to cite; he warns us that things are not at all as our senses tell us they are, that they are not red and green, sweet or salty, that our naive belief that all of our knowledge derives ultimately from our senses is a prejudice of sense- and body-bound youth, a prejudice that must be rejected before we will be able to penetrate to the true nature of things. In his *Meditations,* he begins with a series of skeptical arguments that are directed in large part, if not entirely, against our naive trust in the senses, and in the Fourth Meditation, he *appears* to recommend that we must limit ourselves to knowledge derived from the light of reason; he *appears* to argue that only by limiting ourselves to clear and distinct perception can we guarantee that we do not stray into intellectual sin, that is, error. And if we are to limit ourselves to clear and distinct perceptions, then there would seem to be no room for *any* appeal to experience *at all,* it would seem, even the sort of appeal that I outlined in the previous section.[19]

But, I think, the situation is a bit more complex than this textbook summary of Descartes's epistemology might suggest. Descartes does certainly favor reason over the senses, but he certainly does not recommend rejecting the senses altogether. The fullest account of Descartes's views on the senses and the role that they play in the acquisition of knowledge occurs in the Sixth Meditation.

The reconsideration of the senses, rejected earlier in the First Meditation, begins early in the Sixth Meditation. Earlier and unsuccessful attempts to prove the existence of bodies led the meditator to consider more carefully the faculty of imagination and the closely related faculty of sensation (AT VII, 74). And so the meditator goes back over the considerations that led him first to trust the senses, ending with a review of the considerations that originally led him to question the senses (AT VII, 74–77). At this point, the meditator notes,

> But now, after I have begun to know myself and my author a bit better, I do not think that everything that I seem to get from my senses should simply be accepted, but then I don't think that everything should be rendered doubtful either. (AT VII, 77–78)

The senses loom large in the rest of the Meditation. The meditator first distinguishes between the mind and the body. Then the question turns to the external world, and it is here that the senses make their first positive contribution to the enterprise. The meditator begins: "Now there is in me a certain passive faculty of sensing, that is, of receiving and knowing the ideas of sensible things . . ." (AT VII, 79). We have a passive faculty of sensation. But this would be of use only if there were, somewhere, an active faculty for producing these ideas, a cause. This, Descartes argues, could not be in me, for it seems to involve neither my understanding nor my will, the two faculties I have. So, the meditator reasons, the ideas of sensation he has must come from outside of him, either from God or from bodies (i.e., bodies as understood in the Fifth Meditation, things extended and extended alone) or from something else. The meditator reasons that it must be from bodies themselves that our ideas derive; God has given me a "great propensity for believing that they come to me from corporeal things," while he has given me "no faculty at all" for learning that this propensity might be mistaken (AT VII, 79–80). So, the meditator argues to himself, God would be a deceiver if it turned out that our ideas of bodies come from anywhere else but from bodies themselves. And so, he concludes, bodies exist.[20]

The argument is a very interesting one. A conclusion is established not because we have a clear and distinct perception that bodies exist, exactly, but because the meditator has a "great propensity" for believing something, and God has given him no way of correcting that propensity.[21] Descartes admits here that there are at least some circumstances in which a belief that we seem to get from sensation, the inclination to believe that seems to come to us with the sensation, is worthy of our trust. It may not be *as* worthy of our trust as a genuine clear and distinct perception, as he implies in the Synopsis of the *Meditations* (AT VII, 16), and it may not always be true, as a clear and distinct perception is. But when sensation leads us to a belief, as it does in this case, and when that belief is not overridden, as it were, by a reason for rejecting it, as is the case with our beliefs about colors actually being in things, say, then we can trust the senses.[22] This is the strategy that Descartes pursues in the remainder of the Sixth Meditation in his duscussion of the senses. He argues that what he calls the "teachings of nature," which include the beliefs that appear to arise spontaneously with sensations, can be trusted as being for the most part true when corroborated by reason, that is when reason does not give us better grounds for rejecting a judgment from the senses, or when reason is in accord with that judgment, or when reason is silent on the question.

As with clear and distinct perceptions, Descartes is here dealing with something that God gave us, beliefs that are, in a certain sense, innate: "I am dealing only with those things that God gave me as a composite of mind and body" (AT VII, 82). As such, Descartes argues, they must be in some sense true: "it is doubtless true that everything that nature teaches me has some truth in it" (AT VII, 80). When it is truth about the nature of things that we are interested in, it is the light of reason, clear and distinct perceptions, that we must turn to first. Descartes writes,

> And so, my nature teaches me to flee what gives me pain and to seek what gives me pleasure, and the like. But it does not appear that it teaches us to conclude anything about things outside of us from the perceptions of the senses *without a prior examination of the intellect,* since knowing the truth about things seems to pertain to the mind alone, and not to the composite [of mind and body]. (AT VII, 82–83; emphasis added)

And so, while some of the teachings of nature will turn out to be true, it is only the intellectual examination of them that will establish this. In this way Descartes restores the senses and rejects the hyperbolic rejection of the senses that begins the *Meditations;* indeed, he goes on to reject even the dream argument that is so prominent in the First Meditation (AT VII, 89–90). But though the teachings of nature, what we learn from our senses, are restored, they are subordinate to reason; they may be trusted to some extent and in some circumstances, but only after they have been given a clean bill of health by reason.

It is with this in mind that we should return to the use of experiment in the rainbow case discussed earlier. One can say that insofar as Descartes does allow the appeal to the senses in at least a general way, there is no inconsistency in Cartesian epistemology; as long as what Descartes takes from the experiments to which he appeals falls within the bounds of proper caution, there is no special problem here. But there is something more interesting to be said in this case about the way in which experience is subordinate to reason.

In the previous section, I showed that while experiment might function as an auxiliary to a deduction, it is the deduction itself and not the experiment that yields the knowledge. So, for example, in the anaclastic line case, while experience might suggest to us that there is some lawlike relation between angle of incidence and angle of refraction, it is only through deduction that the actual law can be established (see Rule VIII: AT X, 394). But the point goes deeper still. In the rainbow case, Descartes begins by observing that on his flask, the stand-in for the raindrop, there are two regions of color, at roughly 42 and 52 degrees from the ray of sunlight, which angles are then *deduced* in the end from his theory. After giving his account, Descartes notes that an earlier observer, the sixteenth-century mathematician Franciscus Maurolicus, set the angles incorrectly at 45 and 56 degrees, on the basis of faulty observations. Descartes notes that "this shows how little faith one ought to have in observations which are not accompanied by the true reason" (AT VI, 340; Ols 342).[23] It is only because we can *calculate* the angles of the primary and secondary bows from the account we have of the rainbow that we can be sure of what they are, *despite* the fact that the investigation *began* with an experimental determination of those angles.[24] Though it is an observation that starts the ball rolling, it is only through a Cartesian deduction that the phenomena and causal dependencies observed can actually enter the body of scientific knowledge, strictly speaking. Similarly, it is only because a deduction can, indeed, be made in the reverse order of the causal dependencies that experiment has found, that those dependencies ought to be trusted. Descartes is, of course, aware that color can arise not only from refraction of light, but from the reflection of light off of a surface whose texture is appropriate to cause the changes in the light necessary to produce the color seen. At one point in his discussion of the rainbow Descartes seems prepared to consider such an account of color in the rainbow, because, at first glance, the restriction on the beam of light necessary to produce color through refraction seems to be absent (AT VI, 335; Ols 338–339). And so, it seems, the causal dependence of the colors of the rainbow on refraction and reflection suggested by experiment is only provisional; while the experimental determination of the path the light follows through the droplet may suggest to us a deductive path that we might be able to follow, it is the actual success of the deduction from intuition to phenomena that actually establishes the causal connections that produce the phenomena. Experiment is important in helping to find the deduction, but it is the deduction that, in an important sense, fixes both the causal path and the phenomena. Experience is important, but only under the control of reason, as Descartes took great pains to emphasize in the Sixth Meditation.

This feature of Descartes's position connects in an interesting way with an often discussed problem in the philosophy of science, the question of the theory-ladenness of observation. Whether or not one can have an observation that is not in an important way dependent on some theory or other is a question too often discussed in the abstract. Descartes's appeal to experiment in the rainbow case shows an interesting complexity in the whole dispute. Descartes does use observation to motivate the theory that he is proposing, or, perhaps, to guide us to that theory. In this sense, observation would seem to be a-theoretical for Descartes. But at the same time it is extremely important to realize that the observations Descartes presents as motivating his account of the rainbow, or at least guiding it, are not to be trusted fully *until* we have an account of the matter, until we can derive those observations from more basic principles. There is such a thing as pre-theoretical observation for Descartes, and this does seem to have a role to play in his procedure. But, at the same time, there is an important sense in which observation does not attain the status of *fact* until it becomes integrated with theory, indeed, until it becomes subordinated to theory.

In this way, for Descartes, experiment by itself can establish no facts; while experiment can lead us to facts, it is only the final deduction of a phenomenon from intuited first principles that establishes the credentials of a fact, even if first "discovered" through experiment. In his recent writings, Ian Hacking argues that experiment must be viewed as in an important sense independent of theorization in science; "experiment has a life of its own," he insists.[25] By this he means to point out, among other things, that experiment does not function exclusively in the service of theoretical argument, furnishing premises for theoretical arguments, testing theories proposed, allowing us to eliminate one of a pair of competing theories and accept another, and so forth. This may be true enough for a wide variety of figures. But it is not true for Descartes. For Descartes, at least in the context of the rainbow, experiment plays a carefully regimented role in what is from the start a theoretical project. But, at the same time, neither do experimental phenomena have a role assigned to them in standard hypothetico-deductive conceptions of scientific method, as the touchstone of theory, the a-theoretical facts to which we can appeal to adjudicate between alternative theories. If my account of experiment is correct, then however much experiment might help us to find the correct account, it is ultimately reason, not experiment, that is the touchstone of reality, for theory as well as for the experimental facts that help us construct theories.[26]

On the standard view of things, widely shared since the late eighteenth century or so, there are two sorts of philosophers: rationalists and empiricists. Descartes is traditionally viewed as a rationalist, in fact, the founder of the school, in modern times at least. When the extent of Descartes's dependence on experiment and observation is recognized, there is a temptation simply to think that Descartes must have been placed in the wrong slot, and conclude that he must really be some sort of empiricist.[27] I would resist that temptation. It seems to me that what the case of Descartes shows is how crude the scheme of classification really is. For Descartes both reason and experience are important, though in different ways. His genius was in seeing how experience and experiment might play a role in acquiring knowledge without undermining the commitment to a picture of knowledge that had motivated him since his youth, a picture of a grand system of certain knowledge, grounded in the intuitive apprehension of first principles.[28]

Notes

Other than the abbreviations used throughout this book (AT, CSM, CSMK, HR), when quoting *Meteorology* or the *Dioptrics* I use the following abbreviation.

Ols Paul Olscamp. *Discourse on Method, Optics, Geometry, and Meteorology.* Indianapolis: Bobbs-Merrill, 1965.

1. For a full defense of this view, see D. Garber, "Descartes et la méthode en 1637," in *Le Discours et sa méthode,* ed. N. Grimaldi and J.-L. Marion (Paris: Presses Universitaires de France, 1987), 65–87, and Garber, *Descartes' Metaphysical Physics* (Chicago: University of Chicago Press, 1992), ch. 2.

2. To avoid confusion, I should point out that I am breaking with most commentators, who refer to these as the analytic and synthetic steps, following the distinction Descartes draws in the Second Replies: AT VII, 155–56 or AT IX-1, 121–22. See, for example, C. Serrus, *La méthode de Descartes et son application à la métaphysique* (Paris: Librarie Félix Alcan, 1933), ch. 1; L. J. Beck, *The Method of Descartes: A Study of the Regulae* (Oxford: Oxford University Press, 1952), ch. 11, etc. This is a distinction that has little direct relevance to the stages of the method of the *Rules.* In the *Rules* we are dealing with a distinction between two parts of a single method; though they are distinct, both are necessary for a true application of the method. But the distinction between analysis and synthesis in the Second Replies is completely different. There we are dealing with different ways of setting out a single line of argumentation, and we must choose one or the other. On analysis and synthesis see also D. Garber and L. Cohen, "A Point of Order: Analysis, Synthesis, and Descartes's *Principles,*" *Archiv für Geschichte der Philosophie* 64 (1982): 136–147.

3. Rule IX tells us that in order to understand the notion of a natural power, "I will reflect on the local motions of bodies" (AT X, 402) What this suggests is that the understanding of illumination is, somehow, an intuitive judgment about the simple nature, motion, though it is not clear how exactly he thought this would work.

4. Descartes writes, "If, at the second step, he is unable to discern at once what the nature of light's action is . . . he will make an enumeration of all the other natural powers, in the hope that a knowledge of some other natural power will help him understand this one, if only by analogy" (AT X, 395). In personal correspondence John Nicholas has emphasized to me the importance (and complexity) of this step in the construction. He suggests, plausibly, I think, that "human limitations are such that in practice we commonly cannot carry out the downward deduction, and have to fall back on the surrogate step of analogizing and comparing with other natural agencies than the targeted one." Insofar as this analogizing may depend on our experience with the phenomenon in question, as well as with other phenomena, this suggests to him that there may be another use of experience in Descartes than the one that I emphasize in the following sections. He might well be right.

5. See Pierre Costabel, *Démarches originales de Descartes savant* (Paris: Vrin, 1982), 53–58, for an account of the historical background to this example.

6. See especially the development in Rule XII (AT X, 419) where Descartes discusses the so-called simple natures on which all of our knowledge is supposed to be grounded. The simple natures divide into three classes: intellectual, material, and common. The intellectual simple natures include knowledge, doubt, ignorance, volition. The material simple natures include shape, extension, and motion. The common simple natures include existence, unity, and duration.

7. For a fuller account of the changes, see n. 1 in this essay.

8. See Garber, "Science and Certainty in Descartes," in *Descartes: Critical and Interpretive Essays,* ed. Michael Hooker (Baltimore: The Johns Hopkins University Press, 1978), 114–151, esp. 116–123. Desmond Clarke argues that the term 'deduction' is so broad for Descartes that even hypothetical arguments count as deductions for him. See D. Clarke, *Descartes' Philosophy of Science* (University Park, PA: The Pennsylvania State University Press, 1982), 63–70, 201–202, 207–210.

9. For a survey of the various views taken in the literature, see Clarke, *Descartes' Philosophy of Science,* 9–10.

10. Charles Larmore suggests such a view in "Descartes' Empirical Epistemology," in *Descartes: Philosophy, Mathematics and Physics,* ed. Stephen Gaukroger (Sussex: The Harvester Press, 1980), 6–22, esp. 9, 12. I presented a similar view in "Science and Certainty in Descartes," though I no longer think that it is correct.

11. One might point here to the obvious use of hypotheses in the *Dioptrics* and *Meteorology,* well before the *Principles of Philosophy;* see AT VI, 83ff., 233ff; Ols 66ff., 264ff). But the *Essays* constitute an attempt to give the results of inquiry without revealing the full system, and they are not intended to replace proper argument in natural philosophy, which proceeds from cause to effect. By arguing from hypotheses he thought that he could show some of his results without having to divulge the first principles of his physics, for which, he believed, the public was not ready. But, while pleased with his *Essays,* he was clear that they represent not the definitive treatment of his thought, in accordance with his method of inquiry, but, rather, interesting experiments in exposition. There is an extended discussion of this in Part VI of the *Discourse:* AT VI, 76–77. This theme also runs through Descartes's correspondence in the period; see AT I, 562–564; AT II, 141–144, 199–200; CSMK, 87–88, 103–104, 107. See also Garber, "Science and Certainty in Descartes" and *Descartes' Metaphysical Physics,* ch. 2.

12. See also Descartes's remarks in *Principles* III, a. 4. There he talks about having to turn to the phenomena at that stage in his exposition, "not to deduce an account of causes from their effects," but "to direct our mind to a consideration of some effects rather than others from among the countless effects which we take to be producible from the selfsame causes."

13. My own interest in the rainbow case here is largely as an illustration of the method of the *Rules.* For discussions of Descartes's account of the rainbow that emphasize its place in the history of such discussions and in the history of optics more generally, see Carl B. Boyer, *The Rainbow* (Princeton, NJ: Princeton University Press, 1987), ch. 8, and Jean-Robert Armogathe, 'L'arc-en-ciel dans les *Météores,*' in *Le Discours et sa méthode,* 145–162. Considering Descartes's account in its historical perspective makes it quite clear that despite the impression he gives in the *Meteorology* of having discovered everything himself, he owes a great deal to previous investigators. Interesting and important as these historical considerations are, I will focus instead on Descartes's presentation of his theory in an attempt to untangle the methodological underpinnings of his argument.

14. This is the paraphrase Descartes gives in the *Meteorology;* the passage he is referring to in the *Dioptrics* can be found at AT VI, 89–93.

15. Descartes does the calculation by considering a spherical droplet of water hit by parallel rays over one hemisphere, and calculating where various of the rays would emerge after an appropriate number of reflections and refractions. His conclusion, carefully stated, reads:

> I found that after one reflection and two refractions, very many more of [the rays] can be seen under the angle of 41 to 42 degrees than under any lesser one; and that none of them can be seen under a larger angle. Then I also found that after two reflections and two refractions, very many more of them come toward the eye under a 51 to 52 degree angle, than under any larger one; and no such rays come under a lesser. (AT VI, 336; Ols. 339)

While the conclusion is arrived at by calculation, that calculation must make explicit appeal to the index of refraction for water. When the question comes up in the Second Discourse of the *Dioptrics,* he notes that we must appeal to experience in order to determine the value of this constant for various sorts of materials (AT VI, 101–102). This would seem to be another place in which experiment would enter into the method. However, one presumes that Descartes believed that the index of refraction could itself be arrived at by calculation, were we to know the size, shape, and motion of the corpuscles that make up water.

16. See, for example, Descartes's remarks in *Principles* IV, 204–206; see the discussion of these passages in Garber, "Science and Certainty in Descartes."

17. See the discussion in Rule XIII, AT X, 430–431, where Descartes discusses the importance of specifying in exact terms what is being sought in an investigation.

18. See Descartes, *La description du corps humain,* AT XI, 252ff.

19. For a development of some of these themes in Descartes, see Garber, "*Semel in Vita:* the Scientific Background to Descartes' *Meditations,*" in *Essays on Descartes' Meditations,* ed. A. Rorty (Los Angeles and Berkeley: University of California Press, 1986), 81–116.

20. For a fuller presentation of this argument, see ibid.

21. In the version of the argument given in *Principles* II, a. 1, Descartes does seem to argue from the fact that "we seem clearly to see" that sensation proceeds to us from the object of our idea of body to the real existence of body, and does not appeal to the "great propensity" that is the nub of the argument in the *Meditations.* It is not clear why the later text differs from the earlier one on this point. It may represent a genuine change in Descartes's epistemology. But then it may simply reflect Descartes's desire not to enter into his full account of the senses in the *Principles.* For the relation between the *Meditations* and the *Principles,* see Garber and Cohen, "A Point of Order."

22. That is, we can trust at least some of the judgments that characteristically accompany our sense perceptions. What seems to be at issue here is the third of Descartes's three grades of sensation; see AT VII, 436–437.

23. For a discussion of Maurolycus's theory of the rainbow, see Boyer, *The Rainbow,* 156–163. The implication of Descartes's remarks is that Maurolycus's values for the angles derive from observation alone. This is not entirely fair. Maurolycus had his reasons for setting the angles as he did, reasons based on his (incorrect) analysis of the path the light follows within the raindrop; indeed, he knew that his calculated value differs from what was known through observation, something for which he attempted to offer an explanation (pp. 159–160).

24. We must, of course, remember that the calculation does appeal to an experimentally determined value for the index of refraction; however, as I pointed out earlier, Descartes would surely have thought that a "reason" could be given for that too.

25. Ian Hacking, *Representing and Intervening* (Cambridge: Cambridge University Press, 1983), 150.

26. Descartes does say some things that would appear to go against my conclusion. For example, immediately following the long passage from Part VI of the *Discourse* I quoted earlier, Descartes writes,

> I know of no other means to discover this [i.e., how a particular effect depends on the general principles of nature] than by seeking further experiments [*expériences*] whose outcomes vary according to which of these ways provides the correct explanation. (AT VI, 65)

But, I think, this must be understood in the context of the interpretation I have offered earlier. The experiments in question must be viewed as *leading us down* one deductive path rather than down another, and *not* as a theory-neutral means of choosing between independently constructed theories; for, as Descartes elsewhere insists, we cannot *really* be sure of an experimental fact until *after* we have already determined what the correct deduction is.

27. See, e.g., Clarke, *Descartes' Philosophy of Science,* 205.

28. In addition to its presentation at the San José Descartes Conference, earlier versions of this paper were given in University of Rochester, University of Colorado, Columbia University, Catholic University of America, University of Notre Dame, Georgia Philosophical Association, University of California at San Diego, Virginia Polytechnic Institute and State University, University of Illinois, and the University of Ohio. I would like to thank the audiences there, as well as Peter Dear, Ernan McMullin, John Nicholas, Gary Hatfield, and Beverly Whelton for their very helpful suggestions. Parts of the text also appear in ch. 2 of my book *Descartes' Metaphysical Physics.*

19

Descartes's Physics and Descartes's Mechanics: Chicken and Egg?

Alan Gabbey

One of the nomological bases of mechanics is what is known today as "the principle of virtual work," or of "virtual speeds," to use the term employed by Jean Bernoulli when he announced the first modern formulation in 1717. A version of the principle in terms appropriate to this paper would be that the heights to which heavy bodies can be lifted severally through the expenditure of the same effort are inversely proportional to their respective weights.[1] The principle goes back in one form or another to antiquity, yet there is no version of it to be found in Descartes's *Principles of Philosophy* (Latin edition 1644, French edition 1647), the treatise in which Descartes published the foundations of his mechanical philosophy, of which notably the laws of nature in Part II are generally recognized as pioneering contributions to the establishment of modern "mechanics." Furthermore, nowhere does Descartes tell his readers if or how the principle relates to his laws of nature. Its anomalous absence from the *Principles* seems therefore to have been a curious oversight.

The omission cannot be explained by assuming on Descartes's part an ignorance of or lack of interest in a contemporary (or earlier) version of the principle, or by concluding that he must have thought it trivial or unimportant. Several times in his letters he stated his own version, which was among the clearest in the seventeenth century, and he used it twice in the composition of elaborate minitreatises on the theory of machines.

The first occasion was when he complied with Constantin Huygens's request that he send him a few pages on mechanics, that is, on the five simple machines: the pulley, the inclined plane and the wedge, the windlass, the screw, and the lever. Accompanying his letter to Huygens of 5 October 1637 was an "Explanation of machines with whose aid heavy loads can be lifted with a small force,"[2] the opening paragraphs of which present and demonstrate Descartes's version of the principle of virtual work (if I may call it that for the time being):

> The invention of all these machines is based on only one single principle, which is that the same force [*force*] which can raise a 100-pound weight to a

> height of two feet, for example, can also raise a 200-pound weight to a height of one foot, or one of 400 pounds to a height of half a foot, and so on, as long as the force is applied to it.
>
> And this principle cannot fail to be accepted, if it is borne in mind that the effect must always be proportioned to the action necessary to produce it, so that if the action by which a 100-pound weight can be raised to a height of two feet is required to raise to just one foot another weight, the latter must weigh 200 pounds. for raising a 100-pound weight one foot, and again another 100 pounds one foot, is the same as raising 200 pounds one foot, and it is also the same as raising 100 pounds two feet.[2]

Descartes then proceeds to apply the principle to the theory of the five simple machines.

The second treatment of the theory of machines was sent to Mersenne on 13 July 1638. It is shorter than the account written for Huygens, since the "general foundation for the whole of statics," and the three illustrative examples (the pulley, inclined plane, and lever), serve as starting points in Descartes's solution to "the geostatic question," which was then in dispute among mathematicians and mechanicians.[3] As for the general foundation on which the whole of statics rests, the "General Statical Principle" (GSP), as I can now call it without anachronism, and its employment, the account sent to Mersenne is basically the same as that sent the previous year to Huygens, but with two important differences. In the account Mersenne received, Descartes is clear about the foundational nature of the GSP:

> . . . it seems to me that these three examples suffice to assure us of the truth of the principle I have proposed, and to show that everything customarily dealt with in statics depends on it . . . (AT II, 237).

Equally important is his explicit recognition that for the proper application of the GSP only *small* displacements, subject to the constraints of the system, must be taken into account. Earlier in the letter to Mersenne he distinguishes between "true or absolute weight" and "apparent or relative weight." True or absolute weight is the force with which a weight at rest tends to fall freely along a (vertical) straight line. Apparent or relative weight is the force required to hold a weight at rest on (typically) an inclined plane, or equivalently, the force with which the weight tends to begin moving down the plane under gravity alone. In other words, Descartes's apparent or relative weight is the *gravitas secundum situm*—positional gravity—of the tradition in statics deriving from Jordanus de Nemore (ca. 1220), and all such positional gravities are reducible to positions on an inclined plane.[4] So in the section on the inclined plane, for example, Descartes compares the absolute and relative weights of the body F placed on the plane AC (Fig. 19.1), and notes that although it tends downwards along the straight line DN toward the center of the earth at M, it cannot begin actually to fall except along the plane DP:

> Note that I say *begins to fall,* not simply *falls,* because it is only the beginning of the fall which ought to retain our attention. So if for example the weight F were not placed at the point D on a flat surface, as ADC is

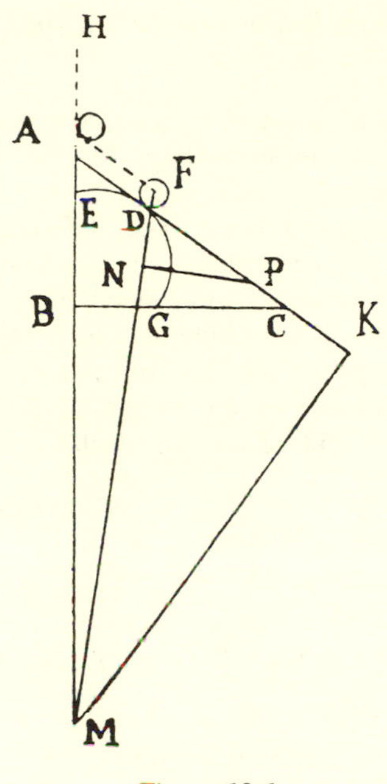

Figure 19.1

> taken to be, but on a spherical surface like EDG, or on a surface curved in some other way, it would weigh neither more nor less, with respect to the power at H, than it does when on the plane AC, provided that the flat surface imagined to touch the curved surface at D were the same as ADC. For although the motion of the weight, rising or falling from D towards E or G on the curved surface EDG, would be quite different from that on the flat surface ADC, nonetheless when at D on EDG, the weight would be determined to move in the same direction as if it were on ADC, that is, towards A or towards C. And it is evident that any change in its motion, once it has ceased to touch the point D, cannot alter anything in the weight it had when it touched it. (AT II, 233–234; Descartes's emphasis)

I have quoted this passage at length to show Descartes's clear understanding of the correct application of the GSP, and although this is not the principle of virtual work properly speaking, it is worth noting that Bernoulli too recognized that only infinitesimal displacements of the bodies in equilibrium ensure the general validity and applicability of his principle of virtual speeds.[5]

So we wonder even more why the GSP did not find a place in the *Principles*. After all, Descartes devoted seventeen or eighteen articles of Part II, and half-a-dozen articles of Part III, to the three laws of nature and the rules of collision, and to analyses of the forces arising from circular motion, alongside all of which the GSP and its applications might have been expected to find a natural place.

The omission becomes all the more anomalous when confronted with

Descartes's claim in the same *Principles of Philosophy* that mechanics is a part or subdivision of physics:

> I recognize no difference between artifacts and natural bodies, except that the operations of artifacts are carried out for the most part by means of components [*instrumentum*] so large that they are easily apparent to the senses, for that is necessary so that they can be made by men. But natural effects, on the contrary, depend almost always on certain organs so small that they escape all our senses. And indeed there are no considerations [*ratio*] in mechanics that do not apply also to physics [*physica*], of which mechanics is a part or species [*pars vel species*]. It is no less natural for a clock with this or that movement to tell the time, than it is for a tree grown from this or that seed to produce such and such a fruit. . . .[6]

Complementing this passage is an intriguing remark in the letter for Fromondus of 3 October 1637. Fromondus had objected that Descartes's general description in *Les météores* (Discours 1) of the diverse particulate compositions of earth, air, water, and all other bodies surrounding us, seemed "excessively crude and mechanical" (AT I, 406). Descartes's reply reads:

> I cannot see what he is objecting to. . . . For if my philosophy seems to him excessively crude [*crassa*] because it considers shapes, sizes, and motions, as in mechanics, he is condemning what I think deserves praise above all else, and in which I take particular pride; namely, that I use that kind of philosophizing in which nothing is argued except what is mathematical and evident, and whose conclusions are confirmed through true experiments [*veris experimentis*], so that whatever may be concluded can be done from its principles, can in fact be done, each time things in an active state are applied, as is appropriate, to things in a passive state.[7] I am surprised he has not noticed that the mechanics that has been in use up to now is nothing other than a small part of the true physics, and which took itself off to the mathematicians, since it found no place with the supporters of the common philosophy. But this part of philosophy remains truer and less corrupt than other parts, because since it relates to use and practice, those who go astray in it are apt to suffer financial loss. So that if he is belittling my way of philosophizing because it resembles mechanics, that seems to me the same as if he were to belittle it because it is true.[8]

To which I might add an even more intriguing remark from a letter the following year to Plempius, on 15 February 1638, in which Descartes argues that his account of the expansion of the arteries explains an experimental discovery of Galen's:

> . . . given the cause of the pulse of the arteries that I advance, the laws of my mechanics, that is of [my] physics, teach that if a rod is introduced into the artery, and the artery ligatured at the rod itself, then the artery ought not to beat beyond the ligature, but ought to beat once the ligature is released, exactly as Galen discovered. . . . (AT I, 524)

Whatever laws of mechanics are covertly at work here, we may ask why the laws of Descartes's mechanics were not therefore included somewhere among the laws of nature in the *Principles,* which laws are presumably a subset of the laws of physics in general.

To add to the anomaly, there is an inconsistency. In the prefatory letter to the 1647 French edition of the *Principles* Descartes specifies the first steps along the path one should follow in pursuit of self-instruction: that is, a provisional morality and logic that unlike that of the Schools will show how to "direct one's reason properly so as to discover truths of which one is ignorant." Then one will be ready, he continues, for "the true philosophy," which as a body of constituted knowledge he describes in the following way:

> . . . the whole of philosophy is like a tree, whose roots are metaphysics, the trunk physics, and the branches growing from the trunk are all other sciences, which reduce to [*se réduire à*] three principal sciences, namely medicine, mechanics, and ethics. (AT IX-2, 14)

On an ordinary reading of this familiar passage, and of the equally familiar context in which it appears, mechanics is not an *integral* part of physics, even a small part, but is one of its three major disciplinary offshoots to which all *other* sciences can be reduced.[9] The relation of mechanics to physics near the top of the philosophical tree does not square, it seems, with the earlier claim that mechanics is in some way subsumed within physics, the laws of mechanics being a subset of the laws of physics.

A further point is that if we consider the central contention of Descartes's program of mechanical philosophy, that all natural phenomena, including sensible and insensible qualities and properties of things, are to be explained in a proper causal manner in terms of the varying motions (and rest) of small pieces of *res extensa,* then it seems that mechanics should be *the* basic science, since it deals typically with interactions between simple bodies in motion and rest. On this view, physics should be a branch growing out of the trunk of mechanics.

To try to disentangle these anomalies and inconsistencies, a good starting point is a clue provided by Descartes himself in the passage just quoted from the letter for Fromondus of 3 October 1637. It will be recalled that Descartes showed surprise (whether feigned or not) that Fromondus was not aware that "the mechanics that has been in use up to now is nothing other than a small part of the true physics, and which took itself off to the mathematicians, since it found no place with the supporters of the common philosophy." Here Descartes is referring to the absence in his day of treatises on mechanics written by authors of Peripatetic manuals of *philosophia naturalis* or *physica.* The treatises on mechanics available to him in 1637 were all written by mathematicians of one sort or another, and from different walks of life, not by promulgators of *physica Peripatetica.* Setting aside published works from antiquity or the medieval period, we have as examples the mechanical treatises of Tartaglia, Benedetti, Commandino, Valerio, Guidobaldo del Monte (whose influential *Mechanicorum liber* of 1577 Descartes read), Maurolico; the commentaries on pseudo-Aristotle's *Mechanica* written by Bernardino Baldi

(1621) and Giovanni di Guevara (1629); and Mersenne's translation (1634) of Galileo's *Le meccaniche.*[10]

These were all important and influential writers on mechanics, yet none of them, as far as I know, published anything that might sit on the shelf alongside the Aristotle commentaries or *summae* of the Conimbricenses, Toletus, Ruvio, Suarez, Eustache de Saint Paul, Abra de Raconis, or other scholastic writers whose works Descartes either knew or would have known.

Conversely, and equally significantly, none of these scholastic writers on natural philosophy, and none of those who preceded them in the Medieval or Renaissance Peripatetic tradition, published anything on mechanics. The principal reason for this *lacuna* in the Peripatetic program for natural philosophy derives from the broad distinction between *sciences* such as natural philosophy and the mechanical or manual *arts.* Since antiquity, the latter had been concerned with the construction and operation of machines and other artifacts designed to move or rearrange things *contra naturam* and for human ends. On the other hand, the definitions of *physica* (equivalently *philosophia naturalis* and *physiologia*) in the traditional Peripatetic manuals typically employ the phrase "the science [*scientia*] of natural bodies, *in so far as they are natural.*" Physics does not deal with artificial things *qua* artificial, so it does not share the concerns of the *artes mechanicae.* The first line of the *Mechanica* of pseudo-Aristotle alludes to the distinction: "Remarkable things occur in accordance with nature [κατὰ φύσιν], the cause of which is unknown, and others occur contrary to nature [παρὰ φύσιν], which are produced by skill for the benefit of mankind."[11]

However, already in pseudo-Aristotle's *Mechanica* (as in Book 8 of the *Collections* of Pappus of Alexandria), mechanics was a theoretical discipline as much as a manual art. More precisely, *qua* science it was a theoretical discipline that dealt in a mathematical way with problems arising out of the use of machines. With the rediscovery of the *Mechanica* in the Renaissance, mechanics became a developed *scientia media,* as optics and astronomy had done during the Middle Ages, that is a *scientia* operating midway between mathematics and physics in the sense that the treatment was mathematical, and therefore the province of mathematicians, while the subjects so treated were physical and sensible. As pseudo-Aristotle put it, mechanical problems "are not altogether identical with physical problems, nor are they entirely separate from them, but they have a share in both mathematical and physical speculations [θεωρημάτων], for the method is demonstrated by mathematics, but the practical application belongs to physics."[12] So mechanics was "subalternated" to both mathematics and physics, though in the Renaissance and early seventeenth century there arose considerable discussion on whether it should be seen as subalternated principally to one or other of the two parent sciences.[13]

In his important study of Galileo and his sources, Wallace has shown that for the Jesuits at the Collegio Romano the science of nature, while employing the general principles of Aristotelian natural philosophy, should not exclude from its province the study of motions originating from "extrinsic principles and thus . . . in some way violent or preternatural." Wallace writes:

> . . . they regarded the pseudo-Aristotelian *Quaestiones mechanicae* and Archimedes' works on weights and on bodies that float in water as equally valid sources, together with Aristotle's *naturalia,* for resolving problems relating to local motion. All of this suggests that they operated under a conviction that there were more general principles that grounded the possibility of a science of mechanics. . . . This attitude of mind was not necessarily shared by other authors in the late sixteenth century, especially those who had been trained as mathematicians and were working in the tradition of mechanical treatises deriving from Greek antiquity. . . .[14]

Later Wallace remarks (p. 207):

> Precisely how the Jesuit mathematicians of that period would go about formulating such a science is not easy to ascertain, since . . . there are no extant mechanical treatises in the archives of the Collegio. Thus it is difficult to know how they would have applied the teachings of the *Posterior analytics, Physics, De caelo,* etc., to answering the questions raised by Tartaglia, Guidobaldo, and Benedetti in their differences over the principles of mechanics. . . .

One writer who addressed himself to these problems was Galileo's friend Giovanni di Guevara, not a Jesuit, but of the order of Clerks Regular Minor. The introduction to his commentary on pseudo-Aristotle's *Mechanica*[15] is an essay on the science of mechanics conceived within an Aristotelian framework, but after a long analysis of the nature of mechanics, and its relations to physics, he concludes with the view that mechanics, though it is partly physical and partly mathematical, is still not quite a true *scientia media,* but a discipline subalternated to mathematics, and is therefore basically a mathematical discipline. Wallace explains (p. 213):

> . . . Guevara maintains that mechanics, considered absolutely and completely, is subalternated not to natural philosophy but to mathematics, and that this is what Aristotle meant when he said that its subject is physical but that its mode of consideration is mathematical; practically all philosophers and mathematicians follow him in this, for they list mechanics under the mathematical disciplines and regard it as subalternated to geometry . . . the subject matter of mechanics is the heavy and light movable body, but it considers this under the formality of the quantity of weight body has or the quantity of force necessary to move or support it.

I cannot say if Descartes read Guevara or knew about Jesuit thinking on these matters within the Collegio Romano, but mechanical treatises had a European readership, and I feel that the situation described by Wallace is exactly what Descartes was hinting at in the letter to Fromondus. He was fully alive to the disciplinary identity of Renaissance authors of treatises in mechanics, who were mostly mathematicians, not *vulgaris philosophiae cultores,* and the tone of the remark in the letter to Fromondus implies regret that the

Peripatetic tradition had not taken mechanics on board as a fully integrated component of the discipline of natural philosophy.

We have seen something of Descartes's official line, to the effect that no difference is to be recognized between artifacts and natural bodies, but the weight of tradition was not to be evaded so easily. The following excerpt nicely serves a double purpose. The last sentence shows Descartes's awareness and acceptance of the disciplinary distinction between *mechanica* (both theoretical and practical) and *physica;* the rest provides the central clue in understanding the relation between physics and theoretical mechanics in Descartes's thought. In March 1638, six months after he had sent him the small treatise on mechanics, Descartes wrote to Huygens in disappointed response to the latter's wish that he get down to elaborating and completing a full-scale version of his mechanics:

> . . . I still cannot see any likelihood of publishing my *Monde,* at least not for a long time; and without that, neither would I be able to finish the Mechanics you wrote to me about, for it depends entirely on my *Monde,* principally in what relates to the speed of motions. And it requires having explained what the laws of nature are, and how she acts in the ordinary way, before one can really explain how she can be applied to effects to which she is not accustomed. (AT II, 50)

The Roth edition of the Descartes–Huygens correspondence gives a variant reading of the last sentence that is worth noting:

> . . . it requires having come to an understanding of what the laws of nature are, and how she acts in the ordinary way, before one can really explain how she can be applied to effects which for her are not ordinary.[16]

So in fact the philosophical tree in the letter-preface to the French *Principles* does present the state of affairs as Descartes wishes it to be understood. Theoretical mechanics depends on physics as its nomological foundation, which in turn depends on metaphysics, and the trunk-branches distinction is that between physics as the general *scientia* of body in motion and rest, and all other *scientiae,* including notably those that will have immediate practical applications in the form of *artes.*[17] We recall Regula V, in which Descartes berates "those who study mechanics apart from physics and, without any proper plan, construct new instruments for producing motion."[18] Also, mechanics as a *scientia media* was very much a major part of the *unfinished* business of the *Principles of Philosophy.* Descartes made that quite clear in the same letter-preface. After a general description of the contents of the four parts of the *Principles,* "by means of which I think I have begun to explain in order the whole of philosophy," he continues:

> But to bring this plan to completion, I ought in the future to explain in the same way the nature of each of the other more particular bodies to be found on earth, namely minerals, plants, animals, and principally man; then finally, to deal in an exact way with medicine, ethics and mechanics.[19] That is what I would have to do to let people have a complete body of philosophy;

> and I still do not feel so old, I am not doubtful about my energy, I do not find I am so far from the knowledge of what remains, that I do not dare to undertake the completion of this plan if I had the facilities to carry out all the experiments I would need to ground and justify my arguments. But seeing that would require great expenditure which an individual like myself could not meet without public aid, I feel I ought from now on to content myself with studying for my own instruction, and may posterity forgive me should I fail to labor henceforth on its behalf. (AT IX-2, 17)

Hence no mechanics in the *Principles* as published, and no GSP.

Let us look more closely at the reasons why Descartes did not include mechanics in his published *summa* of natural philosophy. In the March 1638 letter to Huygens he said something about "the speed of motions" being a principal stumbling block in linking *Le Monde* to the theory of machines. To see what he was getting at, we turn to the letter to Mersenne of 12 September 1638, in which he replied to some difficulties arising out of the GSP he had set out in the earlier letter of 13 July. Descartes asks Mersenne to note that all forces do not have the same number of "dimensions." The force required simply to sustain a weight, by hanging it on a nail in the wall, for example, has only one dimension, since if the nail can support the weight for only an instant, it can support it for a whole year, all else being equal. However, the force required to raise the weight through a certain height will not raise the same weight through a greater height: if the second height is twice the first, the force would have to be doubled. Accordingly, the force that raises a weight has two dimensions, one the weight, the other the distance through which the force raises it. Descartes suspects that failure to appreciate this distinction was part of the reason doubts were expressed about his GSP. But there is, he suspects, a further reason, deriving from a failure to appreciate another important distinction. In the case of forces with two dimensions, that is, the forces involved in the raising of weights, it is important not to assume that the second dimension will be speed, rather than distance. He explains:

> . . . many habitually confuse consideration of distance [*espace*] with that of time or speed . . . [*Descartes uses the example of a balance in equilibrium with one arm twice the length of the other, and the weight on the shorter arm twice the weight on the other arm*] it is not the difference in speed that is the reason one of these weights must be twice the other [for equilibrium to occur], but the difference in distance [through which they rise or fall] . . . for example, to raise the weight F as far as G, you do not need to use a force exactly twice the force you would have used the first time round, supposing you wanted to raise it twice as fast; you would need to use a force that might be greater or less than twice as large, according to the different proportion this speed might bear to the causes resisting it; whereas you need a force exactly twice as large to raise it with the same speed to twice the height. . . . If I had wanted to link consideration of the speed to that of distance, I would have had to attribute to the force three dimensions, whereas I attributed to it only two, so as to exclude [consideration of speed]. And if I have revealed the least bit of ingenuity anywhere in that short piece on statics, I would be happy for it to be known that it is on that simple point more than on all the

> rest. For it is impossible to say anything good and solid concerning speed, without having explained what weight really is, and at the same time the whole system of the world. . . . (AT II, 353–355)

Within the framework of Descartes's mechanical philosophy, the explanation of any (correct) description of the behavior of bodies falling under or rising against the force of gravity must be based on an account of how the forces associated with the rotation of the gravitational vortex round the earth govern in general the motions of those bodies, whether under specified constraints or in free-fall. In turn, a complete causal explanation of this interplay of forces depends reductively on a general account of what happens when two moving bodies collide,[20] which depends finally on divinely grounded laws of nature. The laws of nature, and the collision theory, in all of which speed of course plays a crucial role, form the centerpiece of Part II of the *Principles.* There Descartes's purpose was to say something good and solid concerning the speed of bodies moving in ideal conditions away from the influence of gravity. But he was unable to extend these findings to show why bodies fall the way they do, or why it takes such and such a force to raise a given weight through a given distance in a given time.

Viewed in this light, the GSP, Descartes's version of the work pinciple, is not a *lex* or *principium physicae* in the sense of being irreducible to other than metaphysical considerations. It is a lawlike empirical rule that explains the operation of devices and simple machines under the inviolate influence of gravity. For Descartes the irreducible *leges physicae* are centrally the three laws of nature set out in Part II of the *Principles,* and they are necessarily true of any divinely created possible world containing *res extensae* in motion. On the other hand, the GSP is contingently the case for the actual world God has chosen to create. Ironically, the ultimate *principia* of Descartes's mechanics are not to be found in what he wrote on mechanics *qua* theory of machines, and the single starting point from which the latter was developed, the GSP, cannot do service as a *principium* of his physics in the same foundational sense as the three laws of nature.

The anomaly and the inconsistency with which I began are therefore only apparent. The absence in the *Principles of Philosophy* of the work principle or the GSP is what we should have expected, given the unfinished state of the physics as Descartes saw it. When his great *corpus* of natural philosophy is complete, then the GSP and the properly grounded Cartesian *mécanique* (see n. 19) will form an major branch on the tree, its bases firmly located somewhere among the *leges physicae* as applied to the complexities of Descartes's mechanical theory of gravity. At the same time, mechanics is an integral part of the "true physics," since the latter, once constituted in its final form, will tell us how the motions of the particles responsible for gravity relate causally to the rest and motions of the components of machines and mechanical devices, just as it will tell us how these motions cause the natural fall of heavy bodies. Indeed, the "true physics," in which there would therefore be no significant relevant difference between artifacts and natural bodies, would then retain in a fuller sense the ideal enshrined in the Peripatetic definition of *physica:* "the science of natural bodies, in so far as they are natural."

In the meantime, however, we will have to make do with the melancholy conclusion that Descartes's mechanical philosophy was the undoing of his aspirations as a mechanician.

Finally, there is a message here for historians of mechanics, and also of physics, in the early modern period. It has always been normal to include Descartes's laws of nature, with or without the collision rules and the analysis of circular motion, as part of the story of the evolution of modern "mechanics." If the main arguments of this essay are valid, then that way of writing the history of mechanics misrepresents the state of affairs as it would have been viewed by Descartes and his contemporaries and immediate predecessors. The distinction between physics and mechanics, and the associated disciplinary demarcations, argue for a more contextualized history of mechanics and of the foundations of physics. Such a revised history would not end with Descartes. Isaac Newton called his great work of 1687 *Philosophiae naturalis principia mathematica,* not *Mechanicae principia mathematica,* and neither does a Newtonian formulation of the GSP make an appearance there as an *axioma* or *lex* to accompany the three laws of motion of Book I.

Notes

1. In its modern form the principle states that for any system of forces initially in equilibrium, the total work is zero for infinitesimal displacements of the system of forces consistent with the constraints of the system. Here the total work is the algebraic sum of all quantities given by the product "applied force × distance through which the point of application is moved in the direction of the force." In Bernoulli's account, if in a system of forces in equilibrium any of the forces suffer small displacements (*vitesses virtuelles*) from their equilibrium configurations, the algebraic sum of all the "energies" is zero. Bernoulli's "*energie*" is the term for the product "force × virtual speed," that is, "force × the small component displacement in the direction of the force (in an arbitrary time interval)"; it corresponds to the older concept of "work." The Principle of "virtual work" would be an appropriate nomenclature in a Cartesian context, since Descartes discounted consideration of time in statics. Bernoulli stated his principle in a letter to Pierre Varignon of 26 January 1717: see Varignon's *Nouvelle mécanique ou statique, dont le projet fut donné en m.dc.lxxxvii,* 2 vols. (Paris, 1725), 2: 175–176.

2. AT I, 435–447. Except where otherwise indicated, all translations from French and Latin are my own.

3. The question was whether a body weighs more or less when closer to the center of the earth than when further away; see Pierre Costabel, "Les enseignements d'une notion controversée: le centre de gravité," *IIe Symposium International d'Histoire des Sciences, Pisa-Vinci* (Florence, 1958), 116–125.

4. See Ernest A. Moody and Marshall Clagett, eds., *The Medieval Science of Weights* (*Scientia de Ponderibus*): *Treatises Ascribed to Euclid, Archimedes, Thabit ibn Qurra, Jordanus de Nemore and Blasius of Parma* (Madison: University of Wisconsin Press, 1952), 6, 15–16, 128–129, and 150–151; and Marshall Clagett, *The Science of*

Mechanics in the Middle Ages (Madison: University of Wisconsin Press, 1959), 3, 74–75.

5. The rigorous form of the general virtual work principle must be stated in terms of *infinitesimal* displacements because displacements from equilibrium of a system of forces are in general nonlinear, and the corresponding forces vary continuously with time. Note Descartes's curiously unrigorous use of the same letter 'D' to refer to two quite distinct points. The point D on the line DN along which F tends toward the center of the earth M is the point of intersection of the inclined plane and the line joining the centers of F and the earth, whereas the point D at which F rests on the surfaces ADC and EDG is the point of contact between them and F. Descartes's carelessness here does not invalidate the points he is making, which are clear enough from the text and diagram as they stand.

6. IV, a. 203: AT VIII-1, 326.

7. The application of actives to passives was the traditional form of words used to describe mechanical interventions (in the broad sense) in the ordinary course of nature, and was therefore one way of capturing the distinction between *ars* and *natura. Artes* involve the application of bodies in an active state (e.g. a pulley, a plough) to bodies in a passive state, that is, bodies fitted to receive the action (a heavy weight, the earth).

8. Descartes to Plempius for Fromondus, 3 October 1637: AT I, 420–421.

9. A possible source for the details of Descartes's tree is the account of subalternated sciences in Ludovicus Carbone, *Introductio in universam philosophiam libri quatuor* (Venice, 1599), which took its ideas from Paul Valla's logic lecture notes of 1588 in the Collegio Romano. Carbone writes that physics, as a speculative science, has two practical sciences subalternated to it: ethics, which depends on that part of natural philosophy that deals with the soul; and medicine, which deals with the body. Naturally, Descartes adds mechanics to the tree, because at the time he is writing the *Principles of Philosophy* he is beginning to see mechanics more clearly as the science that deals in a general way with bodies in motion. On Carbone and subalternated sciences, see William A. Wallace, *Galileo and his Sources: The Heritage of the Collegio Romano in Galileo's Science* (Princeton, NJ: Princeton University Press, 1984), 135.

10. See, for example, *Mechanics in Sixteenth-Century Italy. Selections from Tartaglia, Benedetti, Guido Ubaldo, and Galileo,* ed. Stillman Drake and I. E. Drabkin (Madison: University of Wisconsin Press, 1969).

11. Aristotle, *Minor Works,* trans. W. S. Hett, Loeb Classical Library (London and Cambridge, Mass.: Harvard University Press, Heinemann, 1980; 1st ed., 1936), 331. The *Mechanica* was a collection of thirty-five mechanical problems and puzzles, written possibly by Aristotle's pupil Strato, and first published in 1497. It became one of the most influential texts in the history of early modern mechanics. See further Paul Lawrence Rose and Stillman Drake, "The Pseudo-Aristotelian *Questions of Mechanics* in Renaissance culture," *Studies in the Renaissance* 18 (1971): 65–104 and François de Gandt, "Les *Mécaniques* attribuées à Aristote et le renouveau de la science des machines au XVIe siècle," *Les études philosophiques* (1986), 391–405.

12. Aristotle, *Minor Works,* 331.

13. The story is quite complicated. See W. R. Laird, "The Scope of Renaissance Mechanics," *Osiris* 2 (1986):43–68; William A. Wallace's chapter on "Traditional Natural Philosophy" in *The Cambridge History of Renaissance Philosophy,* ed. Charles B. Schmitt, Quentin Skinner, Eckhard Kessler, and Jill Kraye (Cambridge: Cambridge University Press, 1988), 201–235; and Wallace, *Galileo and his Sources,* passim.

14. Wallace, *Galileo and his Sources,* 202.

15. *Ioannis de Guevara Cler. Reg. Min. in Aristotelis mechanicas commentarii: una cum additionibus quibusdam ad eandem materiam pertinentibus* (Rome, 1627).

16. *Correspondence of Descartes and Constantijn Huygens, 1635–1647,* ed. Leon Roth (Oxford, 1926), 71.

17. It should be emphasized that Descartes's tree is of "toute la *philosophie,*" with the branches as *sciences,* not arts—although obviously the three major ones (medicine, moral theory, mechanics) are on the borderline between science and art. This would explain why logic (not a science, but an art) is missing from the tree, though not quite why mathematics is also missing.

18. CSM I, 20–21.

19. At this point in the text Descartes writes that he should "traiter exactement de la médecine, de la morale et *des mécaniques,*" whereas in the tree passage the three principal were "la médecine, *la mécanique,* et la morale." This might be a distinction without a difference, but I suspect that Descartes is using the singular to refer to the body of theory as such, and the plural to refer to specific applications of the theory to explain the workings and construction of machines.

20. Note that such an account would have to include a theory of *oblique* collisions, but Descartes's efforts in that direction were singularly unimpressive. See my "Force and Inertia in the Seventeenth Century: Descartes and Newton," in *Descartes: Philosophy, Mathematics and Physics,* ed. Stephen Gaukroger (Sussex: The Harvester Press; New Jersey: Barnes & Noble, 1980), 256–257.

20

The Heart and Blood: Descartes, Plemp, and Harvey

Marjorie Grene

Although the expression "scientific revolution" may sound simple to some ears, the seventeenth-century events it is often used to refer to are, like any other historical phenomenon, almost infinitely subtle and many-sided. I hope that by looking in some detail at a few letters to and from Descartes in 1637–38 I may add a little to our awareness of that complexity. These are among the first letters Descartes received, and answered, raising questions about his *Discourse on Method* and the essays that accompanied them: his first published work, written in French so as to attract a wide audience (even women, he said, could read them!). (He had said he would publish the essays anonymously, not wanting to be a center of controversy; but whatever sort of self-deception that was, it passed.) What I want to examine, in particular, is the questions Descartes's correspondents raised about the motion of the heart. As everyone knows, Descartes was one of the first men of learning on the Continent to accept Harvey's doctrine of the circulation, but as emphatically as he agreed with Harvey about the blood's course, he disagreed with him about the nature and action of the heart. His correspondence, therefore, with a (by now) obscure Dutch physician—in which he refers explicitly to his disagreement with Harvey—set alongside some of Harvey's own statements about his method, may help us to understand the different ways in which these two scientific reformers perceived their own roles in the stirring events of their time, and help us a little to understand their differences.

Although Descartes first read Harvey's *De Motu Cordis* late in 1632, he had already anatomized sufficiently to have reached independently (or so it seems) the conclusion that the blood does indeed circulate, from arteries to veins and back, through heart–lungs–heart, and so on, from generation to death, in a ceaseless round. At the same time he had formed an opinion opposed to Harvey's about the motion of the heart, and while he willingly gave credit to the English physician for the discovery of the blood's circular course (credit for which Harvey in turn expressed his gratitude), he insisted, from the *Treatise on Man* of 1632, through the *Discourse* and consequent correspondence, to the

Description of the Human Body in 1648, on his alternative and, as he held, better grounded, indeed, indubitably grounded, account of the activity and function of the heart. As he put it to Mersenne in November or December 1632: "I have read the book *De Motu Cordis,* of which you had spoken to me earlier, and I have found myself differing a little from his opinion, although I did not read it before I had finished writing about this matter" (AT I, 263; CSMK, 40). The classic analysis of this concurrence and disagreement is still, so far as I know, Gilson's essay, "Descartes, Harvey et la scolastique," which presents not only the position of the two great revolutionaries, but a summary of the correspondence connected with the *Discourse* between Plemp and Descartes in 1637–38 (Gilson 1975, 51–101). It would be difficult indeed to better Gilson's account, but I hope that a reexamination of the sources in this dispute may nevertheless shed a little further light on what was for Descartes a topic of fundamental significance to the medicine he did not live to write. As he was to say at the close of Part II of the *Description of the Human Body:* ". . . it is so important to know the cause of the movement of the heart, that without this it is impossible to know anything about the Theory of Medicine, since all the other functions of the animal depend on it" (AT XI, 245; CSM I, 319).

So let us look at the correspondence on this topic in 1637–38. The first letter, from Plemp to Descartes on behalf of his teacher Froimond, raises two questions about the motion of the heart. First, Froimond doubts whether a fire like that Descartes envisages in the heart "could produce in man all animal operations except that of the rational soul." "Such noble operations," he believes, "do not seem to be able to flow from so ignoble and brutish a cause" (AT I, 403). Descartes is proud of his mechanical explanation; that is an easy objection for him to answer, and Plemp will not raise it again in his own voice (except, perhaps, very indirectly, in his second round of letters, about continued functioning of the digestive system in beheaded bodies—where something like a lesser soul would seem to be involved). Froimond's third criticism (the second about the heart) will be repeated by Plemp (and later, indeed, by Harvey) and answered by Descartes in the former case in more detail than he accords Froimond: that is the question how the rarefaction of the blood insisted on by Descartes can take place in so short a time as that of a single heartbeat (AT I, 403). Dilatation occurs, Descartes replies, at different rates in different media. The heart would not have to be, as Froimond alleges, as hot as a furnace to accomplish the rarefaction necessary in this case (AT I, 416; CSMK, 63).

Descartes assures Plemp—himself a physician—that he awaits with great interest Plemp's expression of his own opinions in the matter of the function of the heart, and when Plemp's letter arrives, early in 1638, Descartes replies in great detail. Let me run through the exchange (two letters each from January to March 1638), noting some points of special interest both for Descartes's own physiological theory and for his disagreement with Harvey (AT I, 496–499, 521–534; AT II, 52–54, 62–69). Finally, I want to draw from this exchange, as well as from some Harveyan texts, a more general comparison between the scentific programs of Harvey and Descartes.

Plemp raises four objections to Descartes's theory of the motion of the heart and three to the circulation. Before beginning with these he cites the *De Respiratione* of Aristotle to show that the Philsopher himself had spoken of "boiling" in the heart. To this Descartes replies that although, as every one knows, in logic one can reach true conclusions from false premises, that is really as good as no conclusion. Nevertheless, ten years later, in the *Description of the Human Body,* he will cite the same passage, remarking that no one followed Aristotle in this case, while, notoriously, they rushed to follow him in many much less plausible opinions.

The three objections to the circulation are easily refuted—or so it seems, since Plemp did indeed become a convert to the Harveyan view. So let me deal with them quickly before turning to the more controversial issue of the heart's action. They are: (1) that if the blood just passed through the heart, there would not be, as there clearly is, a distinction between venous and arterial blood. Descartes answers that here his own view in fact betters Harvey's, since for Harvey nothing happens to the blood in the heart: it just gets pushed out, while as Descartes sees it, the blood of the arteries, after its rarefaction in the heart, will obviously be brighter than that of the veins (besides, the veins have taken up heavier matter from the digestive system before they arrive at the vena cava and the heart). (It should be noted, however, that Harvey did rightly locate the transformation of venous to arterial blood in the lungs, even though no one could understand their function until Lavoisier and oxygen. Harvey thought the blood was strained, or possibly cooled, by the lungs—though I'm afraid he did try to minimize the difference between venous and arterial blood. Descartes believed, as had Aristotle of the brain, that the lungs were indeed cooling organs. They condensed the blood to prepare it for redistillation in the heat of the heart.)

(2) If the blood circulated, intermittent fevers, with their source in the veins, would have to peak not every three or four days, but many times each day. Descartes refers to Fernel as his authority for a newer theory of the origin of fevers. (Gilson explains in some detail the relation of Fernel to traditional as well as modern medicine; he was obviously a good source for silencing Plemp.)

(3) Plemp argues that if the veins were ligatured and the blood circulated as Descartes (and Harvey) insist, the arteries would swell up, whereas the result is rather "anemia." This plays straight into the pro-circulation hand, however, since the flow of blood from a cut in an artery while the veins are tied in fact proves the circulation. If the veins are tied longer, of course, Descartes admits, there will be "corruption" from other sources; but that is a side issue. In the main, Descartes's arguments here were plainly persuasive. And given contemporary knowledge of cardiac anatomy—as Descartes himself presents it, for instance, even in the *Discourse,* as well as in the later *Description of the Human Body*—that is not surprising.

The questions about the motion of the heart are more vexing. Descartes's answers are long and circuitous; Plemp replies again in March 1638; and

Descartes answers the new criticisms, again somewhat laboriously. Plemp's original objections and Descartes's answers, are as follows:

First, if, as Descartes alleges, it is the entry of blood into the heart (and its rarefaction by the "hidden fire" there) that produces the heart beat, how can he account for the fact that the heart continues to beat when extracted, and so cut off from the flow of blood? Descartes provides *five* answers! (1) There is always some blood; (2) for purposes of distillation, the less, the better; (3) the heart is *used* to dilating, and so goes on doing it (which seems to contradict the first point); (4) perhaps there is "in the folds of the heart some humor resembling a ferment (or yeast), by mixing with which another humor, arriving, makes it [the heart] swell." This is a point Descartes lays much stress on, as we shall see in connection with Plemp's third objection. Indeed, he also places it at the head of his argument on the heart and blood in the *Description of the Human Body.* Finally (5), still answering Plemp's first objection, Descartes points out that his view contradicts, and improves on, the common opinion of those who believe that the heart beat depends on some faculty of the soul. It is a matter of faith, he says, that the rational soul in man is indivisible, with no other sensitive or vegetative soul adjoined to it. So how could an excised heart go on beating? The soul could not exist in this additive (or subtracted) way.

Plemp's second objection concerns a famous experiment by Galen, in which a tube is inserted into an artery, and the artery tied to the top of the tube. The arteries (below the ligature) stop beating, and one infers that it is not the blood (still passing through) but something in the tunics of the vessel that causes the pulse. Descartes has no trouble with this one. Although he has never tried the experiment, "the laws of my mechanics," he replies, "that is, of physics, teach me" that just these results will follow. Some blood is flowing through, but going from a narrower to a wider channel it will not stretch out the arteries to provide a perceptible pulse. He also envisages other ways to perform Galen's experiment, including one that would not slow down the passage of blood. But then, while he is at it, he takes the opportunity to instruct Plemp further about his own experiments in vivisection. (The history of biology is terrible to think about; even those who did not accept the theory of the *bête-machine* happily practiced vivisection.) This passage (if one can bear it) is worth quoting in full, however, since it involves the experiment by which (along with two other observations) Descartes believes he has refuted Harvey. First, a refutation of Galen on the pulse:

> And there is nothing to move us in the authority of Galen, when he asserts in various places "that the arteries are not like bladders that become distended when they are filled, but like bellows . . . that fill up because they are distended, and in this state attract by their extremities and their apertures from all the neighborhood whatever can fill up their folds." For this is refuted by a most certain experiment, which I am not displeased to have seen several times in the past and to see again today while I am writing to you.

Descartes is positively Popperian in his confidence in experimental falsification, although it is of course always the other person's opinion that is refuted. Here, then, is the experiment, one of the three he will use to refute Harvey ten years later. (The other two are: the slight enlargement of the ventricles allegedly observed by "other physicians" when the heart beats, and the change in appearance from venous to arterial blood.) He writes:

> . . . opening the thorax of a young live rabbit and displacing the ribs so that the heart and trunk of the aorta are exposed, I then tied the aorta with a thread at a certain distance from the heart, and separated it from everything adhering to it, so that there could be no suspicion that any blood or spirit could flow into it from anywhere but the heart; then with a scalpel I made an incision between the heart and the ligature, and I saw with the greatest clarity [*manifestissime*] blood leaving in a spurt through the incision when the heart was extended, while, when it was contracted, the blood did not flow.

(It is the supposed enlargement of the heart at the moment of beating that he will later emphasize; the heart beat is a stretching, not a contraction.) But, he continues,

> On the contrary, if Galen's opinion were true, the artery should attract air at each moment of diastole, while it ought to let blood out during systole; nobody, it seems to me, can doubt this.

(As Harvey sees it, however, it is Descartes, with his mysterious dilation of the heart, who will need "attraction"; I will return to that point later.)

Descartes goes on to say that, although if you cut the tip of the heart, it stops beating,

> . . . you will observe, that if the part of the heart near the base beats for some time, it is because new blood arrives there, coming from the vessels and the auricles adhering to it; but it is not the same with the part near the tip. For the rest, after one has cut off the tip of the heart, the base, which is still attached to the vessels, continues to beat for a good while; and I have seen most satisfactorily the two cavities that are called the ventricles of the heart enlarge in diastole and contract in systole. An experiment whereby the opinion of Harvey about the motion of the heart has its throat slit [*quo experimento Harvaei sententia de motu cordis jugulatur*]: for he says the very opposite, namely that the ventricles are dilated in systole, so that they may receive the blood, and contracted in diastole, so that they push it out into the arteries. (AT I, 526–527; CSMK, 81–82)

I have quoted this passage at length, because the comment on Harvey is simply incredible. Descartes said in 1632 that he had read Harvey's book. (He says "*j'ai vu le livre,*" but one assumes he meant this in the sense of "*j'ai lu.*") The how could he have asserted that Harvey believed the heart to be smaller in diastole? Harvey states with complete clarity (and distinctness!) in chapter 2,

> Hence the very opposite of the opinions commonly received, appears to be true; inasmuch as it is generally believed that when the heart strikes the breast and the pulse is felt without, the heart is dilated in its ventricles and is filled with blood; but the contrary of this is the fact, and the heart, when it contracts, is emptied. Whence the motion which is generally regarded as the diastole of the heart, is in truth its systole. And in like manner the intrinsic motion of the heart is not the diastole, but the systole; neither is it in the diastole that the heart grows firm and tense, but in the systole, for then only, when tense, is it moved and made vigorous. (Harvey 1907, 26)

Did Descartes use "diastole" here for systole because he was conforming to ordinary (medical) usage? Or had he only glanced at Harvey's work and not really read it, even through chapter 2? "Diastole" *means* stretching; Harvey simply could not have thought the heart was shrinking when stretching. And he firmly states the very opposite. It is systole he is placing, instead of diastole, and of course correctly, at the moment the heart rises and strikes the chest. His account of diastole, the filling of the vessels, not the heart's relaxation, is another and more complicated story, which I must leave aside for now. The point here is just that Descartes is supremely confident of his throat-cutting experiment, with the mistaken report of Harvey's view that it entails. "I have added this in passing," he concludes, "so that you may see that no opinion different from mine can be imagined, which some experiments of the greatest certainty do not dispute" (AT I, 527; CSMK, 82).

One more point. One must use for this experiment, Descartes adds, a *timid* animal; a dog's heart is too fibrous for the effect to be clear. What fear has to do with it is another mystery! In any event, it is this fibrous structure that has presumably misled those who believe the heart is smaller in diastole. All the same, says Descartes, "it does dilate at that moment, as one can demonstrate by touch itself, since, held in the hand, it feels much harder in diastole than in systole" (AT I, 527–528, n.).

Now we come to Plemp's third objection (repeating Froimond's, and anticipating one by Harvey). The heartbeat would take much longer if it were a question of distillation, of "boiling," as in oil or pitch. And besides, Plemp asks, why would cold-blooded animals' hearts beat if heat were the cause? Descartes explains (as he has done, he says, in *Meteorology*) that there are two kinds of rarefaction, one in which the whole of a fluid is made into air (as in retorts?) and another in which a fluid retains its form but simply increases in volume. The second, in turn, occurs in two ways: either gradually (as explained also in *Meteorology*) or instantaneously. Now it is instantaneous rarefaction that takes place in the heart. Let us look carefully at Descartes's account of this process. He writes,

> As to the other sort of rarefaction, where the fluid increases in volume, this in turn must be divided: either it happens little by little or instantaneously. Little by little, when the parts of the fluid gradually acquire some new motion or shape or location, by reason of which they leave about them larger or more intervals than before (AT I, 529; CSMK, 83).

This, again, was explained in *Meteorology.* But instantaneous rarefaction is what we are really after here. Descartes explains,

> It takes place according to the foundations of my Philosophy, whenever the particles of a fluid, whether all or certainly the greatest number, dispersed here and there in its mass, acquire simultaneously a certain alteration [*mutationem*], by reason of which they require a notably larger space. But this last is the way in which the blood is rarefied in the heart; the thing itself shows it [*res ipsa indicat*]; for diastole takes place instantaneously.

This is a remarkable argument. Plemp, like Froimond, and Harvey to come, objects that rarefaction is a gradual process, and the heartbeat (diastole, in traditional terms) is instantaneous. There *is* instantaneous rarefaction, replies Descartes, which the fundamentals of my philosophy explain, and so the fact that diastole is instantaneous proves the existence of this kind of rapid rarefaction. The very fact alleged against him speaks for his view.

Moreover, he continues,

> If we attend to all those things of which I wrote in the fifth part of the little work *On Method,* we can no more doubt about this matter, than we can doubt that oil and other fluids in a pot are being rarefied when we see them rising in sudden spurts. Indeed, not only the instantaneous stretching of the heart beat [which, he will claim in the *Description of the Human Body,* "the other physicians" all observe], but the whole fabric of the heart [the anatomy lesson of the *Discourse*], its heat [the alleged fact, from which the *Description of the Human Body* too sets out, of the greater heat of the heart—as he says there, too, you can feel it with your hand!—AT XI, 228], and the very nature of blood [its tendency to bubble up when placed near warmth]: all these givens conspire so that we perceive by the senses nothing that seems to me more certain (AT I, 529; CSMK, 83).

Harvey is usually contrasted with Descartes as the great anatomist over against the theoretical mechanist, all of whose physics is geometry, but in these passages at least Descartes himself seems positively to glory in the evidence of the senses, in what can be seen and touched. I shall return to this comparative question, all too briefly, in conclusion.

However, we are still with Plemp's third point. As to the cold-blooded animals, that's no problem. There may not be much heat in hearts, but of course there is more there than in their other organs. Everybody knows *that!* Harvey, by the way, although observing correctly that the heart is no hotter than the rest of the body, does of course retain the traditional concept of animal heat. Two thousand years of medical tradition are not easily abandoned, as we see in Descartes's case as well. Living bodies are warm, after all, and corpses cold. But Harvey locates the vital heat in the blood itself rather than in the heart.

The lingering power of traditional thinking is illustrated again in Descartes's next remarks, as he proceeds to answer another aspect of Plemp's third objection. Plemp had objected that blood is rather earthy and watery (by implication, in terms of the four elements, rather than fiery and airy) and so unfit to undergo such sudden rarefaction. Descartes points out that water itself bubbles up that way (if you are cooking fish in it, for example) and so does flour (surely an earthy substance) when kneaded and fermenting. Milk and blood itself are other examples. It seems that Descartes, although he has reduced the traditional four elements to three and distinguished them solely through size and shape rather than quality, is perfectly happy with traditional four-element discourse.

Now he goes on, "to keep nothing from you," he confides to Plemp, to reveal how he believes (*existimo*) the rarefaction of blood in the heart does in fact take place:

> When the blood begins to boil in the heart, the greatest part of it bursts through the aorta and the arterial vein [i.e. the pulmonary artery]; but a certain part still remains inside, which, filling the inmost recesses of the ventricles, there obtains a new degree of heat, and as it were the nature of a ferment, and immediately thereafter, when the heart is deflated, mixing very quickly with the new blood arriving from the vena cava and the venous artery [i.e., the pulmonary vein], makes it boil up very quickly and pass into the arteries, not without leaving again a bit of itself, to fill the role of fermenting agent. Thus the rising of bread is usually accomplished with a bit of dough that has already risen; the fermentation of wine with the dregs of the grapes; and the fermentation of beer from something like its refuse. Nor is any intense degree of heat required for this, but it varies with the differing nature of the blood of particular animals. . . . So that neither beer, nor wine, nor bread, from which the great part of our blood arises, demand intense heat to make them ferment, but even heat up spontaneously. (AT I, 530–531)

That's clear, isn't it? As you have to keep a bit of sourdough starter to make more sourdough and a bit of yoghurt to make more yoghurt, so a bit of blood lingers in the walls of the heart and serves as leavening agent to the next drops that enter. Canguilhem has inquired why Descartes should have found Harvey's pumping heart, which seems to us to work mechanically, so unsatisfactory, while preferring fermentation, which is a chemical process—and indeed, as we now know, a process demanding the agency of living organisms (Canguilhem 1977, 34). But as Descartes sees it—and he says so explicitly in the *Description of the Human Body*—Harvey will need for his pumping action a pulsative faculty even more mysterious than everything he wants to explain by it (and other faculties, too, to fill the auricles), while, given the heat of the heart, Descartes needs only the one, clearly mechanical, process of rarefaction. The unique, biologically grounded nature of fermentation, of course, was to become clear only in the nineteenth century, and even then, when first proposed, it appeared absurd to the leading chemists of the day. Descartes was happy to distinguish various bubblings—all local motion, relative changes of place in his cosmic plenum, differing in their different, but wholly extensive, circumstances. Why he should not have been troubled by the difference between those, like bread and beer, that need a fermenting agent, and those, like water, that can boil up with only an external source of heat, it would be difficult to say. But there it is: boiling water, rising bread, bubbling blood—it is all explained in terms of extension and motion, that is, changing relations of extension. Harvey *saw* the blood pushed into the ventricle by the contraction of the auricle; Descartes, denying this contraction, would need, Harvey thought, some kind of *attraction* to get the blood into the ventricle (where it was allegedly to undergo rarefaction). So he was using, at least implicitly, an old Galenic notion that had better be forgotten. In Descartes's view, on the contrary, it was Harvey who was retaining overcomplex scholastic notions. His "pumping" theory (which for Harvey was no theory, but what he had seen in countless vivisections in countless different organisms) could not explain (as Descartes's rarefaction could) the change (in the heart, Descartes believed) from venous to arterial blood. And as to the pumping action, that seemed just another mystery. What one has to remember, I think, is that while the notion of the heart's pumping blood seems mechanical to us, there was available in Descartes's time no clear conception of involuntary muscle. Muscles are what you use to move when circumstances dictate motion. What can a muscle be that keeps going from generation to death? True, for Cartesian beasts muscles are not exactly "voluntary" either, since only we, made in God's image, are endowed with wills. But the Fourth Replies' story of the wolf's image in the sheep's eyes and the sheep's consequent flight is easily, and mechanically, told. On the other hand, a muscle that goes on contracting, automatically, indefinitely? Obvious scholastic nonsense!

Plemp's fourth objection, that all the arteries beat at once, had been dealt with in the course of Descartes's intricate answer to the question of Galen's experiment; we can pass it over here. But let me mention briefly some points in the second exchange of letters, before comparing more generally, in conclusion, Descartes and Harvey as scientific revolutionaries.

Descartes deals easily with Plemp's remaining anatomical objections: about the beat in the upper part of an excised heart, about the experience of surgeons that suggests the importance of the tunics for the arterial pulse, and again about the hearts of cold-blooded animals; if they need heat to make them beat, Plemp asks, why doesn't a fish's heart start beating when held in your warm hand? With respect to the last question: Descartes has, conveniently, an eel's heart, extracted a few hours ago; it beats when he puts it by the fire, or in its own blood. Granted, sometimes it will beat even without blood—this is different from the case of warm-blooded animals: its skin seems to split open rather like a roasting apple—and so on. Here, we see again, there is for Descartes no essential difference between fermentation and any other kind of heating.

These humble examples, by the way, seem to be the kind of thing that lead Desmond Clarke to find Descartes still an Aristotelian scientist: he stays too close to everyday experience and too far from the quantitative habits of a proper modern mechanist (Clarke 1982). But the point is that all these everyday analogies, like those in the *Dioptrics,* are pushing the universality of local motion as the one kind of physical change. Light, the heartbeat, you name it, it's all change of position of small portions of extension within the vast plenum that is nature. This is thoroughly, for the study of life, perhaps too thoroughly, anti-Aristotelian science.

Finally, two asides by Plemp are worth noting. Descartes's claim that his account is better than the common opinion means little, Plemp says, since they might both be wrong, and some third view correct. In reply, Descartes says Plemp sounds like someone at the end of a siege, taking desperate measures. But of course Plemp was quite right, both in logic and in fact. At the close, further, apart from raising again the question of the speed of Descartes's cardiac fermentation, he wonders whether that *ferment* may not instead be a *figment* (*quod fermentum vereor ne figmentum sit*) (AT II, 54). Surely, Descartes replies, Plemp cannot think him so helpless as to need this argument. He could demonstrate his opinion in many other ways (I suppose, by the "experiments" he would use to refute Harvey: traditional medical opinion about diastole, the spurting of blood from the young rabbit's heart, and the change from dark, venous to light, arterial blood). Still, the hindsighted reader cannot help enjoying Plemp's little quip.

The correspondence was not continued, but the same year (1638) Plemp published his *De Fundamentis Medicinae,* in which he repeated (and according to Descartes distorted) parts of this exchange. In a later correspondence with Beverwick (who was to publish Descartes's correspondence on the heart in 1644), Descartes expressed his annoyance with Plemp on this score (AT IV, 6: *& quia earum auctor meas responsiones malâ fide distortas & mutilatas in lucem edidit. . . .*).

So much, then, for Plemp. What does this correspondence, combined with the other relevant Cartesian documents, and Harvey's own comments, both on Descartes and on his own methods, suggest about the relation between these two physiological reformers?

They both belong to the class of seventeenth-century innovators who would throw away their books and consult nature itself. They both want their own books (the *De Motu Cordis* and the *De Generatione* in Harvey's case, the *Meditations* in Descartes's) not to be read simply, but to be worked through as exercises. They both believe they have eliminated probabilities and work only with certainties; thus the circulation, Descartes agrees with Harvey, has been proved to all but those who "argue from false and probable principles" (AT XI, 240–241). Nevertheless, as we have seen, each finds the other failing in *his* reform, clinging to antiquated concepts and pseudo-explanations. Each considers himself to be, par excellence, the man of the new time, discarding the tradition for radically new knowledge.

Yet even in what they share, they differ. Harvey, like Descartes and of course many others, can speak of reading the book of nature, but for him it is an easy, open book, needing no intellectual, let alone ontological, decoding; and he can also, or even preferably, speak of looking, directly, at Nature itself. Moreover, in the way of anatomists, he wants his reader to follow him in dissection and vivisection: even the beautiful anatomical drawings of Vesalius and his successors—Harvey's teachers and their teachers—are no substitute for the real thing. It is true that Descartes too suggests to the reader of the

Discourse that he examine carefully the anatomy of a mammalian heart. But on the other hand, in his serious (Latin) work, his aim, as he himself announces it, is to lead the mind away from the senses, in order to return it, purified, to the inspection of nature as pure extension. In contrast, Harvey wants to deepen and intensify the sensory: probing, seeing, touching examination of living, or if necessary recently dead, bodies in ever greater depth. A very uncartesian enterprise! And of course as an anatomist it is, from first to last, sensory certainty that Harvey seeks, while Descartes finds the primary source of certainty in clear and distinct ideas—even though, as in anatomy and physiology, the evidence of the senses may bear out my clear conceptions.

Accordingly, as I have already mentioned, the comparison is often made between Harvey the anatomist, the great observer, and Descartes with his highly intellectual unified mechanistic program. Passmore contrasted them as empiricist and a priorist (Passmore 1958). That, we know, is unfair to Descartes. Gilson, though more subtly, makes a similar contrast between Descartes as mechanist and Harvey as less theoretical experimental explorer. And in a way some such contrast is undeniable. Yet, as we have seen, Descartes believed he had refuted Harvey, not simply through the foundations of his philosophy, though these certainly helped in his replies to Plemp, but by sight and touch. So it can't be quite that simple. And perhaps one should mention also the once authoritative view of Pagel that Harvey was really an Aristotelian, who just believed in circles (Pagel 1967; 1976), as well as the opinion of Whitteridge, according to which Harvey was a modern so-called hypothetico-deductive scientist (Whitteridge 1981). Both these readings, however, are belied, I believe, by Harvey's own words, as well as by a very careful study by Andrew Wear called "Harvey and the way of the anatomists." (Wear 1982. I am grateful to Peter Dear for calling my attention to Wear's paper.) Following the *Historia anatomica* of Andreas Laurentius, Wear argues, Harvey distinguished between the way of *inspection* and the way of *doctrine,* the latter being nobler, but the former more certain. And it was the way of inspection (*autopsia*) that he followed throughout the *De Motu Cordis.* As Harvey himself put it in the second discourse to Riolan:

> This is what I have striven, by my observations and experiments, to illustrate and make known; I have not endeavoured from causes and probable principles to demonstrate my propositions, but, as of higher authority, to establish them by appeals to sense and experiment, after the manner of anatomists. (Harvey 1907, 163)

His conclusion, moreover, he insists, is "true and necessary," if his premises be true; "but that these are either true or false," he holds, "our senses must inform us—ocular inspection, *not any process of the mind*" (Harvey 1907, 162; emphasis added). Surely that is a contrast no Cartesian, including Descartes himself, could happily accept. Indeed, Descartes, in the *Description of the Human Body* warns against Harvey "how experiments themselves can easily give us occasion to deceive ourselves, when we do not examine sufficiently *all their possible causes*" (AT XI, 242; emphasis added). But causes have to be understood, and, for Descartes, understood, ultimately, in the light of the foundations of his physics. Harvey, too, of course, does use causal reasoning. He argues, for example, that the cause of diastole must be different from that of systole: the latter is the contraction of the heart, the former the filling of the ventricles caused by the contraction of the auricles, and the relaxation of the ventricles after systole is another thing again. Every anatomist knows, he says, that different activities have different causes: as when you clench and open your fist, for instance, different muscles do the two jobs. But his way is to look first, to specify what he sees, by careful and arduously trained inspection. We know there are causes, but as an anatomist don't play around with them if you can help it! Causes are classed by him with "probable principles," where for Descartes the consideration of causes has to guide even inspection. It is here, I venture to suggest, in the relation of ocular inspection to causal reasoning, that the difference chiefly lies. Both men share a faith in certainty and contempt for probabilities, but the relation of causality to the source of certainty is different. From our point of view (despite the claim to certainty, which we would have to renounce) Descartes's position is in a way more sophisticated than Harvey's, since most of us recognize by now that "all observation is theory-laden" and so the question *why* is never far removed from the question *what.* In the case of cardiac action in particular, Descartes argued in the *Description of the Human Body* that three observations confirmed *both* his and Harvey's view. The facts that the heart hardens, changes color, and emits blood at the moment of striking could follow equally well from Harveyan contraction or Cartesian dilation. But then there are three observations (which I mentioned earlier) that fit *only* Descartes's reading: the ventricle is enlarged (a little!) while striking, the cut tip of the rabbit's heart stretches, and the blood changes color in the heart. This is good clean scientific methodology. But it just happens that all three uniquely Cartesian observations are mistaken. After all a perceptual (and manual) training like that of the greatest Paduan anatomist and the sustained anatomical investigations that grew out of it contribute to the advance of knowledge something a great geometer and metaphysician, turning his hand relatively late to vivisection, and confident in the conformity of the appearances to his fundamental theory, was almost bound to miss. He did miss it, at any rate. But we can admire the projects of both these reformers without seeing either of them, whiggishly, as practicing the science of our day, the science that in their very different ways they both helped to create.

Bibliography

Canguilhem, G. *La formation du concept de réflexe aux XVIIe et XVIIIe siècle.* Paris: Vrin, 1977.

Clarke, D. *Descartes's Philosophy of Science.* Manchester: Manchester University Press, 1977.

Gilson, E. *Études sur le rôle de la pensée médiévale dans la formation du système cartésien.* 4th ed. Paris: Vrin, 1975.

Harvey, W. *The Circulation of the Blood and Other Writings.* London: Dent, 1907 (after Sydenham Society edition, 1847, trans. Willis).

Pagel, W. *William Harvey's Biological Ideas.* Basel: Karger; New York: Hafner, 1967.

———. *New Light on William Harvey.* Basel and New York: Karger, 1976.

Wear, Andrew. "Harvey and the Way of the Anatomists." *History of Science* 21 (1983): 223–249.

Passmore, J. "William Harvey and the Philosophy of Science." *Australasian Journal of Philosophy* 36 (1958): 85–94.

Whitteridge, G. Introduction to and translation of William Harvey, *De Generatione.* Oxford: Blackwell Scientific, 1981.

Index